THE

PUBLICATIONS

OF THE

Lincoln Record Society

FOUNDED IN THE YEAR
1910

VOLUME 114

ISSN 0267-2634

LAND AND GOD:

THE CITY, COUNTY AND DIOCESE OF LINCOLN OVER NINE CENTURIES:

ESSAYS IN HONOUR OF NICHOLAS BENNETT

EDITED BY

PHILIPPA HOSKIN AND PAUL DRYBURGH

The Lincoln Record Society

Boydell Publishing Services

First published 2025

A Lincoln Record Society publication
supported by Boydell Publishing Services
an imprint of Boydell & Brewer Ltd
PO Box 9, Woodbridge, Suffolk IP12 3DF, UK
and of Boydell & Brewer Inc.
668 Mt Hope Avenue, Rochester, NY 14620-2731, USA
website: www.boydellandbrewer.com

Our Authorised Representative for product safety in the EU is Easy Access System Europe – Mustamäe tee 50, 10621 Tallinn, Estonia, *gpsr.requests@easproject.com*

ISBN 978 1 91065 319 7

A CIP catalogue record for this book is available from the British Library

Details of other Lincoln Record Society volumes are available from Boydell & Brewer Ltd

FSC www.fsc.org MIX Paper | Supporting responsible forestry FSC® C013056

Printed and bound in Great Britain by
TJ Books, Padstow, Cornwall

CONTENTS

Edited documents

ILLUSTRATIONS

Figures

1. The Building of the Medieval and Wren Libraries at Lincoln Cathedral

Plates

Tables

The editors, contributors and publisher are grateful to all the institutions and persons listed for permission to reproduce the materials in which they hold copyright. Every effort has been made to trace the copyright holders; apologies are offered for any omission, and the publisher will be pleased to add any necessary acknowledgement in subsequent editions.

CONTRIBUTORS

Carol Bennett, Independent Scholar, former Interpretation Officer, Lincoln Cathedral

Claudia Capancioni, Bishop Grosseteste University, Lincoln

David Crook, University of Nottingham

Paul Dryburgh, The National Archives, Kew

Julian Haseldine, University of Hull

Philippa Hoskin, Corpus Christi College, University of Cambridge

Sian Hope-Johnson, Bishop Grosseteste University, Lincoln

Andrew Jackson, Bishop Grosseteste University, Lincoln

Elaine Johnson, Bishop Grosseteste University, Lincoln

Michael Jones, University of Nottingham

Alison McHardy, University of Nottingham

Jasmine Mills, Bishop Grosseteste University, Lincoln

David M. Smith†, former Keeper of Archives, Borthwick Institute for Archives, York

David Stocker, Institute of Medieval Studies, University of Leeds

Andrew Walker, Honorary Fellow and Former Vice Principal at Rose Bruford College, Dartford

R. C. Wheeler, Independent Scholar

Louise J. Wilkinson, University of Lincoln

Marianne Wilson, British Library

ABBREVIATIONS

AALT	Anglo-American Legal Tradition, online (http://aalt.law.uh.edu/)
AASRP	*Associated Architectural Societies' Reports and Papers*
BL	British Library, London
CChR	*Calendar of Charter Rolls Preserved in the Public Record Office, 1226–1526*, 6 vols (London, 1903–27)
CCR	*Calendar of the Close Rolls Preserved in the Public Record Office, 1272–1509*, 44 vols (London, 1900–63)
CFR	*Calendar of Fine Rolls Preserved in the Public Record Office, 1272–1509*, 21 vols (London, 1911–62); online edition, 1216–72 (https://www.frh3.org.uk)
CIPM	*Calendar of inquisitions post mortem and other analogous documents preserved in the Public Record Office, Henry III – Henry VII*, 24 vols (London, 1898–2003)
CPR	*Calendar of the Patent Rolls preserved in the Public Record Office, 1232–1516*, 52 vols (London, 1893–1916)
D & C	Dean and Chapter, Lincoln Cathedral
edn	edition
LA	Lincolnshire Archives, Lincoln
LCC	Lincoln Consistory Court
LCL	Lincoln Cathedral Library
LRS	Lincoln Record Society
ODNB	Oxford Dictionary of National Biography, online (https://www.oxforddnb.com)
PRS	Pipe Roll Society
Reg. Sutton	*The Rolls and Register of Bishop Oliver Sutton, 1280–1299*, ed. R. M. T. Hill, 8 vols, Lincoln Record Society, 39, 43, 48, 52, 60, 64, 69, 76 (Hereford, Lincoln and Woodbridge, 1948–86)

SLHA	Society for Lincolnshire History and Archaeology
TNA	The National Archives, Kew
TRHS	Transactions of the Royal Historical Society

NICHOLAS BENNETT – AN APPRECIATION

BY SOME FRIENDS AND COLLEAGUES

Nicholas Hamilton Bennett (b. 1948) has been part of the warp and weft of the scholarly community of Lincoln, city, county and diocese, for over half a century. One might, to borrow from the title of Julian Haseldine's contribution to this festschrift, describe Nicholas as 'The Shining Sun of His Diocese', such has his radiant influence been, and will continue to be. As archivist and librarian Nicholas has worked tirelessly, and with an expertise few have equalled, to research, catalogue and bring to greater public access and attention its vast literary and documentary treasures in manifold ways. Even in retirement, indeed, Nicholas has been key to the success of several high-profile public exhibitions, including the triumphant *Battles and Dynasties* (2017), which brought Domesday Book (its first ever exhibition outside London) and many other global treasures to Lincoln and for which Nicholas wrote the superb catalogue. As importantly, he has always been willing to share his encyclopaedic knowledge, gleaned from generations of the county's leading scholars, patiently and without fear or favour (even better if over a pot of tea – with cake, naturally). He has shepherded many younger researchers in their first steps into the archive and has assisted countless more senior, including many contributors to this volume, in refining and publishing their findings. As his own publications, catalogued at the end of this Appreciation, demonstrate, Nicholas is a fine writer himself across a broad range of topics and one of this country's finest record editors. While a medievalist, Nicholas has catholic interests, from unbeneficed clergy, global exploration and cartography to railways, and does not restrict his local history interests purely to Lincoln(shire). The essays and editions of texts presented here reflect that breadth of interest and expertise. It is our hope that Nicholas and its readers will find each of the contributions to this volume as stimulating as the next.

To an extent, of course, it is Nicholas's lasting contribution to the Lincoln Record Society that is the real catalyst for this volume. Originally envisaged to coincide with his 75th birthday, lockdown and other more minor issues have delayed this tribute. It nonetheless celebrates someone who for over forty years has held multiple roles within our Society, now in its 116th year, and to whom was entrusted the herculean task of writing of its centenary history in 2010. As Honorary Secretary, Honorary Treasurer, Honorary General Editor and now Editor of our Kathleen Major Series of Medieval Records, Nicholas has helped steer the Society through several transitional periods in our history. He has overseen the production of over twenty volumes, assisted in the digital shift while advocating the primacy of print, and has offered immensely wise counsel in managing the Society's recent bequests, always having an eye to the long term. This Appreciation and introductory chapter, then, and the essays which follow, many written by those of us who have worked most closely with Nicholas within the Lincoln Record Society and benefited greatly from his friendship, offers an appreciation on behalf of our members, past, present and future, the wider scholarly community and the general public of all he has done to promote the advancement of public education relating to the ancient city, county and diocese of Lincoln through the edition and publication of historical records. The Society has had no finer servant.

***

Although a schoolboy at Southwell Minster School, unmistakably Nicholas Bennett is a recognisable product of Oxford University, where he matriculated at New College in 1966. He exemplifies – perfectly – many of the old-fashioned virtues that the world beyond associates with those dreaming spires: scholarship; gentility; concern for others and a striving for excellence. Whilst at Oxford, however, Nicholas entirely failed to meet Carol, his future wife, when they performed together in the same concert in 1968 – the couple awaiting a more conventional occasion over coffee in a mutual friend's room in 1970, when Nicholas was mugging up for his Diploma in Archives Administration exams at University College London. They married in June 1971.

Waiting for a permanent post, life for the young couple was precarious. Nicholas had developed research interests in the economics of Banbury, which, given his subsequent career, now sounds a bit random, but it explains why 1972 found them renting a picturesque, thatched cottage opposite the duck pond at Little Ickford, near Thame. It was a cruck-framed building, with ladders to the upper floor and a tin roof to the bathroom, but – like Nicholas himself – the cottage has gone on to make an academic impression. The cruck blades at Little Ickford are now famous as amongst the earliest surviving dendro-dated examples (*c.* 1383). To Nicholas and Carol, however, the cottage is probably more significant as the birthplace of their first son, Patrick. In the event, by the end of the year, Nicholas' first job took him away from the soft Buckinghamshire landscape for good; to the more gritty scenery of the North Yorkshire Record Office in Northallerton, where the medieval cruck-framed cottage was exchanged for a more recent, stone-built, example in Scruton. Here their second son, Laurence, was born in 1973. The family were delighted with this promising start to Nicholas's career, although son Patrick believed at this time that he arranged vinyl discs all day! Edging southwards, however, the stone cottage in Scruton was soon exchanged for a rather grand former

manse in brick at Collingham near Newark from where Nicholas could reach the Nottinghamshire County Record Office, to which he moved in 1976.

At that time the Nottinghamshire Record Office was in the former Judges' Lodgings on High Pavement, Nottingham – near St Mary's church and opposite what is now the Museum of Crime and Punishment. The lure of the criminal justice system was evidently strong, however, and Nicholas joined Lincolnshire Archives Office (LAO) the following year. The LAO employed then a capable and dedicated team, located in the former prison buildings at Lincoln Castle. County loyalty impelled another move, to Forge Cottage in Burton-by-Lincoln – something of a step down from the Collingham Manse architecturally, but in 1983, the family regained appropriate accommodation in another medieval building: within Vicars' Court, Lincoln. Their new home could not have been more suitable; beautifully situated next to the Cathedral, and only a short walk across The Bail from 'the office'. The Bennetts' Vicars' Court residence was part of the south range of the medieval college of Vicars Choral, built under the terms of the will of Bishop Oliver Sutton in *c.* 1300, and came complete with a stone spiral staircase, traceried windows, garderobe tower, and a large garden terraced out above the city and bounded on the south by the Close Wall. It was the envy of tourists and guests alike and the perfect territory for the Bennetts many cats, although black mouser 'Kinny' was more skilled at extracting two breakfasts than catching mice.

Thus, by 1990, the couple had become fixtures within the Close community and that year Revd Canon John Nurser encouraged Nicholas to apply for the post of Cathedral Librarian, which had become vacant, through the retirement of Joan Williams. She had divided her time between the Cathedral Library and LAO, but John Nurser cherished a vision for the Cathedral's library as a centre for research by the surrounding community and he felt it demanded a full-time and senior post. Nicholas's appointment as the first full-time Cathedral Librarian in modern times included responsibility for the Dean and Chapter's own archives, for whose care he was well-qualified. But, to be taken seriously by 'proper' librarians, he felt he required a qualification in library science, which he obtained from Loughborough University. 'The office' was now even closer and, until he retired from the role in 2013, Nicholas's commitment and dedication to the Library's work ensured that a golden period was inaugurated.

It was not, the Bennetts were correct to argue, the weight of their rapidly expanding personal library that caused the serious structural problems in the south range at Vicars' Court during their time in residence, but it was the prospect of extensive repairs that precipitated purchase of a modern house in Nocton, south of Lincoln, in 1992. At the time, this was said to be 'downsizing', but visitors to their lovely home today cannot help noticing that the house has been extended in several directions to accommodate their books, and indeed the apparent garage is, in fact, a disguise for roller-tracking, accommodating those parts of their library not on display inside. As many of us know, Hawthorn House is a warm, airy, comfortable place, where many friends have enjoyed excellent meals and stimulating conversation. Although they no longer have a cat, when Nocton Post Office acquired a kitten Nicholas suddenly discovered how useful the postal service was, so that he could find excuses to play with it. Having suffered a small stroke in 2020, from which he recovered all but his previously boundless stamina, Nicholas has now learned to pace himself, but visitors have found his charm, hospitality and erudition all undiminished. Thanks to the support Nicholas and Carol offer to the astonishing parish church of All Saints Nocton (G. G. Scott 1862), the book-filled house has become a cultural focus for Nocton villagers as well, whilst the church now provides the setting for many of Lincolnshire's most interesting book-fairs and concerts.

The adventurous concert programme at All Saints comes as no surprise – music has always been of great importance to the entire Bennett family. During the 1967–68 season, the Oxford Bach Choir featured both Carol as soprano and Nicholas as bass, but they still contrived not to meet each other, even in the cramped cold and draughty Sheldonian Theatre, at an early performance with period instruments of the Monteverdi Vespers of 1610 (conducted by Sydney Watson and featuring the international counter-tenor James Bowman). No surprise, then, that the two Bennett children were enrolled in the Lincoln Cathedral choir, Patrick in 1980 and Laurence in 1982. Nicholas joined them in the latter year singing bass, as a lay vicar. Nicholas was to sing with the choir for twenty-six years, and between 2009 and 2018 he also served as a lay canon. As someone who knew the history of each of the Cathedral's prebends, it gave him great satisfaction to be granted the stall of Leighton Ecclesia, held between 1626 and 1633 by the poet George Herbert. Even after retirement from his canonry, though, Nicholas continued to sing as Lay Cantor until 2020. Amongst many highlights of his singing career with the cathedral choir, he recalls with particular pleasure the historic visit of Cardinal Hume to the cathedral, and tours to Bruges, Oslo, Paris, Le Mans and Germany.

And it was not just as a fundamental voice in the cathedral choir that Nicholas' offered musical refreshment for the city. During his tenure as Cathedral Librarian, he and Carol organised a memorable series of chamber concerts in the Wren Library, which always played to packed houses and which lit up our Lincoln winters. Particularly memorable was the performance of Dowland songs given by Fretwork and Michael Chance, with the Cathedral's own copy of Dowland's three books of *Songs or Ayres* on display. Making further imaginative use of the library's own collections, more than one concert included the music of William Byrd, alongside a display of Dean Honywood's own collection of Byrd's *Part Books*. Carol also recalls an electrifying evening of Gesualdo's music, by an ensemble from English Touring Opera (visiting Lincoln partly thanks to Alison McHardy) and harpsichord recitals given by their Assistant Director of Music, Charles Harrison. That concert was a huge success, but only thanks to the strenuous efforts of a team of choral scholars and lay vicars, who heaved the valuable and delicate instrument up the three vertiginous flights of stairs to the Wren Library.

It is the building of this magnificent library (1676) and its medieval forebear (*c.* 1422) which forms the focus of the first chapter in this volume, written, appropriately, by Carol Bennett. Books have been collected and used at the Cathedral since the mid-twelfth century, and Carol traces the history of collecting and storage, as well as their role in clerical education, in minute detail through to the present day. She sets the development of Lincoln's library facilities within wider trends in library building and book writing and collecting from Bishop Repingdon's endowment of the fifteenth century through Christopher Wren's commission by Dean Michael Honywood to design a new library in the late seventeenth century to important alterations made in the three centuries since. She also includes analysis of the deleterious effects on the Library of the Reformation and Civil War before a lengthy examination of Wren's design and build within a European setting. Rich in architectural detail and questioning in its approach to comparison between written sources, many of which remain unpublished, and the surviving structures and features – walls, staircases, windows, tracery, roof bosses, desks, benches, bookcases, shelving – the chapter traces and illustrates the various phases of building that have bequeathed the Cathedral an internationally important library. This is also a study in the (sometimes obscure, sometimes world-renowned) personnel who have planned, built and altered the libraries, and the motivations behind some of their (often questionable) decisions. It is tribute to both Nicholas and Carol that both libraries remain in use today, and this chapter will became a key point of reference for scholars investigating the Library and its place within the Cathedral's community of worship, past, present and, probably, future.

Nicholas's strenuous efforts to show Cathedral Library treasures to Lincoln people and to generate a core of support for historical and cultural events in the building had not gone unnoticed. When Patrick Lord Cormack (1939–2024) established the Historic Lincoln Trust to pursue a similar agenda in 2012, he asked Nicholas to become its historic adviser. And so began a dizzying few years in which Patrick's ambitions for his native county seemed to know no bounds. He wanted the new Trust to be a vehicle through which Lincoln's cultural and historical treasures would be to shown off to the world, and which would bring the world to the city. As part of this process, Michael Portillo interviewed Nicholas for the BBC's *Things We Forgot to Remember*, about the Cathedral's own copy of *Magna Carta*, giving Nicholas the opportunity to explain that they also possessed a copy of the 1217 *Charter of the Forest*. Thus began a journey that led to the creation of the new Magna Carta Vault within the refurbishment work at Lincoln Castle – sponsored by David Ross – that displays both documents.

The shift in the position of women in society occasioned by the Great Charter forms the backdrop for Louise Wilkinson's chapter on long-lived Lincolnshire widows in the twelfth and thirteenth centuries. Taking as her focus the thrice-married lady of Freiston barony, Petronilla de Craon (*c.* 1183–1262), interest in whom Nicholas himself had piqued, she explores the experiences of baronial heiresses, widows and mothers within the East Midlands on the decades either side of the enshrinement of Magna Carta into law. This was the period in which the vulnerability of women as daughters, mothers and widows reduced due to the provisions in the Charter and the reaction of Henry III's government in moving away from King John's exploitative rule. Petronilla, daughter and sole heir of Guy II de Craon, a well-connected royal supporter from an Angevin family, exhibits all facets of such vulnerability to male ambition and transition to greater safety during her long life and widowhood: this chapter traces how she was exposed to multiple marriages, had to litigate for her dower and, on occasion, faced violent treatment; but, she also benefited from changes in the law which protected a widow's status and right to remain single. Nevertheless, though indomitable, Petronilla was far from exceptional or unusual among the community of women of baronial rank in the thirteenth-century East Midlands. Indeed, as Louise demonstrates, many of the region's baronies underwent similar transfer to female heirs. Likewise, Petronilla was one of dozens of baronial widows in the king's gift, several of whom lived to similar old age, whose status and landed inheritance were documented as the crown asserted its prerogative.

The status of women in society and law within twentieth-century political debate – unquestionably influenced by more modern understandings of Magna Carta – provides the subject of the chapter by Andrew Jackson, Claudia Capancioni, Sian Hope-Johnson, Elaine Johnson and Jasmine Mills. They, however, recover stark, sometimes startlingly polarised voices of women being trained as teachers at the all-female Lincoln Diocesan Training College, out of which Lincoln's other university, Bishop Grosseteste University (BGU), emerged, in the debate around women's suffrage either side of 1900. Reporting on the fruits of a BGU touring exhibition in 2018 and 2019 – *Vote 100: A Lincolnshire View of Women's Suffrage* – the team explore and analyse two diametrically opposed articles submitted by Winifred Waller (1883–1947) and Annie Royce (1885–1954) to the in-house *Lincoln Training College Magazine* in 1909, a time of forced feeding of hunger strikers and the shouting down of the Home Secretary in Lincoln. These two articles, which take an anti-suffragist and a more militantly suffragist approach, lay bare the debate among educated women as well as both prevailing and more radically insurgent political views and protest strategies before the First World War. They also give insightful vignettes into meetings and rallies and of some of the key personalities involved in the suffrage movement. Their polemics are framed within the contribution of Lincolnshire to the women's suffrage movement over half a century and contemporary debates about gender and class, democracy and equality; they offer new views, not to say, perspectives on emotions, on the tensions between life stories and political activism recorded in the contemporary press, an archival triumph of which Nicholas himself would be proud.

Returning to the unveiling of the Ross Vault in Lincoln Castle, which marked the 800th anniversary of *Magna Carta* in 2015, this inaugurated a period of renewed self-confidence for the city and county. The Vault was the centrepiece of an amazing, multi-venue event called *The Great Lincolnshire Exhibition*. Having acquired the ear of Jeff James, then Chief Executive of The National Archives, and of Alan Borg, a former Director of the Victoria & Albert Museum, Nicholas was given the key role in bringing this wonderful project to fruition. The exhibition was to be found in venues across the city: at Lincoln Museum (then called The Collection), the Usher Gallery and the Cathedral Library, as well as the Ross Vault at the Castle, and aimed to collect a wide range of Lincolnshire-related objects and artefacts from collections around the county and country, and to place them all within their local context. The 'explorers' section included John Smith's map of Virginia and one of Matthew Flinders' maps of Australia, whilst the staggering array of fourteen paintings by George Stubbs, who studied equine anatomy during two years in Horkstow, influenced understanding of this artist across the art world. In his boundless enthusiasm Lord Cormack lined up multiple busts of Sir Isaac Newton. Referring to Lord Jacob Rothschild, Lord Cormack told Nicholas, 'I've spoken to Jacob on the phone and we're going to be able to borrow the bust'. In the end, two fine busts of Newton were displayed! Although Nicholas's role included sourcing many such items for the exhibition, his greatest contribution was in pulling together and editing the catalogue – one of the most worthwhile books on Lincolnshire ever produced.

Later that year Lord Cormack was also a moving force behind a display of four surviving examples of Magna Carta, first at the British Library and then at the House of Lords. Serendipity ensured that it was Nicholas and Carol who won the ballot to stand beside the Lincoln Magna Carta at the British Library event, and to represent Lincoln to the waiting world. Two years later, in 2017, *Battles and Dynasties* opened at Lincoln Museum and at the Ross Vault, and included the astonishing sight of *Great Domesday Book*, open on the Lincoln page. This was another remarkable coup for Historic Lincoln Trust; *Domesday* had not been exhibited outside London since the War. The pretext for this exhibition was the 800th anniversary of the second battle of Lincoln of 1217, at which forces of the young Henry III defeated those of Prince Louis, heir to the French crown, and during which the now rightfully famous Nicholaa de la Haye led the stout defence of Lincoln Castle. Star loans this time included the only surviving contemporary copy of the life of William Marshal (d. 1219), the legendary leader of Henry III's forces, the *Histoire de Guillaume le Maréchal* from the Pierpont Morgan Library, New York, alongside the famous triple portrait of Charles I from the Royal Collection. Nicholas advised on all the exhibits and once again wrote the catalogue. The 2019–20 exhibition was *Victoria and Albert: Treasures from a Royal Marriage,* celebrating the 200th anniversary of both rulers' births. Once again, Nicholas advised and wrote the catalogue. He was delighted that his loan request for one of the greatest treasures of the V&A was granted and the early twelfth-century *Gloucester Candlestick* made the journey to Lincoln. In each of these three exhibitions, Nicholas collaborated with Andrea Martin and Dawn Heywood, curators at The Collection and with Mary Powell of Lincolnshire County Council. Nicholas's critical role in all three was recognised in 2019 by his appointment as Secretary to the Historic Lincoln Trust.

But although Nicholas's work with the Historic Lincoln Trust represents a major achievement, nationally, he is probably better known for his steadfast, dedicated and constructive work at the Lincoln Record Society. Nicholas first met Reg Brocklesby in 1976 – when Reg was editing the section of Archbishop William Melton of York's monumental two-volume register relating to the archdeaconry of Nottingham. It was Reg who encouraged Nicholas to involve himself in record societies and to concentrate his research on the medieval period. The Lincoln Record Society was specifically recommended and, consequently, Nicholas attended his first LRS Annual General Meeting in 1977 – the last to be held in Lincoln's sixteenth-century Guildhall. Here he first met Kathleen Major and Joan Varley, who were to have a significant influence on his subsequent academic and professional development. Once appointed to the Lincoln Record Office the following year, he was encouraged by 'old-school' Lincolnshire County Archivist, Michael Lloyd, to undertake research on the documents in his care during working hours. So, urged on by Alison McHardy, herself a major contributor to the legions of editions of episcopal registers and who presents here an edition of a rare, fascinating but tantalisingly brief eyewitness account, taken from the Lincoln Dean and Chapter muniments, of the enthronement ceremony of Bishop John Buckingham in 1363, Nicholas decided to edit Bishop Fleming of Lincoln's register for publication by the Canterbury and York Society. He chose Fleming simply because he followed Bishop Repingdon chronologically, the edition of whose register for the Society was then being completed by Margaret Archer. The project spread over nearly half a century: the first volume appearing in 1979 and the third (and final) in 2024. On publication of the first volume, that doyen of register scholarship Professor Rosalind Hill wrote congratulating him and addressing him as 'Dr Bennett'; Nicholas responded saying he did not have a doctorate. Rosalind Hill replied that surely this qualification 'would be only a matter of time'. Many years later, she was indeed an external examiner at Nicholas's doctoral viva.

Nicholas's long service as an officer of LRS began in the early 1980s, when Kathleen Major gratefully accepted his offer of help during the Secretary's convalescence from illness; the convalescent in question was his boss, Michael Lloyd. Thus Nicholas became Acting Secretary, taking over as Secretary in 1982 when Michael left Lincoln. Now a member of LRS Council, he was also appointed Treasurer, a role whose scope was gently outlined by David Smith. In 1985 Gershom Knight, Michael Lloyd's successor as County Archivist, relieved Nicholas as LRS Secretary, but Nicholas was to continue as Treasurer for twenty years. Early on, one of his most stressful tasks was to organise the Council lunch at the White Hart under the keen supervision of Kathleen Major, who would check up on him, checking that he had organised a suitable seating plan, amongst other delicate tasks. However, when the White Hart staff asked if the seats should be arranged 'theatre style' Miss Major speculated, 'I don't think the phrase "theatre style" is in Mr Bennett's vocabulary'.

With such training, by 2002 Nicholas was ready to take over the key role of LRS General Editor, a role he performed with great distinction, aplomb and reliability until 2022, since when he has been Editor of LRS's Kathleen Major Series of medieval texts. During such a busy professional life, it is a lesson to us all that Nicholas found the time to play the role of General Editor for some twenty LRS volumes, including eight that he produced himself. So far, the latter have included three volumes of the *Registers of Bishop Henry Burghersh, 1320–42*, two volumes of the *Diaries of Captain Matthew Flinders* and – by way of a gesture to mark the Society's centenary – Nicholas presented us with a history of the LRS under the title *Wonderful to Behold*. Considering how dry such a record society's history might have been, the title does not mislead! This is a marvellous, engaging and very readable account, with many amusing and endearing stories about the scholars and others associated with the Society. Incidentally, the elaborate coloured seal impression placed on this volume's cover was also Nicholas' own discovery in the LRS archives. It was an experimental logo rejected by Canon Foster in 1912. If not the most academically significant volume LRS has published during its long and distinguished history, it is certainly among the most enjoyable to read. Nevertheless, it is likely that even these six volumes will be surpassed by Nicholas's current project, a projected twelve-volume biographical register of *Lincolnshire Parish Clergy c. 1214 to 1968*. This is a distillation of the wealth of primary information about Lincolnshire that Nicholas has encountered during a lifetime amongst Lincolnshire archives. The first two volumes in the series have already been published to acclaim, and they demonstrate that – when complete – this series will take its place amongst those foundational texts of which LRS has made a speciality. Every scholar working on any aspect of Lincolnshire, and beyond, will need to keep it close at hand.

If Reg Brocklesby directed Nicholas's scholarly efforts towards the LRS, it was David Smith, himself a future General Editor and President of the

Society, who encouraged his interest in medieval records, particularly those of an ecclesiastical nature. They first met in 1969, when both were volunteering at Lincolnshire Archives in the Castle. Nicholas recalls that their first meeting involved being closeted in the 'secure' search room in the Gaol (actually a prison cell) with the medieval Lincoln bishops' registers lining the walls. After that, David became a lifelong friend. He was, for example, to be a supervisor of Nicholas's doctorate, alongside the distinguished yet kindly figure of Barrie Dobson. Nicholas's 1989 thesis ('The Beneficed Clergy in the diocese of Lincoln during the episcopate of Henry Burghersh') took seven years to complete, but he was able to deploy his small salary as a lay vicar at the Cathedral to pay his University of York fees. The meat of the thesis was published by the LRS in 1999 as Volume 87. As his supervisions had always taken place either at the Borthwick Institute in the city of York or in a city restaurant, the first time Nicholas went to the History Faculty on the University's imposing and beautiful out-of-town campus was to deliver the completed thesis. He reports that visit induced 'imposter syndrome'. In typically supportive and scholarly manner Professor Smith wanted to contribute to this volume, presenting a calendar from a Dodsworth manuscript at the Bodleian Library of the now lost institution rolls of Bishop Oliver Sutton, whose surviving register was edited for the Society by Professor Hill; these cover the years 1280–90 for the archdeaconries of Buckingham, Oxford and Huntingdon and 1280–6 for the earliest portion of the Leicester archdeaconry roll. His calendar, presented posthumously following Professor Smith's untimely death in Romania in 2022, will no doubt prove invaluable to Nicholas in compiling his monumental register of Lincolnshire parish clergy.

Many of the contributions to this volume unsurprisingly focus on the medieval city, county and diocese of Lincoln, and/or on ecclesiastical records of the era. Julian Haseldine takes on Lincoln's most illustrious episcopal figure, Robert Grosseteste (in office 1235–53). By interrogating Grosseteste's correspondence, that 'carefully curated and highly selective collection of stylised, rhetorically polished Latin letters',[1] which aimed to cement his contemporary posthumous reputation, he aims to get deeper insights into the ideology of one of the medieval period's greatest theologians, philosophers and reformers in sphere of Church governance and pastoral care. The letters both predate and encompass Grosseteste's episcopate in Lincoln and demonstrate his intellectual prowess (often in self-justification) and the variety of concerns with which he dealt, especially with clerical insufficiency, absenteeism or unsuitability for office and royal and lay control of and interference in clerical appointment and monastic settlement. In particular, he shows that Grosseteste was deeply, perhaps unusually thoroughly, committed to the concept of hierarchy within

1 See p. 72 below.

the Church to deliver effective spiritual and moral care for the community, in that personal belief required for salvation would come from priestly communication of and conviction in what would be needed to achieve it, and, in turn, from episcopal appointment of suitable (resident) men as pastors. Here, Grosseteste was rooted in, and staunchly, often aggressively, advocated ecclesiastical and spiritual reforms that had shifted religious culture in Europe since the twelfth century and changed the relationship between clerical authority and laity – those ideals of priestly chastity, moderation and 'purity' (the *vita apostolica*) derived from the monastic vocation – and of more recent developments in mendicant, itinerant preaching, often in urban centres, which he vigorously promoted.

Conversely, this higher ideal of priestly separation from laity and of providing exemplars within communities that would teach and thereby fit parishioners for salvation comes under scrutiny in the contribution of Philippa Hoskin, who has succeeded Nicholas as LRS General Editor. She challenges long-held understanding of benefit of clergy for criminous clerks in England by examining the tensions inherent in the case of Master Thomas of Pontesbury, a beneficed clergyman accused of murder in Shropshire in 1288, who, while claiming benefit and being allowed to compurgate, remained subject to secular sanction, partly of his own volition in pleading before royal justice and pursuit over several years. Pontesbury's case arguably highlights the self-perception of some rectors of parish churches in England as laymen who regarded their appointment as a means to an income and not as a way of life – certainly not in the manner Grosseteste and other clerical reformers would have perceived it. Accusations by witnesses to the violent deed that Pontesbury had subsequently preached in the pulpit of the good character of his victim, and his subsequent maltreatment by the parishioners of Cranfield in Bedfordshire where he took refuge and later also became rector, and another community on the Welsh Marches which accused him of a second murder, would seem to reinforce this viewpoint. Of wider import for studies of clerical criminality is the refusal by Edward I to return Pontesbury's goods seized within the diocese of Lincoln despite his compurgation elsewhere as a Cranfield jury had found him guilty of murder.

In her contribution, Marianne Wilson, the brainchild behind this tribute volume, examines similar issues within the community of the diocesan mother church, Lincoln Cathedral. Taking as her subject its many chantries, their founders and those who staffed them in the later Middle Ages, Marianne weaves together original records, many of which remain unpublished or are available in LRS editions – episcopal registers, chapter acts and chantry certificates – to assess the extent to which high standards of behaviour were met by those whose liturgical life centred on the speeding of souls to Heaven. She reveals the tensions between high spiritual ideals and the reality of administration and of human frailty: the sources document a litany of brawls, brushes with drink and gambling, sexual vices and failure to perform core duties. Nevertheless, they also emphasise the extent of the authority delegated to the Cathedral's dean and chapter to administer chantries and the life of the community; this points to a genuine care and attention, over many decades, by founders and ecclesiastical authorities to fulfilling the wishes of chantry founders and regulating the behaviour of priests, and thereby of the spiritual's interaction with the secular in one of England's great medieval cities.

The blurred lines between clerk and layman, between Church and State jurisdiction, the difficulties of providing adequate pastoral care and of an individual's self-perception and role within the community at large are all at play here. It is a similar interest in the intricate stories legal records can tell about clerical and lay interaction in crime which inspires David Crook's contribution. He discusses, with an appendix of edited plea roll entries, a previously unnoticed early trespass case, brought by a writ *quare* in King's Bench from 1259 to 1260, which revolves around the depasturing, or illicit removal, of crops by grazing animals on them. This was an ultimately unresolved dispute between a parish rector and lay lessee in Welby in rural Kesteven and agents of both the local Cistercian abbey of Vaudey and of the Hospital of St Katherine south of Lincoln, of which the latter were accused of violently breaking the bounds of an estate at night, burning and then grazing crops, as well as stealing sheep. Setting this classic rural dispute in a broader setting, however, reveals much about, not only local landholding and power networks in this corner of Lincolnshire, but also tells us something of the desire of the Montfortian reformers to reach into local judicial matters and, crucially, of the nature of legal knowledge in rural England during the thirteenth century.

Lastly, another former President of the Society, Michael Jones, presents an analysis and an edition of a fourteenth-century survey of the Lincolnshire estates of the honour of Richmond now to be found in the departmental archives of Loire-Atlantique in Brittany. The honour, returned to Duke John IV by John of Gaunt under pressure from Edward III in 1372, provided a reliable income for the exiled Breton leader at a critical stage in the Anglo-French conflict. The surviving documents largely relate to the years 1372–79 and found their way back to Brittany upon his return in 1379. Several of them detail the dukes' relationships with the English crown, and several give intimate detail of over five hundred 'homagers', free and bonded tenants owing homage to the duke in Lincolnshire, as well as other charters relating to Boston. One of the chief insights these records provide is into the administration of honorial lands, differing from manors to groups of estates. Likewise, the financial detail of receipts shows the extent to which the duke could rely on each of his dispersed Lincolnshire estates for his income as well as, for example, the damage from flooding, while the 1377 bailiff's account for Boston gives us the earliest known description of the manor house, its surrounds and the repairs required in preparation for a ducal visit in October of that year. These accounts are a goldmine for socioeconomic history, detailing as they do property tenure, farming and renting of estates, sales of produce, and expenses on maintaining seigneurial buildings. This chapter is, as Michael himself says, presented as a tribute to Nicholas's commitment to making records and research on the historic diocese of Lincoln available to others.

Upon completing his doctoral studies, Nicholas's new post at Lincoln Cathedral Library, to which he was appointed in 2003, proved the perfect setting for his remarkable scholarship. The Cathedral's extraordinary collection of medieval manuscripts and rare books – not solely concerned with theology – were a source of constant discovery and delight and also a stimulus to scholarly projects of all sorts. The increasingly large number of enquiries now arriving at the Cathedral Library prompted many of Nicholas's additional research interests, and engaged not just his existing knowledge of cathedral and diocesan history but also often required further investigation. Such research was the mainspring of a renewed cathedral publication effort – The Honywood Press, of which he was the first editor and which continues today as Lincoln Cathedral Publications. This is an immensely valuable series of short works, each addressing an important theme or topic relating to the Cathedral. Nicholas not only edited the series for more than twenty years but contributed his own delicious volumes on the journey of Charles I into captivity, Thomas de Aston and on Bishop Christopher Wordsworth. Less enjoyable was the writing of various funding bids, the most successful of which enabled the installation of a heating and de-humidification system in the Wren Library in 2000.

Soon after Nicholas was appointed Cathedral Librarian, Carol became a library volunteer, eventually becoming a member of staff with responsibility for administering (*inter alia*) the Library's new *Adopt a Book* programme. In addition to the much-admired concert programme, with her background in adult education she facilitated use of the Wren Library for exhibitions, lectures and study days. In 1994 the library mounted an exhibition on the early colonisation of New England and Virginia, based on Dean Honywood's own contemporary collection, and this included readings and performances. Such work soon attracted a lively team of readers, performers and researchers to the library, including Linda Tilbury, John Wells-Cole, John Davies and Liz Lucas. Sometimes these events were moving – as in the event commemorating the 350th anniversary of Charles I's execution – and sometimes they were hilarious – as when the ladies of Guatemala took revenge on their bishop for banning the drinking of chocolate during long sermons in the Cathedral (according to the Library's copy of Henry Stubbe's 1662 *Discourse on Chocolata*). The Cathedral Library events programme was continued until 2015, with Julie Taylor stepping up on Nicholas's retirement. Simon Armitage came as a reader for one event and later gave a lecture on King

Arthur including his verse rendition of *Morte d'Arthur*, based on a source in the library's fifteenth-century *Thornton Romances*. He described how his project was treated with disdain by the British Library but greeted warmly by Nicholas, whom he described as 'a friendly chap with a bow tie'. Yet it was not until Marianne Wilson told Simon Armitage, 'We studied you for GCSE English', that Nicholas realised how famous Simon was!

During these halcyon days at the Wren Library, when 'Study Days' were such a feature, those organised alongside the Katherine Swynford Society proved the most popular. One year Alison Weir came in whilst preparing for her book about this famous partner of John of Gaunt, and resident of Minster Yard, but Nicholas was always a great supporter of any interesting new research on Katherine's life and times and indeed on any other topic. He will, we hope, be fascinated by the paper presented here by the Society's current President, David Stocker, who presents a view of Katherine as a woman who exerted considerable political independence following the death of Gaunt in 1399 to her own death in 1403. This, Katherine achieved not simply as dowager duchess of Lancaster but also, in retiring to Lincoln Cathedral Close and its surroundings, as countess of Lincoln, by pursuing a tradition of independent political action initiated by an earlier fourteenth-century countess, Alice de Lacy (d. 1348). Alice had, it is argued, used her isolation from court to create a significant endowment of the comital abbey at Barlings to create a mausoleum for the earldom of Lincoln, from which Katherine would later benefit.

Both women, widows, fled from the political heart of the country to Lincoln as the maelstrom of rebellion, in Alice's case in 1322, and the loss of her powerful husband, in Katherine's in 1399, threatened to leave them destitute and at the mercy of a tyrannical king. Both fought hard to negotiate their rights to the ancient core property and status of the earldom of Lincoln, where they would bide their time. The argument presented here is that in 1399 Katherine adopted and adapted the model of passive resistance followed by Alice to her own circumstances to assert her independence from the crown and protect her position as Gaunt's widow and stepmother to the rebel Henry of Bolingbroke, until he took the throne with her support in September 1399. Katherine's own 'passive resistance' continued in taking the veil and becoming a vowess in Lincoln, where she intended to be buried and memorialised, and, in further endowing Barlings, extending her association with Alice de Lacy and an earlier Lancastrian path of resistance.

The period of lively events programming at the Library initiated by Nicholas and Carol proved a mini golden age, connecting the Cathedral's magnificent collection of books and manuscripts with both international scholars and the Lincoln public. Furthermore, all this activity at the Cathedral Library served an additional important function – slowly introducing historians from the new University of Lincoln (founded 1996) to the 'native' academic community, among whom our two remaining contributors might be counted. Without embarrassing either too much, the first, Rob Wheeler, is someone whose catholic interests mirror those of Nicholas himself. Both share a minor passion for railway history. In his chapter, Rob takes us back to the 'Railway Mania' of the mid-1840s. Here, he forensically examines the bubble that dramatically burst in that decade through the case study of the failed Wainfleet Haven Railway. He challenges the established narrative that this – and perhaps other infamous projects approved by Parliament – was a fraudulent endeavour cooked up to attract investors who would be fleeced. Instead, by examining the documentation for the scheme and the local press, and running the biographical rule over its promoters and organisational structure, he reveals not only the kind of man involved in early railway enterprise but also the myriad challenges facing promoters and the methods they explored to overcome them: most notably the difficulties of the proposed route from the marsh to the mainline, and in finding an engineer to survey the line and so attract subscriptions for shares; and their rather fantastical expectations for traffic from Yorkshire and the Midlands. Tracing the plans for the route, Rob digs deep into the early Victorian history of many localities within mid-Lincolnshire, only some of which would become railways hubs, and postulates that a datum error, discovered late in the legal process, and deteriorating relationships with local drainage boards wrecked the scheme and triggered its financial collapse.

The final chapter in this festschrift comes from Andrew Walker, former Head of History at the University of Lincoln and a major figure in both the Survey of Lincoln and the Society for Lincolnshire History and Archaeology. It returns us to one of Nicholas Bennett's greatest passions and contributions to scholarship – the bishops of Lincoln. The subject here, however, is not a distant, enigmatic figure of the Middle Ages but one of Lincoln's most charismatic and radical twentieth-century Church leaders. Edward Lee Hicks, bishop from 1910 to 1919, is one of the diocese's best understood personalities due to the edition of his diaries by Graham Neville published in volume 82. However, rather less studied are Hicks' published responses to war in the *Lincoln Diocesan Magazine*, the documentary focus of this chapter. Over fifty months, Bishop Hicks published short letters to his clergy and the laity of his diocese in which he charts life on the Home Front in a large, rural county with limited means of communication.

For a forum viewed by many contemporaries as dry and dull, Hicks' letters display a radical political edge honed during his earlier career in Manchester and expressed in his opposition to the Boer War. Indeed, he expressed sympathy for the peace movement as war loomed, despite local criticism, but accepted its necessity and sought to walk a fine line between pacifism and patriotic support for the war. He regularly praised the county's troops while arguing against clerical enlistment, save for National Service in the agricultural and munitions industries. He also became a leading advocate of women's involvement in war work in his role as President of the Church League for Women's Suffrage. As the horrors of war came home to the populace, his stance hardened and became more emotive, expressing sympathy for the German soldiers as opposed to the Kaiser and the high command. Further than this, Hicks railed against the influence of drink on the soldiery and the aid it gave men to slide into immorality at a time of crisis. And yet, towards the end of his life, Hicks gave much thought to the postwar world of the returning soldier, the broken family unit, broken communities and terrible social conditions, advocating reform of education to improve teaching standards, class sizes and length of study. Hicks appears in this correspondence every bit the dynamic, compassionate churchmen who Nicholas Bennett has spent much of his life researching.

Throughout his career Nicholas has generously shared his knowledge and experience with scholars at all levels. At Lincoln Castle in the early 1980s his assistance was in constant demand amongst regulars and 'blow-ins' alike. Nicholas was then still a youngster himself, at the start of his Lincolnshire career, yet his regular advisees were people like Jim Johnston (Head of History, later Vice Principal, at Bishop Grosseteste), Ken Cameron (Professor of English Language at the University of Nottingham), Dorothy and Arthur Owen (both librarians and archivists at Cambridge) and Paul Everson (Lincolnshire Investigator for the Royal Commission on the Historical Monuments of England). So, it was a distinguished symposium meeting in that unusual prison search room, but Nicholas managed to foster a spirit of friendly and collaborative enquiry amongst these history Titans – something he still strives for in the very different circumstances of the Rumbold Street search room today. Nicholas still visits Lincolnshire Archives most weeks, where readers frequently ask him to decipher handwriting or translate Latin and the staff often consult him about more technical archival matters. He also still volunteers in the Exchequergate office of Lincoln Cathedral Library, where Claire Arrand – the University of Lincoln's Special Collections librarian, now seconded to the Cathedral – welcomes his profound knowledge of the Cathedral's collections.

At the Cathedral Library Nicholas has also achieved a similar minor miracle to that witnessed at the Castle forty years ago; stimulating a sense of friendly collaborative research amongst the increasing numbers of scholars who used to beat a path to the Library office on the cold and draughty staircase in the cloister – or latterly to Exchequergate. Some of these scholars have become library volunteers, and some have been able to secure employment subsequently, thanks to Nicholas's encouragement. In 2002 for example, Lesley Hollamby invited Nicholas and Carol to their wedding anniversary celebrations, where Nicholas explained to Lesley's husband – Ken – the Treasurer's role at LRS; not too onerous a role, he said! Another library volunteer, Lynn Godson, was persuaded to become LRS Secretary in 2006. Still a chorister, young volunteer Robert Tyrwhitt told his parents he wanted them to meet his new friend. They were surprised to see that Nicholas was considerably older than their son's other friends but in his first job with Christie's, Robert's work involved rare books. Volunteer Katie Lord's career took her to the Royal Collection at Windsor Castle, whilst Katie Cormack (Patrick Cormack's granddaughter) is currently studying to be an archivist. When Marianne Wilson was studying Lincoln Cathedral Close wills for her doctorate at the University of Nottingham, she became a regular visitor to the Exchequergate Library to work with the Chapter Acts, benefiting from Nicholas's unrivalled expertise and support as an honorary thesis supervisor, and establishing a firm friendship with both Nicholas and Carol. Similarly, Paul Dryburgh received warm welcomes and the task of helping to catalogue Dean and Chapter deeds while studying for own Diploma in Archive Administration around that time. Currently, Jess Holt, a University of Lincoln doctoral student working on an edition of the register of Bishop Bek (1342–7), continues this long tradition and benefits from Nicholas's gentle guidance either in the Archives Office, over coffee at Waterstones, or at the Bennetts' enormous Nocton research library.

Nicholas's life, then, has been devoted both to the past itself, managing the records themselves, and to ensuring a future for the past, through his broader educational work and through the many younger contemporaries who have drawn inspiration from his words and example of dedication. This volume contains essays by some of those who have been privileged to have dealings with him, as friends and collaborators in his many historical enterprises. It tackles many themes dear to Nicholas: the Church, its clergy and records, Lincoln and its magnificent cathedral, its history, its people and its manuscripts, and the wider county and diocese.

NICHOLAS BENNETT – A COMPLETE BIBLIOGRAPHY

COMPILED BY PAUL DRYBURGH (WITH ASSISTANCE FROM CAROL BENNETT)

Books (Sole Author)

Wonderful to Behold: a Centenary History of the Lincoln Record Society, 1910–2010, Lincoln Record Society 100 (Woodbridge: Boydell, 2010)

Books (Editor and Contributor)

Victoria and Albert: Treasures from a Royal Marriage (Catalogue for an Exhibition to Mark the 200th Anniversaries of the Births of Victoria and Albert, Victoria and Albert Museum and Historic Lincoln Trust, 2019)

Battles and Dynasties: An Exhibition to Mark the 800th Anniversary of the Battle of Lincoln (Lincoln: Historic Lincoln Trust, 2017)

Lincolnshire's Great Exhibition: Treasures, Saints and Heroes (Scala for Historic Lincoln Trust, 2015)

Lincolnshire Parish Clergy, c. 1214–1968: a Biographical Register. Part I, The Deaneries of Aslacoe and Aveland; Part II, The Deaneries of Beltisloe and Bolingbroke, 2 volumes, Lincoln Record Society 103, 105 (Woodbridge: Boydell, 2013–16)

'Gratefull to providence': the diary and accounts of Matthew Flinders, surgeon, apothecary and man-midwife, 1775–1802, ed. N. H. Bennett and M. Beardsley, 2 volumes, Lincoln Record Society, 95, 97 (Woodbridge: Boydell, 2007–09)

The Registers of Bishop Henry Burghersh, 1320–1342, 3 volumes, Lincoln Record Society 87, 90, 101 (Woodbridge: Boydell, 1999–2011)

Thomas de Aston and the diocese of Lincoln: two studies in the fourteenth-century church, ed. N. H. Bennett and D. Marcombe (Lincoln, 1998)

An Historical Atlas of Lincolnshire, ed. N. H. Bennett and S. Bennett (Hull: Hull University Press, 1993; reprinted Chichester: Philimore, 2001)

The Register of Richard Fleming, Bishop of Lincoln 1420–31, 3 volumes, Canterbury and York Society 73, 99, 113 (York and Woodbridge: Boydell, 1984–2023)

Articles and Chapters in Books

'Hope or Expectation? Papal Provision of Poor Clerks in the Diocese of Lincoln, 1320–1347', in *Popes, Bishops, Friars and Scholars: Studies in Medieval History Presented to Patrick N. R. Zutshi for his Seventieth Birthday*, ed. Michael Robson and Peter D. Clarke (Turnhout: Brepols, 2025)

'Fear and Loathing in Fourteenth-Century Rutland: The Segregation of the Rector of Seaton', in *Christian Culture and Society in Later Catholic England: Studies in Memory of Donald Logan*, ed. Travis Baker (Leiden: Brill, 2024), pp. 584–602

'The Road to Losecoat Field: The Story of the First Lincolnshire Rising', *The Ricardian* XXX (2020), 137–50

'The Face of One Making for Jerusalem: The Chapter of Lincoln during the Episcopate of Robert Grosseteste', in *Bishop Robert Grosseteste and Lincoln Cathedral: Tracing Relationships between Medieval Concepts of Order and Built Form*, ed. N. Temple, J. S. Hendrix and C. Frost (Farnham: Ashgate, 2014), pp. 17–28

A Portrait of Bishop Christopher Wordsworth (Honywood Papers, Lincoln Cathedral, 2009)

'Pastors and Masters: the Beneficed Clergy of North-East Lincolnshire, 1290–1340', in *The Foundations of Medieval English Ecclesiastical History: Studies Presented to David Smith*, ed. C. N. L. Brooke, R. B. Dobson and P. M. Hoskin (Woodbridge: Studies in the History of Medieval Religion 27, 2005), pp. 40–62

Articles in *Oxford Dictionary of National Biography* (https://www.oxforddnb.com):

'Burghersh, Henry (*c.* 1290–1340), bishop of Lincoln'

'Dalderby, John (*d.* 1320), bishop of Lincoln'

'Fuller, William (1608/9–1675), bishop of Lincoln'

'Honywood, Michael (1596–1681), dean of Lincoln'

'Zouche, William (*d.* 1352), administrator and archbishop of York'

'If You Came at Night Like a Broken King': The Journey of Charles I into Captivity (Honywood Papers, Lincoln Cathedral, 1999)

'A. R. Maddison and the development of local history in Lincolnshire', in *Some Historians of Lincolnshire: Lectures Delivered in 1989*, ed. Christopher Sturman (Lincoln: Society for Lincolnshire History and Archaeology, 1992), pp. 27–31

'Blunham rectory accounts 1520–1539', in *Hundreds, Manors, Parishes and the Church: a Selection of Early Documents for Bedfordshire*, ed. J. S. Thompson, Bedfordshire Historical Record Society (Bedford, 1990), pp. 124–69

Forthcoming

Lincolnshire Parish Clergy, c. 1214–1968: a Biographical Register. Part 3, The Deanery of Calcewaith, Lincoln Record Society (Woodbridge: Boydell, 2026)

1

The Building of the Medieval and Wren Libraries at Lincoln Cathedral[1]

CAROL BENNETT

When giving a library tour, former Cathedral Librarian Nicholas Bennett would begin by saying, 'In terms of its buildings and collections, Lincoln Cathedral Library ranks among the top five cathedral libraries in the country'. These buildings are the Medieval Library of *c.* 1422 and the Wren Library of 1676. It is remarkable that both are still in use, that the building of the more modern library did not replace the old one, and that they both retain original fittings that were purpose-made for them. Of outstanding importance is the fact that Dean Michael Honywood's collection of books is still kept in the library he asked Sir Christopher Wren to design. These two buildings, which take up the north side of the cloister, have the appearance of a unified, classical design when viewed from the cloister garth. Most of this expanse is the Wren Library; behind the two cross windows on the north is the Medieval Library. When its length was truncated in 1789, its façade facing the cloister was made to look as if it was part of the classical Wren Library.

Before Building a Library

The first library catalogue was compiled by Chancellor Hamo in the mid-twelfth century, naming donors and the books they gave or bequeathed to the cathedral. It is bound in Volume I of the Lincoln Chapter Bible (MS1), which was given by Archdeacon Nicholas of Huntingdon for use in the new cathedral. Additions

1 I would like to thank the following people for their help and advice in my research: Dan Beal, Mike Belshaw, Nicholas Bennett, Norman and Sheila Bonner, Ian Bristow, John Culverhouse, Michael Czjakowski, Anthony Geraghty, Peter Hoare, the Revd Philip Johnson, Tom Küpper, James Newton, Rebecca Phillips, Gavin Simpson, Julie Taylor and John Wilton-Ely. I would also like to acknowledge the guidance of the late David Vale and Nigel Leaney.

Figure 1. The Wren and Medieval Libraries, from 1676 to 1788 with the Wolsey Tower of the Deanery to the left (DAVID VALE/113, © Dean and Chapter of Lincoln Cathedral).

to this page continued until the early thirteenth century, including three books given by St Hugh, Bishop of Lincoln. The first section lists forty-four books for study, including patristic writings, sermons, Bible commentaries, lives of the saints and books on canon law. Eleven of these survive. The second section lists twenty-six service books, '*qui tunc erant in ecclesia*', which were looked after by the treasurer.[2] These included missals, collectars, homiliars, benedictionals, a breviary, psalters and the martyrologium read daily in chapter.[3] None of these now survive in Lincoln.

According to an inscription on the catalogue page, books for study were kept '*in armario*' in the care of the chancellor. It is unclear if this was this a chest, a cupboard or a cabinet, but Rod Thomson has pointed out that MS 31, the only book with its original twelfth-century binding, was meant to rest fore-edge down in a chest. It had flaps on the spine that would have enabled the book to be pulled out of the chest; these were cut off when the book was chained.[4] As the collection grew, greater provision for keeping them must have been made, but what form this took, and where books were stored, is not recorded. Among the duties of the chancellor outlined in the 1236–37 *Consuetudines* in the *Liber Niger* is the care of books of theology and others like them, kept in the '*armoriolum*', which is a cupboard, closet or bookcase. There is no information where it was situated, only that the list of the books in the chancellor's care, which he was charged with checking regularly, was kept '*in thessauraria*'.[5] Hamo's catalogue records that service books were kept in the cathedral, and as they were in constant use, they were likely to have continued to be stored there up to the Reformation.[6] Books such as the *Martyrologium* were read, and possibly also kept, in the chapter house; indeed, reading there was part of the *Opus Dei*.

Lincoln's chapter house was not only a place for chapter meetings, but a community space, where the men and boys who served the cathedral were informed of their corporate responsibilities in the services. In addition, it was a place for prayer and education. Many English cathedrals and religious houses

2 R. M. Thomson, *Catalogue of the Manuscripts of Lincoln Cathedral Chapter Library* (Cambridge, 1989), I, xiii–xiv. Henceforth referred to as Thomson.

3 N. Bennett, 'The Medieval Library of Lincoln Cathedral', unpublished lecture in the Wren Library, 17 September 1999.

4 Thomson, pp. xiii–xiv.

5 H. Bradshaw and C. Wordsworth (eds), *Statutes of Lincoln Cathedral* (Cambridge, 1892), *Liber Niger: the Black Book of the Dean and Chapter of Lincoln,* 'Consuetudines et officia ecclesie Lincolniensis', 5: *'De officio cancellarii ... libros etiam theologie custodire et alios similiter in armoriolo conseruare*', pp. 284–5. This section dates from 1236–37 (see p. 231) and was transcribed into the Black Book from the now lost *Cancellaria* in 1300.

6 Thomson, pp. xvii–xviii.

had an association between the chapter house and the cloister as places of study. When libraries were built, these rooms were often placed near them, as at Lincoln, Salisbury and Hereford among the secular cathedrals.[7] The pattern of worship in a secular cathedral was very like that of a cathedral served by monks. The cloister provided, at the very least, a place for fresh air and relaxation as a break from the constant round of services.[8] Lincoln's clergy were not obliged to observe set hours for study, as the Benedictines at Gloucester would do, using the carrels in the great cloister. [9] Yet at Lincoln the cloister may have provided a place for study in the training of priests. According to the Clerical Poll Tax for 1377, there were as many as 130 men and boys listed as living in 'the Close of the Mother Church at Lincoln'. Of these, eleven were Poor Clerks, most of whom would be destined for ordination as priests. Among the Vicars Choral there were three in the minor order of acolytes, and in the major orders there were three subdeacons and three deacons.[10] A '*magister scholarum*' is mentioned in the *Liber Niger*, and Richard Gravesend (bishop 1258–79) made provision for a Master of the Choir Boys.[11] Aside from formal lessons in grammar and singing,[12] from the mid-thirteenth century, those training for the priesthood would be encouraged to read manuals for priests, which were collections of texts mostly on the sacraments and pastoral care.[13]

7 N. Pevsner, rev. B. Cherry, *The Buildings of England*, Wiltshire (Harmondsworth, 1985), p. 419; J. Williams, 'The Library', in G. Aylmer and J. Tiller (eds), *Hereford Cathedral, a History* (London and Rio Grande 2000), p. 512. Hereford's 1487 library was above the west walk of the Bishop's Cloister, facing the chapter house, which was off the east walk.

8 At Lincoln there were ten major daily services. Matins, followed by Lauds, were begun at midnight in winter and dawn in summer; Lady Mass was at around 8 a.m., followed by Prime sung in St Hugh's Choir; Tierce, High Mass, Sext and None were sung in the Choir in succession – and all of this took place before 11 a.m. In the afternoon there was Vespers, followed by Compline. In addition, chantry priests, some accompanied by choristers, sang Mass at chantries at various altars at different times of the day. See M. Bowker, 'Historical Survey 1750–1949', in D. Owen (ed.), *The History of Lincoln Minster* (Cambridge, 1994), chapter 6, p. 169.

9 N. Pevsner and D. Verey (eds) *The Buildings of England, Gloucestershire: The Vale and the Forest of Dean* (Harmondsworth, 1970), p. 220.

10 A. McHardy (ed.), *Clerical Poll Taxes of the Diocese of Lincoln 1377–1381*, LRS 81 (Woodbridge, 1992), pp. 1–2.

11 C. Wordsworth, *Notes on Medieval Services in England* (London, 1898), p. 275.

12 For a list of medieval schools in Lincoln see N. Orme, *Medieval Schools from Roman Britain to Renaissance England* (New Haven and London, 2006), pp. 358–9.

13 J. Shinners and W. J. Dohar (eds) *Pastors and the Care of Souls in Medieval England* (Notre Dame, 1998) Chapter 2, 'Education', pp. 33–48. It is unclear if any of the few priests' manuals in the Cathedral Library's collection were at Lincoln in the Middle Ages.

The partial glazing of the cloister was a nod to comfort for anyone spending time there. There are rebates for glass in the geometric tracery of the cloister arcades, both in the tracery of each bay, and in the tops of the double pairs of lancets below.[14] Salisbury Cathedral used the same glazing system as Lincoln,[15] but there the cloister has retained its original appearance, with lancet openings practically down to the ground. At Lincoln the lancets were shortened by the addition of low walls within each bay, most likely to strengthen the buckling arcades, as will be discussed later. Originally the glazed part covered about one third of the opening in each bay – perhaps enough to keep the worst of the weather out when resting or reading between services.

Building the Medieval Library

When clergy borrowed books, and for whatever reason failed to return them, the collection of valuable manuscripts for study suffered losses, even though a borrower was required to replace a lost book with another of similar value.[16] But, like other cathedrals, the chapter did not provide a purpose-built room for the storage and reading of books until the fifteenth century. By 1450 it seemed as if no cathedral worth its salt was complete without one. York's original library of 1418–20, now the Minster Shop, is a two-storeyed building of four bays, the top floor being the library room, situated south of the east end of the nave.[17] At Wells, Bishop Nicholas Bubwith left a bequest in 1424 for a large library over the east walk of the cloister.[18] St Paul's library was established by Walter Sherrington, prebendary from 1440–49, over the east wing of the Pardon Churchyard cloister.[19] Salisbury's library of 1445 was built above the north half of the east range of the cloister, near the chapter house.[20] Among monastic foundations, Archbishop Chichele's library in Canterbury Cathedral was built over the Prior's Chapel by 1444,[21] and by 1450 Gloucester had built

14 I am grateful to former head glazier Tom Küpper for his guidance, and to cathedral glazier Dan Beal for pointing out that some of the tracery rebates have been chipped away in a regular fashion, where glaziers needed to create some easement to fit the glass into awkwardly shaped openings.

15 Dan Beal, *pers. comm.*

16 See Thomson, I, xvi.

17 N. Pevsner & J. Nairn (eds), *The Buildings of England, Yorkshire: York and the East Riding* (Harmondsworth, 1972), p. 93.

18 N. Pevsner, *The Buildings of England: North Somerset and Bristol* (Harmondsworth, 1979), pp. 310–12.

19 C. M. Barron and M. H. Rousseau, 'Cathedral City and State', in D. Keene, A. Burns & A. Saint (eds), *St Paul's the Cathedral Church of London 604–2004* (London, 2004), p. 42.

20 N. Pevsner, rev. B. Cherry, *Wiltshire* (Harmondsworth, 1985), p. 419.

21 R. B. Dobson, 'The Monks of Canterbury in the later Middle Ages', in P.

their library.[22] Lincoln's Medieval Library was built by 1422. After Philip of Repingdon resigned his bishopric in 1419, he gave a book 'to the new library to be built within the church at Lincoln'.[23] On 14 November 1421, thirty beams of timber were assigned '*ad opus fabrice nove librarie*';[24] and an inscription in a book given by Chancellor Thomas Duffield states that he gave this book to the new library in 1422.[25]

Like the others listed above, Lincoln's library was situated at first-floor level, where there was more daylight than at ground floor level, and less danger of damp. (See fig. 1) Timber-framed, with cob infill,[26] and roofed in lead, it was originally of five bays, extending from the northeast corner of the cloister to the chapter house. Three bays survive; two further bays originally rested on top of the east walk of the cloister. Access from a pre-existing newel staircase in the north turret of the chapter house vestibule connected to the library at a higher level, necessitating a few steps down from the turret door into the new room. Within the turret, the former doorway to the library has a male head stop. On the exterior, the position of the old door in the staircase turret can be seen clearly; the machine sawn ashlar blocking of the lower half of the straight headed opening, which turned it into a window, appears to be J. L. Pearson's work in the late nineteenth century. The site for the library was chosen for its proximity to the chapter house: not only was it convenient for taking books to read in the chapter house or cathedral and returning them, it was also secure. The new system of chaining books to desks dramatically reduced losses. Eventually a new catalogue was drawn up, describing the books as 'newly chained'.[27] It lists 109 titles, of which eighty-eight survive, demonstrating the effectiveness of chaining.[28]

Collinson, N. Ramsay, and M. Sparks (eds), *A History of Canterbury Cathedral* (Oxford, 1995), III, 110.

22 Rebecca Phillips, Gloucester Cathedral Archivist, *pers. comm.* She has revised the Gloucester library's date from the fourteenth century to *c.* 1400–50, based on library masons' marks matching marks in the *c.* 1450 tower, and the cathedral's 1390 *Historia*, which does not mention a library, but does raise concern for the care of the archives.

23 Thomson, III, xvii, n. 44. Repingdon's book is now in the Royal Collection: BL, MS Royal 8 G. iii).

24 G. Simpson, *et al.*, *Lincoln Cathedral: Archive Report on the Medieval and Later Roofs* (Nottingham, 1998), citing LA, A/2/32, fol. 14, p. 39. Henceforth referred to as Simpson.

25 Thomson, III, xvii, n. 44. This is MS 86 in Lincoln Cathedral Library's [hereafter LCL] collection.

26 Simpson, p. 39.

27 LA, D & C, Bij/3/12, n.d.; R. M. Woolley, *Catalogue of the Manuscripts of Lincoln Cathedral Chapter Library* (Oxford and London, 1927), item 295, p. 182.

28 Thomson, III, xvii.

The Medieval Library has a complicated building history, so an outline is needed here. When the Wren Library was completed in 1676, another access to the Medieval Library was made to create an entrance to the new library. This consisted of a staircase that rose in the northeast corner of the old north cloister walk through the floor of the Medieval Library, opposite the door of the Wren Library.[29] Both libraries stood side-by-side, and complete, until 1789, when the two bays of the Medieval Library over the east cloister were demolished. At the same time, a new staircase was built in a new annex, which connects to the cloister through the large late thirteenth-century arch in the northeast cloister wall. This staircase was altered about a hundred years later by J. L. Pearson during extensive works to the cloister, chapter house and Medieval Library, to make it ascend in the opposite direction to the eighteenth-century staircase, for reasons which will be explained later.

Measuring approximately 7 by 6.01 metres,[30] the Medieval Library projects more than a metre beyond the east wall of the cloister; less beyond the north wall.[31] J. L. Pearson renewed the east and north walls of the timber frame between 1893 and 1896,[32] but the low-pitched roof is original.[33] The oak timbers have never been stained; their rich colour is due to the natural ageing process. The principal trusses have tie beams, which support short king posts. Each tie beam is decorated with a circular carved boss directly below the foot of the king post, depicting roses, a grotesque face and a quatrefoil. Brackets on either side of the king posts are decorated with human heads, except for the south one, which is the head of a fanciful beast. Each bay has seven rafters on each side. The middle rafters of each bay have circular bosses, and another boss where the rafters join the ridge. They include two angels playing lute-like ouds, two roses, an imaginary bat/snake figure, a lion's face with mouth foliage, a foliage swirl, a dog fighting a wyvern, and a phoenix. At the foot of these rafters are sole pieces supporting six characterful three-quarter-length angels, covered in feathers, with diadems in their effulgent hair. Their style would not be out of place in East Anglia. They are six-winged seraphim, each having one pair of wings descending from the elbows like sleeves, and a second pair, like a girdle around the

29 B. Willis, *A Survey of the Cathedrals ...* (London, 1730), vol. 3, plan in 'Lincoln Cathedral', pp. 25–35. Henceforth referred to as Willis.

30 Simpson, p. 39.

31 The timbers supporting the floor are medieval. There is a dragon beam to support this jettied arrangement in the northeast corner of the floor, exposed during building work when heating was installed in 2000.

32 LA, D & C, uncatalogued, *Lincoln Cathedral. Statement of Expenditure on Fabric and Church Furniture Accounts from 1874 to [1897].* The first payment for the library staircase was in 1893; the last payment to Thompson the builders was in 1896.

33 Simpson, p. 39.

Figure 2. The Medieval Library from 1422 to 1788 (DAVID VALE/7, © Dean and Chapter of Lincoln Cathedral).

torso, which disappears into carved stylised clouds. The third set of wings on the back, enabling the seraphim to fly, can only be seen clearly on a seventh angel, displayed on the south wall of the library, salvaged from the building when it was reduced in length.

Pearson's plan of his alterations to the room states that the roof is to keep its 'present rafters', and the quatrefoil decoration running along below the wall plate is to be refixed.[34] The quatrefoil band sits on top of a dentil course, and beneath that is a groove for panelling, now lost.[35] This quatrefoil decoration can also be found, in a pierced form, on the stretcher that strengthens the desks between their poppy heads. It is a pleasing detail that conveys the unity in design of the library building and its furnishings. No expense was spared. The room was lit on the east and west by two-light windows, one window on each side for each bay; the outline of an original window, later plastered over, can be seen in the west wall, to the left of the door. There are two original glazed windows of five lights. The large window in the north wall is in its original position; the one in the east wall presumably was salvaged from the south wall of the library as originally built. It is marked 'old window refixed' on Pearson's plan.[36] The desks were positioned at right angles to the east and west walls, placed centrally under the two-light windows, allowing daylight to fall equally on both slopes of the reading desks. There would have been room for up to ten desks, although, allowing space for the stairs, one may have been half the size of the others, with a single slope. The 109 chained books then in the collection could all fit on the desk slopes. Surviving marks of staples on some of the manuscripts show the book chains were attached on the bottom of the front cover, in the middle.[37]

There are three original desks and one bench. Early examples of flat pack furniture, the desks come apart in fourteen pieces; the components could be carried up the small winding staircase or hoisted through a window opening, and then assembled in the room. The pieces are marked with Roman numerals as a guide to construction. The tops of the desks are decorated with poppy heads at each end, with another one in the middle. Below the stretchers connecting the poppy heads are wooden dowels, modern replacements for the metal rods to which the books were chained. On the side of a desk facing into the room can be seen the mark of a hole in the wood where a hinged hasp was fixed at the end of the rod. The outline of locks can be seen where the wood was

34 J. L. Pearson, uncatalogued plan from the D & C Works Department archives, 'Lincoln Cathedral Old Library', dated 26 April 1892, with the address of Pearson's office, 13 Mansfield Street, London. One plan of three for the building and the staircase.

35 Norman Bonner, former cathedral head carpenter, *pers. comm.*

36 Pearson plan, 26 April 1892, uncatalogued D & C Works Department archive.

37 The more usual chaining on the fore-edge allows books to be stored upright in a row, but Lincoln's staple position would not allow for this.

pieced when the lock was later gouged out. When the hasp was closed over the lock, a key was turned to lock it in place to secure the rod. There is room in each bay for one bench to serve one side of each desk. Mouldings on both the bench and the desks were continuous until sawn apart. Originally each desk was connected by a plinth to a bench either side, like a picnic table.[38]

The desks are a remarkable survival of the Zutphen type of lectern desk, with two slopes and a rod above for chaining books, still to be found in the chained library of the Church of St Walburga, Zutphen, in The Netherlands.[39] Lincoln's desks are impressively tall and heavy, measuring 2.2 metres high by 2.1 metres in length, and just less than one metre in breadth.[40] Once common in English libraries, this type of desk was often adapted to hold more books by removing the slopes to make room for a bookcase and a flat desk. However, as libraries broke away from the medieval format, most of the Zutphen type desks were removed and replaced with new presses comprising tall bookcases and flat desks. A striking example of this can be found in Duke Humfrey's Library in Oxford's Bodleian Library. In 1960, Sir Thomas Bodley's 1601 three-decker book presses with flat desks were pulled away from the walls when the floor was repaired. This revealed shadow-like marks made on the walls by the ends of the Zutphen-type desks, original to the library when it was built in 1488.[41] Lincoln's system could not provide for the greater availability of books created by the printing press, so to make more room, a shelf was added beneath the slopes of each desk.[42] Indentations at regular intervals under the slopes' ledges mark where metal plates were fixed, allowing additional books to be chained.

Reformation, Civil War and Restoration

John Leland visited the library in 1533–34 and listed eleven manuscripts for the king; six or seven survive, of which four are in the Royal Collection.[43] By 1536 when the treasurer Henry Litherland drew up his inventory of the revestry (presumed to be in the treasury annex), it was full of numerous chalices, pyxes, reliquaries, images, candelabra, thuribles, mitres, copes and other treasures. A few books were listed under '*Textus Evangelorium*', now lost.

38 B. H. Streeter, *The Chained Library, a Survey of Four Centuries in the Evolution of the English Library* (London, 1931) pp. 17–18. Henceforth Streeter.

39 J. W. Clark, 'On Ancient Libraries: (1) Lincoln Cathedral…', *Cambridge Antiquarian Society Proceedings*, vol. 9, New Series 3 (1894–8), pp. 43–5.

40 Streeter, p. 16.

41 D. Rogers, *The Bodleian Library and its Treasures 1320–1700* (Nuffield, 1991), p. 17, figs 9 and 10; pp. 46–7, fig. 38.

42 Streeter, pp. 21–2.

43 Thomson, p. xx.

Four were covered in plates of silver or silver-gilt with religious imagery, and two were also set with precious stones;[44] their valuable covers would have merited them space in the treasury. As cathedrals were allowed to continue, and religious houses were not, the library gained books from Lincoln Greyfriars, Nocton Park Priory, Heynings Nunnery and Louth Park Abbey.[45] In the next century, Civil War damage to the cathedral was widespread, random and devastating. The library saw action in 1648, when Edward Reyner, the Puritan rector of the Lincoln church of St Peter at Arches, was chased by royalists. He fled to the chapter house, ran up the turret stairs and shut himself inside the library, chased by men with drawn swords. When they threatened to take his life, he opened the door. The raiders stole his coat and purse and led him off in triumph. However, one of the captains recognised Reyner as his old schoolmaster at Market Rasen and released him.[46]

In the autumn of 1660 Michael Honywood was appointed dean, tasked with restoring order to a broken cathedral. A Fellow of Christ's College Cambridge, he had served as university taxor (1623) and proctor (1628). Concerned about the Parliamentary Army's threat to Cambridge, he fled to Leiden in 1643, later moving to Utrecht,[47] and lived in exile until the return of the king. Using his administrative skills, he led the chapter in reinstating Church of England services in a building ruined by war and seventeen years of neglect without a dean and chapter. On 11 May 1661, 'out of the zeal to God's glory and the good affection to the Church', the chapter pledged £1,000 of their own money 'to be put in the Chest of the Common Chamber' to be spent on the fabric, and further financial support followed.[48] A great bibliophile, Dean Honywood had amassed a large library while in Cambridge, which was seized after he fled. Luckily, by 1647 his brother Henry, a colonel in the Parliamentarian Army, was able to redeem the books.[49] While in Holland he bought many more books, which he loaned to his fellow exiles.[50] On his return he was able to combine his two collections, amounting to around 4,000 books.[51] On

44 William Dugdale *et al.*, *Monasticon Anglicanum*, 11 vols (London, 1846), vol. XI, part III, 1278–86.

45 MSS 208 and 221 from Lincoln Greyfriars; MS 73 from Nocton Park Priory; MS 199 from Heynings Nunnery, and MS 47 from Louth Park Abbey. See Thomson, pp. 168–9, 181–2, 53, 159–61 and 33, respectively.

46 J. W. F. Hill, *Tudor and Stuart Lincoln* (Cambridge, 1956), p. 162.

47 N. Bennett, 'Honywood, Michael', ODNB.

48 LA, D & C, A/3/9, fols 223 (11 May 1661), 231v (27 October 1662) and 239 (26 March 1664).

49 J. H. Srawley, *Michael Honywood, Dean of Lincoln (1660–81)* (Lincoln, 1950), p. 6.

50 Honywood's notebook of book buying and loaning survives in the library's collection (MS 276).

51 Julie Taylor, Cathedral Librarian, *pers. comm.* The book titles with the dean's

his arrival in Lincoln he found the cathedral's library in disarray. He and the chapter made an appeal to Lincoln Corporation to return the books 'that had been lately plundered' for use in the Grammar School in the old Greyfriars building. The Corporation agreed that 'they shall have a view of what books we have in the school library, and such of them as they shall sufficiently make appear did belong to their library to be forthwith restored unto them'.[52] This resulted in 'the fetching of 3 loads of Books from the School House below the hill to the Common Chamber'.[53]

But what about Honywood's own library? Unmarried, and of advancing years, his thoughts must have turned to his intention of bequeathing his books to the cathedral. To keep his collection together, and to provide more space for the library's own books, a new building was required. A line in the fabric accounts for 1671–72 may be the first record of the dean's intention: under 'Masons bill' there is a small payment 'to Alexander Cooper for halfe a day for helping to view the Cloysters when the man came from London'.[54] Although the cloister was in a bad state of repair, especially the ruinous north walk, the cathedral masons and plumbers would have been competent to repair it without taking advice. The Londoner may have been 'Mr Tompson', who made the model for the new library.[55]

Reordering St Hugh's Choir and Planning the Wren Library

A little more than a year separates the dates of the articles for repairing and reordering St Hugh's Choir (25 March 1673) and the articles for building the new library (2 June 1674). The focus of Honywood's attention since his installation towards the end of 1660 had been on urgent repairs to the roofs, glass and bells, clocks and locks, commissioning a new organ, recruiting a new choir and finding a satisfactory organist. In the 1670s it was time to restore St Hugh's Choir and repair the north walk of the cloister by building a library

---

MH monogram number 3,827, but this does not include titles with no marks of ownership, which are known from his notebook to have been bought in Holland.

52 *Historical Manuscripts Commission*, Fourteenth Report (London 1895), Appendix, Pt VIII, 'The Manuscripts of the Corporation of Lincoln', p. 104; N. Linnell, 'Michael Honywood and Lincoln Cathedral Library', *The Library* (1983), 135–6.

53 LA, D & C fabric accounts for 1662–63, p. 74. As the financial year for the periods in this article began in September, either for a year from Holy Cross Day (14 September), or a year from Michaelmas (29 September), references to D & C fabric accounts dates will follow this system.

54 LA, D & C, Bj/1/9. Another explanation could be a quarry man's visit to estimate a quantity of stone to be ordered. As payments were made at this time for stone from Ancaster (limestone), and Tickhill (most likely sandstone) it would not seem necessary to buy stone from London.

55 LA, D & C, Ciij/31/1.

over it. Taking on both projects together was ambitious: it can be argued that the dean seeking advice from Sir Christopher Wren was an impetus. Honywood's strongest link with Wren was through his close friend and fellow exile in Holland, William Sancroft. He was recommended to Charles II as one of his chaplains, an appointment that aided his meteoric rise in the Church. Successively master of Emmanuel College (1662–64), dean of York for nine months, then dean of St Paul's (1664–78), and finally Archbishop of Canterbury from 1678, he resigned in 1690 as a non-juror.[56] Sancroft worked closely with Wren on designs for Emmanuel College Chapel and St Paul's Cathedral. He could easily have facilitated a meeting between Honywood and Wren to discuss reordering the choir and building a library at Lincoln. It is more than likely Wren obliged by asking a colleague, Edward Woodroofe, to design the reredos and associated panelling for the high altar. As for the library, Wren would design it himself, and Honywood would pay for it. William Evison was entrusted with the execution, as well as certain design elements, for both. To understand the library building, the work in the choir should be examined jointly with it.

The articles for the repair and reordering of St Hugh's Choir were drawn up between the Bishop of Lincoln jointly with the dean and chapter, and 'William Evitson [*sic*] Joyner of the City of Lincolne'. In the first item, Evison agreed to make a new setting for the altar, 'according to Mr Woodruffes design'. He was to 'sett up & ffix ... The Wainscoat upon the Topp of the wall behind the Altar in the Choir ... both inward & outward, and the Cornishes inward toward the said Choir ... and the Pillars & Pillasters on both sides, wth other inrichm^{ts} according to Mr Woodruffes designe on that side wch have kneelings in the Pannels'.[57] An illustration for this scheme after Wenceslaus Hollar in Dugdale's *Monasticon* shows a reredos for the high altar joined to a panelled screen. The reredos had a segmental arch in the centre, supported by a pair of columns *in antis*, and a pair of pilasters on either side of them. Two bays of panelling, decorated with swags along the top, stood on each side of the reredos.[58] This ensemble was erected in front of the medieval sanctuary room, evidenced by the fact that this narrow room behind the altar was still there in Browne Willis's later cathedral floorplan.[59]

56 R. A. P. J. Berrard, 'William Sancroft', ODNB.

57 LA, D & C, Ciij/31/1, part one.

58 Dugdale *et al* (eds), *Monasticon*, vol. XI, part III (London, 1846), St Hugh's Choir after Hollar, engraved by J. Lee, between pp. 1266 and 1267. The choir stalls are inaccurately shown, making it look as if there is no space for the bishop's throne on the south side. The original Hollar engraving is dated 1672, presumably based on plans for future work. It has not been possible to locate a clear image of the choir from the 1673 edition.

59 Willis, vol. 3, plan in 'Lincoln Cathedral', pp. 25–35.

Figure 3. Detail of an engraving after Wenceslaus Hollar of the 1673 reredos and panelling in the sanctuary of St Hugh's Choir (William Dugdale *et al* (eds), *Monasticon Anglicanum*, vol. XI, part III (London, 1846)).

'Mr Woodruffe' was almost certainly Edward Woodroofe (*c.* 1622–75), one of the surveyors appointed to rebuild the City churches after the Fire of London, along with Christopher Wren and Robert Hooke. He was surveyor to the dean and chapter of Westminster (1662–75) and an assistant surveyor of St Paul's Cathedral from 1669 onwards. In 1671–72 he designed three houses in Amen Court for residentiary canons of St Paul's, and around the same time, he was involved in building the St Paul's deanery for William Sancroft.[60] Woodroofe worked closely with Wren; Anthony Geraghty describes him as 'Wren's first draughtsman', explaining that Wren would do a sketch in pencil, and Woodroofe would work it up into a finished drawing.[61]

William Evison contributed designs of his own for the reordering, which are set out in the second item. Among other things, he agreed to 'make sett up & ffix one new Rayle att the Altar … and the Lord B[isho]ps throne in the said Choir …' He would 'New make and Repair 'all the Pyramids or Capitalls over the stalls of the Dignitarys and Prebendaryes of the said Choir' (i.e., the crocketed canopies over the medieval stalls), and to 'new make the Ornam[ts] which are broken down and defaced at the west end of said Choir'. He was to use the old altar rails to surround the new Eagle lectern, placing the litany desk on these rails to the east, and making a gate to the rails in the west. All of this was to be done 'according to a Designe made and delimn'd by the said William Evitson [*sic*]'.[62] There is also a contract of 2 August 1673 for two masons from Tickhill, John Hurt and John Cophy, to be paid fifty shillings by the dean and chapter to follow 'Mr Evison's draught book' in re-laying the stone floor between the altar and the altar rails in the sanctuary. The masons provided stone, took up the old pavement, and laid a new 'Pavement before the High Altar'. They agreed (somewhat chillingly) to 'smooth out all the Axestrokes and hollowings in the footpace.'[63]

A century later, when James Essex reordered the sanctuary again, part of the Restoration scheme was removed to St Denys's Church in Sleaford. The Lincoln antiquary Edward James Willson (1787–1854) recorded, 'A screen of the Corinthian order brought from Lincoln Cathedral forms the Altarpiece',[64] providing the information that the columns and pilasters had Corinthian capitals. The Lincoln bookseller William Brooke recorded, by 1859, that the

60 H. M. Colvin, 'Edward Woodroffe', *A Biographical Dictionary of British Architects, 1600–1840* (New Haven and London, 2008) pp. 1145–6. Colvin attributes new fittings in the choir of Lincoln Cathedral to Edward Woodroffe, p. 1146.

61 A. Geraghty, 'Edward Woodroofe: Sir Christopher Wren's First Draughtsman', *Burlington Magazine*, vol. 143, no. 1181 (August 2001), pp. 474–9.

62 LA, D & C, Ciij/31/1 part one.

63 LA, D & C, Dvii/3/B/41.

64 London, Society of Antiquaries, Willson Collection, 786/1–2 (old reference), p. 758 b. Henceforth W. Coll.

Figure 4. The 1673 altar rail from Lincoln Cathedral in Sleaford St Denys Church (© James Newton).

'wainscoat screen was to be seen recently in the chancel of Sleaford Church ...; being found equally out of place there, it was lately sold, and fragments of it decorate some of the shops in that town'.[65] Not mentioned in either of these accounts is William Evison's magnificent Communion rail, which also went to St Denys Church and is still in use today.

Comparing it with the view in *Monasticon*, it has been reconfigured to run north to south in a straight line, rather than in its form at the cathedral, where it turned at right angles around the altar in accordance with Laudian principles.[66] The altar rails have richly ornamented balusters, and festoons of leaves and fruit on the posts; the variety of interpretation in the carving of the balusters indicates that there was a team of carvers under Evison's supervision. These rails reveal a direct link with the library: the acanthus and single bead

[65] From a pamphlet with no author or title page, n.d., bound in *Lincoln*, a compilation of pamphlets presented to Mr and Mrs Reuben Trotter in 1859, Lincoln Central Library LCL.

[66] L. Gibbs, *Lincoln Cathedral and Close Conservation Plan* (Lincoln 2001), vol. 1, pp. 73–4.

and split reel carvings under the rail are a match for elements in the cornice and doorcase decoration in the library. Unusually, the bishop is named along with the dean and chapter in the 1673 articles agreed with Evison, indicating that William Fuller (Bishop of Lincoln, 1667–75) provided some funding for the project. He took great interest in restoring the cathedral in general, and St Hugh's Choir in particular; he restored the tomb of an illustrious predecessor, the cathedral's founder Bishop Remigius, on the north side of the sanctuary. In a letter to Sancroft he declared he intended to present a new altar cloth for feast days, and a pair of candlesticks.[67] Given the importance of restoring the bishop's throne, it is surprising that the 1673 articles hardly mention it. Its story is complicated, but it is necessary to summarise it to convey the strong connection of the new choir furnishings with the building of the Wren Library. Considering the wording of the agreement's third item again, it states that 'the said two Rayles, and all the carved works in and about the said Choir, and all the said Pyramids or Capitalls shall be made of good seasoned and sound Oake'.[68] A strict interpretation of this passage is that it relates solely to the altar rail, the rearranged old rails, and the repairs to the choir stalls; the reredos would have been described as wainscot, as it is in item 1. Evison agreed in item 2 to 'waynscoat that place that is now matted under the Organ in the said Choir'. Panelling beneath the organ loft is visible in the illustration in *Monasticon,* on the north side of the choir, opposite the bishop's throne.[69] As the setting for the bishop's throne is hardly mentioned in the agreement, it is unlikely that it was to be an elaborate and expensive design, as at St Paul's Cathedral; it is more likely that this, too, was a wainscot. The agreement does not mention what kind of wood was to be used for the wainscots;[70] however, it can be verified that the carved work of the Communion rail sent to Sleaford St Denys is made of oak. The plans for the wainscots may have specified the type of wood to be used, but these do not survive. If these features were to be painted and gilded, they would have been made of cheaper deal, which can be fir or pine. Given the enormous expense of repairing the cathedral, the cost implications of choosing between either oak or painted deal for the choir and library must have been a consideration.

67 N. Bennett, 'William Fuller', ODNB, vol. 21, p. 169. In a separate endeavour associated with Fuller, the tombs of Katherine Swynford and her daughter Joan, countess of Westmorland, were set in a line, rather than side-by-side, so that they and the chantry's railings no longer intruded into the sanctuary. Then their chantry chapel was given a classical roof to its canopy, presumably as a repair: J. H. Harvey, *Catherine Swynford's Chantry*, a Friends of Lincoln Cathedral pamphlet, n.d., pp. 10–11.

68 LA, D & C, Ciij/31/1 part one.

69 Dugdale et al., *Monasticon,* vol. XI, part III, St Hugh's Choir after Hollar, between pp. 1266 and 1267.

70 LA, D & C, Ciij/31/1, 'Rates of Gilding'.

An undated page in Sir Christopher Wren's hand, and signed by him,[71] is preserved along with the Wren Library building accounts. It lists rates of payment for gilding and various paint finishes.[72] Long associated with the Wren Library only, it is referred to in the 1676 contract for the decoration of the panelling and bookcases agreed between Honywood and the painter and gilder Thomas Rowley, where it states that the work is to be carried out 'at the rates in Sir Christopher Wren's paper'. But if this paper was intended for the library only, why did Wren address it 'For Dr. Gardiner (subdean 1671–95), with the humble service of Chr: Wren'? As Honywood paid for the library, the documents setting out the building programme in stages, with deadlines on saints' days, were agreements made between Honywood and Evison; and likewise between the dean and Thomas Rowley for the decoration. When chapter members' signatures appear, it is only as witnesses to the documents. If this paper was intended for the library decoration alone, Wren should have addressed it to the dean. Another observation is that there are more paint and gilding items in Wren's list than were executed in the library. For example, there is pricing for gilding 'round carving' such as 'Maske heads', which are present in the library. The same 'double worke' rate also applied to 'festoones' which are not found in the library, but they are on the Communion rail posts, and there are swags on the panelling either side of the reredos. The library was begun in the year following the start of work in the choir; Wren's paper could have been used for both projects. Subdean James Gardiner was joint Master of the Fabric with Chancellor Samuel Fuller in 1673, 1674 and 1676.[73] The library was completed by the end of 1676; if Wren's paper was meant for both projects, its likely date is either 1673, when the articles were agreed for the choir, or 1674, when work was ongoing in the choir and the library was being built.

In William Lumby's 1778 estimate for executing James Essex's design for a new bishop's throne and associated seats,[74] Lumby states that the new bishop's throne is to be 'erected in the same Place as the Right Reverend the Lord Bishop's Seats now stand', that is, on the south side of the choir, east of the chancellor's stall, near the entrance from the southeast transept. There are

71 Professor Anthony Geraghty, *pers. comm.,* confirmed in a letter written to the author of 19 January 2006 that the whole of the Rates of Gilding 'document … is without question in Wren's hand'.

72 LA, D & C, Ciij/31/1.

73 LA, D & C, A/3/11, fols 24, 46 and 46v. I am grateful to Nicholas Bennett for looking this up.

74 LA, D & C, A.4.15, 14 March 1778; T. Cocke, 'The Architectural History of Lincoln Cathedral from the Dissolution to the Present Century', *The British Archaeological Association Conference Transactions for the Year 1982, Lincoln Cathedral, vol. VIII* (1986), p. 152. Cocke assigns the date 1779 to the throne. The last payment to Thomas Lumby for it was on 10 March 1780 (LA, D & C Bj/1/16).

two components to a bishop's throne: one is the actual seat, and the other is a stall, canopy or some other backdrop to the seat. Essex's throne is flanked by stalls either side: one seat is for the vicar general and the other for the diocesan registrar. Judging by Lumby's estimate to remove the previous 'Bishop's Seats', the Restoration setting for the throne was designed for more than one seat, and probably accommodated three seats like its successor. Stored in the cathedral is a wainscot topped by a triangular pediment, marbled and gilded, measuring 3.5 metres high by 2.6 metres wide. It has been preserved in the cathedral from at least 1906, when E. Mansel Sympson wrote about St Hugh's Choir: 'Before [the] work of Essex there was a Classical reredos, attributed to Wren, which is now in the cloisters under the stairs to the Library'.[75]

However, Mansel Sympson's assessment of the wainscot does not agree with Hollar's view of the choir, in which the reredos has a segmental pediment. This mystery object could still be seen under the library stairs until around 1988, when it was moved to the chapter house.[76] Currently it is stored in a room at triforium level above the northeast transept. It has lost its original plinth.[77] This is a provincial piece, which, if all original, shows a lack of sophistication in the handling of classical ornament.[78] It is right for a date in the 1670s. At the top is a triangular pediment ornamented with egg and dart, dentil and waterleaf. The architrave beneath the pediment rests on pilasters decorated with 'festoones', as mentioned in Wren's paper, of pomegranates and flowers. Below in the centre is a gilded, broken segmental pediment, with a single bead and split reel ornament, which matches decorative carving

75 E. Mansel Sympson, *Lincoln, a Historical and Topographical Account of the City* (London, 1906), p. 264.

76 N. and C. Bennett *pers. comm.* It was moved to the chapter house to make way for a noticeboard with a photograph of Dean Fiennes showing Magna Carta to President Reagan when it was on tour in the USA in 1987.

77 Could this have been the doorcase in the chamber in the deanery's Wolsey Tower that connected with the passage in the thickness of the wall to the Wren Library? According to E. J. Willson's notes of the deanery before demolition, the height of that room was 12 feet (3.66 metres); as that is roughly the same height as the top of the pediment, it means the area of unpainted panelling where the door would be was too low. See W. Coll., 786/7, p. 65: 'Tower Chamber 16.5 N & S x 15.4 E & W. fire in east side. height 12 ft. Two windows N & S. wainscoted & partly papered. Door in the corner leading to the Minster Library'. In addition, the wainscot is 2.4 metres wide – too wide to be set in the angle of this room. I am grateful to cathedral verger James Newton for looking at this wainscot with me, for measuring, photographing and advising.

78 Gibbs, *Conservation Plan, Vol. 2, Cathedral Gazeteer*, p. 77. She suggests the wainscot may be composite, that the triangular pediment may not belong to the rest of it, citing 'differences in the detailing and construction on the back'. As the wainscot is in storage it was not possible to inspect the back at the time of writing.

Figure 5. Wainscot associated with the reordering of St Hugh's Choir, 1673 (© James Newton).

in the Sleaford altar rail and in the Wren Library. This pediment is supported by pilasters decorated with festoons, which are almost identical to the ones on the posts of the Sleaford St Denys Communion rail. A gilded bracket beneath this pediment forms the keystone of a round arch supported by fluted pilasters. All the flat panels are marbled, except for the panels in plain wood in the centre. There is a faint red stain around the sides of this unpainted area, which arches at the top. This could be a mark from red silk or other cloth,[79] which might have been upholstered with a flange around the edges, made in a similar way to a drop-in seat in a chair, and inserted where the unpainted wood is. Again, the 1673 articles for repairing and reordering the choir provide more information, i.e., that the part of the reredos above the high altar was covered in cloth. Evison agreed to carve the 'Copartm^t just over the Altar Cloath',[80] referring to the pulvinated frieze and the segmental pediment above the cloth set into the panelling over the altar, like the red silk panel in the centre of the marble reredos of the 1680s chapel at Belton House. As there was cloth over the altar it is feasible that it was matched by red cloth in the bishop's wainscot, centred on the figure of the prelate seated on his throne immediately in front of it.

The base colours of the marbling are predominantly cream and off white, figured to look like veins in marble. The central feature stands out against the wine-coloured Rance marbling above and to the sides of it – a paint effect listed in Wren's paper. There is ample evidence of painting in the choir at this time. In 1671–72, Richard Haslewood was paid 7s. [?d.] 'for colouring of the Pulpitt'; in the same year he was paid 1s. 6d. 'for colering the Pulpitt doores with other places'.[81] John Lane was paid for his work in the choir as a mason in 1672–73, with an additional payment of 18s. 'for scafilling for the painter'.[82] In 1674 Haslewood was paid 2s. [?d.] for 'colouring the Pulpitt'.[83] It is difficult to understand why there were so many payments for colouring the 'pulpitt' unless the term was equally applied to a pre-existing pulpit[84] and to the bishop's throne wainscot. A Puritan minister who preached during the Interregnum requested that the pulpit be moved to the bishop's late seat for warmth, as the minster windows were broken, and the stall provided

79 Red soft furnishings for St Hugh's Choir can be traced back to the eighteenth century. See LA, D & C Bj/1/15, 1763–64 fabric accounts payment to Mr Lely for half a yard of Scarlet Cloth for the Choir; Bj/1/16, 1786, a payment of £19 14s. 8d. 'for the Crimson Curtains over the Iron gates in the Choir'. The current seat cushions are red.

80 LA, D & C, Ciij/31/1/1 part one.

81 LA, D & C, Bj/1/9.

82 *ibid.*

83 *ibid.*, fabric accounts for 1673–74, 17 April 1674.

84 The pulpit would have been an unlikely target for destruction, as Puritan preachers gave sermons in the cathedral during the Civil War and interregnum.

shelter.[85] If there was a conflation of terms, it could explain why John Lane was paid 'for amending the pavem^{t} in the Choire and fixing the Screwes for the Pulpitt',[86] possibly meaning installing a new wainscot for the throne. There are other less specific payments to Haslewood for painting at this time; some of these may have been for varnishing rather than applying colour. He was still at work in 1676–77, when he was paid 'For colouring the doores in the Choirsters Seats'.[87] However, a note of caution should be interjected here. It is more likely this payment refers to applying dark stain or varnish to the wood; there was an earlier payment of 1661–62 to 'the Paintor' for painting the railes at the high altar, the bishop's arms, and 'Collering of the Seates'[88] and another in the following year for 'painting the seats in the Quire'.[89] These seats are still in the choir, and there are no traces of polychromy on them, or on the altar rail now at Sleaford.

As for the bishop's throne itself, the Restoration seat was in part a copy of the medieval throne of around 1330,[90] which had survived the Civil War, although 'brutally hacked in several places' according to Venables.[91] Either because of its poor condition, or because it did not fit into the new classical setting, Evison based his throne on the ancient seat, adding classical mouldings that had the potential to be marbled and gilded. This Restoration throne was in the chapter house[92] when it was drawn by S. H. Grimm in 1784,[93] by which time Essex's bishop's throne had replaced it in the choir. Evison's hand can be seen in the mouldings on the back, on the side that is visible, and below the seat, consisting of waterleaf and his signature single bead and split reel. As for the soft furnishings, before the articles for woodwork in the choir were

85 *Calendar of State Papers Domestic 1655*, ed. Mary Anne Everett Green (London, 1881), pp. 260 and 205, as quoted in Hill, *Tudor and Stuart Lincoln*, p. 163.

86 LA, D & C, Bj/1/9, 21 March 1673/4.

87 LA, D & C, Bj/1/9, fabric accounts for 1676–77, p. 29.

88 LA, D & C, Bj/1/8, fabric accounts for 1661–62, p. 59.

89 LA, D & C, Bj/1/8, fabric accounts for 1662–63, p. 30.

90 C. Tracy with A. Budge, *Britain's Medieval Thrones* (Oxford, 2015), p. 99.

91 E. Venables, 'Ancient Chair, Lincoln Minster', *Archaeological Journal* 47 (1890), 407. Venables thought this chair might have been made for King Edward I's Parliament in Lincoln, rather than for the bishop's throne. In 1891, the ancient throne was removed from the Medieval Library, restored, and given a canopy by J. L. Pearson, then placed in the chapter house, where it remains today. See LA, D & C, uncatalogued, *Lincoln Cathedral. Statement of Expenditure on Fabric and Church Furniture Accounts from 1874 to* – (a ledger for expenditure on the fabric, which ends in 1897). In the ledger it is described as 'Desk, Canopy and Floor to Chair of State'.

92 N. Bennett, *pers. comm.* A seat for the bishop was needed in the chapter house if there was a bishop's visitation, but the dean would sit in the seat when attending chapter meetings there as well.

93 BL, Add. MS 15541, fol. 124.

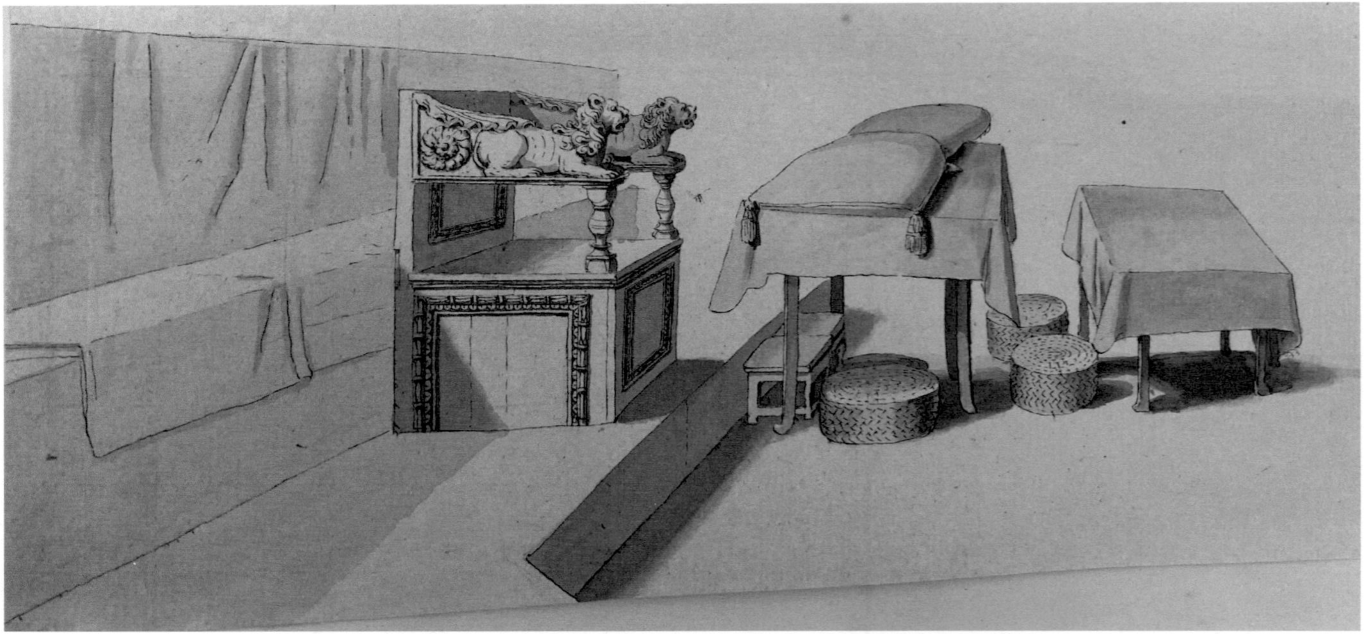

Figure 6. The Restoration bishop's throne, moved to the chapter house, where it was drawn by Grimm in August 1784 (BL Add. MS 15541, fol. 124).

agreed, Mr Kyte was paid £3 9s., in the 1670–71 fabric accounts, for five yards of cloth 'for the Ld Bpp seat' and this is followed by payments for cushion fringes.[94] If cushions for the seat, its desk and a kneeler were being made for it, it may be that Evison had already made the new throne before building work was agreed. The 1670s throne disappeared without a trace, and the seats associated with it, but the fate of the wainscot after Essex's reordering was recorded by the antiquary Edmund Venables (precentor of Lincoln 1867–95):

> What the altar-piece was, you may see from a plate in Dugdale's Monasticon – a wide expanse of plain oak panelling with a curved pediment in the centre. The Throne was doubtless of the same character ... Some fragments of it did duty in St Peter's-in-Eastgate until the church was rebuilt in 1870.[95]

Elsewhere, Venables wrote that the church of St Peter-in-Eastgate 'was rebuilt in a very un-ecclesiastical fashion in 1781 (when the wainscot of the former Bishop's Throne in the Minster was converted into the altar screen)'.[96]

The Restoration setting for the bishop's throne is likely to be the pedimented wainscot that has been preserved in the cathedral from at least 1906, returned to the cathedral after it had served as the reredos in the church of St Peter-in-Eastgate. There would have been ample room in St Hugh's Choir for this feature to stand in the space where the current bishop's throne is. The wainscot is 2.6 metres wide; the current throne and associated seats measure 4.05 metres. There is a section of panelling, east of these seats, which fills in the rest of the bay. The Restoration bishop's throne was probably flanked by panelling either side to close off the choir in a similar fashion, and to provide a backdrop for the seats of the diocesan registrar and the vicar general. If this theory is correct, the timing is of interest. The parish church, which had been in ruins since the Civil War, was rebuilt from 1778 to 1781, at the same time as Essex's reordering of the choir and installation of the present bishop's throne. The parish was probably grateful to borrow a second-hand wainscot for their

94 LA, D & C, Bj/1/9, fabric accounts for 1670–71.

95 E. Venables, *A Walk through Lincoln Minster, a Lecture Delivered by the Rev. Edmund Venables, M.A., Precentor of Lincoln, to the Young Men's Christian Association, on the Evening of December 12th, 1884* (Lincoln, n.d.), p. 34. Venables' description of the throne being 'doubtless of the same character' as the reredos in the choir indicates he never saw it, although he was precentor from 1867 to his death in 1895. The library staircase was completed in 1893 or 1894: *AASRP*, XXII (1893–94), Part I, Report, p. viii. If the wainscot was put under the library stairs around this time, it would have been in place for E. Mansell Sympson to record seeing it there in 1906.

96 Venables, *A Walk through the Streets of Lincoln, a Lecture Delivered by the Rev. Edmund Venables, M.A., Precentor of Lincoln, to the Young Men's Christian Association, on the Evening of December 11th, 1883* (Lincoln, n.d.), p. 22.

reredos, which they returned after their new Gothic church was built in 1870.[97] The altar rails in Sleaford are still on loan from the cathedral.[98]

Building the Wren Library

Detailed documents for building the library, and for furnishing it with bookcases and decorating it, survive from May 1674 to November 1676. There can be no doubt that Sir Christopher Wren was the architect. The memorandum of 18 May 1674[99] is an agreement 'between Mr Deane of Lincoln & Mr Evison, Wherein Mr Evison did undertake to build the library over the decayed Cloyster according to Mr Surveyors direction and Mr Thompsons modell'. The 'Mr Surveyor' was Wren, who was appointed Surveyor of the King's Works in 1669; Mr Thompson was probably John Thompson, who appears in the St Paul's building accounts as a mason and a model maker.[100] Whether the model was three-dimensional and made of wood, or a 'modello' in the sense of a drawing, is not known. The articles dated 2 June, and indented articles of 30 June, state the library was to be built 'according to Sir [Christ]opher Wrens directions and Mr Tompsons modell'.[101]

Aside from the undated page by Wren setting out the rates for gilding and painting there is an agreement in which Thomas Rowley agreed to decorate the room 'at the rates in Sir Christopher Wren's paper'.[102] The contracts reveal that the work was completed speedily: built and wainscoted in two and a half years – a testament to the dean's good management and Evison's skill in marshalling his work force. In the contract for marbling and gilding of 11 November 1676, Rowley agreed to work at astonishing speed and finish by Christmas.[103] Honywood would turn seventy-nine that autumn; it appears he did not want to waste any time. The new library not only accommodated the dean's and the cathedral's books, it put right the ruined north walk of the

97 N. Pevsner, rev. N. Antram, *The Buildings of England, Lincolnshire* (Harmondsworth, 1995), p. 500.

98 The Revd Philip Johnson, Vicar of Sleaford, *pers. comm.*

99 LA, D & C, Ciij/31/1, memorandum of 18 May 1674. This reference number comprises eleven documents to do with agreements and estimates for building and decorating the Wren Library. There is a twelfth document, Wren's 'Rates of Gilding', which may have been consulted for decorating both the choir and the library.

100 *The Wren Society* (Oxford, 1933), vol. XV, p. 6, records a payment of 5s. to 'John Tompson … for … making a Modell for the Head of the 2 Staircases over the Consistory …' in St Paul's Cathedral, in accounts dated Jan./Feb., 1695/6, among other payments.

101 LA, D & C, Ciij/31/1, articles for building the library between Dean Honywood and William Evison, 2 June 1674; indented articles for the same, 30 June 1674.

102 103 *ibid.*, 'Contract for painting the Library by measure. 11 Nov. 1676'

103 *ibid.*

cloister, and created a long gallery for the deanery, accessed from the Wolsey Tower. The north cloister was in such a bad state after the Civil War that Evison was allowed to use uncarved stone from it 'and that parcel of lead, that remains of the roofe of the North Cloyster & [j]oynes to the Old Library, about a yard breadth more or less'.[104] The north wall of this walk survives; the scars where the medieval wooden vault was attached to it can be seen clearly. But as the lead had been stripped from virtually the entire walk, and left for thirty years, it was no wonder that the arcade facing the garth, which was never strong, had collapsed into ruins.

Did Honywood and Wren consider a library that would blend in with the rest of the cloister? Crafts people who worked on old church or collegiate buildings at that time could still build in the Gothic style.[105] Although the appearance of a classical library in the midst of a Gothic cloister has been criticised by later generations, it should be noted that originally the new building's volumes integrated with the lofty Wolsey Tower to its northwest and the two bays of the Medieval Library advancing over the east walk of the cloister. (See fig. 1.) To appreciate how a classical building could look among older buildings, Honywood may have investigated recent developments in Cambridge. Wren's first building, Pembroke College Chapel, was commissioned by his uncle Matthew Wren, bishop of Ely, and consecrated in 1665. It was the first chapel in Cambridge or Oxford in the classical style. Sancroft probably showed Honywood Emmanuel College Chapel, designed by Wren like a classical temple, the basic structure of which had been built by 1672[106] when Honywood was planning his library. Although Wren was capable of building in a Gothic style (e.g., the later buildings of Tom Tower, Christ Church College, Oxford, as well as three City churches) he disliked 'the Saracen Mode', especially as Gothic buildings did not wear well.[107] The dean and his chapter had already chosen a classical reordering of the sanctuary in St Hugh's Choir; a straightforward modern building that would be easier to maintain would have appealed to Honywood's practical nature. Many years before, when he was at Christ's College, he had been involved in planning the Fellows' Building of 1640–42. With its classical pilasters and pediments, it is a stylish modern building for its time.[108]

104 LA, D & C, Ciij/31/1, articles for building the library, 2 June 1674.

105 K. Clark, *The Gothic Revival*: *an essay in the history of taste* (Middlesex, 1964), p. 9.

106 P. Collinson, 'Restoration and Transmogrification', in S. Bendall, C. Brooke & P. Collinson, *A History of Emmanuel College Cambridge* (Woodbridge, 1999), 9, p. 274.

107 'Sir Chr. Wren's Report on the Abbey in 1713, to Dean Atterbury', from *Parentalia*, Section VII, 295–302, taken from *The Wren Society*: Original Drawings (Oxford, 1924–43), XI, 17.

108 Srawley, *Michael Honywood*, p. 3.

Wren's design for Lincoln's library echoes his scheme for Emmanuel College. The five bays on either side of the chapel, with high-hipped roofs, are comprised of upper rooms with a loggia beneath.[109] The round-headed arches rest on square piers and the rooms above have cross windows with aprons below them. Disregarding the central feature of the chapel, these wings look very like the Lincoln library. Where Emmanuel has square piers, Lincoln's south front has Tuscan Doric columns; Lincoln's cross windows have frames that are lugged rather than plain, and there is a lower hipped roof. At Lincoln, the keystones of the arches attach to the platband, which itself forms a base for the aprons under the windows. (See fig. 1) This tying together of classical features is a characteristic of the Baroque style, as is the sense of rhythm created by placing single plain oak-framed cross windows over the arches at the north and south ends, then progressing from both ends towards the centre, featuring two windows with straight entablatures set on brackets, ornamented with swags of drapery, then two plain windows either side of the central window with a straight entablature embellished with a floral swag. Set into the tops of the window frames on either side of the central window are escutcheons with Honywood's arms. The north front, originally above the roofline of the dean's stables, is windowless, allowing a complete run of bookcases inside. On its narrow west side, the entrance at ground floor level from the deanery (now the visitor centre garden) has Tuscan Doric columns, a pulvinated frieze, and a segmental pediment. It is tied by an apron to the large window above, which has volutes at the bottom and a straight entablature at the top. Inside, like the doorcase opposite, this window is framed by bolection moulding, carved with a flowing acanthus, and single bead and split reel. On either side of the window and doorcase are Corinthian half columns, fluted and gilded. To the left of the door is Dean Honywoood's portrait by Cornelius Johnson, and to the right is a likeness by an unknown artist of his grandmother Mary Honywood.[110]

On entering the room from the Medieval Library to its east, the advancing and receding planes in the bookcases and panelling skilfully distract the eye from the deficiencies of a long, narrow room. Addressing the narrowness of the north cloister walk below, Wren stole a bay from the east and west walks to widen the room.[111] The cornice has a pulvinated frieze, gilded grotesque masques (one playfully sticking its tongue out), waterleaf and egg and dart mouldings, and plaques meant for shelf marks. The exaggerated stepping out of the top of the cornice emphasizes the movement – the equivalent of a lively skyline on the exterior of a Baroque building. Yet the cartouche over

[109] Bendall, Brooke & Collinson, *A History of Emmanuel College*, plate 4.

[110] Mary Honywood was noted for her piety, and for living to see 367 descendants, as recorded on Michael Honywood's ledger stone in Lincoln Cathedral retrochoir.

[111] The scars of the medieval wooden vault can be seen.

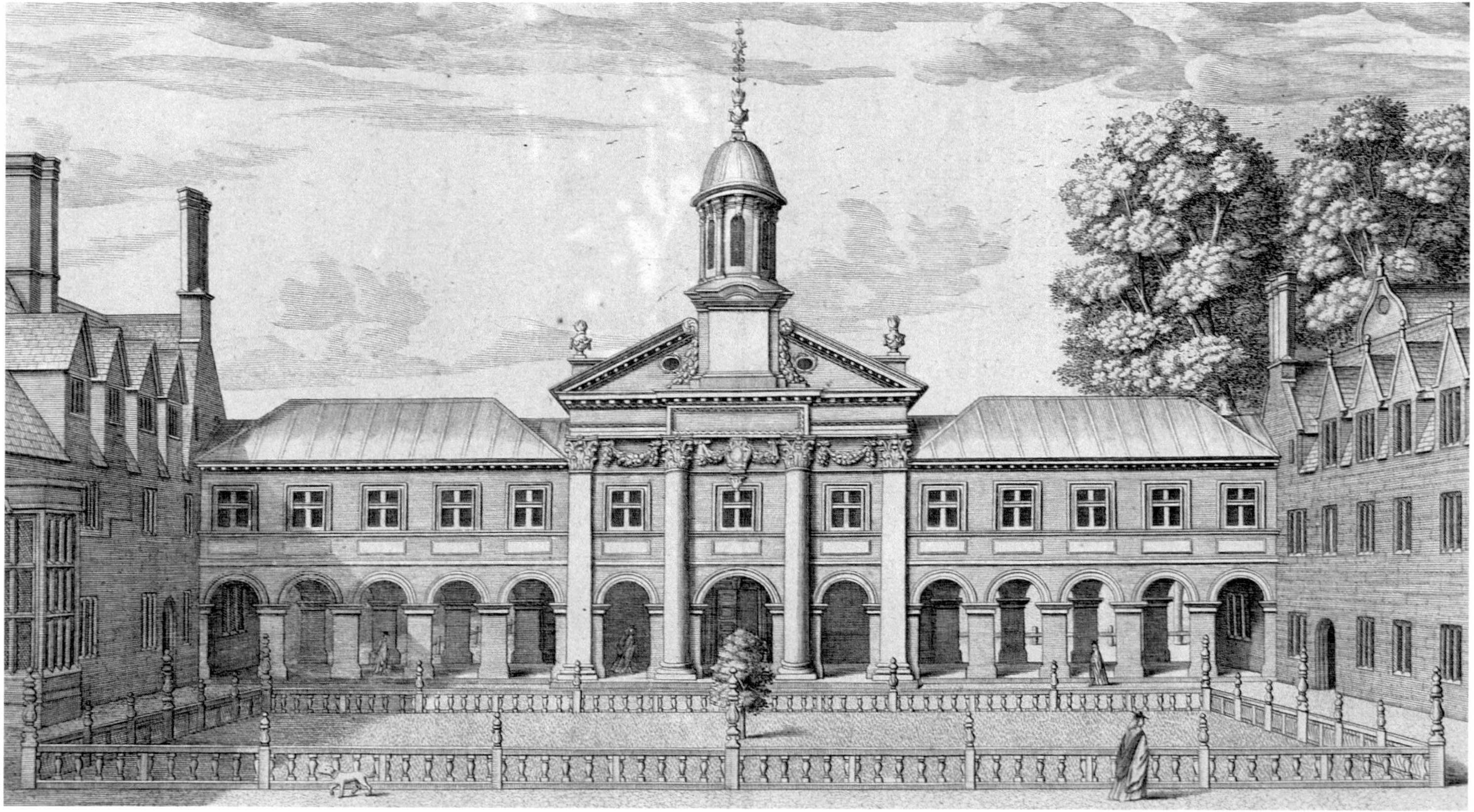

Figure 7. Emmanuel College chapel range, designed by Christopher Wren and begun in 1668 (detail of a plate in D. Loggan, *Cantabrigia Illustrata* [Cambridge, 1690]).

Figure 8. The Wren Library interior, with the Medieval Library next door (© James Newton).

the door, with Honywood's arms, echoed by the cartouche of the cathedral and diocesan arms over the window, are both framed in strapwork – a vernacular touch – but not uncommon for the time. E. J. Willson noted that 'the north side is appropriated to the books, the lowest range being originally shut off with doors, which have since been thrown open to prevent dampness'.[112] Although eventually removed, there are surviving marks for hinges for a cupboard at the base of the press in the northeast corner.[113]

Evison designed 'the staircase at the West end of the building according to his own modell'.[114] His elegant set of four graduated semicircular stone steps descend from the threshold of the two-leaved door from the deanery garden into the north walk of the cloister.[115] The entrance to the library upstairs was by means of a staircase in the northeast corner of the cloister that rose through the Medieval Library floor.[116] Evison agreed to 'make two leaved doors out of the new into the old Library with railes and banisters to the steps there'.[117] The two-leaved door to the Wren Library was changed to a single door in the late eighteenth or early nineteenth century, as will be discussed later.[118] The bookcases are set against the wall, not extending at right angles in bays as they do in Wren's later Trinity College Library, where the arrangement echoes the medieval lectern desk model. An indented agreement of 13 December 1675 binds Evison, before 1 June, to 'make the Wainscoat on the windowed side of the Library … lately built at the cost and charges of the said Michael Honywood, which Wainscot shall consist of large and fair Mouldings (according to a pattern to be given in and agreed on) …'[119] The contract goes on to specify the type and thickness of wood – whole deals or split deals as appropriate, and that the backs of the panelling and the bookcases are to be 'pitched' in the way a ship would be caulked against the damp with tar. The phrase 'according to a pattern to be given in

[112] W. Coll. 786/7, p. 66.

[113] Two small keys for these cupboards survive, attached to a label on which is written in a copperplate hand, 'Wren Library Bookcases'.

[114] LA, D & C, Ciij/31/1, memorandum of 18 May 1674, and 'Mr Evisons Bond for the Steps in the Cloyster. Dec. 13.75'.

[115] It is unclear if the staircase from the northeast corner of the cloister through the floor of the Medieval Library was also designed by Evison.

[116] Willis, plan. The first three steps of this winding staircase are plotted in the northeast corner of the cloister, running from south to north before turning east.

[117] LA, D & C, Ciij/3/1, articles of 2 June 1674.

[118] The staircase emerged through the floor in the middle bay of the three surviving bays. The beam running north to south in this bay was moved from the centre of the bay to the east, to allow space for the stairs. This was exposed in 2000 during the installation of heating.

[119] LA, D & C, Ciij/3/1, indented agreement between Honywood and Evison for the panelling and bookcases.

and agreed on' is a window into how Evison, and others, collaborated with Wren. Wren would originate the overall concept and leave the finer design details to a crafts person. They would then present various alternatives to him, or in the case of the City churches, the design might be presented to one of the other surveyors working with him. Then one option would be chosen and agreed upon.[120]

The restored *trompe l'oeil* marbling is one of the most memorable features of the Wren Library. In a double deception, wood is painted to look like marble, then given a dark border, called 'revaling' (a reveal). This is a three-dimensional effect, creating the illusion that the flat panels are raised and fielded panelling. In Wren's paper on rates for decorating, he described the paint effect in this room as 'veined work like black or White Marble … extraordinarily well done so as to deceive the Eye and be taken for Naturall …'[121] On the back of the agreement with Thomas Rowley for painting the panelling and gilding the masks, columns and coats of arms, is a memorandum stating that 'Mr Dean agreed to allow Mr Rowley half the Charges of the Carriage of his Materialls from London to Lincoln'.[122] If Rowley was a Londoner he was probably recommended by Wren. A page of figures, in an unknown hand, states that the 'the wainscot in the thickness of the wall into Mr Deans Chamber' was to be 'vaned in black and revaled'.[123] In another page of figure checking is a measurement of 68 feet, 5 inches (20.85 metres) of wainscot, measured by the linear foot, for 'the plane Wainscoote in to Mr Deans chamber'.[124] These details show that the entire chamber's wainscot and decoration were included in the library project. Evison provided a small door in the northwest corner of the library for a passage through the thickness of the medieval Wolsey Tower wall to this room. Unlike the unheated library, the chamber had a fireplace by which the dean could sit and read.[125] The door is still there, but the passage was reduced to a cupboard when the deanery was demolished in 1847.[126]

The figures were gone over and checked by the dean and others. The figure

120 J. Summerson, *Sir Christopher Wren* (London and Glasgow, 1953), pp. 82–3.

121 LA, D & C, Ciij/31/1, 'Rates of Gilding'.

122 *ibid.*, contract for painting the library.

123 *ibid.*, 'The Wainscot on the Window Syde'. On the back of the dean's door, Nigel Leaney found evidence of Rance marbling, simulating a red/wine colour of marble quarried in Rance, Belgium. It seems there was a change in plan for this chamber, away from the library's black and white scheme.

124 *ibid.*, 'Measure of Painting in the Library'. This fits E. J. Willson's measurement of the room as 16 feet, 5 inches by 15 feet, 4 inches (5 metres by 4.7 metres). See W. Coll., 786/7, p. 65.

125 W. Coll., 786/7, p. 65.

126 S. Jones, K. Major & J. Varley, *The Survey of Ancient Houses,* III (Lincoln, 1990), 19–33.

of £780 was for the building only. According to an indented agreement of 13 December 1675 for the making of the deal panelling and bookcases, £50 was to be paid to the workmen when they began work, and a further £50 by Candlemas in the new year, and 'the rest (if it shall come to more) when the said work shall be completed finished and measured according to the manner form and method aforementioned'.[127] A page of figuring, partly in Honywood's hand, which included 'plane Wainscot into Mr Deans chamber' proved to be so complicated that it was inconclusive.[128] The figure written on the back is £189 4s. 3d., with a cryptic comment about the forty-two grotesque mask heads: '42 times the measure of the mask heads to be deducted out of this rate of the whole'.[129] Separate from the building accounts is an undated and torn page, possibly an audit voucher, bundled with other documents dating between 1665 and 1725.[130] The account is for £149 17s. 6d. for 'the window side … the casing of the back … the shelves … the upright standards … the cornices … the wainscoat under the shelves … the two ends'. The amounts paid per foot for each type of work is listed beneath, but the bottom quarter of the page is torn, making a direct comparison with the agreement impossible. If this is an audit voucher, there may have been other vouchers for the rest of the payments, but there are few surviving audit vouchers from this period. Perhaps, although Honywood paid for everything, he wanted his donation to go through the cathedral's books; it is clear that the library bills do not appear in the fabric accounts. The difference between the total of £189 4s. 3d., written on the back of the 'Measure of the Wainscoat' page, and the sum of £149 17s. 6d. on the presumed audit voucher is around £40. Perhaps the difference has to do with the forty-two mask heads. Mr Rowley's bill for painting and gilding was £61 6s. 1d., bringing the total to slightly over £991 3s. 7d. If the two £50 payments were additional, and not part-payment of £149 7s. 6d., the figure would go up accordingly. No record of payment for Wren's design or the model has come to light; it is possible that, as at Trinity College Library, Wren did not ask for a fee.[131]

The library's oak tables, having drawers with drop handles, and baluster legs with stretchers, are of the period.[132] They were designed to fit in the recesses of the panelling under the windows; this was discovered during the installation of conservation heating in 2000, when it was decided that dehumidifiers and

127 *Ibid.*, indented agreement for panelling and bookcases, 13 December 1675.

128 *ibid.*,'The Measure of the Wainscot in the Library'.

129 *ibid.*, indented agreement for the panelling and bookcases, 13 December 1675.

130 LA, D & C, A/2/19/3/3. I am grateful to Nicholas Bennett for finding this document.

131 H. Colvin, 'The Building', in D. McKitterick (ed.), *The Making of the Wren Library, Trinity College, Cambridge* (Cambridge, 1995), p. 37.

132 Michael Czajkowski, furniture restorer of Woodhall Spa, *pers. comm.*

heaters could be placed under these tables without intruding too much on the appearance of the historic interior. Although some of the tables had been dispersed in the cathedral and the bishop's house, seven tables were found, and a further three were replicated. Their original position under the windows made sense. In a room without lighting, a book removed from a shelf could be taken across to a table to be read in the daylight. Might these tables have been Wren's idea? The drawings that he and Nicholas Hawksmoor made for the furnishings at Trinity College Library survive,[133] but there is no documentary evidence for Lincoln's library tables.

The Wren Library Builders

William Evison is a shadowy figure, known only for his work at the cathedral, but he must have impressed the chapter with work elsewhere before his employment there. He styled himself a gentleman in his will of 1685, of the Lincoln parish of St Mary [le Wigford], where he wished his body to be buried. Although there is no mention of a family in his will, his inventory lists 'some cloaths of Mrs Evisons', which implies he was a widower. He had a well-appointed and roomy house, with a cooper's shop where lumber was stored, and another shop where there was a wagon, a cart, and extensive amounts and varieties of timber; his appraised wealth was £381.[134] Evison's will named many beneficiaries, especially among the younger generation. To one son of William Darwin of South Kyme he gave a chest of tools and £30 towards apprenticing him to a joiner; the other son, who received £40, was to be apprenticed to a freemason.[135]

At the same time, the fabric accounts of 1673–74 record that Samuel Marsh[136] was being paid an annual fee of £1 6s. 8d. under the heading '*Solutiones Ministrorum*', or 'Servants' Wages'. This continued until the last payment was made 'to Marsh's widow for his fee as mason' in 1687.[137] Samuel Marsh the Elder was head mason and patentee for masonry and stone cutting.[138]

133 Colvin, 'The Building', p. 48; plates 42 (All Souls I, 49) and 43 (All Souls, I. 48).

134 J. A. Johnston, (ed.), *Probate Inventories of Lincoln Citizens 1661–1714*, LRS 80 (Woodbridge, 1991), p. xxxiv and pp. 88–92. There was so much timber that Dr Johnston described him as a timber merchant.

135 LA, LCC, 1685/i/196.

136 LA, LCC Wills 1687/ii/81, p. 81. He appears as 'Samuel Marsh the Elder, of Welby in the County of Lincoln, ffreemason'.

137 LA, D & C, Bj/1/9, fabric accounts for 1686–87.

138 His name is not found in the LA calendar of Lincoln Cathedral patentees until after his death, when on 29 October 1687, John Sutton of Ancaster was appointed the patentee *lathomo* (shortened form of *lathomo seu fabro lapidario,* meaning stone cutter or stone mason), at an 'annual fee of 26s:8d and all endowments as Samuel Marsh

There were at least three generations of masons in the villages of Welby and Culverthorpe called by the same name. When Samuel Marsh the Elder died in 1687 at the age of forty-six, it was only five years after his father's death. As his father was also called Samuel Marsh, it creates a confusing picture. (In the next generation, Samuel the Elder's son, born in 1670/1, was called 'the younger'.) George Vertue records that a Samuel Marsh was the 'architect' employed by the First Duke of Newcastle to design parts of Bolsover Castle in the 1660s and Nottingham Castle in the 1670s. The duke also employed a Samuel Marsh at Welbeck Abbey. It is not always clear which of the two older men designed or oversaw building work at these houses, but according to Howard Colvin, 'in Midland England they were among the leading master builders of their day'.[139] In 1685–87, while Samuel Marsh the Elder leased the quarry at Heydour from John Newton of Culverthorpe, he supplied stone for building Belton House.[140] At the cathedral, he worked on the reordering of the choir, paid £9 5s. 'for his last work in the Quire' in 1675–76.[141] It is likely Marsh supervised cathedral mason John Lane and the masons from Tickhill, while Evison supervised woodwork and carving repairs, as well as new work in wood.

Aside from Evison's work in the choir and library, the chapter paid him for smaller jobs, such as providing 'new flooring the Common Chamber and other work there' in 1675–76.[142] He was not given an annual fee, perhaps because Marmaduke Ryall was head carpenter and there was not sufficient need for a head joiner. Given the name that the Marshes were making for themselves in the 1670s, and the fact that Samuel Marsh the Elder was head mason at the cathedral, it raises the question whether Marsh supplied the stone for building the Wren Library. Might he also have had a supervisory role? It appears the latter is not the case: unlike the work in the choir, the agreements made it clear that it was Evison who supervised and paid all the people working under him. Given the opportunity he had to work with someone as talented as Samuel Marsh, he may have been pleased to have the freemason's advice on the fabric of the building. However, it was Evison, and not Marsh, who had to promise 'that he will mainteine the stone wall with arches & pillars

had the same'. See R. E. G. Cole (ed.), *Chapter Acts, Lincoln Cathedral, AD 1526–36*, LRS 12 (Horncastle, 1915), p. 194, 'Letters Patent for the Chief Stone-Mason of the Cathedral', which explains that in addition to the stipend for the office, the patentee would be paid for work done. I am grateful to Nicholas Bennett for his advice on this.

139 Colvin, *Biographical Dictionary of British Architects, 1600–1840*, pp. 678–9.

140 *ibid.*, p. 678.

141 LA, D & C, Bj/1/9, fabric accounts for 1675–76.

142 *ibid.*

upright & good for ten years, that is against such defects as may proceed from ill workmanship or bad materialls & no other'.[143]

The Libraries in the Eighteenth Century

Honywood's books were a rich and varied addition to the cathedral library's collection, including works in many languages on history, science, mathematics, geography, atlases, the Law, literature, politics and current events. He bought old manuscripts and incunabula as well as books on current religious disputes. The newspapers, broadsides and pamphlets documenting the reign of Charles I, the Civil War and Interregnum form a unique collection. This was no longer a library confined to theology, biblical studies and the writings of the Church Fathers. In 1700, the antiquarian Thomas Tanner, later bishop of St Asaph, took an interest the medieval manuscripts, notes on which he published in *Bibliotheca Britannico-Hibernica*, published in 1728.[144] Gentlemen visitors, such as John Loveday of Caversham, wrote in 1732, 'this Library is an handsome Room … The MSS. Are kept in an old Room just by'.[145] When John Byng, Fifth Viscount Torrington, visited on 28 June 1791, he wrote, 'Climb hill to the cathedral; was shown the cloisters, now in great disorder, but going to be repair'd … and to the library, where a great collection of old manuscripts are soon to be arranged: but my guide knew nothing; and I could not find any finely illuminated'.[146]

The repairs to which Byng referred were to the cloister, which resulted in the removal of two bays of the Medieval Library. The surveys for this work are undated, but the fabric account payments reveal the work dated from 1788–89.[147] There is an oft-repeated story that the truncation of the Medieval Library was to make good after a fire there in 1609.[148] While it is true that some manuscripts kept in the old library were damaged by fire, some of Honywood's books that were given later were also damaged by fire. Upsetting a candle could happen at any time; perhaps there were several mishaps over the years. Looking at the evidence for fire damage to the fabric, the points to consider are, why did it take from 1609 until 1789 to address the damage, and why would Honywood make the entrance to his library through a fire damaged Medieval Library that he did nothing to repair? Furthermore, there

143 LA, D & C, Ciij/31/1, articles of 2 June 1674, item 10.

144 Thomson, p. xxiii.

145 J. Loveday, https://www.johnlovedayofcaversham.co.uk/the-tours-of-john-loveday, Tour 23, pp. 181–2.

146 C. Bruyn Andrews (ed.), *The Torrington Diaries*, (London, 1935), vol. II, p. 346.

147 LA, D & C, Bj/1/16, fabric accounts for 1788–89: head carpenter Thomas Lumby was paid 'for Work in the Cloyster'.

148 For a full examination of this subject, see Thomson, xxii.

is no evidence of scorching in the roof timbers of the remaining three bays of the Medieval Library today.[149]

Previously, in 1761, when James Essex wrote his first report on the fabric as surveyor, he commented on the poor condition of the three remaining medieval walks of the cloister, suggesting that they might have to be removed:

> … if ever it should be thought advisable to take [the cloisters] down rather than repair them, care should be taken to secure the Library, as the Stone arches at each end of it, having no other abutments on one Side but a Slender Pillar, cannot long stand when the Walls of the Cloister are taken down.[150]

On Essex's death in 1784 the head mason William Lumby succeeded him. In his 1787 survey Lumby wrote, 'Cloisters much out of repair in places; the Spouts are out of Order, and suffers the Wet to run upon the Walls …'.[151] The concern was for the poor state of the cloister, rather than the Medieval Library above, but the dean and chapter concluded that the weight of the building, full of heavy oak desks and manuscripts, was more than the cloister beneath could support. This was no longer the main library; by removing two bays, the load would be lessened on the weak east cloister beneath, and three bays of the old library could be preserved. The truncating of the Medieval Library and the building of the new staircase in its annex was part of a bigger plan to move cathedral workshops into the cloister. Luckily during their time there, the workshops are not known to have occasioned accidents or fires that impacted the libraries above. The fabric accounts show payments for the work on the Medieval Library from 1787 to 1789. The estimates are not dated, but William Lumby was paid £5 5s. 2d. for drawing plans in September, 1787,[152] and his father, head carpenter Thomas Lumby, presented a bill for £12 2s. 2d. for 'Work in the Cloyster and Stamp' in 1788–89.[153] The estimate for the carpenter's work outlines the following steps:

> Taking down the old Library, that is the Timber Sides & End, Board floor, Joists and Roof … Making good the Roof, up to the front of the Library Wall, same pitch as the Cloister Roof … Boarding ditto … Taking down the old Strings and bannisters… Making good the Space with Naked flooring …

149 Simpson, p. 40.

150 LA, D & C, The Ark, 22/7, Architect's Reports, Survey of Lincoln Cathedral by Mr Essex Sept. 1761.

151 *ibid.*, item 7, 'A Survey of Dilapidations of the Cathedral Church of Lincoln', 1787.

152 LA, D & C, Bj/1/16, fabric accounts for 1786/7.

153 LA, D & C, Bj/1/16, fabric accounts for 1788/9.

At the same time, an annex would be built off the northeast corner of the cloister, to accommodate a staircase leading to a new door at the southern end of the east side of the old library, and through that room to the Wren Library. Material from the old staircase was to be re-used: 'Putting up the old Stairs and making good such stuff as may be required'.[154] The estimate for masons' work states the annex walls would be of 'Common Walling Stone' and plastered. There was to be an 'Ashlar wall in the line of the [Wren] Library'. This façade, which can be seen from the cloister, has been done so well that it looks like part of Wren's design; only the straight join in the masonry gives it away. To make up for the gap created by removing the part of the library over the cloister, a 'Battlement wall' was to be built from the new south wall of the Medieval Library to the chapter house 'in the same manner as the Battlements at the South End of the same building ...'.[155]

Of the two cross windows in the new south wall of the Medieval Library that were designed to match the Wren Library, only one can be seen from the cloister. The other one was provided with glass, like its neighbour, but as it abuts the 'battlement wall', it is blocked by masonry and does not function as a window. It must have been put there for the sake of the internal symmetry of the room.[156] At some point the two-leaved door into the Wren Library was replaced with a single door.[157] This was made to look Gothic on the Medieval Library side, where the door's design of Gothic arches and quatrefoils continues as panelling on the wall to the north of the door. This door and panelling take up the entire bay, disguising the fact that the door is set to one side in the bay. Once again it seems symmetry was a priority. The design of pointed arches resembles the Gothic door into the Canons' Vestry off the southeast transept, designed by Essex and made by the head carpenter Thomas Lumby.[158] On the Wren Library side, a Georgian door has been spliced to the Gothic door. During the restoration of the interior decoration of the Wren Library in the 1980s, Nigel Leaney found there was a brown varnish on this door, and that it was not marbled until the first redecoration in 1814,[159] revealing

154 LA, D & C, A.4.13, 'An Estimate of Carp^{t} work ...', (fair copy), n.d.

155 *ibid.,* An Estimate of Masons Work of Several Intended Alterations to be made at the Cathedral Church in Lincoln'.

156 At the time of writing, the glass in this window is covered by a noticeboard.

157 The remodelling of this door is not listed in the estimate for carpenters' work, but a 'Gothick Door & frame with Caseings, out of the Cloisters into the new Intended Staircase' is listed. From at least the time of Browne Willis's plan of 1730, the large medieval arch had been filled in, presumably with wooden boards, leaving a small opening for a door.

158 LA, D & C, A.4.16, 1–5.

159 From a photocopy of Nigel Leaney's diary notes in the author's possession, dated 28 February 1986; *pers. comm.* Nigel Leaney.

that these alterations were made by then. It is likely the door and panelling were made during the 1789 alterations or soon after: it would not have been necessary to apply varnish if the door was new in 1814 and marbled then.

The Libraries from the Nineteenth Century to the Present

The Wren Library ceiling is not original. An addition made during the first redecoration in 1814, it rests heavily on the segmental arches over the door and window. Writing around 1817, E. J. Willson observed:

> The interior was repainted about 3 years back, exactly as at first, & a great improvement was done at that time in the ceiling ... a well-proportioned curve connects the whole design so well that the spectator would wonder the original architect omitted it ... Before this the ceiling was quite rough and rude, without any moulding, as if it had been left unfinished ...[160]

The decorator who marbled the library for the second time was so proud of his work he painted over the door, 'James Cooper in the year 1814'.

Changes to the Medieval Library, both when the staircase was inserted through the floor in 1676, and when two bays were removed in 1789, led to a rearrangement of the desks. Each bay of the room is marked by a pair of slender columns supporting braces for the roof. When the room was altered each time, not all of the desks could be positioned in the centre of each bay; some had to be shunted along, and no doubt some benches were removed. Where the braces of the roof got in the way, the poppy heads on the wall side of a desk were cut off, and that side of the desk was hollowed out slightly to fit around the slender columns supporting the brace. Two of the three surviving desks show this adaptation. The poppy heads were retained, and later put back on these desks.

In the early 1800s, the dean and chapter decided to sell some books to pay for the refurbishment of the Wren Library and to buy new books and bind others. In 1811, three Caxtons were sold, now in the John Rylands Library, Manchester. The Reverend Thomas Frognall Dibdin visited Lincoln in 1814, when the books had been moved to the chapter house during the Wren Library's refurbishment. He paid 500 guineas for twenty valuable items, of which many were *incunabula* and early printed books.[161] The bibliophile Beriah Botfield was scathing in his criticism of Dibdin's 'Lincoln Nosegay', stating that 'the unlettered spoiler has deprived [Honywood's Collection] of

[160] W. Coll., 786/8, pp. 75–6.

[161] C. Hurst, *Catalogue of the Wren Library of Lincoln Cathedral* (Cambridge, 1982), p. xi. Henceforth Hurst. There was a third sale of more modest proportions in 1817.

some of its brightest ornaments'. Botfield visited the libraries in 1833, noting that manuscripts were still kept in the 'Manuscripts Library' and that there was a library of printed books, numbering 4,451, 'in a spacious Gallery one hundred and four feet by seventeen'. Traces of nineteenth-century lettering stating these statistics can be seen in the panel over the door in the Wren Library. Botfield recorded a shocking practice that he hoped had been stopped: '… as formerly a few shillings were sufficient to induce the verger to allow the excision by any "curious stranger" of the illuminated capitals, many of the volumes are lamentably mutilated and defective'.[162] When the Reverend John Skinner toured Lincolnshire in 1825, he noted the Roman mosaic floor (discovered in 1793) below ground in the cloister garth, covered by a little building.[163] The mosaic was moved to a space under the library stairs in 1867.[164] He admired other antiquities, such as the Greek sepulchral stone kept in the cloister, and in the library, 'Roman vessels of various shapes and sizes, and some iron heads of missive weapons'.[165] During the course of the century, in the absence of a local museum, archaeological finds that were not only from the cathedral, but from other places in Lincoln and the county, continued to find a home in the cloister and library.

Meanwhile, by gift or bequest, the number of books was increasing, including many volumes from the personal collection of James Jeremie, dean of Lincoln, 1864–72. New bookcases were added on the south side of the Wren Library,[166] and a stove for heating was introduced on the north wall.[167] This stove was in place by 6 May 1862, when the dean and chapter agreed an annual payment of £5 to the vergers to keep the library in order. They were to open and close windows, dust, and light a fire if need be, and were urged 'not to admit anyone in the Library without special leave'.[168] A showcase was made for the cathedral's 1215 exemplar of Magna Carta in 1864.[169] In 1867 chapter resolved, 'that in order to enable the Clergy of the Diocese to use the Cathedral Library more frequently the library be open every Friday throughout the year from 11 a.m. to 2 p.m. and the librarian or some authorised

162 B. Botfield, *Notes on Cathedral Libraries of England* (London, 1849), pp. 268, 269, 283.

163 A. White (ed.), 'The Revd. John Skinner's Tour to Lincolnshire 1825', *Lincolnshire History and Archaeology*, SLHA 19 (Gainsborough 1983), p. 94.

164 LA, D & C, A/3/18, p. 253.

165 White (ed.), 'The Revd. John Skinner's Tour to Lincolnshire 1825', pp. 95 and note 13, p. 96. The Greek stone was later sent to the City and County Museum.

166 Hurst, p. xii.

167 A round hole for a stove pipe in the panelling, later filled in, is hidden behind the portrait of Mary Honywood.

168 LA, D & C, A/3/18, 6 May 1862, p. 124.

169 LA, D & C, Bj/1/20, fabric accounts for 1864–65.

person on his behalf will be in attendance'.[170] Gone were the days when the vergers cut illuminations from the manuscripts for visitors. Later that year it was agreed that the verger George Logsdail would receive a salary of £5 per annum as deputy to the librarian for Friday openings.[171] This general sorting out included moving the manuscripts from the Medieval to the Wren Library. In 1881 Precentor Venables recorded they 'were arranged in lock-up cases at the west end of the Library'.[172]

Although J. L. Pearson was appointed cathedral architect in 1870,[173] his ambitious and wide-ranging restoration programme did not begin until after he had completed his survey of the fabric in June 1875. He wrote of the cloister:

> The removal of the North side of the Cloister arcade and part of the East and west sides and the subsequent erection of a colonnade with a library over in the Classic style is much to be deplored; it would however be neither a very difficult not very costly work to take down the library and colonnade … and rebuild them on an adjoining site.[174]

He would return to this radical idea several years later; there were many more urgent repairs needed, including work to the west front, chapter house, and the medieval cloister, which by this time was close to collapse. The Architectural Society reported in 1882:

> The restoration of the cloisters has been commenced on the western side. The inclination of the walls outwards, which, for want of a proper foundation, commenced almost immediately on their first erection, rendering necessary the addition of buttresses, has increased so much that their security was endangered. The only satisfactory mode of procedure was to take down the whole of the cloisters … bay by bay, and rebuild it stone by stone, replacing the decayed parts with new work. The whole is being executed with the most scrupulous attention to the original design.[175]

170 LA, D & C, A/3/18, p. 243.

171 *ibid.*, 4 November 1867, p. 248. George Logsdail's son was William Logsdail, the artist. The librarian by tradition was a priest vicar.

172 R. J. King, *Handbook to the Cathedrals of England, Eastern Division, a new edition edited by the Reverend Edmund Venables* (London 1881), p. 389.

173 D. M. Thompson, 'Historical Survey, 1750–1949', in D. Owen (ed.), *History of Lincoln Minster* (Cambridge, 1994), p. 274. Henceforth Thompson. LA, D & C, Bj/1/20 fabric accounts for 1870–71 records the first payment to Pearson of £128 11s. 11d. for 'Architect's charges'.

174 LA, D &C, Ark 22.13.

175 *AASRP*, XVI (1881–2), Part II, Report, ci–cii.

The cloister was not fully restored to its original design; the low wall that had been inserted below the tracery in each bay to add strength was re-instated, but the large buttresses added for the same purpose were removed.[176] The late eighteenth-century Westmorland slate roof was replaced with lead.[177]

The success of the ongoing restoration of the cloister may have led the chapter to consider returning the north walk to its medieval appearance. This would necessitate moving the Wren Library stone by stone and rebuilding it, but having seen how methodically this was done in the cloister under Pearson's supervision, the chapter were ready to consider it. In 1885 they reported to the Church Commissioners that over £70,000 was needed for repairs to the fabric, according to Pearson's estimate, and if the north cloister 'were to be replaced and a new library erected, which would be a necessary consequence of the restoration of the cloisters, an addition of £4,800 would be required'.[178]

In 1891, the industrialist Alfred Shuttleworth began negotiations to remove the old houses stretching between the chapter house to Eastgate, including College House with its medieval hall, as well as the run-down cottages, butcher's shop and The Dolphins Inn on the northwest corner of Priorygate.[179] He lived across the street from the cathedral's east green, in Eastgate House (now the Lincoln Hotel); clearing the site would improve the view from his house and enable the widening of Eastgate and Priorygate. Shuttleworth would pay to have the buildings demolished and compensate the chapter for lost rents, to which the chapter agreed.[180] The Wren Library could be moved to a site in front of the deanery stable yard's east wall, changing its orientation from south to east facing.[181] On 12 March 1892, *The Builder* published the wording of a circular from Dean William Butler, inviting the public to a meeting to discuss the proposal:

> It has probably come to your notice that Mr Shuttleworth has made some very acceptable proposals to the Dean and Chapter. He wishes to effect a long-desired public improvement on the north-east of the Minster Green by removal of the eight houses now standing thereon, and the keeping for the future, as an open space, almost

[176] Pearson wanted to keep the additional buttresses, but in 1884 the chapter decided against it. See LA, DIOC/Bishop Greaves, Box 3, the Reverend Edward Leeke's notes on Chapter meetings, 1 March 1884.

[177] C. Brighton, *Lincoln Cathedral Cloister Bosses* (Lincoln, 1985) pp. 7–8.

[178] 'Answer of the Dean and Chapter to the Cathedral Commissioners in Appendix to their Report, 1885', as quoted in J. W. F. Hill, *Victorian Lincoln* (Cambridge, 1974), pp. 267–8. The figure was based on Pearson's 1875 survey (Ark 22.13).

[179] S. Jones *et al., The Survey of Ancient Houses*, III, pp. 44–50; L. Elvin, *Lincoln as It Was*, III, Victorian photos.

[180] Hill, *Victorian Lincoln*, p. 268.

[181] LA, D & C, Ark 22.32.

> all the ground so cleared. These proposals include also, by request of the Dean and Chapter, another, which seems to them a not less important improvement, *viz.*, the removal of Sir Christopher Wren's Library and its re-building, as near as possible, stone for stone, upon the Western boundary of the ground cleared, together with the rebuilding of the ancient North Walk of the Cloisters – destroyed after the Civil War. Mr Shuttleworth, however, makes it a condition of the assistance which he offers to give that the Library be removed and rebuilt without delay'.[182]

Worse was to come. A week later it was announced in *The Builder*:

> The meeting in the Chapter House last Saturday … appears to have resolved on the demolition of Wren's Library without a dissenting voice … Cathedral cities are usually about fifty years behind the rest of the world in their ideas, and Lincoln seems no exception to the rule'.[183]

On 2 April *The Builder* reported that the Director of the Society of Antiquaries, H. S. Milman, had written to the dean, and that he had replied, 'The Dean and Chapter are acting under the strongly-expressed opinion of their highly-competent architect, Mr Pearson, and they have no doubt that his judgement is right in the matter'. The Antiquaries made clear they did not doubt Pearson's competency, but questioned 'whether it is proper to demolish a piece of architecture of undoubted historic interest and of considerable beauty to make way for a presumed reproduction …' and 'ample room might be found for the extension of the library without interfering with the present buildings', and that as 'this is the only example of a cathedral cloister of post-Reformation date in England' they viewed the proposal 'with the greatest possible concern'.[184] But Pearson had already begun voicing his own concerns about the cost of the project during the previous winter, writing to Subdean Jacob Clements: 'The cost of the rebuilding of Wren's work would be much more than 2,000£ … besides which it will be necessary to make a new library wider than the present one, the arrangements of the Staircase would also have to be different …'[185] On 29 May he advised the subdean that there would need to be 'an additional room with a staircase … and a room over, this being a new building it will cost £3,500 …'[186] The plans show not

[182] Editorial, *The Builder*, vol. LXII, 12 March 1892, printed in London, p. 201.
[183] *ibid.*, 19 March 1892, p. 220.
[184] *ibid.,* 2 April 1892.
[185] Letter to Subdean Clements from J. L. Pearson, 19 January 1892, D & C archive, uncatalogued.
[186] *ibid.,* 29 May 1892, D & C archive, uncatalogued.

one but two new structures either side of the rebuilt library. As the building would have lost its context once removed from the cloister, these pavilions were needed to anchor the design. Pearson's plan narrowed the walkway under the library, creating a space behind it for 'architectural fragments', no doubt meant for tidying away all the archaeological clutter then kept in the cloister, and at the foot of the library stairs.

By the end of the year, the force of the public outcry, coupled with concern over the increasing expense, put an end to the scheme. Chapter instead decided to repair the existing library for £900, to which Shuttleworth contributed £400.[187] In the restoration of the Medieval Library from 1893–96, Pearson rebuilt the timber-framed north and east walls, hid the rough walling of the staircase annex with machine-sawn ashlar masonry, inside and out, gave it windows of a late medieval appearance, and replaced the staircase. The 1789 stairs had ascended clockwise, leading to a door Lumby had created at the southern end of the east wall of the Medieval Library.[188] Pearson changed this door back to a two-light window, and wound his staircase in the opposite direction, leading to a door of his own design at the north end of the east wall. A few steps below this door is a landing, which was provided with a blank north wall into which was set a relieving arch – an arrangement repeated on the floor below.[189] Now that the houses had been demolished on the northeast green, the cleared space provided an ideal site for a future library extension. By running the staircase the other way, doors could later be inserted below the relieving arches to access the two floors of the Wickham Library, given by Dean Edward Wickham for use as a diocesan lending library, completed after the dean's death in 1914.[190]

In the early twentieth century, all was well with both historic libraries. When the heating throughout the cathedral was upgraded just before World War I,[191] the stove in the Wren Library was replaced with a hot water pipe running under a metal vent along the south side of the room. Having been

187 Thompson, p. 285.

188 J. W. Clark, 'On Ancient Libraries: (1) Lincoln Cathedral …', *Cambridge Antiquarian Society Proceedings*, vol. 9, New Series 3 (1894–98), 38. The plan describes this as 'modern window, 1893, formerly a door'.

189 D & C, uncatalogued, Pearson's staircase plan (no. 138, 8 December 1892). This is one of three uncatalogued plans by Pearson; the other two are 'Staircase to Old Library', i.e., south and east exterior elevations of the staircase annex (no. 140, 8 December 1892); and 'Old Library' (no. 159, 26 April 1892). At the time of writing, the author consulted her photos of the plans, but the actual plans had not yet been transferred to Lincolnshire Archives and they could not be located.

190 Thomson, pp. 290-1; LA, D & C, A.3.24.

191 Thomson, p. 294.

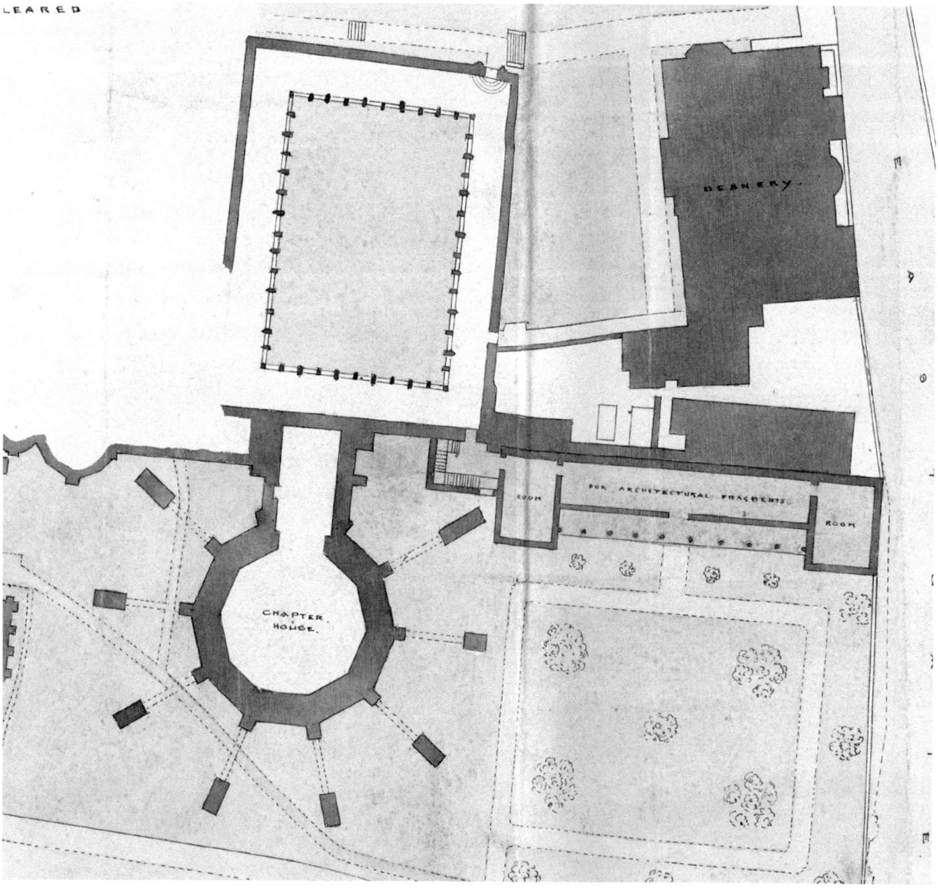

Figure 9. Detail of J. L. Pearson's unexecuted plan of 1892 to move the Wren Library to Lincoln Cathedral's east green. Positioned at right angles to the north walk of the cloister, the rebuilt library was to have additional wings at each end (LA, D & C, Ark 22.32, reproduced with the kind permission of the Dean and Chapter of Lincoln Cathedral).

painted a stone colour earlier, the Wren Library was painted green in 1902, then painted green again in 1951.[192] In 1983 it was discovered that there was death watch beetle in the Wren Library's roof, and the floor joists were coming away from the south wall. A major programme of works, undertaken by the architectural firm of Maguire and Murray, necessitated the removal of the manuscripts and rare books to the University of Nottingham. A nineteenth-century bookcase was pulled away from the wall, revealing the original marbling on the panelling behind. This created great excitement, and chapter made the bold decision to return the library to the time of Wren. The newer bookcases and their books were moved to Exchequergate (the west gatehouse in the Close Wall), and the heating was taken out. Beginning in 1986, Nigel Leaney led students from the Conservation and Restoration course at the Lincolnshire College of Art and Design in reinstating the painting and gilding scheme. They began by scraping through four layers of paint down to the original marbling, exposing one corner of the room around the door. The marbling was then replicated in the rest of the room, using paints, as well as a crayon recipe for the streaks in the marbling, based on an analysis of the original scheme.[193] On its completion in 1990, the airiness and beauty of the library could be seen as it would have looked when it was first built. Unfortunately, the removal of the heating created a humidity problem for the rare books. In 2000, conservation heating and dehumidifiers were added which improved the situation. The library could be open to the public, and used for concerts, lectures and readings, to tie in with exhibitions of books and manuscripts in the Medieval Library, but only in the warmer months, as the system was designed for books and not for people. Around this time, it was noticed that there was a worrying crack developing in the ceiling. Twenty years later, investigations revealed that most of the Wren Library oak roof trusses were buckling. At the time of writing, the books have been removed once again, and the roof and ceiling are being repaired. There are plans to update the heating and dehumidification system, and to renew the ceiling of the north walk of the cloister beneath.

When Nicholas Bennett began his library tours by saying that these historic libraries were a remarkable survival, it was true on several levels. The Medieval Library could have burned down by when a candle was upset, or it might have been swept away to make room for Wren's new library. The Wren Library could have become a Victorian pastiche if it had been re-sited, but it is still there, despite spreading floor joists, death watch beetle and buckling roof trusses. Standing up to the vicissitudes of time, Lincoln Cathedral Library's buildings, furnishings, and its unique collections continue. They are a treasure worth preserving.

192 *Lincoln Diocesan Magazine*, 67, No. 2 (February 1951), p. 43.

193 N. Leaney, *pers. comm.*

2

Long-lived Lincolnshire Widows: Petronilla de Craon and her Contemporaries

LOUISE J WILKINSON

In 1242–43, the monks of Spalding priory recalled how 'Lucy, countess of Bolingbroke' had granted them twelve carucates of land in Pinchbeck in pure alms more than a century earlier, together with further properties in Spalding, Weston and Moulton.[1] By the thirteenth century, there was a long tradition of prominent secular female landholders in Lincolnshire and its neighbouring counties. Pauline Stafford's seminal study, *The East Midlands in the Early Middle Ages*, highlighted the importance of women landowners in this region in the ninth, tenth and eleventh centuries, who successfully laid claim to shares of paternal inheritances, transferred estates to others and acted as valued benefactors of religious houses, especially as widows.[2] There were also strong associations between the East Midlands and royal women before and after the Norman Conquest. Domesday Book recorded how Edward the Confessor's wife, Queen Edith, held land in dower in Lincolnshire in Gayton le Wold, Grantham, Great Ponton, Horncastle, Nettleham, Stamford and Torksey in 1066.[3] Property in Rutland, located immediately to the south

1 Spalding was possibly founded or re-founded by Lucy's first husband, Ivo de Taillebois, as a cell of St Nicholas, Angers: N. Sumner, 'The Countess Lucy's Priory? The Early History of Spalding Priory and its Estates', *Reading Medieval Studies* 13 (1988), 81–103. The abbey of St Nicholas, Angers, also held property in Moulton in frankalmoign by Countess Lucy's gift: *Liber Feodorum. The Book of Fees commonly called Testa de Nevill*, 3 vols (London, 1920–31), vol. 2, p. 1008 (1242–43 survey).

2 Pauline Stafford, *The East Midlands in the Early Middle* Ages (1985), pp. 150–1.

3 C. W. Foster and Thomas Longley (ed. and trans.), *The Lincolnshire Domesday and Lindsey Survey*, LRS 19 (Lincoln, 1924), pp. 10–11 (Stamford; seventy messuages which belonged to Rutland), 12–13 (Torksey; Edith also appears in a list of persons with rights of sake and soke and toll and team in Lincolnshire), 16 (Grantham), 17 (Great Ponton), 19 (Nettleham), 23 (Gayton le Wold and Horncastle), 203 (Fillingham, held by a tenant from Edith). See also Pauline Stafford, *Queen Emma and Queen*

of the county, was routinely assigned to Mercian, and later, English queens, including Ælfthryth, Emma, Edith, Matilda of Scotland, Eleanor of Aquitaine, Berengaria of Navarre and Isabella of Angoulême.[4] Local heiresses also came to prominence in the immediate aftermath of the invasions of Cnut of Denmark (1016) and William of Normandy (1066), when incoming Danish and Norman lords married Anglo-Saxon and Anglo-Scandinavian women as a means of legitimising their English conquests.[5] It was, after all, in Lincolnshire that there were two notable aristocratic heiresses of Anglo-Saxon/Scandinavian descent in the first generation or so after the Norman Conquest, both of whom married Norman husbands: Muriel, the descendent of Colswein of Lincoln, heiress of Picot FitzColswein and wife of the Norman Robert de la Haye, constable of Lincoln Castle;[6] and the aforementioned Lucy (d. 1136–38), the daughter of Turold, a Norman sheriff of Lincoln, by a daughter of William Malet, a half-Norman, half-English companion of William the Conqueror.[7] Lucy was wife, in turn, of Ivo de Taillebois, Roger FitzGerold and Ranulf le Meschin, who was created earl of Chester during their marriage.[8] Lucy left a

---

Edith: Queenship and Women's Power in Eleventh-Century England (Oxford, 1997), pp. 135–6.

4 Charles Phythian-Adams, 'Rutland Reconsidered', in Ann Dornier (ed.), *Mercian Studies* (Leicester, 1977), pp. 63–84, at p. 64; Stafford, *Queen Emma and Queen Edith*, pp. 127, 129–30, 132, 135–6, 148; Lois L. Huneycutt, *Matilda of Scotland: A Study in Medieval Queenship* (Woodbridge, 2003), pp. 69–72.

5 Eleanor Searle, 'Women and the Legitimisation of Succession at the Norman Conquest', *Anglo-Norman Studies* 3 (1980), pp. 159–70. The strength of women's property rights in this region more generally is demonstrated by the separate bequests of land made in their will by Ulf and his wife Madselin in 1066: Dorothy Whitelock (ed. and trans.), *Anglo-Saxon Wills* (Cambridge, 1930), pp. 94–7; Doris Mary Stenton, *The English Woman in History* (London, 1957), pp. 18–19.

6 J. F. Hill, *Medieval Lincoln*, rev. edn (Stamford, 1990), pp. 87–8. Muriel's estate comprised Brattleby, which was held by her father Colswein in 1086 and by her husband Robert at the time of the Lindsey survey of 1115–18: Peter Sawyer, *Anglo-Saxon Lincolnshire* (Lincoln, 1998), p. 207; Foster and Longley (ed. and trans.), *The Lincolnshire Domesday and Lindsey Survey*, pp. 118–24, 238–41, 243, 245, 251–3, 257, 259. Muriel's inheritance was noted in a charter issued by Henry I: J. H. Round (ed.), *Calendar of Documents preserved in France, Illustrative of the History of Great Britain and Ireland, Vol. I, A. D. 918–1206* (London, 1899), pp. xlviii–xlix, 329–30, no. 923.

7 For Lucy's background, see: Katharine S. B. Keats-Rohan, 'Antecessor Noster: The Parentage of Countess Lucy made Plain', *Prosopon: Newsletter of the Unit of Prosopographical Research* 2 (1995), 1–3; Susan M. Johns, *Noblewomen, Aristocracy and Power in the Twelfth-Century Anglo-Norman Realm* (Manchester, 2003), pp. 55, 59–61.

8 Lucy's three husbands were named in her gift of Spalding manor to Spalding Priory: Geoffrey Barraclough (ed.), *The Charters of the Anglo-Norman Earls of*

significant mark on Lincolnshire's religious and secular landscape as foundress of Stixwould, a religious house for women in Lincolnshire, which claimed, initially, the status of an abbey.[9] It was also Lucy who, as a widow, fortified a tower at Lincoln Castle, which was known as 'Lucy's Tower' by the thirteenth century.[10] Furthermore, it was Muriel's granddaughter, Nicholaa de la Haye, who inherited Brattleby and a claim to the constableship of Lincoln Castle.[11] As the chronicler Richard of Devizes noted, Nicholaa defended Lincoln Castle during a forty-day siege in 1191, when she and her second husband, Gerard de Camville, became embroiled in John, count of Mortain's war with the royal chancellor.[12] Later, in widowhood, Nicholaa held both the offices of constable of Lincoln Castle and sheriff of Lincolnshire and defended the castle and county against the baronial rebels during the First Barons' War of 1215–17.[13]

The presence of women, such as Countess Lucy and the women of the de la Haye family, may well have facilitated a degree of acceptance of aristocratic female landholding in the East Midlands in a patriarchal era.[14] This chapter takes as its central focus the life of a hitherto neglected and long-lived Lincolnshire widow, Petronilla de Craon (*c.* 1183–1262), the thrice-married lady

---

Chester, c. 1071–1237, Record Society of Lancashire and Cheshire 126 (Stroud, 1988), no. 16. Ivo de Taillebois was sheriff of Lincoln in 1086 and held Lucy's manor of Bolingbroke and its sokeland: Foster and Longley (ed. and trans.), *The Lincolnshire Domesday and Lindsey Survey*, pp. 86–7.

9 TNA, C 47/19/3, no. 16; BL, Add. MS 46701, fol. 1r; Barraclough (ed.), *The Charters of the Anglo-Norman Earls of Chester*, nos 18–19. More than fifty years after Countess Lucy's death, her anniversary was still being celebrated at Stixwould, as was noted in a charter issued by the nuns: BL, Harleian charter 44 i. 29.

10 Hill, *Medieval Lincoln*, p. 91; Jonathan Clark, Justin Garner-Lahire, Cecily Spall and Nicola Toop, *Lincoln Castle Revealed: The Story of a Norman Powerhouse and its Anglo-Saxon Precursor* (Oxford, 2021), pp. 54–5.

11 For Henry II's charter, confirming Nicholaa's father, Richard de la Haye in possession of his father Robert's lands and of the constableship of Lincoln castle, see TNA, DL 10/24; J. H. Round (ed.), *Ancient Charters: Royal and Private prior to A.D. 1200, Part I*, PRS 10 (1888), no. 36. For Richard I's charter of 1189, confirming Gerard de Camville and Nicholaa as his wife in possession of these lands and this office, see TNA, DL 10/40; Round (ed.), *Ancient Charters*, no. 55.

12 J. T. Appleby (ed. and trans.), *The Chronicle of Richard of Devizes of the Time of King Richard the First* (London, 1963), p. 31; *The Great Roll of the Pipe of the Third and Fourth Years of the Reign of King the First, Michaelmas 1191 and Michaelmas 1192*, PRS, New Series 2 (1926), p. 1.

13 On this, see Louise J. Wilkinson, *Women in Thirteenth-Century Lincolnshire* (Woodbridge, 2007), pp. 18–23.

14 On the presence and responsibilities of women as landholders among the lesser aristocracy in twelfth-century Lincolnshire, see Hanna I. Kilpi, 'Lesser Aristocratic Women in Twelfth-Century Charters: A Lincolnshire Case Study', *Medieval Prosopography* 31 (2016), 67–96.

of Freiston barony in Lincolnshire and South Warnborough in Hampshire.[15] It considers Petronilla's experiences as a baronial heiress during the reigns of four English kings, those of Henry II (d. 1189), Richard I (d. 1199), John (d. 1216) and Henry III (d. 1272). This chapter examines how far Petronilla's experiences as an heiress, widow and mother resonated with those of other elite women landholders in the East Midlands during the decades immediately before and after Magna Carta (first issued in 1215) became established in English law. This period was critically important in the transition of aristocratic women's rights from vulnerability to improved security.[16] As Thomas Keefe's analysis of the proffers and income for heirs and heiresses received by the crown has shown, the years after John's accession in 1199 witnessed 'a more intense exploitation [by the king than before] of wardships and marriages as a financial resource'.[17] Yet, it was in response to this 'exploitation' that Magna Carta's clauses that protected heiresses against disparagement (marriage to social inferiors) guaranteed widows free and relatively swift access to their property and safeguarded widows against the threat of forced remarriage by removing the danger of distraint were conceded, first by John to the baronial rebels in 1215 and later by Henry III's government to his English subjects.[18]

Petronilla de Craon and the barony of Freiston

The principles governing female succession to estates held from the king and other lords by military service were reasonably well established, not only in Lincolnshire but also throughout England, by the thirteenth century. As a rule, proximity of kinship informed inheritance customs and determined who should succeed as an heir to the lands of a dead tenant-in-chief. Estates held of the king by knight service descended from one generation to the next by patrilineal primogeniture, so that the eldest son succeeded to his father's properties. In the absence of a son, daughters of the same generation inherited lands as co-heiresses and the family estates were divided equally between the daughters. In the absence of lineal descendants, property passed to collateral heirs – brother, brother's children, sisters, sisters' children,

15 I am grateful to Nicholas Bennett for first stimulating my interest in Petronilla.

16 J. C. Holt, *Magna Carta*, 3rd edn (Cambridge, 2015), pp. 71–2.

17 Thomas K. Keefe, 'Proffers for Heirs and Heiresses in the Pipe Rolls: Some Observations on Indebtedness in the Years before the Magna Carta (1180–1212)', *The Haskins Society Journal: Studies in Medieval History* 5 (1993), 99–109, at p. 104.

18 William Stubbs (ed.), *Select Charters and Other Illustrations of English Constitutional History*, ninth edn by H. W. C. Davis (Oxford, 1913, reprinted 1960), pp. 294 (1215 Magna Carta, caps 6–8), 337 (1216 Magna Carta, caps 6–8), pp. 341–2 (1217 Magna Carta, caps 6–8), p. 350 (1225 re–issue, caps 6–7, with caps 7–8 of 1217 merged into cap. 7).

uncle, uncle's children and aunts, aunts' children – provided the heir or heirs had been born to a married couple.[19]

Despite the preference given to sons as heirs, it was quite usual for English baronies, in the sense of honours held by greater lords, to descend to a woman as an heiress or to multiple women as co-heiresses.[20] Scott Waugh calculated that out of a total 192 English baronies between 1200 and 1327, sixty-one (or 32%) descended solely through male heirs, of which thirty-six passed from father to son and another twenty-five were transmitted to collateral male heirs. 110 baronies (57%) descended through women on at least one occasion, forty-three of which passed to single heiresses and sixty-seven to co-heiresses. Another twenty-one baronies suffered forfeiture or were transmitted to new holders by grant or sale.[21] Baronies routinely descended not only to daughters, but also to sisters, nieces and other female kin.[22]

Petronilla de Craon was one such heir to a barony in Lincolnshire. She was the sole daughter of Guy II de Craon (d. *c.* 1205), a tenant-in-chief of Richard I and participant in the Third Crusade.[23] The Craon family originated in Anjou but flourished in England in royal service under the early Norman kings. They had already acquired Freiston, the caput of their barony, and other Lincolnshire lands by 1086.[24] In 1114, Petronilla's ancestors, Alan de Craon, dapifer of King Henry I, Muriel de Beauchamp his wife and Maurice, their son, founded a Benedictine priory at Freiston

19 G. D. G. Hall (ed. and trans.), *The Treatise on the Laws and Customs of the Realm of England commonly called Glanvill*, revised edn (Oxford, 1991), pp. 75–9; George E. Woodbine (ed.) and Samuel E. Thorne (trans.), *Bracton: On the Laws and Customs of England*, 4 vols (Cambridge, 1968–77), vol. 2, pp. 190–1, 194–8.

20 Baronies typically comprised ten or more (sometimes considerably more) knights' fees and their holders were tenants-in-chief or the tenants of other lords: Robert Bartlett, *England under the Norman and Angevin Kings, 1075–1225* (Oxford, 2000), pp. 212–13. On aristocratic female inheritance, see J. C. Holt, 'Feudal Society and the Family in Early Medieval England: IV. The Heiress and the Alien', *TRHS*, 5th series 35 (1985), 1–28; S. F. C. Milsom, 'Inheritance by Women in the Twelfth and Early Thirteenth Centuries', in Morris S. Arnold, Thomas A. Green, Sally A. Scully and Stephen D. White (eds), *On the Laws and Customs of England: Essays in Honour of Samuel E. Thorne* (Chapel Hill, 1981), pp. 60–89.

21 Scott L. Waugh, *The Lordship of England: Royal Wardships and Marriages in English Society and Politics, 1217–1327* (Princeton, NJ, 1988), p. 19, table 1.1.

22 *ibid.*, p. 21.

23 Ian L. Bass, 'Lincolnshire and the Third Crusade: The List of Crusaders from the Deanery of Holland', *Historical Research*, 93:261 (2020), 577–98, at pp. 589–90.

24 Foster and Longley (ed. and trans.), *The Lincolnshire Domesday and the Lindsey Survey*, pp. 179–85; E. M. Poynton, 'The Fee of Creon', *The Genealogist*, New Series 18 (1902), 162–6, 219–25.

as a cell of Crowland Abbey.[25] Although the date of Petronilla's birth was not recorded, a late medieval genealogy of the founders of Freiston indicates that her mother's name was Isabella.[26] An entry on the Pipe Roll for Michaelmas 1182 records how Guy, Petronilla's father, incurred a debt of 200 marks when he purchased the right to marry Isabella, the daughter of Thomas Basset and widow of Albert Gresle (*alias* Grelley), and have her dower from her first marriage.[27] Petronilla married for the first time by the early 1190s, when she was a young girl. She succeeded to Guy II's barony in around 1205 and had outlived no fewer than three husbands by the time of her death in 1262.[28] Petronilla's marital career highlights the fluctuations in fortunes that individual ladies faced as landholders; the vulnerability of young heiresses to the ambitions of senior royal officials and to the king's will, especially in the years before Magna Carta; and their relative safety from royal interference during Henry III's personal rule. This safety existed in spite of contemporary complaints about the marriages of English comital heirs and heiresses to the king's and queen's Lusignan and

25 John Caley, Henry Ellis and Bulkeley Bandinel (eds.), *Monasticon Anglicanum: A New Edition*, 6 vols in 8 (London, 1846), vol. 2, pp. 101, 120, no. xx; vol. 4, pp. 124–8, esp. pp. 125–6, no. i (Freiston Priory); vol. 6, pt 1, p. 136, no. ii (Chronicle of Llanthony Abbey); *CChR, 1300–1326*, p. 102 (*inspeximus* and confirmation of Edward I, 10 June 1307); William Page (ed.), *A History of the County of Lincoln, Volume 2*, Victoria County History (London, 1906), pp. 128–9; Dorothy M. Owen, *Church and Society in Medieval Lincolnshire* (Lincoln, 1990), p. 148; K. S. B. Keats-Rohan, *Domesday People: A Prosopography of Persons occurring in English Documents 1066–1166: II. Pipe Rolls to Cartae Baronum* (Woodbridge, 2002), p. 417. Peter of Blois's additions to the history of Crowland Abbey includes a dramatic tale of how Alan became violently ill, summoned the abbot of Crowland to him, established a cell for monks at Freiston and endowed it with seven churches: Henry T. Riley (trans.), *Ingulph's Chronicle of the Abbey of Croyland, with the Continuations by Peter of Blois and Anonymous Writers* (London, 1854), pp. 260–1.

26 *Monasticon Anglicanum*, vol. 4, p. 126, no. iii.

27 *The Great Roll of the Pipe for the Twenty-Eighth Year of the Reign of King Henry the Second, A.D. 1181–1182*, PRS 31 (London, 1910), p. 57. Isabella's marriage to Guy de Craon, following a period in Thomas Basset's custody after her first husband's death, was documented in 1185: John Walmsley (ed. and trans.), *Widows, Heirs and Heiresses in the Late Twelfth Century: The Rotuli de Dominabus et Pueris et Puellis* (Tempe, Arizona, 2006), pp. 22–3, no. 28. See also Keats-Rohan, *Domesday People: II. Pipe Rolls to Cartae Baronum*, p. 167.

28 Petronilla's recent death is recorded in *CFR, 1261–62*, no. 285 (11 April 1262), when her eldest son and heir performed homage for South Warnborough. See also I. J. Sanders, *English Baronies: A Study of their Origin and Descent, 1087–1327* (Oxford, 1960), p. 47.

Savoyard relations, documented by contemporary writers, such as the St Albans chronicler, Matthew Paris.[29]

Petronilla de Craon's first marriage, probably arranged between 1189 and 1191, was to William de Longchamp the younger, a kinsman of the bishop of Ely, Richard I's controversial royal chancellor.[30] One of the complaints lodged against the bishop by the chronicler Roger of Howden was the way in which this chancellor's nephews and kinsmen 'sought ardently to unite themselves in matrimony with earls, barons and magnates of the kingdom' despite their relatively lowly birth.[31] The behaviour exhibited by the Longchamp family was remarkably similar to that of William Brewer, the son of a royal forester from Bere in Hampshire, whom another writer, Roger of Wendover, described as one of King John's evil counsellors. Brewer assiduously enriched himself, his five offspring and his nephew by acquiring profitable wardships and marriages.[32]

Petronilla de Craon's marriage was one of the unions engineered by the Longchamp family, which was negotiated between the bishop and her father, Guy. The documents recording the terms of her marriage settlement strongly convey Petronilla's own lack of involvement as a child in negotiations and the efforts to which the Longchamp family went to secure possession of both Petronilla and her lands. The marriage agreement stipulated that if William the younger died, then his younger brother Henry would take his place as Petronilla's bridegroom; if Henry died, then a third brother would marry Petronilla. Altogether, no fewer than three Longchamp boys were effectively lined up to secure Petronilla's hand for the Longchamp dynasty, demonstrating Petronilla's material value as a baronial heiress.[33] Although William de Longchamp the younger inherited lands of his own in Herefordshire, his marriage to Petronilla brought him a valuable barony, whose principal estates lay in Kesteven and Holland in Lincolnshire,

29 Henry Richards Luard (ed.), *Matthæi Parisiensis, Monachi Sancti Albani, Chronica Majora*, Rolls Series, 7 vols (London, 1872–83), vol. 4, pp. 627–9.

30 Nicholas Karn (ed.), *English Episcopal Acta 31. Ely, 1109–1197* (Oxford, 2005), p. 184, no. 142. On the Longchamp family's rise to wealth through royal service, see David Balfour, 'The Origins of the Longchamp Family', *Medieval Prosopography* 18 (1997), 73–92.

31 '... comites et barones regnique magnates sibi summa aviditate in matrimonium copulare ardebant': William Stubbs (ed.), *Chronica Magistri Rogeri de Houedene*, Rolls Series, 4 vols (London, 1868–71), vol. 3, p. 142.

32 In July 1213, for example, William agreed to pay King John £666 for custody of all the land of Hugh de Auberville, together with the marriages of Hugh's heir and his widow Joan: Thomas Duffus Hardy (ed.), *Rotuli de Oblatis et Finibus in Turri Londiniensi Asservati, Tempore Regis Johannis* (London, 1835), p. 474. His nephew married Joanna de Morville of Burgh by Sands, Cumberland: J. C. Holt, *The Northerners* (Oxford, 1961, reprinted 1992), p. 235.

33 Karn (ed.), *English Episcopal Acta 31. Ely, 1109–1197*, p. 184, no. 142.

thereby greatly increasing his personal wealth.[34] Holland was, arguably, an area of particular interest and ambition for the Longchamp family, since the chancellor successfully contrived to secure the appointment of another Henry de Longchamp as abbot of Crowland in 1191.[35] Petronilla, for her part, was promised thirty pounds' worth of land in Herefordshire as her dower should her groom, William de Longchamp the younger, predecease her, in a document issued by Bishop William, Henry her father-in-law (d. 1203) and William the younger her husband.[36]

Petronilla's marriage to William de Longchamp the younger saw the couple facing litigation, when the Knights Templar sued them in a plea of warranty of charter in 1201.[37] Petronilla's involvement in the management of her family's estates is suggested by the way that she was personally called to warranty in the same year by William her husband in another case brought by Thomas of Moulton, an important local landholder, which sought to determine if Thomas's mother had been seised in demesne on the day that she died of 'a toft and two messuages' in Boston, which William now held.[38] By 1202, however, Petronilla's husband was overseas in the king's service and his absence may well have left the couple's lands vulnerable to localised disorder.[39] When the justices in eyre visited Lincolnshire in that year, for example, William Gering accused William the Cook of seizing him and forcibly imprisoning him in William de Longchamp the younger's house in Freiston, although the case was later dismissed.[40]

The precise nature of Petronilla's personal relationship with William the younger during their years of marriage is difficult to unravel. Yet, it may be significant that she chose to include the Longchamp arms on her portrait seal, especially since William the younger was the father of her oldest son and heir, Henry, a daughter named Alice and a younger son named William, who

34 For the Longchamp family's Herefordshire properties, see Balfour, 'The Origins of the Longchamp Family', 82–3.

35 Henry de Longchamp, a former monk at Evesham, was abbot of Crowland until his death in 1236. Perhaps the Longchamp family saw his appointment and the marriage into the Craon dynasty as a means of securing a foothold in a region where there were opportunities for land reclamation and trade on the Lincolnshire coast: *Monasticon Anglicanum*, vol. 2, pp. 101–2; Page (ed.), *A History of the County of Lincoln*, vol. 2, pp. 105–18.

36 Karn (ed.), *English Episcopal Acta 31. Ely, 1109–1197*, pp. 184–5, no. 143.

37 *Curia Regis Rolls of the Reigns of Richard I and John, preserved in the Public Record Office, 3–5 John* (London, 1925), pp. 54–5.

38 *ibid.*, p. 57.

39 Petronilla was not named in this suit and may have been with her husband or in residence elsewhere on their estates: D. M. Stenton (ed.), *The Earliest Lincolnshire Assize Rolls, A. D. 1202–1209*, LRS 22 (Lincoln, 1926 for 1924), p. 205, no. 1161.

40 *ibid.*, pp. 159–60, no. 968.

served as constable of the bishop of Lincoln.[41] On her seal, Petronilla was depicted standing on a carved corbel, wearing a flat headdress and a mantel over her gown. On her dress were 'lozengy' bearings for her natal family of Craon, while in her right hand was a shield with three crescents, representing the Longchamp family. The seal legend, although damaged, indicates that Petronilla used her natal family name of 'Crov[n]' to authenticate documents, reflecting the prestige that was attached to her as a baronial heiress.[42]

By the end of 1203, Petronilla was widowed for the first time in her life. An entry on the Liberate Rolls, dated 17 September 1203, indicates that King John ordered Geoffrey FitzPeter to place Petronilla, the wife of William de Longchamp, in possession of the vill of Freiston for her sustenance, an order that was required, perhaps, if her husband had died or was incapacitated.[43] On 5 December 1203, the king issued letters patent to put arrangements in place for the widow of William de Longchamp and her sons to be delivered to him in England.[44] After William the younger's death, Petronilla quickly remarried and her second husband was a man called Henry Delamare.[45] The new match first comes to light in the records in a curious entry on the Fine Rolls for 1205, which records how Henry Delamare promised to pay the king 500 marks (£333 6s. 8d.) so that he might take possession of his wife Petronilla's lands in Hampshire, Lincolnshire, Sussex and Wiltshire. This sum satisfied the king and the local sheriffs were ordered to place Henry and Petronilla in possession of Petronilla's estates immediately.[46] What is intriguing about this entry is that there is no reference to Henry offering money so that he might marry Petronilla in the first place, as one might perhaps

41 Agnes Ethel Conway, 'The Family of William Longchamp, Bishop of Ely, Chancellor and Justiciar of England', *Archaeologia Cantiana* 36 (1924), 15–30, at p. 27.

42 Walter de Gray Birch, *Catalogue of Seals in the Department of Manuscripts in the British Museum*, 6 vols (London, 1887–1900), vol. 2, p. 382, no. 6622.

43 T. Duffus Hardy (ed.), *Rotuli de Liberate ac de Misis et Praestitis Regnante Johannis* (London, 1844), p. 63.

44 T. Duffus Hardy (ed.), *Rotuli Litterarum Patentium in Turri Londinensi Asservati, Vol. I. Pars I. Ab Anno MCCI. Ad Annum MCCXVI* (London, 1835), p. 37. On 27 December 1204, William de Cantilupe was awarded seisin of William de Longchamp's former lands in Lincolnshire: T. Duffus Hardy (ed.), *Rotuli Litterarum Clausarum in Turri Londinensi Asservati, Vol. I, Ab Anno MCCIV. Ad Annum MCCXXIV* (London, 1833), p. 16b.

45 A Henry Delamare held estates in Oxfordshire and Wiltshire: *Liber Feodorum*, vol. 1, pp. 11, 12 (1198 survey); Hubert Hall (ed.), *The Red Book of the Exchequer*, 3 vols (London, 1896), II, 486 (1210–12 survey). A Petronilla Delamare held nine and a half knights' fees in Rendcombe, Gloucestershire, as a tenant of the earl of Gloucester in 1262–63, although she may have been the widow of another man: *CIPM*, vol. 1, p. 158, no. 530; p. 164, no. 544; N. M. Herbert (ed.), *A History of the County of Gloucester: Volume 7, Victoria County History* (Oxford, 1981), pp. 218–27.

46 Hardy (ed.), *Rotuli de Oblatis*, pp. 315–16.

have expected him to have done under King John, especially when the marriage of a widowed heiress was at stake. Perhaps Petronilla and Henry had incurred John's disfavour by marrying without the king's consent.

Petronilla and her second husband certainly encountered difficulties later in claiming her dower in Wilton, Herefordshire, from her first marriage to William de Longchamp the younger. In 1207, Henry de Longchamp (a Longchamp kinsman) offered the king three palfreys so that the royal justices would *not* hear the plea that was before them between Henry de Longchamp, on the one hand, and Henry Delamare and Petronilla his wife, on the other, concerning the dower for which Petronilla and her new husband were suing him in Herefordshire.[47] Unfortunately for the couple, Longchamp's efforts to block this lawsuit were successful, since an entry on a royal plea roll for 1207 records King John's order to the justices to stop the suit 'because he does not wish that plea to be held'.[48] King John had listened to Longchamp's request, accepted the palfreys he offered and stopped Petronilla and Henry Delamare from suing Longchamp, in a case that Longchamp otherwise might have lost.[49] Such was the sometimes-prejudicial handling of royal justice under King John for members of the aristocracy.[50]

The couple met with greater success in securing recognition of Petronilla's rights over other estates that formed part of her inheritance. A final concord of 17 November 1208 recorded a settlement reached between the couple and the abbot of Swineshead, whereby the abbot recognised Petronilla's right to a bovate and a half of land in Burton, Lincolnshire. The couple, for their part, granted the abbot the disputed property in return for an annual payment of 5s.[51] Yet, Petronilla's marriage to Henry Delamare proved to be short lived.

47 *ibid.*, p. 410. See also Thomas Madox, *The History and Antiquities of the Exchequer of the Kings of England in Two Periods, Volume I*, 2nd edn (London, 1769), p. 100 n. y. A royal charter issued on 7 March 1205 granted Henry, with the assent of Geoffrey his older brother, Wilton in Herefordshire and its castle, which Hugh his grandfather had given to Henry's father and also stipulated that neither Henry nor his heirs could be sued in the future over this property by writ of mort d'ancestor: Thomas Duffus Hardy (ed.), *Rotuli Chartarum in Turri Londinensi Asservati, Vol. I, Pars I* (London, 1837), pp. 146b–147.

48 *Curia Regis Rolls of the Reigns of Richard I and John, 8–10 John* (London, 1931), p. 72.

49 The impression that Henry Delamare had lost the king's favour is confirmed by an entry on the patent rolls. On 5 September 1207, King John issued letters close which ordered the sheriff of Hampshire to seize the lands of Henry Delamare the Norman due to Henry's failure to satisfy a debt owed to the crown: Duffus Hardy (ed.), *Rotuli Litterarum Clausarum*, p. 91b.

50 On this, see Holt, *Magna Carta*, chapter 5.

51 The couple also quitclaimed their right in the foreign service in return for four marks: W. O. Massingberd (ed.), *Abstracts of Final Concords temp. Richard I, John*

By 1211, she had been widowed and, once again, she quickly remarried. The findings of an inquiry into the tenants of the honour of Craon in 1211–12 listed around twenty knightly tenants, who each owed the service of between a thirteenth of a knight and five knights.[52] Petronilla's third husband was Oliver de Vaux, who came from a family of East Anglian landholders. This time, Petronilla may have had little choice in the matter of her remarriage. An entry on the Pipe Roll for 1211 noted a debt of 500 marks (£333 6s. 8d.) and five palfreys, which Oliver had incurred for both marrying Petronilla and acquiring her lands.[53] Although Oliver and Petronilla possibly negotiated their union beforehand, it is important to acknowledge that King John was a ruler who was perfectly prepared to use the threat of distraint to coerce a widow into a second marriage that he favoured. In October 1204, for example, the king had written to his local officials, informing them that he had ordered another Lincolnshire lady, Alice, the widow of Sir John Belet, to take Ralph Riddel as her new husband; Ralph had offered King John fifty marks (£33 6s. 8d.) and two palfreys to buy Alice's hand in marriage.[54] The officials were instructed to seize Alice's lands if she refused this match.[55] When Alice subsequently rejected Ralph's suit, John proved that he was as good as his word and her estates were confiscated.[56] Alice only disentangled herself from this situation when her father, Sir Fulk (III) de Oyry, agreed to pay the king one hundred marks (£66 13s. 4d.), double the sum originally offered by Riddel, for the right to arrange Alice's next marriage and for Alice to have her dower.[57]

By 1211, the value of Petronilla de Craon's marriage had apparently increased by five palfreys since her second marriage in 1205. Perhaps this was linked to the additional dower properties she had secured through her earlier Delamare marriage. At the time of the 1212 survey of tenants-in-chief, Petronilla's third husband, Oliver de Vaux, held thirty knights' fees of the honour of Craon in Lincolnshire and further property in Hampshire 'in barony' in the right of Petronilla his wife.[58] The trade in the marriages of elite widows under King

and Henry III, Vol. I, Part I (London, 1896), p. 86 (no. 24). For another suit involving the couple, see *Curia Regis Rolls of the Reigns of Richard I and John, 11–14 John* (London, 1932), pp. 5, 33.

52 Hall (ed.), *The Red Book of the Exchequer*, vol. 2, pp. 610–11.

53 Doris M. Stenton (ed.), *The Great Roll of the Pipe for the Thirteenth Year of the Reign of King John, Michaelmas 1211*, PRS, New Series 28 (London, 1953), p. 1; Poynton, 'Fee of Creon', 220.

54 Hardy (ed.), *Rotuli de Oblatis*, p. 226.

55 Hardy (ed.), *Rotuli Litterarum Clausarum*, p. 12b.

56 *Curia Regis Rolls of the Reigns of Richard I and John, 5–7 John* (London, 1926), p. 257.

57 Hardy (ed.), *Rotuli de Oblatis*, pp. 287–8.

58 *Liber Feodorum*, vol. 1, pp. 75, 195.

John and his predecessors was still documented in Henry III's reign.[59] When the royal justices visited Lincolnshire in 1219, local jurors reported that Oliver de Vaux 'has Petronilla, who was the daughter of Guy de Croum [*sic*], of the gift of the lord king John and her land is worth £50 per annum'.[60] The same was reported in 1226–28, when it was also noted that Oliver had her 'through the king'.[61] When the justices in eyre visited Hampshire in 1236, the local jurors there also stated, quite factually, that Petronilla de Craon 'was married to Oliver de Vallibus by King John' and reported a valuation of £20 for her estates there.[62]

During the First Barons' War of 1215–17, Oliver and Petronilla joined the rebels, like many other Lincolnshire landholders, causing Oliver to forfeit his lands, temporarily.[63] After the conflict ended, Oliver returned to the king's faith and later served as a justice in eyre under Henry III in the mid-1230s.[64] On Oliver's death, in or before 1242, Petronilla his wife finally assumed independent control of her lands – her inheritance and her dower.[65] When, in 1249, local jurors in Hampshire reported on Petronilla's situation, they described how she was in the king's gift and was marriageable, once more.[66] Fortunately for Petronilla, Henry III's reign was generally a safer time for aristocratic widows who wished to avoid remarriage than that of his father.[67] The 1215 Magna Carta and its later reissues of 1216, 1217 and 1225 famously included those clauses noted at the beginning of this chapter that offered protection for widows in securing access to their lands after their husbands' deaths and from the threat of forced remarriage.[68] The continued currency of these ideas in royal circles is reflected by an entry on a royal memoranda roll for 1250, which recorded how, on 7 October, King Henry III 'came … with his council to the Exchequer', where he ordered all his sheriffs not only

59 Holt, *Magna Carta*, p. 71.

60 *Liber Feodorum*, vol. 1, p. 285.

61 *ibid.*, vol. 1, p. 363.

62 *ibid.*, vol. 2, p. 1367. See also *ibid.*, vol. 1, p. 420 (1235–36, Hampshire).

63 Oliver's lands in Hampshire, Lincolnshire, Norfolk, Nottinghamshire and Suffolk were confiscated and granted to Reginald Croc and others: *Rotuli Litterarum Clausarum*, pp. 235, 252, 253b, 255b, 257b, 270b, 274b; Holt, *The Northerners*, p. 55.

64 David Crook, *Records of the General Eyre* (London, 1982), pp. 90–1, 95.

65 Oliver was alive in 1238, when he was serving the crown: *Close Rolls of the Reign of Henry III, 1237–42* (London, 1911), p. 40. Petronilla held her lands as a widow in 1242–43: *Liber Feodorum*, vol. 2, pp. 1088–90.

66 On this occasion Petronilla's lands in South Warnborough were valued at £15 per annum: *Liber Feodorum*, vol. 2, p. 1418.

67 David Carpenter, *Magna Carta* (London, 2015), pp. 450–2.

68 Stubbs (ed.), *Select Charters*, pp. 294 (1215 Magna Carta, caps 7–8), 337 (1216 Magna Carta, caps 7–8), 341–2 (1217 Magna Carta, caps 7–8), 350 (1225 Magna Carta, cap. 7).

that they should observe and maintain the liberties of the Church, but also that they should 'similarly' maintain all orphans and widows.[69]

After the death of her third husband, Petronilla de Craon did not remarry, but retained possession of her barony and administered her lands with the assistance of her officials and servants until her death in 1262. Like other widows, she answered to the crown for debts owing from her estates and for new charges demanded by the king from his tenants-in-chief. When, for instance, inquisitions were held to determine who was liable to pay scutage to the crown in Lincolnshire in 1242–43, ten men were found to be liable for scutage as Petronilla's under-tenants or as tenants of property that was then in her custody. As the guardian of the heir of Thomas Rat, Petronilla was also answerable herself for 4s. 2d. for property that was then directly in her care.[70] Around seventeen years later, the Pipe Roll for Michaelmas 1259 recorded how she owed £27 for the aid demanded by the king for knighting his son.[71] The royal officials clearly did not pursue this debt, since Petronilla still owed this sum in the year of her death.[72]

Petronilla and those who served her remained watchful in her widowhood for potential encroachments on her rights. In January 1248, she reached a legal settlement with Roger of Huntingfield, another baron, whom she had sued for the wardship of William, the son and heir of Thomas of Pinchbeck, her tenant. Under the terms of this agreement, Petronilla resigned her right in the wardship in return for a cash payment of £20.[73] In a slightly more sinister turn of events, on 26 September 1252, Petronilla purchased a writ *quare vi et armis* to enable her to bring a case before the justices at Westminster.[74] Furthermore, the extant records of a royal inquisition, which may or may not have been related to this case, document how eighteen named men and their accomplices had pursued Petronilla's men to the vill of Orby and kept Petronilla and her men shut up in the house of John of Orby for a night and half a day, so that it was not safe for them to leave.[75] The origins of the

69 M. T. Clanchy, 'Did Henry III have a Policy?', *History* 53:178 (1968), 203–16, at pp. 215–16 ('Appendix: Speech of Henry III in the Exchequer on 7 October 1250').

70 *Liber Feodorum*, vol. 2, pp. 1002–3.

71 Richard Cassidy, 'The 1259 Pipe Roll' (unpublished PhD thesis, King's College London, 2012), p. 114, no. 1740.

72 TNA, E 372/106, rot. 4, m. 2. In the following year, she was still shown as owing £13 10s for the scutage for Wales: E 372/108, rot. 3, m. 1.

73 'Final Concords for Lincs: 30–33 Henry III (Case 130, File 33)', in C. W. Foster (ed.), *Final Concords of the County of Lincoln 1244–1272* (Horncastle, 1920), pp. 33–51, no. 35, online at British History Online: http://www.british-history.ac.uk/lincoln-record-soc/vol2/pp33-51 [accessed 30 December 2022].

74 *CFR, 1251–52*, no. 1143.

75 *Calendar of Inquisitions Miscellaneous (Chancery) preserved in the Public Record Office, Vol. I* (London, 1916), p. 578, no. 2162.

dispute and what it was that had prompted Petronilla to be treated in this way were not recorded. If anything, it suggests that Petronilla was not the most beloved of local lords; perhaps her men had been too vigorous in pursuit of her rights. In the following year, an entry on a royal plea roll recorded how a member of the Wells family sued Petronilla for custody of Matilda and Elizabeth, the sisters and heirs of Thomas of Woodthorpe, although Petronilla failed to appear to answer his suit.[76]

Petronilla pursued her rights to her Longchamp dower, originally assigned to her in the early 1190s, in the royal courts throughout the late 1250s and early 1260s. The plea rolls for 1259–61 indicate that she sued Reginald de Grey and Matilda de Longchamp his wife and Hawise, widow of Henry de Longchamp, respectively, for her third share of Wilton Castle and of lands there.[77] Elsewhere, Petronilla maintained her rights and properties with fewer challenges. A charter issued in June 1253 by Richard FitzHerbert of Newport, rector of Faldingworth, which sought to establish a chantry at the altar of St Giles in Lincoln Cathedral, named Petronilla as the lady of the fee to whom 3s. in rent was owed each year at the feast of St John the Baptist for a toft in the Bail of Lincoln that formed part of the endowment.[78]

On her death in 1262, Petronilla may well have been in her late seventies. The results of an inquisition post mortem found that Petronilla held the manors of Warnborough and South Warnborough in Hampshire and a further twenty-two and a half knights' fees in Lincolnshire. Her heir, Henry de Longchamp, was reportedly more than forty or fifty years old at the time of her death, although he may have been more than sixty as his father had died by the end of 1203.[79] As the mother of more than one son from successive marriages, Petronilla was not indifferent to the future financial security of her younger offspring. Shortly before she died, she settled lands and tenanted estates in Freiston, Butterwick, Whaplode and Boston on John de Vaux, her son by her third husband, Oliver; this was a transaction which Henry de Longchamp (d. 1274), John's older half-brother, later saw through to completion following litigation in the king's court.[80]

76 TNA, KB 26/149, rot. 14d.

77 Cited in Conway, 'The Family of William Longchamp', 26.

78 C. W. Foster (ed., vols 1–3), C. W. Foster and Kathleen Major (eds, vol. 4), Kathleen Major (ed., vols 5–10), *The Registrum Antiquissimum of the Cathedral Church of Lincoln*, LRS, 10 vols (Lincoln, 1931–72), vol. 2, pp. 107–11, no. 395.

79 TNA, C 132/26/3; *CIPM,* vol. I, p. 144, no. 508. The extant documents do not cover her Lincolnshire lands in detail.

80 Poynton, 'Fee of Creon', 221–2.

Petronilla de Craon in context: Heiresses and co-heiresses in the East Midlands

Petronilla de Craon lived a long and eventful life, but was it an exceptional or unusual one for a woman of baronial status in Lincolnshire? The remainder of this chapter will place Petronilla's life as an heiress and widow within the wider context of female landholding in the East Midlands under the Angevin kings and consider how far her experiences mirrored or differed from those of other women of the Lincolnshire baronage. Heiresses were certainly more commonly encountered in thirteenth-century Lincolnshire than they were elsewhere in England. Here, the careers of earlier prominent female landholders noted at the beginning of the chapter and contemporary inheritance customs supported an acceptance of property transmission in the female line. Between 1199 and 1327, accidents of birth and mortality meant that nine of the thirteen baronies (69%) whose chief holdings were situated in Lincolnshire descended to heiresses on at least one occasion. Of these nine, two – Ashby (held by the Neville family) and Thoresway (held by the Bayeux family) – passed to a single heiress on one occasion, and another two lordships – Freiston (Petronilla de Craon's barony) and Stainton-le-Vale (home of the Scotney family) – descended in the female line twice.[81] A further two baronies – Bolingbroke and Brattleby – descended to heiresses on three occasions, although by the third occasion Bolingbroke and Brattleby had been united by marriage, so that both honours passed into the hands of Alice, the daughter of Henry de Lacy, earl of Lincoln and lord of Bolingbroke, by Margaret, countess of Salisbury and lady of Brattleby.[82]

[81] Sanders, *English Baronies*, pp. 3, 47, 81–2, 88.

[82] *ibid.*, pp. 18, 109, 112.

Table 1: The Descent of Lincolnshire Baronies to Heiresses and Co-Heiresses, 1199–1327.

Barony whose caput lay in Lincolnshire	**Number of occasions and year when it passed to an heiress or co-heiresses**	**Number of heiresses or co-heiresses (or their immediate descendants and heirs) to whom it passed on each occasion**
Ashby	1 (1227)	1 (1227)
Blankney	0	0
Bolingbroke	3 (1232; 1243; 1311)	3 (1 in 1232; 1 in 1243; 1 in 1311)
Bourne	0	0
Brattleby[83]	3 (1230; 1261; 1311)	3 (1 each in 1230, 1261, 1311)
Folkingham	1 (1298)	3 (1298)
Freiston	2 (*c.* 1205; 1274)	2 (1 in *c.* 1205; 1 in 1274)
Nocton	0	0
Redbourne	1 (1253)	5 (1253)
Sotby	0	0
Stainton-le-Vale	2 (1202; 1232)	5 (2 in 1202; 3 in 1232)
Tattershall	1 (1306)	3 (1306)
Thoresway	1 (1250)	1 (1250)
Total	**15**	**26**

83 Brattleby was already in the hands of Gerard de Camville, husband of Nicholaa de la Haye, daughter and co-heiress of the barony in 1199.

The barony of Redbourne, which owed the king the comparatively small service of three knights, passed to the greatest number of co-heiresses in the same generation, when it was divided in 1253 between Joan, Margery, Elena, Juliana and Cecily, the sisters of Alexander III de Neville, who each received one fifth of the barony.[84] The baronies of Stainton-le-Vale and Folkingham similarly felt the impact of multiple co-heirs. After the death of Lambert de Scoteny in 1202, his two nieces, Agnes and her sister, whose name is not known, inherited the family lands centred upon Stainton-le-Vale. When William, the son of Agnes's sister, then died in 1232, the heirs to his half of the barony were women – his three daughters, Frethesancia, Cecily and Helen, who each received one sixth of the barony.[85] The Gants' barony of Folkingham was shared between three co-heirs in 1298, when it was divided between Juliana de Gant and her nephews, Roger and Peter, the sons of her sisters Margaret and Nicholaa.[86] Only the baronies of Blankney, Nocton and Sotby, held by the families of d'Eincourt, Darcy and Kyme, respectively, passed from one generation to another uninterrupted in the male line.[87]

If this survey of female inheritance is extended to cover baronies, such as Shelford in Nottinghamshire and Skelton and Skirpenbeck in Yorkshire, whose caputs were situated in a neighbouring county, but whose holders held significant estates in Lincolnshire, it is possible to identify further instances where baronies descended to heiresses:[88] Shelford passed to a single heiress in 1230,[89] while Skelton was divided between four co-heiresses in 1272,[90] and a half-share of Skirpenbeck descended to a single female heir in 1322.[91] The honour of Richmond, whose caput was in Yorkshire and whose estates similarly included Lincolnshire properties, was held by its heiress Constance of Brittany (d. 1201) and her second husband, Guy de Thouars, until he sided with the French crown in 1203.[92] Later in the century, Peter of Savoy bequeathed his interest in the honour to his niece, Henry III's queen, Eleanor of Provence, even though Richmond had been granted to Eleanor's son-in-law, John of Brittany.[93] The bishop of Lincoln's tenants also numbered men who held

84 Sanders, *English Baronies*, p. 74.

85 *ibid.*, p. 82.

86 *CFR, 1272–1307*, p. 401; Sanders, *English Baronies*, p. 46.

87 Sanders, *English Baronies*, pp. 15–16, 67–8, 79–80.

88 My calculations here exclude the baronies of Chester, Chitterne and Pontefract, whose holders merged with those of Bolingbroke in Lincolnshire during the thirteenth century.

89 Sanders, *English Baronies*, pp. 76–7.

90 *ibid.*, p. 77.

91 *ibid.*, pp 78–9 (this half-share descended to Isabella, who was one year old in 1322).

92 *ibid.*, p. 140.

93 John compensated Eleanor with 800 marks per annum: *ibid.*, p. 141.

estates of sufficient size to be counted as barons. The Condet family, the lords of Thorngate Castle situated just outside Lincoln's city walls, held properties at Wickhambreaux in Kent and Eagle, Skellingthorpe, South Carlton and Thurlby in Lincolnshire, as well as other lands in Nottinghamshire. In the early thirteenth century, their holdings were in the hands of an heiress, Agnes de Condet, and her husband Walter Clifford (d. 1222–23).[94] Heiresses were therefore relatively common figures in this region in this era.

Admittedly, the prevalence of female heirs ultimately meant that three Lincolnshire baronies whose caputs lay within the county fragmented and fell into abeyance through passing into the hands of co-heiresses and their descendants, demonstrating the corrosive impact of the succession of multiple females on baronial estates. The question therefore arises of whether heiresses who inherited baronies with caputs in Lincolnshire benefited at all from the implementation of Magna Carta's provisions touching heiresses. Some apparently did not. On 17 March 1227, for example, an entry on the Fine Rolls recorded how the king had taken the homage of Robert FitzMaldred, husband of Isabella, the sister and heiress of Henry de Neville of Ashby and 'made fine with the king for his relief by 200m'.[95] It is not clear why this inflated sum of 200 marks, rather than the £100 set down in Magna Carta, was demanded of Robert for admission to his wife's barony. The heiresses to portions of baronies, however, sometimes fared better. In March 1232, Walter of Killingholme and Frethesancia his wife and Philip de Fauconberg and Cecily his wife offered two palfreys to secure seisin of Frethesancia's and Cecily's shares (two thirds) of William de Scoteny's half-barony in Lincolnshire, while the third share of Helena, their unmarried sister, remained in the king's custody as she was underage.[96] According to the Pipe Roll for Michaelmas 1232, Walter and Frethesancia rendered five marks at the Exchequer for one palfrey, while Philip and Cecily's palfrey (or its equivalent sum) was still outstanding.[97] With access to William's lands also came the responsibility for rendering his outstanding debts to the crown. By October 1232, all three heiresses and Walter and Philip had secured an arrangement, whereby they undertook to settle William's outstanding debts at a rate of £10 per annum, divided equally between them in accordance with the size of

94 Foster (ed.), *The Registrum Antiquissimum*, vol. 1, pp. 282–95.

95 *CFR, 1226–27*, no. 146 (addressed to the sheriff of Yorkshire), no. 147 (addressed to the sheriff of Lincolnshire).

96 *CFR, 1231–32*, no. 77. Brian FitzAlan offered the king 100 marks for Helen's custody, marriage and the keeping of her inheritance in Lincolnshire and Yorkshire, together with the rights to the marriage of Matilda, William de Scoteny's widow, so that she could not marry without Brian's permission and agreement: *ibid.*, no. 102.

97 TNA, E 372/76, rot. 10d, m. 1.

their shares.[98] The impact of the division of Stainton-le-Vale barony between two generations of co-heirs, so that Frethesancia inherited a sixth share and married a county knight, was strongly felt in the next generation, when her son and heir, William of Willoughby, promised to pay a relief of twelve and a half marks in September 1259, for one and a half knights' fees and a third part of half a knight's fee in Lincolnshire, in order to succeed to his mother's inheritance.[99]

Petronilla de Craon in context: Widows in the king's gift in Lincolnshire

Under the Angevin kings, the marriages and lands of widowed heiresses who were tenants-in-chief, of the widows of tenants-in-chief and of the underage heirs of tenants-in-chief were all in the king's gift, placing immensely valuable sources of patronage at the crown's disposal. When Petronilla de Craon was listed as a widow whose marriage was in the king's gift in 1219, her situation was similar to that of other near-contemporary and contemporary baronesses in England and the East Midlands.[100] Lincolnshire is one of the twelve English counties for which the detailed returns survive of a national survey conducted by the crown and its agents in 1185 into the boys, girls and widows who ought to be in the king's gift and their properties.[101] In this region, at around the time that Petronilla's parents married, there were no fewer than twenty-two widows who were then in the king's gift, whose age, children, lands and their lands' current and/or potential value, were all painstakingly documented so that the crown could maintain its rights over them.[102] The information for

98 *CFR, 1231–32*, no. 271. See also *ibid.*, no. 156.

99 *CFR, 1258–59*, no. 744.

100 See p. 57 above.

101 John Horace Round (ed.), *Rotuli de Dominabus et Pueris et Puellis de XII Comitatibus [1185]*, PRS 35 (1913), pp. 1–21; Walmsley (ed. and trans.), *Widows, Heirs and Heiresses*, pp. 2–35.

102 The number rises to twenty-five if we include widows who were mentioned in the entry for an heir. The twenty-two women included in this survey were the widows of tenants-in-chief or of the tenants of fees then in the king's hand as escheats or during an ecclesiastical vacancy. They were: 1. Rose, daughter of William Trussebut and widow of Everard de Ros; 2. Matilda de St Liz, daughter of Robert FitzRichard and widow of William d'Aubigny of Belvoir; 3. Alice, widow of Peter of Billinghay (in the king's gift through the archbishopric of York being vacant); 4. Countess Margaret, sister of the King of Scots and countess of Richmond; 5. Elizabeth, daughter of William FitzWalter and widow of Robert FitzHugh of Tattershall; 6. the daughter of Robert FitzErnis of Goxhill and widow of Simon de Crevequer; 7. Alice Basset (probably the widow of Thomas Basset); 8. the widow of Geoffrey de Turs and Herbert FitzGilbert (in the king's gift through the archbishopric of York being vacant); 9. Rose,

this slightly earlier generation of widows provides some valuable points of comparison with Petronilla's personal situation.

The wealth of individual landholding widows from Lincolnshire named in the 1185 survey varied considerably. The wealthiest widows were women of comital and baronial status, who held land as their dower, marriage portion (*maritagium*) and/or inheritance in this one county alone. Margaret, sister of the king of Scots and countess of Brittany and Richmond, held land in dower worth £21 in Kirton wapentake, in addition to receiving income from Boston's fairs, '£4 per annum from the farm of the vill of Boston' and 10s. from a furlong of land there.[103] Countess Margaret also held estates worth £28 per annum in dower in Suffolk and twenty pounds' worth of land in Cambridgeshire.[104] Matilda, countess of Chester, held Waddington in Lincolnshire, valued at £40, while Bertrada, countess of Chester, the widow of Matilda's son Earl Hugh, held land in Belchford, Hemingby and Donington which had the potential to be worth £40 if fully stocked, in addition to dower and *maritagium* overseas and elsewhere.[105] Matilda, daughter of William de Vernon, widow of Richard de la Haye, the former baron of Brattleby and constable of Lincoln Castle, and mother of Nicholaa, on the other hand, held Swaton in dower, which was valued at £30 with its existing stock.[106] Of a similar social status and wealth was Elizabeth, widow of Robert FitzHugh of Tattershall, whose dower in Horncastle was estimated to be worth £20 if fully stocked and whose marriage

daughter of Baldwin FitzGilbert de Clare and widow of William de Bussy; 10. Agnes, daughter of Colgrim de Weleburn' and widow of Walter of Hacconby; 11. Matilda, daughter of William de Vernon and widow of Richard de la Haye; 12. the daughter of Richard Basset and widow of Robert de Caux; 13. the widow of Albert Grelley and wife of Guy de Craon (and Petronilla de Craon's mother); 14. Matilda, daughter of Walter of Waterville and widow of William de Dives; 15. Matilda, countess of Chester, daughter of Earl Robert of Gloucester and widow of Earl Ranulf of Chester; 16. Bertrada, countess of Chester, daughter of the count of Evreux and widow of Earl Hugh of Chester; 17. Avice de Crevequer; 18. the mother of Ralph of Humberston and kinswoman of Ralph FitzDrogo; 19. Helewis of Swinhope, a Fleming, widow of Simon de Canci; 20. the daughter of Thomas de Neville and widow of Walter Furmage; 21. Alice, widow of John d'Eincourt; and 22. Matilda, widow of Reginald de Crevequer. The three widows mentioned within entries relating to heirs were the widow of Peter Paynel, the widow of William FitzChetel and the widow of William de Vesci: Walmsley (ed. and trans.), *Widows, Heirs and Heiresses,* pp. 2–35; Johns, *Noblewomen, Aristocracy and Power*, appendix 2, pp. 232–5.

103 Walmsley (ed. and trans.), *Widows, Heirs and Heiresses*, pp. 8–9, no. 8, pp. 12–13, no. 12.

104 *ibid.*, pp. 94–5, no. 160, pp. 124–5, no. 216.

105 *ibid.*, pp. 24–7, nos 30–1.

106 *ibid.*, pp. 20–1, no. 24.

portion in Calcewath wapentake yielded rent of 100s. (£5) per annum.[107] Other widows of Lincolnshire baronial families held lands variously valued in their present state at 310s. (£15 10s.), £12, ten librates of land and five marks of fixed rents.[108] The widow who held lands or rights with the smallest value was Ralph of Humberston's mother, whose two bovates of land held in dower supplied her with half a mark in income per annum.[109]

Throughout the thirteenth century, the articles of the general eyre also regularly included similar questions to those of the 1185 survey about later generations of landholding widows. Although the records compiled from the later surveys included fewer details, they still provide some fascinating comparative information. In 1219, for instance, local jurors reported, wapentake by wapentake, the names of nine widows in Lincolnshire who were in the king's gift and the value of their properties, which are listed in Table 2 below.[110]

Table 2: Widows in the King's Gift in Lincolnshire, 1219

Name of Widow	Nature and Value of Property
Cecily d'Aubigny	Rents worth 14s. in Bigby, 4 marks (53s. 4d.) and 5s. 2d. in Habrough (Yarborough wapentake)
Matilda Banastr'	Land worth 10 marks per annum (133s. 10d.) in Kirmington (Yarborough wapentake)
Matilda de Lacy, widow of Roger, constable of Chester	Land worth £15 in Ingoldmells (Candleshoe wapentake) and further properties worth £13 (Manley wapentake)
Agnes Wake	Land worth £20 (Ness wapentake)

[107] *ibid.*, pp. 8–9, no. 9, pp. 16–17, no. 17, pp. 18–19, no. 21.

[108] *ibid.*, pp. 12–13, no. 13, pp. 28–9, no. 37 (both – the daughter of Robert FitzErneis of Goxhill and widow of Simon FitzReginald de Crevequer, baron of Redbourne), 22–3, no. 27 (the daughter of Ralph Basset, widow of Robert de Caux and mother-in-law of Ralf FitzStephen, holder of a barony whose caput lay in Laxton in Nottinghamshire), pp. 32–3, nos 39, 41 (Alice d'Eincourt, widow of John; Matilda, widow of Reginald de Crevequer, baron of Redbourne). Avice, another Crevequer family widow, held lands worth £14 in Croxton: *ibid.*, pp. 26–7, no. 33. Albert de Grelley's widow held lands in Bloxholm that rendered £9 3s 8d from the farm of her lands and 101s. from the sale of grain over an eighteen-month period before her marriage to Guy de Craon: *ibid.*, pp. 22–3, no. 28.

[109] *ibid.*, pp. 26–7, no. 34.

[110] *Liber Feodorum*, vol. 1, pp. 283–6.

Nicholaa de la Haye	Land worth £20 in Swaton (Aveland wapentake)
Matilda de Hauville	Land worth 10 marks (133s. 10d.) per annum and other property of Roger le Gros's escheated fee (Aveland wapentake)
Matilda de Caux	Land worth £12 (Loveden wapentake) and £15 (Flaxwell wapentake)
Matilda de Vesci	With land worth £50 per annum which she held by the service of three knights (Loveden wapentake)
Isabella de Dover	Land worth £9 per annum (Graffoe wapentake)

A further two men, Gilbert of Beningworth and Oliver de Vaux (Petronilla de Craon's third husband), were noted as holding land by virtue of their wives' inheritances. Beningworth, a local knight associated with Ranulf, earl of Chester and Lincoln, held lands in Salmonby and Scrafield worth 100s. 'in serjeanty for carrying one goshawk in season'.[111] Vaux was recorded holding Petronilla's lands worth £50, indicating that she was one of Lincolnshire's wealthiest widowed heiresses at the time, alongside Matilda de Vesci.[112] Just as there had been in 1185, there were significant differences in wealth among the landholding widows. In stark contrast to Petronilla and Matilda, Cecily d'Aubigny's rental income from properties in Lincolnshire was just £3 12s. 6d. per annum.[113]

Petronilla de Craon in context: Longevity, children and succession

Somewhat frustratingly, the ages of widows in the king's gift were often not recorded in the later surveys like that of 1219. Yet, some of the Lincolnshire widows named in the 1185 survey certainly enjoyed, like Petronilla de Craon, long lives by the standards of their day and had at least several children. Avice de Crevequer was the eldest at seventy years old; she was the mother of three daughters and her heir was her twenty-two-year-old grandson, Robert de Bonesboz.[114] Both the mother of Ralph of Humberston and Matilda, widow

111 *ibid.*, p. 285. For Gilbert, see Barraclough (ed.), *Charters of the Anglo-Norman Earls of Chester*, nos 292, 295–9, 314, 355, 413.

112 *Liber Feodorum*, vol. 1, p. 285. Petronilla was erroneously described as Guy de Craon's widow.

113 *ibid.*, vol. 1, p. 283.

114 Walmsley (ed. and trans.), *Widows, Heirs and Heiresses,* pp. 26–7, no. 33 (Avice de Crevequer).

of Reginald de Crevequer, were more than sixty years old, while Matilda de St Liz, widow of William d'Aubigny of Belvoir and mother of William d'Aubigny junior, was said to be sixty by the local jurors.[115] Matilda, Richard de la Haye's widow, was fifty-seven and the mother of three daughters; and the widow of Robert de Caux, Matilda, countess of Chester, and Helewis of Swinhope, widow of Simon de Canci, were all believed to be over fifty.[116] Elizabeth, widow of Robert FitzHugh, was fifty, as was Rose de Clare, widow of William de Bussy.[117] Other widows were in their late twenties, thirties and forties. The youngest widows were two twenty-four-year-old women: the daughter of Robert FitzErnis, widow of Simon de Crevequer and mother of two living sons and two living daughters (the eldest son was five years old);[118] and the daughter of Thomas de Neville, widow of Walter Furmage and mother of a daughter who was not yet one year old.[119] The average age of the twenty-one widows for whom an age was given in 1185 was forty-two and a half years and this figure may have been a little higher, since five widows were recorded as being over a particular age. If it is borne in mind that life expectancy at birth in England in 1200 was around twenty-five years and it was unusual to live past one's forties, the ladies who held lands in Lincolnshire in the 1185 survey were a relatively long-lived group, whose wealth presumably afforded them a better diet and lifestyle than the lesser free tenantry and peasantry.[120]

No fewer than twenty-one widows with lands in Lincolnshire had living children at the time of the 1185 survey.[121] In the case of those widows for whom local jurors provided both their ages and those of their children, it would appear that most widows had given birth to their eldest surviving son or heir when they were in their early to mid-twenties and were therefore perhaps a few years older than Petronilla de Craon had been when her eldest surviving son was born in her late teens.[122] Some Lincolnshire widows clearly had large numbers of offspring

[115] *ibid.*, pp. 2–3, no. 2 (Matilda de St Liz), pp. 26–7, no. 34 (mother of Ralph of Humberston), pp. 32–33, no. 41 (Matilda, widow of Reginald de Crevequer).

[116] *ibid.*, pp. 20–1, no. 24 (Matilda, widow of Richard de la Haye), pp. 22–3, no. 27 (widow of Robert de Caux), pp. 24–5, no. 30 (Countess Matilda of Chester), pp. 28–9, no. 35 (Helewis of Swinhope).

[117] *ibid.*, pp. 16–17, no. 17 (Elizabeth, widow of Robert FitzHugh of Tattershall), pp. 20–1, no. 22 (Rose de Clare).

[118] *ibid.*, pp. 12–13, no. 13, 28–9, no. 37.

[119] *ibid.*, pp. 28–9, no. 36.

[120] Chris Given-Wilson, 'Introduction: The Late Middle Ages in England', in idem (ed.), *An Illustrated History of Late Medieval England* (Manchester, 1996), p. 5.

[121] This figure is out of a possible twenty-five named in the survey and includes the three women mentioned in the entry for an heir. It is possible that some children may have been stepchildren.

[122] Walmsley (ed. and trans.), *Widows, Heirs and Heiresses*, pp. 2–3, no. 1 (Rose, widow of Everard de Ros), pp. 18–19, no. 20 (the widow of Geoffrey de Turs and

who were still living at the time of the 1185 survey. By the age of thirty, for example, the widow of Geoffrey de Turs and Herbert FitzGilbert had already outlived two husbands and borne seven surviving boys, the eldest of whom was ten in 1185.[123] By the time she was fifty, Elizabeth, the widow of Robert FitzHugh of Tattershall, had ten living sons.[124] Another, valuable point of comparison for the number of children borne to individual ladies is provided by Agnes de Condet's testament, which was drawn up before 1222–23; she bequeathed a gold ring to each of her five sons, Walter, Roger, Richard, Simon and Giles, and a gold ring to each of her daughters, although the latter were not listed by name.[125] Although Petronilla de Craon was among the longest-lived of her contemporaries and near-contemporaries, she was clearly not alone among women of her rank in giving birth to multiple children and in raising offspring who survived childhood illnesses in an era of high infant mortality.[126] Demonstrable fertility, as well as landed wealth, helps to explain why some Lincolnshire widows, like Petronilla de Craon, were attractive as marriage partners.

There were several other heiresses to Lincolnshire baronies in the period 1199 to 1327, who married and outlived one husband or more. These women included Isabella de Neville, lady of Ashby; Hawise of Chester (*alias* Hawise de Quincy), Margaret de Lacy and Alice de Lacy, countesses of Lincoln and heiresses of Bolingbroke; Nicholaa de la Haye and her granddaughter Idonea de Camville, ladies of Brattleby; Cecily de Crevequer, a co-heiress of the barony of Redbourne; Joan, a co-heiress of Tattershall; and Matilda, the heiress of Thoresway.[127] Strikingly, there do not appear to have been disputed successions to the baronies these women held when they died. After Nicholaa de la Haye died in 1230, for example, William Longespée, the husband of Nicholaa's granddaughter and heir, Idonea de Camville, performed homage for Nicholaa's Lincolnshire properties which she held as a tenant-in-chief, as well Nicholaa's former dower lands in Charlton and Henstridge in Somerset.[128] On the death of Hawise of Chester, countess of Lincoln and lady of Bolingbroke, in the

Herbert FitzGilbert), pp. 20–1, no. 23 (Agnes, widow of Walter of Hacconby), pp. 24–5, no. 29 (Matilda, widow of William de Dives), pp. 28–9, no. 36 (the widow of Walter Furmage).

123 *ibid.*, pp. 18–19, no. 20.

124 *ibid.*, pp. 16–17, no. 17.

125 The only daughter named elsewhere in her testament was Basilia: Foster (ed.), *Registrum Antiquissimum*, vol. 1, pp. 293–5.

126 On infant mortality, see Nicholas Orme, *From Childhood to Chivalry: The Education of the English Kings and Aristocracy, 1066–1530* (London, 1984), p. 3.

127 Sanders, *English Baronies*, pp. 3 (Ashby), 18 (Bolingbroke), 74–5 (Redbourne), 88 (Tattershall), 88–9 (Thoresway), 109 (Brattleby).

128 *CFR, 1230–31*, nos 41–2. A schedule of Nicholaa's Lincolnshire lands was stitched onto the fine roll: *ibid.*, no. 72.

early months of 1243, the king awarded seisin of all the estates that Hawise had held from him in chief to Walter Marshal, earl of Pembroke, the husband of Hawise's daughter Margaret.[129] Intriguingly, the Pipe Roll for Michaelmas 1243 recorded that Hawise of Chester, or rather her heir, still owed £50 for Hawise's relief as one of the co-heirs of her brother Earl Ranulf of Chester, who had died in 1232.[130]

Conclusion

In conclusion, Petronilla de Craon was undoubtedly a long-lived Lincolnshire widow, who outlived no fewer than three husbands and survived into her late seventies. Yet, many of her experiences as a landed heiress, widow and mother resonated with those of her near-contemporaries and contemporaries. She secured seisin of her inheritance, accumulated successive dowers from her marriages and was an active litigant in the royal courts when disputes arose over her access and title to property. She also incurred debts and obligations to the crown as a tenant-in-chief. During her marriages, she gave birth to multiple children, some of whom survived to adulthood. The emergence of Magna Carta and the adoption of its clauses on heirs and widows did not make a significant impact upon her life since her marriages took place in the reigns of King Richard and King John. The sums demanded by King John from her second and third husbands demonstrate the profitability of the 'trade' in widows, especially widowed heiresses, for the crown. In Lincolnshire and in the East Midlands more generally, however, there was a well-established and continuing pattern of female, secular landholding that created a strong expectation that aristocratic women would and could possess and manage land. Whether individual women did this successfully and without interference from others depended heavily on each woman's circumstances, their neighbours' ambitions and the crown and its local agents' interests in the region. In advancing old age, as the mother of mature sons and in the more benevolent environment of Henry III's personal rule, Petronilla retained and administered her barony on her own behalf after 1242; her tenure was not without incident, but it endured until her death, nonetheless.

[129] *CFR, 1242–43*, no. 199; TNA, E 372/87, rot. 2d, m. 2.
[130] TNA, E 372/87, rot. 2, m. 1.

3

The Shining Sun of His Diocese: the Portrayal of the Ideal Bishop in Robert Grosseteste's Letter Collection

JULIAN HASELDINE

Introduction

Robert Grosseteste stands out, even among so illustrious a group as the medieval bishops of Lincoln, as an exceptional character. In modern times he has been celebrated as a pioneer of scientific method, as the first chancellor of the University of Oxford and as an energetic reformer of the Church who defied both pope and king. Grosseteste's career was certainly remarkable. For most of his adult life he was a student, teacher and scholar at the nascent university of Oxford, with, possibly, a period of study at Paris, the predominant centre of theological study in Europe. By 1213 or 1214 he was master of the schools at Oxford, a position generally agreed now to be the chancellorship in all but name. Here he established an international reputation as a theologian and philosopher and produced a substantial body of works on theology, biblical exegesis and natural philosophy (what we might call science), as well as writing on pastoral instruction and composing poetry. He was in his late sixties when, evidently to his surprise, and likely as a compromise candidate in a contested election, he was chosen as Bishop of Lincoln, a position which he was to hold for eighteen years (1235–53). Rising to the challenge of such a momentous change at this age, he went on to become an extraordinarily energetic proponent of reform in the diocese, his tenure characterised in particular by his strenuous and indefatigable efforts to improve the standards of pastoral care in his diocese, striving constantly to ensure the provision of suitable priests, to correct abuses, and to encourage preaching.[1]

1 For a full account of Grosseteste's life and thought, see J. McEvoy, *Robert Grosseteste* (Oxford, 2000), and P. M. Hoskin, *Robert Grosseteste and the 13th-Century*

Grosseteste's concern for pastoral care dominated his episcopate and has defined his reputation as bishop. Pastoral care has, indeed, been identified as the leitmotif of his thought, connected in some way to everything that he wrote in his long career as a theologian and philosopher.[2] The same concern is evident in the two most critical sources for Grosseteste's years as bishop, his rolls, the central records of the administration of the diocese, and his letters, of which almost all that survive come from his years as bishop. Grosseteste's rolls are far from typical of such documents; they reveal, as Philippa Hoskin has shown, a bishop who prioritised pastoral and spiritual concerns over administrative efficiency, running counter to trends traditionally identified in thirteenth-century episcopal governance.[3] His letters, by contrast, are very typical of a long tradition of medieval epistolography. Medieval letters have been characterised as quasi-public documents, written not as confidential communications but as open statements, directed to a wider readership than the named addressees alone. Like almost all of the correspondence that has come down to us from the ancient and medieval worlds, Grosseteste's survives in the form of a carefully curated and highly selective collection of stylised, rhetorically polished Latin letters, preserved and circulated as part of his literary legacy and intended to present his achievements and ideas to posterity. The value of Grosseteste's letters, then, lies not in any insights into the personality or feelings of the man, nor primarily into his working practices, although they do preserve many details of these, but in revealing the ideology which dominated his episcopate, centred as it was on his beliefs about pastoral care.[4]

Diocese of Lincoln: An English Bishop's Pastoral Vision, Late Medieval Europe 19 (Leiden, 2019). For a brief overview, see J. McEvoy, *Robert Grosseteste Bishop of Lincoln 1235–1253* (Lincoln, 2003); McEvoy differs in some important respects from the older R. W. Southern, *Robert Grosseteste. The Growth of an English Mind in Medieval Europe* (Oxford, 1986). On the position of Master of the Schools, or chancellorship, of Oxford, see J. McEvoy, *The Philosophy of Robert Grosseteste* (Oxford, 1982), pp. 8–10. On Grosseteste's prolific writings (predominantly in Latin, but including some prayers and poetry in the Anglo-Norman vernacular), see S. H. Thomson, *The Writings of Robert Grosseteste, Bishop of Lincoln 1235–1253* (Cambridge, 1940, repr. 2013), which is currently being updated – on this and other recent projects in Grosseteste studies, see the website of the International Robert Grosseteste Society (www.grossetestesociety.org, accessed 5 July 2022).

2 See McEvoy, *Robert Grosseteste*, pp. 140–5; idem, *Robert Grosseteste Bishop of Lincoln*, p. 31.

3 P. M. Hoskin (ed.), *Robert Grosseteste as bishop of Lincoln, The Episcopal Rolls, 1235–1253*, LRS, Kathleen Major Series of Medieval Records 1 (Woodbridge, 2015), pp. xxv–lxxiii.

4 The letters are edited in H. R. Luard (ed.), *Roberti Grosseteste Episcopi quondam Lincolniensis Epistolae*, Rolls Series (London, 1861) and translated in F.

Pastoral care in the thought of Robert Grosseteste

For Robert Grosseteste, the things for which he was and is famous, natural philosophy, theology and pastoral care, were not separate. Over the years, he developed a philosophical vision of great originality and sophistication, which united natural law, divine law and the theology of salvation. His reputation as a proto-scientist rests on his celebrated studies of optics, but these were themselves integral to a metaphysics in which light was a fundamental phenomenon of natural law, which was itself an expression of divine order; light was the first created phenomenon, the agent of divine creation, the life-giving power in bodies and the illuminating force of the intellect. The harmony of God and nature, which this system implied – the unity of natural and divine law, exemplified by the simultaneously physical and metaphysical nature of light – had been broken by the Fall and could be restored only by human salvation. Salvation alone could reunite God with nature and restore thereby the universal order. Salvation, in turn, was the personal responsibility of the individual believer, a position which aligned with predominant medieval understandings of the implications of human free will.

This sense of the personal responsibility of the believer for their own salvation ,which thus lay at the heart of Grosseteste's cosmology, was further amplified in his approach to pastoral care by another important philosophical concept – hierarchy. During his years as bishop, Grosseteste was translating and producing commentaries on the works of the sixth-century Greek theologian Pseudo-Dionysius, including his treatises on *Celestial Hierarchy*, dealing with angelology, and *Ecclesiastical Hierarchy*. For Grosseteste, the hierarchy of the Church, a clearly articulated chain of command running from pope to bishops to lesser clergy, a hierarchy which was both divinely ordained and reflected the heavenly hierarchy, was not merely a means to ensure and protect ecclesiastical authority but was the effective force to deliver pastoral care. The personal responsibility of the individual believer for their own salvation depended on the personal responsibility of the priest for leading them to understand what was needed to achieve salvation, and this in turn depended on the personal responsibility of the bishop to ensure the provision of effective pastoral care through the appointment of suitable pastors. Hierarchy conferred power with grave responsibility. This in turn explains a final idea commonly cited as axiomatic to Grosseteste's view of authority, that it must be exercised always in

A. C. Mantello and J. Goering, *The Letters of Robert Grosseteste, Bishop of Lincoln* (Toronto, 2010). A good introduction to medieval epistolography remains G. Constable, *Letters and Letter-Collections*, Typologies des Sources du Moyen Âge Occidental 17 (Turnhout, 1976); see also J. P. Haseldine, 'Letters and Letter-Collections', in *Routledge Resources Online, Medieval Studies* (https://www.taylorfrancis.com/rroms, accessed 6 May 2024).

such a way that mercy tempers justice: the aim is to lead the believer through understanding to salvation, not merely to impose obedience.[5]

Acknowledging the importance of pastoral care and of the rights and responsibilities of the Church, however, are not in themselves original or even surprising concerns for a bishop. Neither the need to provide effective pastoral care, nor the will to ensure it, depend on the adoption of a complex metaphysical cosmology. Grosseteste the original philosopher and Grosseteste the committed bishop were two rather different aspects of a complex character. As James McEvoy, perhaps the most important modern scholar of Grosseteste's philosophy, noted:

> Most of Grosseteste's ideas about the Church, the pastoral office, and the realm, were not original with him, but they were profoundly personal to him. His uniqueness lies in the thoroughness with which he brought them to their furthest practical conclusions and turned them into a programme for the reform of the Church. ... His intellectual interests remained alive and continued to evolve after his elevation; his public life was, as it were, their dramatization on the stage of history.[6]

Grosseteste's own letters certainly reveal an exceptional sensitivity to the personal responsibility of the bishop for ensuring effective pastoral care. In one letter from the very beginning of his episcopate, in reply to an accusation that he had been excessively severe in refusing to institute an unsuitable candidate as a rector, he asks:

> Should I not at least have spoken out against the damnation of those souls that I feared and saw was imminent? Am I not answerable for the death of those souls if I do not resist their death as much as possible and use all my strength to repel it? Shall I not speak even a word of truth to oppose the death of souls, a death I am bound to oppose with my own blood, with my own life and death? Should I have softened the truth in the face of such an imminent death of souls ...[7]

Nevertheless, one might reasonably ask whether Grosseteste's attitude to pastoral care has any wider interest beyond the personal motivations and evidently passionate commitment of one bishop. That an important and original thinker should associate his metaphysical system with some respectable

5 The most detailed analysis of Grosseteste's theological and metaphysical system is McEvoy, *The Philosophy*; on his theory of pastoral care, see also Hoskin, *Robert Grosseteste and the 13th-Century Diocese*, pp. 47–78, and Mantello and Goering, *The Letters*, pp. 18–22.

6 McEvoy, *The Philosophy*, pp. 432–3.

7 Mantello and Goering, *The Letters*, pp. 84–5.

reforming positions is perhaps understandable – academic theology had always been regarded as providing the foundation for the Church's mission. That Grosseteste pursued his agenda with such evident energy and articulated it with the power and feeling which the above quotation illustrates may be a testament to his character. Nevertheless, it is important to consider whether his actions and ideals can tell us more about the role and concerns of bishops and about the state of the Church in the thirteenth century, especially as this is a period commonly identified as one of critical importance for the growth of the power and organisational structure of the Church.

Indeed, for all its sophistication and intensity of expression, Grosseteste's beliefs about personal responsibility for salvation and its implications for the quality of the priesthood and for the exercise of episcopal power, ideas which animate both his thinking and his practice, do have a wider resonance. They are a response to one of the most profound religious and political transformations in European history, a transformation deeper and more far reaching in some respects even than the Reformation, which was in many ways its epilogue. They reflect the central concerns of what the ground-breaking historian Herbert Grundmann, advancing a thesis which would transform the study of medieval religion, called 'the religious movement of the twelfth century'.[8] By this, Grundmann meant not a single or coherently directed movement for reform, but a profound shift in the religious culture of Europe, when the relationship between the Church and the laity was changed radically and when the nature and roles of the clergy and of the religious orders, and the place of the Church in Christian society, were all questioned and in some fundamental respects redefined. This is the context in which Grosseteste's letters, the most public articulation of his ideas about the role of bishop, must be set.

Robert Grosseteste and the religious movement

The opening essay in the volume of the *Cambridge History of Christianity*, which covers the European Central Middle Ages (*c.* 1100–*c.* 1500), identifies two fundamental changes that shaped what is often seen as the classic period of medieval Christendom; these are the 'monasticisation of the clergy' and the 'pastoral revolution of the twelfth and thirteenth centuries'.[9] These are less familiar, perhaps, than the well-known litany of Crusades, cathedral building, knights and merchant princes popularly associated with the 'culture of

[8] H. Grundmann, *Religiöse Bewegungen im Mittelalter* (Leipzig, 1935, rev. edn Darmstadt, 1961), transl. by S. Rowan as *Religious Movements in the Middle Ages* (Notre Dame, 1995), see esp. pp. 7–22.

[9] H. Leyser, 'Clerical purity and the re-ordered world', in M. Rubin and W. Simons (eds), *Christianity in Western Europe* c. *1100*–c. *1500*, The Cambridge History of Christianity 4 (2009), pp. 11–21, phrases quoted at pp. 14, 17.

Christendom', but they nevertheless describe profound changes in the religious and social life of all Europeans. The first refers to a series of reforms intended to redefine the relationship between the priesthood and the laity. It is most commonly associated with the drive by reformers and the papacy, beginning in the later eleventh century, to enforce celibacy on the clergy, a position now taken as definitive of Catholic priesthood but then often an unwelcome novelty to a body of men who were commonly and uncontentiously married. This was, however, only one of a broader range of measures designed to set priests apart from the society and the communities of which they had often been – ordination notwithstanding – indistinguishable members. Now they were to be both visibly distinct from and morally superior to those around them, sober, modestly dressed, abstaining from hunting and gaming, sufficiently educated to teach the basics of the faith and, above all, chaste. The driving ideal was that of establishing the 'purity' of the clergy through their visible and moral separation from the world around them, an ideal drawn from that of monastic vocation. Priests, of course, were not to withdraw physically from the world like monks, but rather their separation was to make them not only worthy providers of the sacraments but also exemplars and teachers of the faith.[10]

This became inextricably linked to the second of these critical transformations, the pastoral revolution. Increasingly, the Church moved not only to promote the reform of the clergy but also to expand its pastoral provision, particularly where the rapid growth of urban centres, which was so characteristic a feature of the booming economy of the twelfth century, led to urban parishes being overwhelmed by the numbers of incomers. New parishes and better educated priests became goals of a papacy shifting its attention and resources from the promotion and cultivation of the monastic orders to its pastoral mission. This was to be achieved and sustained by strengthening the hierarchy of the Church, putting in place a system of provincial and diocesan councils to ensure that the reform ideals and the administrative authority of the papacy were disseminated effectively and uniformly. Rome was to be not only the symbolic heart of the Church but now its administrative and legal centre.

Once again, what in retrospect might seem normal, the central authority of the papacy, presented challenges to bishops accustomed to a far greater measure of autonomy and with powerful loyalties to the secular rulers whom they often regarded as pious supporters with legitimate interests in the control of their churches.[11] These changes arose in the context of the greatest economic, demographic and geopolitical transformation in European

[10] For a good introduction to this complex topic, see K. Cushing, *Reform and the Papacy in the Eleventh Century, Spirituality and Social Change* (Manchester, 2005).

[11] A good recent introduction to this area is A. Larson and K. Sisson (eds), *A Companion to the Medieval Papacy, Growth of an Ideology and Institution* (Leiden, 2016).

history between the end of the Roman Empire and the industrial revolution, in the period, between the eleventh and thirteenth centuries, which has now come routinely to be referred to as the 'making', 'birth' or 'origins' of Europe, reflecting a growing historiographical consensus that it was then that many critical features of modern European society emerged. In a series of what historians have labelled revolutions – commercial, administrative, religious and intellectual – education, social mobility, access to wealth and opportunity for self-expression were, for many, dramatically expanded.[12] At the same time, Christianity remained the dominant ideology of this society, and the relationship between the Church and people a central political issue for contemporaries.

In the early Middle Ages, this relationship had been centred on intercession. It was the prayers of the pious, offered continuously to Heaven on behalf of sinners, which could, above all, lead the rest of the faithful to salvation, and no prayers were believed to be more effective than those of monks and nuns. Over the centuries, the monasteries had grown enormously in wealth and power largely on the basis of this intercessory function, of the pious donations and cultural influence which their prayers, directed to Heaven on behalf of rulers, of patrons and of all of society, attracted. At the same time, the function of the priesthood was to administer the sacraments to the faithful, a function fulfilled primarily through the performance of rites in a language unintelligible to most and requiring little more than their mute presence – it was only in the thirteenth century, for example, that the duty to partake in communion at least once a year was placed on the laity.[13] By the end of the eleventh century, monks themselves were beginning to question their role, as breakaway groups moved to isolated locations to pursue a life of contemplation and prayer in a movement that would lead to the creation of the so-called new religious orders, such as the Carthusians and the Cistercians, and to a great period of monastic reform and revival wherein the pursuit of personal spiritual growth took precedence over the duty to intercede.

The pressure for change, however, came also from without the Church, as the laity took up the ideal of clerical purity and began to demand higher standards of their priests. Already in the eleventh century, the Patarines, an armed movement which emerged in northern Italy, were attempting, often through violence, to enforce reformed standards on the clergy. Others promoted outright anticlericalism, as in the case of the ascetic preacher and former monk

[12] Seminal contributions to the thesis of the 'making' of Europe at this time included C. H. Haskins, *The Renaissance of the Twelfth Century* (Cambridge MA, 1927); R. L. Benson and G. Constable (eds), *Renaissance and Renewal in the Twelfth Century* (Oxford, 1982); R. Bartlett, *The Making of Europe: Conquest, Colonization and Cultural Change, 950–1350* (London, 1993), and R. I. Moore, *The First European Revolution, c. 970–1215* (Oxford, 2000).

[13] In canon 21 of the Fourth Lateran Council (1215): see below & n. 19.

Henry of Le Mans, whose followers took control of the city of Le Mans in the early twelfth century, assaulting the clergy and boycotting their services, until he was driven out, only to pursue a preaching campaign in southern France which was described by his contemporary St Bernard of Clairvaux as leaving the churches empty. Across Europe, chroniclers recorded outbreaks of what they denounced as heresy, in which diverse groups, some clandestine, others aggressively anticlerical, met in secret to share their beliefs or openly denounced the clergy. These were groups motivated not by differences of Trinitarian or Christological theology like the great heresies of late antiquity against which the Church had defined its core doctrines – Manicheanism, Pelagianism, Arianism, Monophysitism and the rest – but rather by a deep distrust of the conduct of the clergy and of bishops.

While they espoused a wide variety of different positions – some refusing tithes, others rejecting marriage or child baptism, others denying the need for an institutional Church – the most common recurrent concern was that the sinfulness of the priest could invalidate the sacrament, endangering thereby the salvation of the believer. This led some to urge strong action to enforce celibacy and other reformed standards on the clergy, and others to deny the need for clergy at all; some claimed the right to administer sacraments themselves while still others rejected belief in sacrament outright. Most of these so-called heresies thus reflected the real fears of a population for whom the Christian faith set the parameters of their world view. The Church's position, that the sacrament remained valid irrespective of the sinfulness or otherwise of the officiant, only fuelled the conviction of many that the priesthood, as the necessary mediator of salvation, was redundant.[14]

But these extreme positions reflected only a small part of a much broader religious movement, more often growing alongside than against the Church. Popular preachers, often from the laity, were increasingly drawing crowds across Europe, travelling from place to place, calling their hearers to repent and to live true Christian lives, speaking not in churches but in squares and market places, and often inspiring large movements of lay renunciants.[15] This was the

[14] The changes in understandings of the nature of the Church, priesthood and sacrament, and the relationships between laity and clergy, are particularly well explored in Rubin and Simons, *Christianity in Western Europe*; see also J. H. Arnold (ed.), *The Oxford Handbook of Medieval Christianity* (Oxford, 2014). The modern debate about the nature of medieval heresy was sparked by R. I. Moore, *The Origins of European Dissent* (London, 1977); the revised edition of M. Lambert, *Medieval Heresy: Popular Movements from the Gregorian Reform to the Reformation* (3rd edn, Oxford, 2002) offers a good introduction to what remains a controversial field; for an account of Henry of Le Mans (also known as Henry of Lausanne and Henry the Monk) including St Bernard's response, see Moore, *The Origins*, pp. 82–105.

[15] The topic of preaching runs through much of the literature cited above; an

context in which Francis of Assisi (to be canonised as St Francis), a member of a wealthy merchant family, was to embark on his own career of itinerant miracle working, asceticism and preaching, attracting a large following who likewise renounced their wealth and possessions to take up the life of wandering holy men begging for alms, adding to an already substantial body of preachers feeding the religious needs of a population hungry for their message, while alongside them growing numbers of hermits and recluses became foci of enthusiastic devotion.[16] Beyond this, and nourishing the religious movement, there was an unprecedented groundswell of lay engagement with the sacramental and devotional practices of the religion, a dramatic growth in pilgrimage, in the popularity of saints' cults, of participation in religious guilds and in festivals, an emerging adoption of the idea of the seven sacraments as defining the parameters of lives understood more firmly as a progression through the Christian symbolic order.[17]

It was Herbert Grundmann's insight that all of these movements, clerical reform, monastic reform, popular heresy, the preaching movement, the lay renunciant movements, the eremitical movement, each of which had been studied separately by historians, arose from the same roots and shared the same concerns. All were driven by the ideal of the *vita apostolica* ('apostolic life'), the desire to live a life in imitation of the Apostles, primarily through the adoption of religious poverty or asceticism and through preaching. For Grundmann, this made up one 'religious movement', and the fates of these groups and their leaders, whether they were accepted as orthodox or denounced as heretical, depended not on what they said or did as upon the reaction of the Church authorities to their activities, above all upon whether they were seen as pious supporters or as dangerous critics of the Church.[18]

The result was both an unprecedented and complex engagement of the laity with Christian sacramental, penitential and devotional practices and, at the same time, a growing crisis of trust in the Church as the legitimate leader of the Christian people. This religious movement reflected not a contrast to any sort

excellent introduction is K. Jansen, 'The Word and its diffusion', in Rubin and Simons, *Christianity in Western Europe*, pp. 114–32.

16 See e,g, Lambert, *Medieval Heresy*, pp. 67–107; C. H. Lawrence, *The Friars, The Impact of the Early Mendicant Movement on Western Society* (London, 1994), pp. 26–42; H. Leyser, *Hermits and the New Monasticism* (London, 1984).

17 See especially M. Rubin, 'Sacramental Life', in Rubin and Simons, *Christianity in Western Europe*, pp. 219–37.

18 Grundmann, *Religious Movements*, pp. 1–30, 209–35. Grundmann also argued that the apparent exception, the Cathars, who did espouse a fundamentally different theology (dualism), arose from the wider religious movement and developed distinct doctrines only gradually, owing their success primarily to their adoption of the *vita apostolica*.

of earlier age of supposed spiritual lethargy, but rather the new and different needs of a society experiencing explosive economic and demographic growth, bringing new opportunities for social movement but also social dislocation and new and visible gulfs between rich and poor. Religious poverty and the sense of personal responsibility that drove the popularity of penitential preachers were the moral responses to these circumstances. The wealth of the Church, once genuinely valued as honouring the greatness of God and inspiring faith in its intercession, was now re-defined as corruption. The Church needed both to restore trust in its clergy and to regain the initiative over a pastoral mission often being taken over by others.

By the late twelfth century the Church was moving from coercion alone, the prosecution of individuals or groups as heretical, which only led to further growth of the movement, to itself adopting the principles of the *vita apostolica*. This was exemplified by the conviction of Dominic Guzman, later canonised as St Dominic, that to compete with heretics it was necessary to appear like them, as poor, ascetic preachers. This led to the foundation of the Order of Preachers, the Dominicans, while leading members of Francis of Assisi's growing body of followers, commonly known as the Franciscans, set out to take his movement in the same direction, succeeding, against the resistance of Francis himself, and at the cost of bitter internal splits, in turning the most radical of the lay religious movements into an arm of the Church's preaching mission. Thus the preaching movement was brought relatively rapidly under the control of the Church while the final and most fundamental goal, the expansion of the pastoral system, a much larger and necessarily slower project, was set in train.

These developments culminated in the Fourth Lateran Council, convened by Pope Innocent III in 1215, generally regarded not only as the most important of the medieval Church councils but also as the crowning achievement of the period's most powerful pope. This was the Church's response to over a century of political conflict, religious turbulence and heresy, legislating to enforce Catholic dogma, to control the proliferation of new religious orders and lay preachers, to prescribe minimum requirements on the laity for attending confession and communion, to raise the standards of the priesthood, and above all to establish a functioning hierarchy and effective system of administration by which the aims and standards promulgated at the centre could be disseminated across the whole Church. It set out both a vision of a united church and a mechanism to achieve it, and at the centre of this was the bishop, now no longer seen as the autonomous head of his church but as the vital link between centre and locality.[19]

19 On Innocent III, see J. Sayers, *Innocent III, Leader of Europe 1198–1216* (London, 1994); J. C. Moore, *Pope Innocent III (1160/61–1216): To Root Up and Plant* (Leiden, 2003). A translation of the canons of Lateran IV can be found in Fordham University's

Robert Grosseteste was born probably sometime in the late 1160s, a near contemporary of St Dominic and nearly a generation older than St Francis, growing to maturity when the religious movement was at its height.[20] In Oxford, where he was teaching at the schools from shortly before 1200, and in Paris, if he did indeed spend time there, he would have experienced the impact of the challenges to the Church from the vantage point of two of its most important intellectual centres. In 1214, when the Oxford schools were formally constituted as a university, he became its first head, just a year before the convening of the momentous Fourth Lateran Council.[21] The Council itself was to be the defining event in the careers of Grosseteste's generation of theologians and churchmen. In Oxford he also associated himself closely with the Franciscans, the most radical of the lay poverty movements which had been brought into the Church, teaching at their schoolhouse from 1229 until his election to the see of Lincoln.

The concerns of the religious movement, for the personal responsibility of the believer for their own salvation, for preaching as a means to implant understanding of what was required for salvation, as well as the intense focus on the propriety of the priesthood and the efficacy of the sacrament, shaped the environment in which Grosseteste lived, taught and wrote. And while the more extreme manifestations of the religious movement, anticlerical violence and heresy, remained far from Lincoln, the concerns and values of the religious movement and the growth of popular engagement with the changing sacramental and devotional culture of the time, did not.[22] The response of the Church, articulated most fully in the canons of the Fourth Lateran Council, the drive for an invigorated pastoral mission enforced by an effective hierarchy binding together the churches under the control of Rome, provided the template for Grosseteste's priorities and actions as bishop, and he brought this new vision of the Church to Lincoln with particular force. The implementation of this vision through his activities in the diocese of Lincoln is the leitmotif of his letter collection, a work compiled to convey his legacy as bishop.

---

online *Medieval Sourcebook* (https:/www.sourcebooks.fordham.edu, accessed 12 July 2022). On the reception of Lateran IV in England, see Hoskin, *Robert Grosseteste and the 13th-Century Diocese*, pp. 24–46.

20 On the possible date of Grosseteste's birth, see McEvoy, *The Philosophy*, pp. 4–5. Southern proposed a slightly later date: Southern, *Robert Grosseteste*, pp. 63–4; St Dominic was born in 1170, St Francis in 1181 or 1182.

21 On the chronology of Grosseteste's life in these years, see McEvoy, *The Philosophy*, pp. 6–10.

22 The foundation of the Gilbertines, the only English reformed order, in Sempringham in the early twelfth century was only the most prominent example of the early spread of the new religious culture in Lincolnshire.

Robert Grosseteste and his letters

It is not unreasonable to approach Robert Grosseteste's letter collection as a public statement of his views and ideals rather than as a window into his personality or inner thoughts. Since antiquity, the letter collection had been the most important literary vehicle for presenting the public personae, achievements and ideals of prominent figures, and the medium through which they could most closely control their intellectual or political legacies. Medieval letters were neither written nor read as personal or private communications but composed and circulated as public pronouncements. Robert Grosseteste compiled his collection consciously in this long tradition of epistolography, whose conventions and rules were well established.[23]

His collection is typical in many respects of medieval letter collections. Firstly, it was a sender's collection, one of the most common types, comprising copies of letters sent by the author, not those received by him, and so presenting only one side of his correspondences.[24] Secondly, it relates almost entirely to his years as bishop, with only ten of the 130 letters pre-dating his election, and these, as we shall see, were relevant to the image he wished to present of his episcopate; medieval letter collections commonly reflected not the broader life or career of the author but their period of tenure of a particular office.[25] Thirdly, like most other letter collections, Grosseteste's includes some other documents that would not be considered letters today, such as his constitutions and statutes of the diocese, which had previously been circulated to his clergy, or his formal deposition to the Council of Lyons of 1245 in his dispute with the chapter of Lincoln.[26] It was normal for documents such as these, and others such as treatises, political manifestos or legal judgements, to be cast in epistolary form and included in letter collections. Grosseteste's collection was originally compiled around 1246, under his supervision, and contained 129 letters.[27] To this, only one further letter was later added, no. 128, written in 1253 and having initially been circulated separately.[28] Other than this letter, no correspondence from the final seven years of his episcopate is included.

[23] See e.g. Constable, *Letters and Letter-Collections*. Mantello and Goering suggest that it may have been a sort of 'companion piece' to his theological *Dicta*: 'Just as the *Dicta* ... illustrate the master's activities in the schools, so the *Epistolae* [letters] ... illustrate the life and duties of the bishop': Mantello and Goering, *The Letters*, p. 18.

[24] In fact, most sender's collections did include a very few letters received; Grosseteste's is unusual in including none at all.

[25] See e.g. the discussion in J. P. Haseldine, 'The Creation of a Literary Memorial: The Letter Collection of Peter of Celle', *Sacris Erudiri*, 37 (1997), 333–79, at pp. 336–8.

[26] Letters 52* and 127 (on the numbering of the letters see n. 28 below).

[27] On Grosseteste's role in the compilation of the collection, see Mantello and Goering, *The Letters*, p. 18.

[28] Luard included 133 letters in his edition for the Rolls Series, but, unwilling to change the numbering of the earlier, 1690, edition, assigned the numbers 52, 52*

One of the more common conventions of letter collections was that they should display variety (*varietas*), demonstrating the author's ability to command a range of subjects and modes of writing. Thus, a combination of petitions, spiritual or devotional exhortations, letters of friendship, examples of theological or philosophical learning, advice or erudite jesting were common. This range typically served to illustrate the author's piety, learning, championing of their institution or of good causes, connections with the renowned and the pious, spiritual direction of others, and command of rhetoric, and to stand testimony to their accomplishments and achievements. Variety, however, was not miscellany, and the selection and arrangement of letters within the conventional parameters of the genre is the key to understanding the self-images or messages which authors sought to project through their collections.[29]

The ten letters which pre-date Grosseteste's election to Lincoln are not arbitrary remnants of earlier correspondences now otherwise lost, but were selected to establish his credentials as a reforming bishop. The earliest, written in early 1229, is a lengthy response to two questions on theological matters put to him by a former pupil, Adam Rufus. Perhaps surprisingly for a theologian of Grosseteste's eminence, and especially considering that theological letters were frequently included in letter collections, this is the only such letter in this collection. It serves, however, both to establish Grosseteste's persona as a theologian and, by its opening place in the collection, to draw attention to his change of life: the original collection, as put together around 1246, is bracketed by this illustration of his theological prowess and by the great claims for his episcopal and pastoral rights of letter 127 with which it closes.[30] Adam Rufus also went on to become a Franciscan; he is the subject of letter 2, a letter of consolation to the Franciscans as he prepared to depart on a missionary journey to preach to Muslims.

Here, then, Grosseteste endorses both abandoning of study for a pastoral vocation, a theme which recurs in his later letters,[31] and the sort of missionary

---

and 72, 72* where he had added letters. He also included some letters which had survived separately in other manuscripts but were never part of the original collection and some since identified as inauthentic: Luard (ed.), *Roberti Grosseteste*. Thus the original collection of *c.* 1246 comprises those letters today conventionally numbered 1–52, 52*, 53–72, 72* and 73–127. Mantello and Goering use these numbers in their translation, placing the items extraneous to the original collection at the end: Mantello and Goering, *The Letters,* pp. 4–18.

29 Grosseteste's collection is presented in chronological order, which was by no means typical of medieval letter collections, where ordering by theme or by rank of recipient were equally common. The history of this collection is complicated by the facts that the earliest surviving manuscripts are fourteenth-century and that many are incomplete or do not preserve the same order of letters: Mantello and Goering, *The Letters*, pp. 3–23.

30 See below and n. 53.

31 See below, n. 51.

endeavour for which the Franciscans were to become celebrated. By the time this letter was written, Grosseteste had been appointed to the archdeaconry of Leicester, in the diocese of Lincoln, with a prebend in Lincoln Cathedral. In 1231, after an illness, but, significantly, also shortly after he began his association with the Franciscans' school in Oxford, he resigned the archdeaconry and other benefices, retaining only his prebend to support his teaching, an action signalling both his sympathy with Franciscan principles of religious poverty and his concerns over absentee tenure of benefices, a theme which, again, is prominent in his later letters. His decision is explained and defended in letters 8 and 9. The other early letters show him actively engaged in the business of his livings, defending his rights and those of his parishioners, as well as offering spiritual counsel to a leading aristocrat, the earl of Pembroke, and upbraiding an immoral scholar, all common components of letter collections. In these opening letters, then, Grosseteste is presenting himself as a scholar who takes religious poverty, pastoral responsibilities and spiritual mentorship seriously.[32]

The bulk of the collection then goes on to present exemplary interventions by Grosseteste in a number of disputes and affairs during his episcopate. Particularly striking is the number of letters defending his refusal to institute unsuitable candidates to positions with cure of souls. These run throughout the collection and are often lengthy, carrying elaborate justifications of Grosseteste's position. Most are responses to complaints by the candidates' patrons or by powerful supporters to whom the patrons have evidently turned. Together, they encompass a range of reasons for unsuitability, often backed up by reference to conciliar regulations.[33] The very first letter written after his election to Lincoln, when Grosseteste was still styled bishop-elect, no. 11 (early 1235), is his defence of his denial of a preferment to an unsuitable candidate quoted

[32] Letter 5, to Margaret de Quincy, countess of Winchester, has attracted attention for Grosseteste's sharp criticism of the protection she had offered to the Jews of Leicester, expelled by Simon de Montfort, including inviting some to settle on lands in Grosseteste's prebendal parish. While anti-Semitism, and anti-Semitic attacks endorsed by those in power, had been increasing dramatically for more than a century, Grosseteste was here not simply replicating prejudices common to his time but had adopted one of the more intolerant and uncompromising of the positions then current: Southern, *Robert Grosseteste*, pp. 244–9. The letter, which also deals with another matter, was included in the collection primarily to illustrate Grosseteste's close involvement in his parish. The other letters mentioned here are nos 4, 6, 7 and 10, respectively; he also defends himself for abandoning a proposed pilgrimage, a matter touching his personal reputation, in letter 3.

[33] See also Hoskin, *Robert Grosseteste as bishop*, pp. lv–lviii; many of the cases discussed below are covered in detail in Hoskin, *Robert Grosseteste and the 13th-Century Diocese*, pp. 101–79.

above.[34] In this case, the candidate, a deacon, was 'in dress and behaviour a layman, or rather a knight' and 'practically illiterate'. Grosseteste argues that, while some may say that such clothing does not constitute unsuitability for the cure of souls, it nevertheless constitutes disobedience of 'the council's regulations', a reference to canon 16 of the Fourth Lateran Council.[35]

Ignorance is cited for similar refusals in letter 19, where Grosseteste alludes to canon 27 of Lateran IV forbidding ordination of the ignorant and unformed and forwards copies of the candidate's examination answers in support, and letter 72, where the presentee is described as 'almost totally illiterate'. In letter 17, inexperience is the reason: the candidate 'is a minor and not sufficiently educated, still a boy, in fact, who thinks Ovid the greatest letter writer!'[36] Youthful predilections for classical pagan authors being replaced by mature appreciation of Christian works was a very common literary trope, with roots in Patristic literature, and in this case Grosseteste grants the young man an annual payment until such time as he is ready to be appointed elsewhere. In one case, Grosseteste has been outmanoeuvred and outranked as the papal legate has intervened on behalf of a presentee, the son of an earl, who is ineligible by age and not in holy orders; here Grosseteste's resort is to ask that a suitable vicar be appointed to ensure pastoral care on the ground under the, presumably to be absentee, rector.[37] In another case, he declines to admit a candidate to a benefice because he does not know him, referring the matter to the archbishop-elect of Canterbury, who does. This was no light concession; Grosseteste's relations with Canterbury were often far from harmonious and he was also a keen defender of his rights in his see, but where pastoral care was concerned, no doubt was permissible, for:

> Not only is he guilty of this kind of murder [i.e. of souls] who knowingly and deliberately hands over the souls he must save to one who is unable to do so, or ignorant, or negligent, but so in many cases is the person who entrusts those souls to a man concerning whom he is completely ignorant as to his ability or knowledge or willingness to care for them.[38]

Pastoral care also raised wider questions than personal suitability. The appointment of royal justices to benefices with cure of souls was a particular

34 See above, and n. 7.

35 Mantello and Goering, *The Letters*, p. 83 & n. 3, noting that it may also refer to canon 33 of the Council of Oxford, 1222.

36 *ibid.*, p. 95.

37 Letter 52; the issue here was also that the earl of Derby had recently recovered the right of presentation to the parish to which he was now presenting his son. Another dispute over presentation where age is the issue is treated in letter 26.

38 Letter 87, trans. Mantello and Goering, *The Letters*, p. 293.

concern of Grosseteste's. This was the principal reason for his refusal to institute the powerful and well-connected clerk and justice Robert Passelewe, a refusal which set him against both the king and the archbishop of Canterbury.[39] The relationship between secular and priestly power had been one of the central ideological pillars of the reform papacy since the eleventh century, and the involvement of priests in judicial matters was treated in canons 16 and 18 of Lateran IV. Grosseteste also objected to the appointment of abbots as itinerant royal justices,[40] which for him was as much a pastoral as a jurisdictional matter as he considered his responsibilities to ensure effective pastoral care to extend to the heads of religious houses. Indeed, he frequently intervened in the pastoral affairs of religious houses, quashing the elections of many unsuitable candidates for abbacies and priories, opposing monasteries farming out churches with cure of souls, and in one case involving himself in the affairs of a dependency of the powerful French monastery of Fleury.[41]

These cases were related to his ambitious and, in scope and rigour, unprecedented programme of visitations across the diocese, which Southern described as 'a huge extension of the bishop's pastoral function.'[42] Episcopal control over monasteries had long been a source of friction throughout Europe, exacerbated by the will and capacity of the administratively centralised new orders to exempt themselves from episcopal oversight. This, however, was an area where Lateran IV sought to strengthen bishops' authority, partly under the influence of theologians such as Grosseteste.[43] For Grosseteste, pastoral responsibility in all contexts and episcopal power were inextricable: the appointment of abbots as justices and the coercion of bishops who refused to institute presentees were two of the principal issues in his great manifesto on royal and ecclesiastical jurisdictions which is preserved in his collection as letter 72*.[44]

Another important threat to pastoral care, and one perhaps more commonly encountered in the sources more generally, was absenteeism, which often went hand in hand with pluralism. In the one case in the letter collection of Grosseteste agreeing to an appointment, he stresses the nature of the pastoral

39 Letters 124 to the king and 126 to the archbishop of Canterbury.

40 Letters 27, 28 and 82.

41 See letters 30, 18, and 53, 54 and 108, respectively.

42 Southern, *Robert Grosseteste*, p. 259, who estimates, for example, that Grosseteste deposed more than a quarter of the heads of Augustinian houses in the diocese.

43 Canon 12 preserves the bishop's rights and role in the regulation and visitation of religious houses. On Grosseteste's influence on papal policies, see S. Vanderputten, *Medieval Monasticisms, Forms and Experiences of the Monastic Life in the Latin West* (Berlin, 2020), p. 113. Grosseteste also based his practice on precedent in Lincoln: Southern, *Robert Grosseteste*, p. 258.

44 Mantello and Goering, *The Letters*, pp. 230–57, with a summary at p. 464.

responsibilities involved both to the sponsor, a cardinal, and the appointee.[45] The collection also records two disputes over attempts by the papal legate to have prebends in Lincoln conferred on his clerks,[46] a rebuke to an absentee[47] and his concern that a suitable vicar be appointed for a priest who has been asked to accompany the newly appointed English cardinal, Robert of Somercote, to Rome.[48] Papal provisions to English benefices, which were to become a growing focus of political tension, were also often the occasion of absenteeism. Letter 128, the document added to the end of the collection in 1253 after being widely circulated independently, is a resounding refusal of a papal provision. A final illustration of the seriousness with which Grosseteste pursued pastoral matters is his letter to a character identified only as 'T', threatening him to accept a living, after he had previously declined another offer, 'to avoid … being found guilty of not loving God, of not offering to him the sacrifice of your zeal, and thus of not being eligible to enter into the joy of the Lord'.[49]

Two further issues stand out in the collection. One is preaching, and in particular Grosseteste's efforts to bring Franciscans and Dominicans into the diocese and to promote their interests both there and in Rome,[50] as well as his exhortations to individuals to return home from studies abroad to devote themselves to the pastoral mission.[51] The other is his long-running conflict with the Dean and Chapter of Lincoln over his jurisdiction, both pastoral and administrative, over them, and in particular his right of visitation. This dispute lasted from 1238 until 1245, when Grosseteste successfully took his case to the Council of Lyons. The collection preserves fifteen letters relevant to the course of the dispute, addressed to the Dean and Chapter, to the pope and papal legate and to others involved, and two more on the subsequent planned visitation. [52] In these letters, Grosseteste clearly makes the dispute a matter of saving souls rather than of rival jurisdictions or the traditional liberties which the Chapter claimed. Letter 127, the copy of his submission to the Council of Lyons which closed the original version of his collection, contains Grosseteste's

45 Letters 46 & 47.

46 Letters 49 & 74.

47 Letter 25.

48 Letter 65; here Grosseteste adds the request to a letter of congratulation, a very common type of letter and normally the occasion for pious exhortations and reflections on the duties of office.

49 Letter 118, trans. Mantello and Goering, *The Letters*, p. 358.

50 Franciscans: letters 31, 34, 38, 41, 42, 58, 59, 69, 70, 109, 115; Dominicans: letters 14, 15, 16, 40, 100.

51 Letters 13, 16, 51, 120.

52 Letters 71, 73, 77, 79–82, 90–4, 96–8, and on the subsequent visitation, 121–2 (cf. letter 50).

fullest statement on the nature of the episcopal office. It shows his mastery of a remarkable range of biblical exegesis and philosophy, but also demonstrates his approach. As Southern put it: 'Considering that the whole affair was at bottom a legal and jurisdictional one, nothing is more remarkable than the almost complete absence from it of any reference to canon law, which from a practical point of view, provided the only texts that mattered'.[53]

All in all, those letters that concern these different aspects of pastoral care, from suitable appointments, to promoting preaching, to episcopal rights, account for some 60% of the letter collection. The remainder includes many letters of the sort usually found in twelfth- and thirteenth-century collections, petitions and requests for help, letters dealing with conflicts and disputes, or with the business of the see, cases of ecclesiastical discipline or the reform of abuses, and letters cultivating relations with sympathetic cardinals. At the same time, however, the collection lacks some kinds of letters which are very common in the genre more widely: there are no letters of friendship, for example, or jesting letters or letters accompanying loans of manuscripts and the exchange of literature, and the only letters of spiritual exhortation are those few which predate his episcopate. His focus is clear.

Reading Robert Grosseteste's letter collection

Robert Grosseteste's letter collection, then, was his testament to what he saw as the principal achievements of his episcopate. A brief selection of early letters establishes his credentials as a bishop fully committed to his new pastoral responsibilities. The bulk of the collection demonstrates a range of actions in the diocese but is dominated by the overriding concern to ensure effective pastoral care. The collection, in its original form, then concludes with letter 127, representing the culmination of his campaign to assert his authority over the Chapter, which was for Grosseteste, as we have seen, primarily a pastoral matter. It may be that he planned to issue an extended version of his collection representing the later years of his episcopate – later material does survive[54] – but it is equally possible that he considered this a sufficient record of his achievements and ideals. In the event, only one further letter, no. 128, his statement against papal provisions discussed above, was added to some later copies of the collection, perhaps to add one final element to an otherwise complete picture of the ideal bishop in his diocese.

There is, however, one final aspect of Grosseteste's letter collection which is crucial to understanding its purpose and its impact as a public statement of his views on salvation, pastoral care and episcopal authority. The masterful command of epistolary style which the letters demonstrate was no mere

53 Southern, *Robert Grosseteste*, p. 265.

54 See Mantello and Goering, *The Letters*, p. 17.

ornament but was as important as the content in conveying Grosseteste's message. Since antiquity, letter writing had been considered, and formally taught as, a branch of rhetoric, as oratory in written form, and in the Middle Ages it was the preeminent medium of diplomatic, political and legal communication. Exactly as in politics or international diplomacy today, where the rhetorical framing of communications is often more important in determining real outcomes than the content of what is said, signalling attitudes, according respect or offering calculated insult, so medieval actors framed their approaches and interventions in the shared conventions of Latin epistolary rhetoric. Just as learning to interpret political and state rhetoric is an essential practical skill for diplomats and political scientists today, so historians must be sensitive to the rhetorical conventions of medieval letters. One of the most important of these was the so-called *captatio benevolentiae*, the 'securing of the goodwill' of the recipient, an often elaborate introduction to a letter, presenting relevant moral or literary themes before proceeding to the specific details of the case in hand. One short extract from one of the letters defending Grosseteste's refusal of a preferment discussed above, no. 11, will serve to illustrate his use of this technique. The letter opens:

> Benevolentiae dilectionis vestrae, qua soliciti estis de processu et successu negotii mei, gratiarum actiones multiplices refero et affectuosas. Multipliciores tamen et magis devotas et affectuosas ago gratias quod me in misericordia et dilectione corripere et increpare voluistis super correptione et increpatione mea, quae, ut creditur et videtur a multis, modum et moderamen excessit.[55]

Here, Grosseteste deploys the language of affection and gratitude to set the tone for what was a sharp dispute and a rebuff. He uses this language not in a literal sense but following the shared conventions of diplomatic rhetoric, of which the vocabulary of love, friendship and affection was a prominent and well-established part, in order to present his refusal as respectful and principled, as firm but without personal invective or partiality. His skilful use of this language is important to the effect, and while Mantello and Goering's translation is excellent, the English language cannot fully replicate this style, with its measured rhythms, resonant assonances, sonorous pairings of rhymed words, emphatic repetitions and dramatically nested phrases, which can only

[55] *Rolls*, p. 50; Mantello and Goering, *The Letters*, p. 83: 'I send you many heartfelt thanks for the loving concern with which you watch over the progress and outcome of my affairs. But my thanks are greater and even more sincere and heartfelt because you have been good enough to rebuke and reproach me with compassion and affection for my own rebuke and reproach, which, as many believe and feel, exceeded all measure and moderation'.

fully be appreciated as they were intended to be received, by being read aloud, slowly. The style, which can often seem overblown and repetitive to modern tastes, could at its best have a fluent and imposing gravity, and was highly valued by medieval writers. Its use, which required great erudition, care and skill, in itself signalled a serious and respectful communication. A fine example is this extract from Grosseteste's great statement on episcopal authority in letter 127:

> In congregatione igitur fidelium sibi commissa, oportet quod episcopus praedictam solis refulgentiam praedicto modo circuendo exhibeat, nihil dimittens per anni circulum sua praesentia non illustratum propter hoc; et in Ecclesiastico scriptum est, Sol illuminans per omnia respexit. Et qualiter per omnia respiciet episcopus tanquam sol suae dioecesis, nisi per omnia possit visitare, corrigere, et reformare, et sic per lucem occulta in lucem manifestationis producet, ut quae tenebrosa sunt, purget, et quae vitalia amplius vivificet?[56]

Here we see the same rolling crescendos of phrases, powerful assonances and dramatic repetitions, the same careful layering of ideas but with yet more complexity. The soaring rhetoric is skilfully punctuated with the double use of the characteristically scholastic term *praedictus* ('aforesaid'), lending a sense of theological precision to the extravagant metaphor by which the circuit of the bishop on his visitation becomes the circuit of the life-giving sun. References to Scripture are woven together with natural philosophy to ground the argument, while the reader is carried on past the statement of the harsh necessity of duty – to inspect, to correct, to reform – to the culminating proclamation of the vital power of light and of the bishop. This encapsulates perfectly the authentic public voice of Robert Grosseteste, articulating the response of an intellectual to the religious movement, the commitment of his generation of ecclesiastics to the new pastoral mission of the Church, and his own personal sense of assuming the responsibility to become the shining sun of his diocese.

[56] *Rolls*, pp. 391–2; Mantello and Goering, *The Letters*, p. 402: 'The bishop must therefore make his circuit in the way indicated [i.e. his visitation] and thereby display the sun's brilliance in the congregation of the faithful entrusted to him, leaving nothing throughout the course of the year that has not received the light of his presence as a result. Also in Ecclesiasticus it is written: "The sun looks down on everything with its light". And how will the bishop look down on everything, as the sun of his diocese, unless he is able to bring what has been hidden into the light where it may be seen, thereby purging what is dark and bringing more life to living things?'

4

Depasturing in Welby, Lincolnshire, in 1259: an Early Trespass Case in the Court of King's Bench

DAVID CROOK

Nicholas Bennett has long been a keen student of the activities of the clergy of the diocese of Lincoln, and continues to be engaged on the editing both of the massive episcopal register of Bishop Burghersh (1320–42) and of a biographical dictionary of the Lincolnshire clergy between the early-thirteenth and the late-twentieth centuries. He well knows that clerics sometimes came into significant conflict both with lay people and with each other, and that this could involve physical violence resulting in court action.[1] Many of the legal disputes involving clergy were of a kind that were dealt with not by the church courts but by the royal courts of justice, the surviving records of which become increasingly voluminous in the second half of the thirteenth century. Lincolnshire was the second largest county in England, and one of the most prosperous and well populated, so it is not surprising that a very significant proportion of the pleas dealt with by the Bench, or Common Bench (later known as the Court of Common Pleas), and the Court *Coram Rege* (later known as King's Bench), arose within its boundaries. The King's Bench came into continuous existence during the reign of Henry III, in the later 1230s, and the two courts subsequently continued to work side by side, and also in competition with each other, for 600 years.[2] Most of the records of their proceedings to the year 1250 are now in print, in the twenty volumes

1 The register of Bishop Sutton includes some examples of violence involving clergy in several of the counties in the diocese: *Reg. Sutton*, III, LRS 48 (Lincoln, 1954), xxxi, xxxix–xli, 11–12, 19–22, 40, 125–7, 146–7, 154, 159–60, 166, 172–4, 177–8; *Lincolnshire Parish Clergy, 1214–1968: A Biographical Register*, ed. N. H. Bennett, 2 vols, LRS 103, 105 (Woodbridge, 2013, 2016).

2 C. A. F. Meekings and David Crook, *King's Bench and Common Bench in the Reign of Henry III*, Selden Society Supplementary Series, 17 (London, 2010).

of *Curia Regis Rolls*, the last volume being published in 2006.[3] Many of the later rolls, and also those of the itinerant royal justices in eyre periodically holding royal pleas in the counties, have subsequently been digitised by the late Professor Robert Palmer of the University of Houston, Texas, and they are among nearly ten million images now readily available on the Anglo-American Legal Tradition website, currently maintained by the O'Quinn Law Library of the University of Houston Law Center.[4]

A key development in the royal courts during the middle and later thirteenth century was the increasing use of writs of trespass *quare* (why) to seek monetary recompense for actions which had caused damage or material loss to a complainant and his property, usually in a rural setting. By the fourteenth century an array of different forms of trespass litigation had evolved, a great number of them illustrated by Morris Arnold in the second volume of his detailed account of the development of trespass in that period, published in 1987.[5] They included the wrongful distraint of animals in a variety of mainly rural contexts, such as breach of a pound, taking agisted animals without payment, taking animals, killing animals and inciting dogs, and other rural issues such as hunting, fishing, ploughing, digging, reaping, cutting trees, polluting or changing the course of streams, flooding, breaking closes and burning.

Another trespass not so far mentioned is that of depasturing, the act of denuding growing crops by grazing animals on them. Arnold illustrated that offence by using a case of trespass *vi et armis* (by force and arms), which came before the King's Bench in 1309, when six men led by William the Reeve were accused of having depastured, on 13 November 1306, at Feltwell in Norfolk, £20 worth of the grain of Henry of Barsham, using Henry's own cows, bullocks, sheep and pigs, and were sued by him for damages to the value of £40. The defendants denied trespass on the grounds that 'the usage and custom of the vill is such that the third part of all the lands of Feltwell shall lie unsown in every third year, so that each of the commoners of the vill can common there with every kind of beast'; and that Barsham had in that year sown his land in that third part, so the reeve and the rest of the defendants depastured the land to serve as their common for the whole with

3 *Curia Regis Rolls Preserved in the Public Record Office, XX, 34–35 Henry III (1250)* (London, 2006). The volume contains nearly 2000 entries and covers only two terms/six months, so it was increasingly obvious that further printed publication would be impossibly expensive. The earlier complex and very detailed subject index was not included in the last three volumes, the last being the one in volume XVII (1242–3).

4 Available online at http://aalt.law.uh.edu/.

5 M. S. Arnold, *Select Cases of Trespass from the King's Courts, 1307–99*, II, Selden Society, 103 (London, 1987).

their own beasts, as they were entitled to do. Barsham agreed that it was the normal custom but, with the consent of the commoners, he had sown the land in that year and held it in several until the day of the trespass about which he had now complained.[6]

Writs of depasturing like the one used in that case are first mentioned in a legal treatise written in 1318–20, and in which references to examples from Yorkshire and Lincolnshire predominate over those from other counties.[7] The identity of the compiler is not clear, but it is possible that he was Master Roger de Croxton, a servant of Joscelin de Kirnington, archdeacon of Stow and dean of Lincoln and then, from 1318–21, treasurer of Lincoln.[8] It is however clear from a case that arose in a Lincolnshire village in 1259–60 that the writ was already in use by legal practitioners in the King's Bench by that much earlier date, although it may then have been a rarity. It was known to the legal advisors of a parish rector and a lay lessee in a parish in rural Kesteven by that date, and used in a dispute between them and an important monastic house, supported by a hospital very close to Lincoln itself. It is to this dispute, involving men of substance and a leading monastic house in this area, that this contribution will now turn to examine the consequences of local violence and intimidation and the network of local politics at play, as well as the nature of legal knowledge in rural society in thirteenth-century England.

At the octave of Hilary [about 20 January] 1260 Thomas son of Edus of Welby appointed an attorney (Roger de Cauz or Geoffrey of Welby) for a case against Henry de Lek and others in a writ concerning a plea of trespass 'of which he complains'.[9] Records of three hearings in the case are found in the *Coram Rege* rolls for Easter and Trinity terms 1260, and the texts of the entries are here printed in full.[10] The first was on about 12 April 1260, in the King's Bench in the time of Hugh Bigod as justiciar of England. Bigod was the baronial justiciar appointed by the rebel barons who had taken control of government from the king at the Oxford Parliament of 1258.[11] Thomas son of Edus of Welby, represented by an unnamed attorney, began proceedings under a writ of trespass in the due form against Brother Henry de Lek, monk

6 TNA, KB 27/196, rot. 32d, printed in Arnold (ed.), *Select Cases of Trespass from the King's Courts*, II, p. 302.

7 Oxford, Bodleian Library, MS Rawlinson C 292.

8 *Early Registers of Writs*, ed. E. de Haas and G. D. G. Hall, Selden Society, 87 (London, 1970), pp. lv–lxx, and 178, no. 305.

9 TNA, KB 26/161, rot. 16d [AALT IMG 0141].

10 A full transcription and translation are provided in the Appendix below.

11 For most of the voluminous records of proceedings before him, see *The Special Eyre Rolls of Hugh Bigod*, ed. A. H. Hershey, Selden Society, vols 131, 133, for 2014, 2016 (London, 2021), continuously paginated. For the list of sessions held in various counties, see pp. 773–5.

of the Cistercian abbey of Vaudey in Beltisloe wapentake in the southwest of the county, William of Ropsley, lay brother of Vaudey, and Brother Geoffrey the Buyer (le Acatur or Achatur), lay brother of St Katherine's hospital in Lincoln, in a plea concerning why, with a multitude of armed men, they came to Thomas's land in Welby and depastured the grain there against the king's peace.[12]

The defendants did not attend, committing default because the sheriff, Hamo Hauteyn, had been ordered to have them in court on that day. He had done nothing, so he was subject to an amercement of £5.[13] He was ordered to have the defendants in court at the following octave of Trinity, about 7 June 1260. The other plaintiff, Master Alan of Rockland, parson of the church of Welby, also appeared to prosecute the trespass, and the sheriff had again been ordered to have the defendants in court at the same date; for a second time he had failed to do so, and was penalised as before. At that second hearing in June the basic details of the offence were rehearsed by the plaintiffs, but with the time and the precise details of the charge elaborated. These were: that the offence took place at night on Saturday 28 June 1259; that the multitude of armed men who came to depasture the land of the parson in Welby carried weapons which included axes, hauberks, swords, crossbows and arrows; that they had burned about fifteen acres of his land sown with wheat, depastured it with his beasts (sheep), burned his hedges and thrown down his folds, broken his closes therein and plundered his sheep, against the king's peace. He alleged that because of their actions he had suffered damages and injury to the value of forty marks.

This time Brother Henry and the other defendants duly appeared and denied using force and causing injury on that day, and any trespass against Master Alan. They confirmed that the abbot and his monks had lands and tenements in Welby, and stated that in every second year half of the fields in the village lay fallow with all its beasts, and that none of those who had lands or tenements there could without the agreement of the others enclose or cultivate any of their land, nor put it in defence, so that all those in the village who had lands and tenements would be able to common in the lands lying fallow during that time. They also

12 At the octave of Hilary [about 20 January] 1260 Thomas son of Edus of Welby appointed an attorney (Roger de Cauz or Geoffrey of Welby) for a case against Henry de Lek and others in a writ concerning a plea of trespass 'of which he complains': TNA, KB 26/161, rot. 16d [AALT IMG 0141].

13 Hauteyn was sheriff of Lincolnshire from Michaelmas 1259 to 11 December 1261: E. F. Jacob, *Studies in the Period of Baronial Reform and Rebellion, 1258–1267* (Oxford, 1925), p. 267; TNA, E 368/45, rot. 7 [AALT IMG 6776], given incorrectly by Jacob as m. 6, and his term in office is not given in that entry, for which see Public Record Office, *List of Sheriffs for England and Wales to 1831* (London, 1898), p. 78. For his remaining debts of over £171, see E 368/45, rot. 16 [AALT IMG 6794].

said that Master Alan had formerly, in some of his land lying in the part of the field of Welby which at that time lay fallow, enclosed and cultivated it without the assent and licence and others of the village according to the custom of the parties, in the peace of the lord king and not against that peace, entered that close with his beasts to common there without any other trespass against him.

They therefore 'put themselves on the country', requesting a jury of local men to decide the issue. Master Alan replied that he had enclosed that piece of land with the agreement of the chief lords of the fee of Welby, and seeded it with wheat and also with summer corn, peacefully and without objection or hindrance from the abbot and monks or anyone else of the village of Welby until Henry, William and Geoffrey, with a multitude of armed men, came there on that day and depastured that corn with his beasts, and committed other offences against him. He also asked for a jury to decide the issue. The sheriff was therefore ordered to cause a jury of twelve men to come to the court three weeks after the feast of St John the Baptist (about 15 July), and Henry and the others also, and give a verdict. Robert de Lek and William Skyrebek (Skirbeck) undertook to have them there at that term. The same defendants also came to answer to Thomas son of Edus of Welby concerning a similar plea about burning a hedge belonging to the parson, and for burning a crop of three acres also belonging to the parson, so causing Thomas forty shillings of damage. Again, the defendants denied force and injury, and answered in the same way as they had to the parson, and also submitted themselves to a jury, which was to appear at the same date.

In the record of this hearing it becomes clear that Thomas son of Edus, although he seems to have made the first complaint, was in fact the lesser of the two plaintiffs, since he claimed less than the parson in damages, a lesser amount of property was involved, and it was the property of the parson rather than his own that had allegedly been damaged. It must have been for that reason that the record of the second and third hearings treated the parson as the main plaintiff, but the record of the first hearing suggests that the original initiative in taking legal action came from the layman rather than the cleric. Furthermore, the references to the variety of weapons used by the raiders should not be taken literally. It was in the interests of the plaintiffs in such cases to exaggerate the level of lawlessness to ensure that the offence could be regarded as a serious breach of the king's peace and so readily justiciable by the king's justices. If the attack really did take place at night, as alleged, it would be difficult to be sure of such details in any case. It seems likely that the attack was carried out by initially by stealth, and that any actual violence may have been minimal.

The next hearing, set for the octave of Trinity, did take place at that date, about 6 June 1260.[14] It was recalled that the sheriff had been ordered to empanel

14 TNA, KB 26/167, rot. 13 [IMG0036].

twelve jurors who had no affinity with any of the parties to come to the court and confirm or deny whether the alleged events at Welby, described again in detail but this time said to have taken place on Friday before the feast of the Apostles SS Peter and Paul (27 June 1259), had taken place or not. Again, no jury appeared because the sheriff had done nothing to summon one, because he said the writ arrived too late for it to be executed. It was ordered by the court that the jury should now come to Hugh Bigod's court at the octave of Michaelmas following, about 6 October 1260, to deliver a verdict in the court wherever it then was. No jury appeared, as so often happened, and the case was apparently not resolved. There is no record of the outcome. It is worthwhile to set these events in their local and then wider judicial and political contexts.

The village of Welby lies four and a half miles from the important market town of Grantham, half a mile east of Ermine Street, the Roman road which runs along the eastern side of Lincoln Edge between Stamford and Ancaster and then on to Lincoln itself. It lay in Threo wapentake, which also included other parishes on the western side of the road as well as the east, from Londonthorpe (usually but not always rendered as 'Lunderthorp' in thirteenth-century records) and Harrowby, and running down the slope of the Edge to the bottom at Belton and Barkston, but leaving Grantham in a neighbouring wapentake. Immediately to the south of Welby lay Ropsley, which by 1336 and probably earlier yielded more tax revenue to the crown than Welby, and was second in value only to Haydour, immediately to the east of Welby, in the wapentake as a whole.[15] As already mentioned, the first-named plaintiff in the earliest record of the dispute, which clearly had a major, but perhaps only short-term, impact on life in Welby, was Thomas son of Edus of Welby. A little more is known about his presumed descendants and relatives. In 1298 a Thomas Edus of Welby, possibly his son, was a pledge for a sub-taxer for the levy of a ninth in that year in Welby, and for the appearance of another man before justices of oyer and terminer at Stamford.[16] The second-named plaintiff was the rector of Welby, Master Alan

15 *The Lay Subsidy of 1334,* ed. R. E. Glasscock (London, 1972), p. 172.

16 *A Lincolnshire Assize Roll for 1298*, ed. W. S. Thomson, LRS 36 (Hereford, 1944 for 1939), pp. 37 (entry 191), 109 (415), 165. The name 'Edus' or 'Edusa' was relatively unusual, and was female. Two other Lincolnshire females called Edusa occur in 1202 and 1206, respectively Edusa wife of Herbert de Crossholme and Edusa the third daughter of Alexander the Carter: *The Earliest Lincolnshire Assize Rolls, 1202–1209*, ed. D. M. Stenton, LRS 22 (1926), pp. 123 (no. 710), 268 (no. 483). In 1212 Edus widow of Robert de Biker, or de Bichere, from whom the prior of Spalding claimed a bovate of land in Moulton, appointed an attorney to represent her: *Curia Regis Rolls,* VI (1932), pp. 342, 351–2. An Edusa sister of Gunilda was living in Alkborough in 1219 (*Rolls of the Justices in Eyre, Lincolnshire 1218–19, and Worcestershire 1221*, ed. D. M. Stenton, Selden Society, 53 (1934), nos 241, 330). A Geoffrey son of Edusa was a pledge in a Whaplode case in 1242: *Curia Regis Rolls*, xvii, no. 28. Outside Lincolnshire, Sewardsley priory, a Northamptonshire nunnery, received a bequest of

de Rokeland, whose name probably derived from Rockland in Norfolk. He had been instituted as rector of Welby by Bishop Robert Grosseteste in 1251–52, on presentation by the bishop of Rochester, Laurence of St Martin, who at the time was warden of the prebend of Grantham Australis not far away.[17]

Their principal opponent was Vaudey Abbey, a Cistercian house lying between Swinstead and Edenham about fifteen miles south of Welby, founded by William count of Aumale in 1147 at Bytham, and which moved to the Vaudey site two years later.[18] It is now obliterated above ground except for the base of a clustered pier and a few grass-covered mounds.[19] Vaudey had a significant annual income of about £230 by 1291, and a grant of free warren by Edward I in 1299 mentions that the abbey had demesne lands in Welby, as well as in Edenham, Ropsley, Burton [le Coggles], Corby [Glen] and Little Bytham.[20] No cartulary has survived, but there is nevertheless considerable evidence about the property of the abbot in Welby. King Richard confirmed at the very beginning of his reign, on 7 September 1189, a charter of John son of Ingebrand to Vaudey, making a grant of an unspecified portion of land with common of pasture over all his land in Welby, while Robert Spron and his son John, Alan the Clerk, Fegge, and William son of Osbert granted the house some other parcels of land there.[21] The abbey had ten and a half bovates in Welby by gift of John Fitz Roger, and one member of the Gant family, lords of Folkingham, Robert son of Walter de Gant, was buried at Vaudey in 1162.[22] The abbey therefore had major interests in Welby by the time of the judicial eyre held in Lincolnshire in 1202.[23]

During the latter part of the reign of King John and the minority of Henry III the abbey was involved in legal action over its substantial landed interests in

---

land in Hulcote from an Adam son of Edus de Esteneston (Easton Neston) at an early date: *The Heads of Religious Houses: England and Wales, II, 1216–1307*, ed. D. M. Smith and V. C. M. London (Cambridge, 2001), p. 604; TNA, E 326/3977.

17 *Robert Grosseteste as Bishop of Lincoln: The Episcopal Rolls, 1235–1253*, ed. P. M. Hoskin, LRS, Kathleen Major Series of Medieval Records, 1 (Woodbridge, 2015), no. 507.

18 *Heads of Religious Houses: England and Wales, 940–1216*, ed. D. Knowles, C. N. L. Brooke and Vera London (Cambridge, 1972), p. 146. The earlier name of the site was 'Bracthuait'.

19 www.heritagegateway.org.uk/Gateway/Results_Single.aspx?uid=348506&resourceID=19191.

20 *Victoria County History of Lincolnshire*, II, ed. W. Page (London, 1906), p. 143; *Calendar of Charter Rolls*, II, p. 576.

21 John Caley, Henry Ellis and Bulkeley Bandinel (eds), *Monasticon Anglicanum: A New Edition*, 6 vols in 8 (London, 1846), V, 490–2; F. M. Stenton, *The Free Peasantry of the Northern Danelaw* (Oxford, 1969), nos. 211–12.

22 *Monasticon Anglicanum*, V, 491; M. Abbot, 'The Gant Family in England', unpublished University of Cambridge D. Phil. thesis (1973), pp. 241–2.

23 Stenton (ed.) *The Earliest Lincolnshire Assize Rolls*, pp. 1 (no. 3), 52 (no. 302).

the parish, often jointly with the master of the Gilbertine priory of St Katherine and St Sepulchre's Hospital outside Lincoln.[24] In 1213–14 the two houses were sued both by Robert de Evermue and Robert de Willoughby, respectively, over three bovates and five bovates of land in Welby.[25] In 1221 the then abbot brought a writ of *pone* in the Common Bench against Thomas de Reinville concerning a hundred acres of pasture in Welby, litigation which continued until at least 1224. In 1223 a grand jury of sixteen Lincolnshire knights was empanelled to decide the case. The jury had however still not appeared in court by the autumn of 1224, when there was a further postponement until Easter term 1225, for which no roll has survived, so the outcome of the case is unknown.[26]

The feudal survey of England made in 1242–43 gives some details about the Vaudey holdings in Welby at that date. The abbot held three-quarters of a knight's fee, with several sub-tenants holding of him by military service. He had eighteen bovates of land, and St Katherine's outside Lincoln also held five and a half bovates.[27] The tenurial situation in Welby therefore clearly accounts for the interest and the involvement of both Vaudey Abbey and St Katherine's in the dispute which arose there in 1259. The abbot of Vaudey in particular had a crucial interest in good communications between the abbey and Welby, via the intermediate parishes of Irnham, Ingoldsby and Ropsley. In 1230 Abbot Nicholas found it necessary to initiate a lawsuit in the king's court against Maurice de Gand, lord of Irnham, in which he sought damages of £5 for impediments to the passage of his men, horses and carts to Irnham through Gand's field, headland and wood, then through the land of William de Coleville, and finally through Maurice's land to the great way next to the head of that wood. In January that year the sheriff was instructed by the justices of the Bench to visit Irnham in person, taking with him twelve [knights],[28]

24 The Gilbertine priory of St Katherine was founded in about 1148 by the bishop of Lincoln but the origins of the priory are unusual in that the Gilbertines were specifically given the responsibility of caring for the inmates of the hospital of St Sepulchre that had been founded not long before by Bishop Robert Bloet (1094–1123). The priory was established beside and to the south of the hospital but the two closes remained distinct, and this indicates that the hospital was considered to be an important institution in its own right.

25 *Curia Regis Rolls*, VIII, pp. 40, 55, 183.

26 *Calendar of Fine Rolls 1216–1224*, ed. P. Dryburgh and B. Hartland (Woodbridge and London, 2007), 5 Henry III, no. 342; *Curia Regis Rolls*, XI, nos 631, 1476, 2663 (where the defendant is called Thomas de Sumardeby); see also no. 763. A subsequent unrelated case of 1250 involving land in Welby refers to 200 acres of pasture there: *Curia Regis Rolls*, XIX, no. 1512.

27 *The Book of Fees*, ed. H. C. Maxwell-Lyte, 3 vols (London, 1920–31), pp. 1004, 1037, 1038, 1091.

28 The actual word is replaced by the abbreviation 'etcetera' in the text.

to inquire into the rights of the abbot's servants to pass through without impediment, and to report back to the justices in mid-June. As a result, the right of way for the abbot's men from the abbey to Irnham and through Maurice de Gand's estate there was confirmed, so securing their passage to Welby.[29]

The abbot of Vaudey at the time, in office by 1251 and still in place in 1264, was a Henry, of whom no details are known.[30] Henry de Lek, the monk of the abbey who was the first-named defendant in the case, cannot himself have been the abbot, since in July 1258 abbot Henry appointed 'Brother Henry de Leyk, his monk' as his attorney to conclude a foot of fine in the Common Bench at Westminster.[31] William of Ropsley, the *conversus* or lay brother of the abbey named as the second defendant, seems likely to have been one of Henry's subordinates with responsibility for Vaudey property away from the immediate neighbourhood of the abbey itself. If he did indeed come from Ropsley, as his name indicates, his home village was immediately to the south of Welby, and he may well have been responsible for the abbey's property in that area. The abbey had a grange in Ropsley, already in existence by 1189–90, on Ropsley Heath.[32] The third defendant, Brother Geoffrey le Achatur, or 'buyer', was a lay brother from the priory of St Katherine outside Lincoln.[33] Geoffrey's occupational name suggests that it was his duty to buy or otherwise obtain food for St Katherine's and that some of it might regularly have come from Welby.

So much for the local setting. In terms of the wider judicial context, there had been no recent eyre by royal justices for common pleas in Lincolnshire since the one that ended in February 1257, long before the offences at Welby were committed on 27–28 June 1259.[34] The revolutionary Oxford Parliament of June 1258 effectively took control of government from the king, and initiated a special series of judicial hearings before a newly appointed justiciar, Hugh Bigod, the first holder of the office since 1234. Initially these took place in the south of England, from 16 June until 28 August 1258, but from 1 to 18 September Bigod was in what we now might call the east midlands, successively at

29 *Curia Regis Rolls*, XIII, nos 2552, 2569; XIV, no. 167. Gand in fact died in July 1230 in France while taking part in Henry III's campaign there, so these proceedings must mainly have involved his manorial servants at Irnham rather than him personally: Nicholas Vincent, 'Gant, Maurice de', ODNB.

30 *Heads of Religious Houses, II*, p. 319.

31 *Final Concords of the County of Lincoln 1244–1272*, ed. C. W. Foster, LRS 17 (Horncastle, 1920), p. 163, no. 10.

32 For its site, see Lincolnshire Heritage Monument record MLI30069. No grange is recorded in Welby itself.

33 *Heads of Religious Houses* II, p. 523; 'The Priory of St Catherine's Outside Lincoln', *Victoria County History of Lincolnshire*, II, pp, 188–91. For its site, see Lincolnshire Heritage Monument record MLI70159.

34 D. Crook, *Records of the General Eyre,* Public Record Office Handbooks, 20 (London, 1982), p. 122.

Oakham in Rutland; Sandiacre in Derbyshire; Nottingham and Southwell in Nottinghamshire; Grimsby, Lincoln and Stamford in Lincolnshire; and finally at Bradcroft 'outside Stamford in the county of Rutland'.[35] The event which was the subject of the case therefore took place a year after the parliament at Oxford and six months after Bigod held the final session of his special hearings at Stratford in Essex on 14 January 1259. He subsequently continued in office as justiciar until October 1260, when he was replaced by Hugh le Despenser. The *Coram Rege* roll for Easter 1260, when the king was abroad, and when the case first came to the court, is headed *Placita coram domino rege de tempore Hugonis le Bigod justiciarii Anglie*; the second and third entries were in Trinity term, whose roll is headed *Placita coram H. le Bygod justiciario Anglie*. All three hearings in the Welby case were therefore pleaded before the justiciar, wherever he then was, in place of the king, so the Court of King's Bench sat as it normally had earlier in the reign before the events of the summer of 1258.[36]

As in so many legal disputes, there is no record of the outcome, but it is extremely unlikely that the rector of Welby and his lay parishioner eventually received the satisfaction that they sought. The dominance of the abbot of Vaudey in the affairs of the parish of Welby certainly continued during the subsequent decades. In 1280 the then abbot explicitly and successfully used statute law to prevent the distraint of his plough beasts and sheep by William de Freskenard and Peter of Barkston at a named location in the fields of Welby, but that is another story, for another day.[37]

[35] Hershey (ed.), *Special Eyre Rolls of Hugh Bigod, 1258–60, I*, nos, 152, 154–8, 162, 166–229, 231–5, 237–325, 327–8, 371–80, 392–7. Only a single case involving the depasturing of land was recorded during these sessions; it related to Wollaston in Northamptonshire and was heard on 25 August 1258 (no. 131). As it happens, St Katherine's priory representatives were also in Bigod's court at Lincoln on 13 September 1258 as the plaintiff against Robert of Metheringham and Robert son of William of Metheringham in a dispute over a free tenement in Blankney (no. 289), during which the prior sent men to a meadow, mowed it in three places and carried away the hay. It may be suggested that this case was what made the advisors of the parties in the Welby suit of two years later aware of the new procedure and its possibilities.

[36] *King's Bench and Common Bench*, p. 142; TNA, KB 26/167, rots 1, 11 [AALT IMG 0003, 0028].

[37] TNA, JUST 1/495, rot. 49 [AALT IMG 5488], presumably under the terms of the Statute of Marlborough (1267): P. Brand, *Kings, Barons and Justices: The Making and Enforcement of Legislation in Thirteenth-Century England* (Cambridge, 2003), Chapter 14 and Appendix 3.

APPENDIX

The texts of the entries relating to the case of Thomas son of Edus of Welby and Master Alan of Rockland *versus* Henry de Lek, monk of Vaudey Abbey, William of Ropsley, *conversus* (lay brother) of Vaudey and Brother Geoffrey le Achatur, *conversus* (lay brother) of the Hospital of Lincoln.

1. TNA, KB 26/167, rot. 1d (AALT IMG 0080) Heading on rot. 1 of this membrane for quindene of Easter 44 Henry III [1260] reads PLACITA CORAM DOMINO REGE DE TEMPORE HUGONIS BIGOD JUSTICIARII ANGLIE IN CRASTINO CLAUSE PASCHE ET A DIE PASCHE IN QUINDECIM DIES ANNO XLIIII [Easter term, 1260, *c.* 12 April and *c.* 19 April]. This entry is at the very beginning of the roll and must relate to 12 April 1260.

> *Linc'* Thomas filius Edus de Welleby [per attornatum suum *interlined*] optulit se quarto die versus fratrem Henricum de Lek monachum de Valle Dei fratrem / Willelmum de Roppel' conversum eiusdem loci et fratrem Galfridum le acatur conversum hospitalis Linc' de placito quare ipsum / cum multitudine armatorum venerunt ad terram ipsius Thome in Welleby et blada sua in eadem terra existen/cia cum averiis suis depasti fuerunt contra pacem etc. Et ipsi non venerunt etc. Et plures fecerunt defaltas ita quod precep/tum fuit vicecomiti quod haberet corpora eorum ad hunc diem. Et quod (vicecomes *interlined)* esset auditurus judicium suum etc. Et vicecomes nichil / inde fecit ideo ipse in misericordia scilicet Hamo Hauteyn et amerciatur ad centum solidos. (C s. *in the margin*) Et sicut pluries preceptum est vicecomiti / quod habeat corpora eorum in octabis Sancte Trinitatis ubicumque etc. (Et vicecomes audiendum judicium etc. *interlined*). Et sciat etc. Et quod gravius etc.

> *Linc'*. Magister Alanus de Rokelond persona ecclesie de Welleby optulit se iiij die versus eosdem Henricum et alios de placita / predicte transgressionis. Et ipsi non venerunt etc. Et plures fecerunt defaltas ita quod preceptum fuit vicecomiti quod haberet corpora eorum / ad hunc diem. Et vicecomes nichil inde fecit ut supra. Et ideo ipsi in misericordia ut prius. Et preceptum est vicecomiti sicut / pluries quod habeat corpora eorum ad eundem terminum. (Et vicecomes sit audiendum judicium etc. *interlined*). Et sciat etc. et quod gravius etc.

2. TNA, KB 26/167, rot. 13 (AALT IMG 0036) ADHUC DE OCTABIS SANCTE TRINITATIS (*c.* 7 June 1260). Right-hand margin slightly damaged by ?water.

> *Linc'.* Henricus de Lek monachus de Valle Dei frater Willelmus de Roppele conversus eiusdem loci et frater Galfridus le achatur conver/ sus hospitalis Lincoln' attachiati fuerunt ad respondendum Magistro

Alano de Rokelond (persone ecclesie de Welleby *interlined*) de placito quare ipsi cum multitudine / armatorum venerunt ad terram ipsius persone in Welleby et blada sua in eadem terra existentia cum averiis suis depasti / fuerunt et alia dampna ei intulerunt contra pacem etc. Et unde predictus Magister Alanus dicit quod predicti Henricus Willelmus et Gal' / nocte diei sabati proximi ante festum apostolorum Petri et Pauli anno xliij [28 June 1259] cum multitudine armatorum scilicet cum / hachiis haubergellis gladiis arcubus et sagittis venerunt ad terram ipsius persone in Welleby et (vestura *interlined*) circa quindecim / acrarum terre seminate de frumento cum averiis suis depasti fuerint et hayas suas combusserunt et eciam faldam eiusdem / persone prostraverunt et cleyas inde fregerunt et blada predicta cum bidentibus eiusdem persone similiter depredaverunt / contra pacem etc. Et unde dicit quod deterioratus est et dampnum habet ad valenciam xl marcarum. Et inde producit sectam.

Et Henricus et alii venerunt et defendunt vim et iniuriam quando etc. et bene defendunt quod ipsi predicto die non fecerunt predictum Magistro / Alano predictam transgressionem set dicunt quod volunt cognoscere quadam veritatem. Dicunt enim quod Abbas suus de Valle Dei / et ipsi monachi habent terras et tenementa in predicta villa de Welleby et quod medietas camporum eisdem ville quolibet secundo / anno iacet ad warettum et dicunt quod consuetudo est in partibus illis quod singuli tenentes predicte ville usi sunt communi/candi in medietate illa que iacet ad warettum cum omnimodis averiis suis et quod nullus eorum qui terras vel tenementa / habeat in predicta villa sine assensu aliorum aliquid de terra sua ex illa parte campi iacente includere potest nec / excolere nec eciam in defensum ponere quominus omnes de predicta villa qui terras et tenementa habent dum ibidem / communicare possint dummodo medietas illa iacet ad warettum. Et dicunt quod quia predictus magister Alanus quandam partem / terre sue (iacentem *interlined)* ex illa parte campi de Welleby que tunc temporis jacebat ad warettum includere fecit et excolere sine assensu / et licencia ipsorum abbatis et monachorum et aliorum de predicta villa ipsi secundum consuetudinem partium illarum cum pace (domini regis *interlined*) et non contra / pacem intraverunt clausum illud cum averiis suis ad communicandum ibidem absque alia transgressione qua in eidem magistro Alano / fecissent. Et quod ita sit ponit se super patriam.

Et Magister Alanus dicit quod ipse de (assensu *deleted*) (licencia *interlined*) et voluntate capitalium dominorum feodi de Welleby includi fecit predictam peciam terre / sue et etiam seminari fecit de frumento et similiter de tramesio pacifice sine contradicione vel impedimento predictorum abbatis et / monachorum seu aliorum de predicta villa de Welleby et terram illam seminatam pacifice possedit quousque predicti Henricus / Willelmus et Galfridus cum multitudine armatorum predicto die venerunt ibidem et blada illa cum averiis suis depasci fuerunt / et alias transgressiones predictas ei fecerunt. Et quod ita sit ponit se super patriam. Et predicti Henricus et alii similiter. Et ideo preceptum / est vicecomiti quod venire faciat a die Sancti Johannis Baptiste in tres septimanis xij etc. per quos etc. Et qui nec etc. ad recognoscendum in forma predicta / etc. Quia tam etc. (et concessum est etc. *interlined*). Et Robertus de Lek et Willelmus Skyrebek manucepit habendum eis ad prefatum terminum etc.

[*blank space of about ten lines*]

Linc'. Iidem Henricus, Willelmus et Galfridus attachiati fuerunt ad respondendum Thome filio Edus de Welleby de placito consimili transgressione / combustione haye predicti persone. Et queritur de vestura trium acrarum terre etc. ad dampnum ipsius Thome xl solidorum etcetera. / Et Henricus et alii venerunt. Et defendunt vim et injuriam quando etc. Et respondent eodem modo ut supra. Et ponunt se inde super / patriam et Thome similiter. Et ideo preceptum est vicecomiti quod venire faciat ad prefatum terminum [xij *hole in membrane*] ut supra etcetera. Quia tam.

3 TNA, KB 26/167, rot. 20d (AALT IMG 0137) Bigod's roll Easter 44 Henry III, St John the Baptist three weeks *coram domino rege c.* 15 July 1260 [from the heading on the dorse of the previous membrane].

Linc'. Preceptum fuit vicecomiti quod venire faceret ad hunc diem xij etc. per quos etc. et qui nec magistrum Alanum de Rokelund / personam ecclesie de Welleby et Thomam filium Edus de Welleby nec Henricum de Lek monachum de Valle Dei fratrem Willelmum / de Roppel' conversum eiusdem loci et fratrem Galfridum le Achatur conversum hospitalis Sancte Katerine extra Linc' aliqua / affinitate attingerent ad recognoscendum super sacramentum suum si predicti Henricus Willelmus et Galfridus cum multitudine armatorum / die veneris proxima ante festum apostolorum Petri et Pauli noctanter anno regni nostri quadragesimo tercio venerunt / ad terram ipsius Thome in Welleby quam ipse de licencia et voluntate capitalium dominorum feodi illius (de Thom' *interlined and deleted*) seminari fe/cerat de frumento et tramesio et blada illa serclari fecerat et pacifice tenuerat usque ad predictum diem blada illa / cum averiis suis depasti fuerunt et faldam eiusdem Thome prostraverunt et blada predicta cum propriis bidentibus ipsius / Thome similiter depasti fuerunt sicut predictus Thomas dicit. Et similiter si predicti Henrici et alii cum multitudine armatorum / predicto die noctanter anno predicto venerunt ad terram ipsius magistri Alani in Welleby quam ipse de licencia et volun/ tate capitalium dominorum feodi illius seminari fecerat frumento et tramesio et blada illa serclari fecerat et pacifice / tenuerat usque ad

> diem predictum blada illa cum averiis suis depasti fuerunt et hayas suas combusserunt et etiam / faldam eiusdem persone prostraverunt et blada predicta cum propriis bidentibus ipsius persone similiter depasti fuerunt / contra pacem etc. sicut predictus magister Alanus dicit vel si predicti Henricus Willelmus Galfridus statim postquam predictus Thomas et / magister Alanus terras predictas seminaverunt eas cum averiis abbatis de Valle Dei et prioris hospitalis Sancte Katerine / extra Linc' intraverunt tanquam communem pasturam suam eo quod terre ille tunc temporis iacere debuerunt ad warettum / secundum consuetudinem parcium illarum et blada in eisdem terris existencia postquam seminata fuerant de die in diem / et similiter predicto die cum averiis suis depasti fuerunt absque vi vel armis vel absque hoc quod aliquam aliam transgressionem / eidem Magistro Alano fecissent sicut predicti Henrici et alii dicunt. Et vicecomes nichil inde fecit set mandavit quod breve tam / tarde venit quod non potuit exequi. Et ideo sicut prius preceptum est vicecomiti quod venire faciat in octabis Sancti Michaelis ubicumque / H. le Bygod etc. xij etc. per quos etc. et qui nec etc. ad recognoscendum in forma predicta. Quia tam etc. Idem / dies datus est predictis Henrici Willelmo et Galfrido qui venerunt pro defectu recognitorum etc.

Editorial note: The King's Bench roll for Michaelmas term 1260 (TNA, KB 26/168), in the heading of which no justice is named, survives but contains nothing further about this case. That for Hilary term 1261 survives only as a damaged single membrane (TNA, KB 26/234), which was recovered from miscellanea before 1939 and eventually added to the series by C. A. F. Meekings in December 1956. It seems overwhelmingly likely that the jury never appeared, a very frequent occurrence in pleas even in more ordinary times, so it would appear that proceedings were never concluded.

5

Rethinking Criminous Clerks: Church/State Relations in the Late Thirteenth Century

PHILIPPA HOSKIN

The clergy of medieval Western Europe got away with murder: both in spiritual terms, through their neglect of the souls of their parishioners, and literally, by using the *privilegium beneficii* (known more often in England as 'benefit of clergy') to escape capital punishment, even when secular courts declared them guilty of a felony. This was, at least, the claim of their contemporaries, and the belief of later historians.[1] Thirteenth-century episcopal and papal legislation (as well as that later and earlier) spoke anxiously of the absence and ignorance of many of the parish clergy who were responsible for guiding their parishioners towards Heaven, and sought ways to remedy these failures. The secular courts knew that they must hand over felonious clergy to the Church courts. They were, equally, certain that in doing so, they allowed many guilty men to be found innocent, by undergoing the simple process of compurgation in which the accused swore to their own innocence, supported by others who testified, on oath, to their good reputation.

However 'bad' or 'good' the clergy were – the assessment of which depends very much on the values held, and filters applied to them, by their contemporaries and historians – one thing is usually taken for granted: that the 'clergy' were regarded as, and thought of themselves as, part of a separate caste from the laity, answerable to ecclesiastical, rather than

1 Frederick Pollock and Frederic William Maitland, *The History of English Law Before the Time of Edward I*, 2 vols (Oxford, 1895, rev. 1971), II, p. 443; J. G. Bellamy, *Crime and Public Order in England in the Later Middle Ages* (London, 1973), p. 144; L. Gabel, *Benefit of Clergy in the Later Middle Ages* (New York, 1969), pp. 104–7; A. K. McHardy, 'Church Courts and Criminous Clerks in the Later Middle Ages', in M. J. Franklin and Christopher Harper-Bill (eds), *Medieval Ecclesiastical Studies in Honour of Dorothy M. Owen* (Woodbridge, 1995), pp. 165–83; R. H. Helmholz, *The Ius Commune in England: Four Studies* (Oxford, 2001), pp. 87–9.

secular, jurisdiction and that contemporary secular administrations shared this view. There are some exceptions. For instance, we know that in England, in opposition to canon law, clergy could be called in civil law cases, even though this was not the case elsewhere in Western Europe. Generally, though, we assume that those clergy who had agreed to take on roles in parish churches saw themselves as clergy, maybe bad clergy, or negligent clergy or clergy who had extra-parochial aspirations, but still as clergy. This was not, however, always the case. This contribution examines the story of one man who committed both spiritual and physical murder. Putting this story in its broader context demonstrates the need for a reassessment of the relationship between secular and ecclesiastical law in late thirteenth-century England and highlights a set of records hitherto ignored.

On 12 November 1288, Thomas of Pontesbury, a priest, beat out the brains of John of St Edward, rector of Pulverbatch, in Shropshire, while he lay sleeping and then, to finish the job, broke his neck. The following day Thomas performed mass in that church, and, the day after that, he boldly climbed into the pulpit and told the parishioners that John had 'died'. Unfortunately for Thomas, there was at least one witness to the crime, and even before that witness had made his confession, Pulverbatch parish suspected Thomas of murder. The parish was in uproar, and the dead rector's wife (itself a challenging statement) and his family were outraged. Over the next three years, they tried to bring Thomas to justice, which he, in turn, tried to evade. He even claimed the murder accusation was malicious and tried to clear his name using the remedies of secular law. To complicate things, during this period, Thomas was accused of a second murder. Eventually, Thomas's case found its way to the ecclesiastical courts (despite the fact Thomas seems to have been unclear how that could and should happen). In these courts he was found innocent (by process of compurgation) of these felonies, but his 'innocence' was still formally contested by secular authority, and he was subject to secular sanctions for the rest of his life.

For those familiar with traditional narratives of clerical life in the thirteenth century, there is much in this story to raise eyebrows. The way to become a rector was not to kill the incumbent and then occupy his pulpit. And it is certainly unusual to find a rector with a legal wife (*not* a concubine) to pursue justice on behalf of her deceased husband. Additionally, if clergy were accused of capital crimes, the normal way forward for them was to claim benefit of clergy, moving them out of the secular and into ecclesiastical jurisdiction, with its much lighter penalties. Clergy had no good reason to engage in risky secular lawsuits which, potentially, would lead to the gallows. Finally, we are used to thinking that by this date the state accepted, even though a little grudgingly, the verdicts of the church courts regarding clerical felony, not that they made their own assessment and enforced their own secular penalties after the judgement of the ecclesiastical courts.

Thomas's case, his actions and choices allow us to see that not all men who described themselves – and were described – as rectors in parish churches considered themselves clergy. Some of them regarded themselves as laymen, for whom being a rector was an appointment with an income, which may or may not have anything to do with their career or way of life. Such worldviews were an additional obstacle to bishops' attempts to improve pastoral care and they deserve further study. This case also demonstrates that the late thirteenth-century English royal administration maintained their right to treat the secular property of clergy accused of felony as they would that of the laity, a point that historians have overlooked. Although this is one case, in a particular time and place, the similar conditions in medieval Western Europe,[2] and the Church's continued struggles to have its parish clergy comply with canon law, suggest that the lessons learnt here are relevant to historians of other places and times too.

Three and a half years after John's death, in May 1292, Master Thomas of Pontesbury,[3] as rector of Cranfield in Bedfordshire, stood accused of John's murder at the gaol delivery sessions at Bedford. His plea of benefit of clergy, and his release into clerical hands here, was the culmination of a case which had been going through the secular courts, in one form or another, since around April 1289.[4] As was usual from the mid-thirteenth century, the king's

2 On pastoral care across thirteenth-century Europe see, for example, Anthony Perron, 'Metropolitan Might and Papal Power on the Latin-Christian Frontier: transforming the Danish Church around the time of the Fourth Lateran Council', *The Catholic History Review*, 89 (2003), 197; Piotr Gorecki, 'Parishes, Tithes, and Society in Earlier Medieval Poland *c.* 1100–*c.* 1250', *Transactions of the American Philosophical Society*, 83 (1993), 53–4; Paul B. Pixton, *The German Episcopacy and the Implementation of the Fourth Lateran Council, 1216–1245* (1995), pp. 450–4. English and French bishops complained that clergy were hung before their status could be affirmed, and in Denmark and England the nature of compurgation caused concern: F. M. Powicke and C. R. Cheney (eds), *Councils & Synods with other documents relating to the English Church. Vol.2: 1205–1313* (2 parts, Oxford, 1964), II, 1122; W. A. Pantin, *Oxford Life in Oxford Archives* (Oxford, 1957), p. 57; Niels Skyum-Nielsen (ed.), *Diplomatarium Danicum*, series 1, vol. 5 (Copenhagen, 1957), no. 140; Gabel, *Benefit of Clergy in the Later Middle*, pp. 104–7; McHardy, 'Church Courts and Criminous Clerks', pp. 165–83; Jolanta N. Komornicka, *'Saisie du Temporel*: The Parlement of Paris and Ecclesiastical Jurisdiction in the Fourteenth Century', *Journal of the Western Society for French History*, 38 (2010), 29–46.

3 It should be noted at the outset that there are two men called Master Thomas of Pontesbury who can be found in Lincoln diocesan records. Both were rectors of Cranfield but the second took his degree in Oxford in the year that the Thomas discussed in this paper died: A. B. Emden, *A Biographical Register of the University of Oxford to 1500*, 3 vols (Oxford, 1957), III, 6–7.

4 At least according to Thomas's own assertions in Michaelmas 1291: TNA, KB 27/128, rot. 22d.

court gave Thomas up to the Church, but first exercised its right to 'decide the character' in which he was to be handed over, that is whether as a guilty or innocent man. First, therefore, it held an inquest of office into his guilt amongst the jurors and representatives of the four local townships assembled for this Bedford court. This was not a trial; officially, the trial was to be held by the Church, and would result either in Thomas being found of good reputation and freed, or losing his clerical status and being imprisoned for life.[5] For our purposes this part of the secular process is fortuitous, though, as it means that the 1292 court records report Thomas's story in detail.

On 12 November 1288, after dark, whilst most people slept, Thomas had left his rooms, carrying with him a large staff.[6] Accompanied by his clerk, who held a candle to light their path, he made his way to the hall where John of St Edward (also known as John Loverich)[7] was in bed, asleep. There Thomas, in a planned attack, hit John around the head from side to side, severely damaging his face and nose. When John tried to struggle up to defend himself, Thomas knocked him down by hitting him on the top of the head so hard that his brains spilled out. The staff broke during this beating, so Thomas finished his work with his hands, breaking John's neck. Then he carried the body back to his own rooms, washed it, and wrapped it in a shroud.[8] The next morning, having

5 R. H. Helmholz, *The Oxford History of the Laws of England Volume 1: The Canon Law and ecclesiastical jurisdiction from 597 to the 1640s* (Oxford, 2004), pp. 511–13.

6 In both the gaol delivery rolls for Bedford belonging to the two justices present (TNA, JUST 3/88, rot. 2; JUST 3/89, rot. 11) these events are dated 'on the Friday night immediately after the last Martinmas'. That cannot be right; that would place Thomas's crime in 1290 and he was arraigned before the court in 1289. The whole gaol delivery roll account is, though, full of small errors of the sort that suggest the clerk was copying information from an earlier document, one he only partially paid attention to as he adapted it. He is confused about whether Thomas committed his crime at his parish of Cranfield or in Pulverbatch for example, although the plea rolls are very clear that it was a crime committed in Shropshire. So, the dating in the roll was quite possibly taken directly from the original statement at Thomas's 1289 arraignment. The case first appears on the rolls with a return date of 3 November (the morrow of All Souls) 1289: KB 27/121, rot. 38. If we take this as the literal first appearance of the case, then the feast of St Martin in question cannot be that of 11 November. It would therefore be the 4 July feast of St Martin that is meant, giving a date of Friday 8 July for these events. However, in 1291 Thomas claimed that he was first brought before the King's Bench in Easter 1289: KB 27/128, rot. 22d. This suggests that these events can be dated to November 1288, which would be 12 November. That makes better sense of the claim that Thomas was working under cover of darkness, needing a candle to light his way.

7 Here he is described as the son of Henry of St Edward, but other court records make it clear that his father's name was Hugh. This is another of the small errors in this Bedford court record.

8 The detail of Thomas washing the body is a curious one. Possibly this was

sent his servants on various errands to get them out of the way, he buried the body before going to the nearby parish church of Pulverbatch (where John had been rector) and celebrating mass.

The following day was Sunday, and Thomas returned to the church. Here he celebrated mass again, for the gathered parishioners, and preached to them. He told them that John, whom he described in complimentary terms as strong and brave, had died on the Friday, and he read what he said was John's will out to them, with what the court record calls 'various bequests'. The implication is that some of those present discovered themselves to be beneficiaries, which was meant to soften their attitude to this sudden event. Some of the parishioners went to the parsonage house to pray for John's soul, expecting to find his body still there. Thomas remained in the church. He declared to those who stayed that because of John's death, he was now the rector and, when some of the congregation accused him of murdering John, he threatened to excommunicate them.[9]

The court record also notes that Thomas's clerk, who had accompanied him to hold his candle, and had witnessed the murder, had by 1292 confessed and abjured the realm. His confession explains the amount of detail the men of Bedfordshire provided about the crime.[10] But the court need never have heard this information at all. Previous to this hearing in Bedford, through 1289, 1290 and the first half of 1291, Thomas's case had appeared regularly before the King's Bench and had presumably been settled, even if only by

---

intended to emphasise that he – a man ordained to higher orders – had continued to handle blood, something circumscribed in Canon Law: Darryl W. Amundsen, 'Medieval Canon Law on medical and surgical practice by the Clergy', *Bulletin of the History of Medicine* 52 (1978), 42; R. H. Helmholz, 'Conflicts between Religious and Secular Law', *Cardozo Law Review* 12 (1991), pp. 717–18; Bettina Bildhauer, 'Medieval European conceptions of Blood: truth and human integrity', *Journal of the Royal Anthropological Institute* (2013), 559.

9 Possibly Thomas was being physically threatened at this point. Violence against the clergy brought automatic excommunication and the parishioners should have known that. Every year, English parish clergy were expected to read the list of these automatic excommunications (excommunications *lata sententia)* in their churches, and late medieval parish priests' handbooks record the list in English, for ease of comprehension by the listeners: *Councils & Synods* 2, II, 1089–90, 1195, 1275–7; Elisabeth Vodola, *Excommunication in the Middle Ages* (Berkeley, 1986), pp. 28–9; Lincoln, Lincoln Cathedral, MSS 66 and 229 for priests' handbooks of the fourteenth and early fifteenth century, including the general excommunication in English.

10 Those abjuring the kingdom had frequently taken sanctuary beforehand and were required to make a public confession of the circumstances of their crime before the church before leaving. Given that Thomas was rector of a Bedfordshire parish church, it is likely that his clerk made this confession in Bedfordshire.

lack of information provided, as it quietly vanishes in early 1291.[11] But then in Trinity 1291, instead of letting things lie, Thomas requested a writ of *odio et athia* – claiming that a malicious accusation of murder had been made against him – in this instance by Hugh of St Edward, father of the murdered John.[12] In Michaelmas 1291, Hugh defended himself against Thomas's claim that he, abetted by Laurentia, described in the king's court records as John's wife, had made a malicious presentment.[13]

Hugh asked to be allowed to prove his innocence on inquisition (a standard process in these cases) and he and Thomas were ordered to appear before the courts at Easter. This appearance never happened because, by 17 December 1291, Thomas seems to have found it prudent to take sanctuary in his church of Cranfield, where he was not being well treated by the parishioners: they were said to be threatening him and refusing to bring him food.[14] Oliver Sutton, bishop of Lincoln, wrote to the archdeacon of Bedford's official and the local

[11] In Michaelmas 1289 Thomas appeared accused of murder and claimed benefit of clergy – at this point claiming that he was under the jurisdiction of the archdeacon of Westminster – but he was not claimed by the archdeacon in the given fifteen days, so the case continued before the King's Bench. In Hilary and Easter 1290 the case was put in respite and a date given in the next term. It is in Trinity 1290 that we first hear that Laurentia daughter of Robert de Wotton had accused Thomas to the court. In Michaelmas 1290 Thomas Morel, representing the abbot of Ramsey (the abbey were patrons of Thomas's Bedfordshire church of Cranfield), was meant to appear against Thomas in a plea of trespass (felonies were all trespasses – though not all trespasses were felonies – so it is entirely possible that the abbey was pursuing the same, not a parallel, case against Thomas. See Pollock and Maitland, *The History of English Law*, II, 472). Morel did not attend, and Thomas and his pledges were put in mercy. In Hilary 1291, the sheriff of Shropshire was instructed to hold an inquisition. In Easter 1291 the case appears again (under Shropshire) where Richard de Beretevill appeared against Thomas for the king. Again, the case was put in respite for lack of witnesses, although Thomas appeared in person: TNA, KB 27/121, rot. 38; KB 27/122, rot. 29d; KB 27/123, rot. 23d; KB 27/124, rot. 26; KB 27/125, rot. 21; KB 27/126, rot. 46; KB 27/127, rot. 52. I am grateful to Dr Paul Dryburgh and Dr David Crook for their advice on these records.

[12] He put in his place Nicholas de Redimel, William Brettevill and Robert Bovey: TNA, KB 27/128, rot. 22d.

[13] It is at this point that we see Thomas claiming that he was presented by Laurentia in Easter 1289. On the same day, Thomas presented Beatrice, wife of the said Hugh, and one Geoffrey Rouland for the same crime, but they did not appear: TNA, KB 27/129, rot. 44.

[14] If Thomas had been in sanctuary for more than forty days – as he could well have been after a case in Trinity 1291 – the parishioners were entirely within their rights to try to starve him out of sanctuary: Helmholz, *The Ius Commune in England,* p. 61; idem, *Oxford History of the Laws of England*, pp. 55–6. Sutton shows no concern with how long he had been there, and at least one clergyman during Sutton's episcopate,

rural dean (both of whom answered to Sutton, since Bedford was in the diocese of Lincoln) to complain about the parishioners' hostility towards their rector who was described as having taken refuge from an unfair accusation of murder. This, Sutton said, was to stop, even if achieving that meant that the whole parish had to be excommunicated.[15] The parishioners were, however, clearly obdurate as, in January 1292, the bishop was once again writing about events at Cranfield. This time he addressed the church's patrons, Ramsey Abbey, and agreed, at their request, to suspend the sentence of excommunication which had been declared against the parish, and to carry out a fuller inquiry into events.[16] What Thomas had hoped to gain from taking sanctuary is not clear, but if he feared that the murder accusation was coming back to bite him, he was correct. Requiring Hugh to prove his innocence by inquisition meant that Hugh gathered a jury of men living locally to him, who knew of these events and would have to consider the veracity of those claims once again. As a result of his ill-judged challenge of John's father, five months later, in May 1292, he was back before the secular courts, facing the justices at Bedford.

At this point Thomas wisely sought benefit of clergy and was claimed by the bishop's representative. A clergyman in this position in the thirteenth century would usually expect to make compurgation and then return to their parishes, cleared of their crime. There might be some delay in making compurgation – some clergy complained of spending months or even years in the bishop's prison awaiting their opportunity – but their path after that was usually smooth.[17] Even after being claimed in the bishop's name, however, things did not run smoothly for Thomas. That Michaelmas, he found himself at another secular hearing, this time in Shropshire, now being accused of the murder of another man, Stephen son of William le Champeneys of Doddington.[18] We have no background to the case but since Doddington is less than thirty miles from Pulverbatch, the two cases could have been related. Thomas again pleaded benefit of clergy and was handed over as a clerk, this time to the archdeacon of Shropshire, acting on behalf of the bishop of Coventry and Lichfield, in whose diocese Doddington lay, and once again, he was given over to the bishop's men with the secular opinion that he was guilty.

For this Shropshire case, Thomas was required to make a second compurgation. But very soon he also needed to make a third. Pulverbatch, although close to Doddington, lay in a different diocese, the diocese of Hereford. Although Thomas did not, in law, hold a benefice in that diocese (that is he

---

in Oxfordshire, took sanctuary for over five months: Karl Shoemaker, *Sanctuary and Crime in the Middle Ages, 400–1500* (New York, 2011), p. 125.

15 Hill (ed.), *Reg. Sutton*, III, 172–3.

16 *ibid.*, 181. It is not clear if Thomas was still claiming sanctuary at this date.

17 Helmholz, *Oxford History of the Laws of England*, pp. 518–19.

18 TNA, JUST 1/741, rot. 47d.

had not been properly presented or instituted according to canon law), he had *claimed* to be rector of Pulverbatch after he had murdered John. This made the parish of Pulverbatch's position difficult. Thomas was not legally rector; killing one's predecessor was no way to gain a benefice. But for the bishop's administration to remove Thomas would have been difficult. The bishop's legal authority over a man he was claiming was not a clergyman in his diocese would have been questionable and the dispute would in any case have required a protracted court case, which Thomas could have dragged out simply by refusing to attend, leaving Pulverbatch without a legitimate clergyman.[19] The bishop of Hereford's administration found a path of compromise. Thomas undertook compurgation in the diocese for John of St Edward's murder and was cleared. A document was issued in the name of Bishop Richard Swinfield of Hereford, which declared that Thomas, described as rector of Pulverbatch, had made that successful compurgation and proved himself of good reputation, and thus requested the return of Thomas's secular property by the king on this account.[20] At the same time, Thomas gave up any claim to the benefice of Pulverbatch in favour of one Owen of Montgomery.[21] The diocese of Hereford thus achieved its end of obtaining a legitimate rector for Pulverbatch.

By mid-June of that year, then, Thomas had completed compurgations in every diocese which could claim an interest in his recent conduct and so, in theory, he was a free man.[22] He had been found innocent; he was able to hold benefices, act as a clergyman and to receive back his secular property. In getting that secular property released, however, he encountered distinct reluctance on the part of royal administration. On 11 June, King Edward I wrote to the sheriff and coroners of Shropshire informing them that the bishop of Coventry and Lichfield had notified him of Thomas's successful compurgation there. But before Thomas's temporal goods were returned to him, as the bishop had requested, Edward instructed that a secular inquisition into

19 Whether this also meant without pastoral care is unclear. The church was not wealthy and neither John nor Thomas was a resident, working rector. Vicars could substitute for absentee rectors, but no vicar or chaplain however is mentioned in the administrative or court records. If there was a vacancy for a vicar, the lack of a rector could itself have prevented it being filled – vicarages were usually in the gift of the rector. In 1239, the Papal Legate Otto had noted that disputes over rectories could leave parishioners' souls uncared for: *Councils & Synods* 2, I, 249–50.

20 William W. Capes (ed.), *Registrum Ricardi de Swinfield episcopi Herefordensis A.D. MCCLXXXIII–MCCCXVII*, Cantilupe Society and Canterbury and York Society, 6 (1909), p. 297. The document is undated, but it was probably issued around the same time as the January 1293 document by which Thomas gave up any right to Pulverbatch.

21 Capes (ed.), *Reg. Swinfield*, pp. 287–8.

22 The compurgations in the dioceses of Lincoln and Coventry and Lichfield are noted in Edward I's instructions to the sheriffs of 9 and 11 June: TNA, C 144/8, no. 23; C 145/54, no. 36.

Thomas's reputation in this matter should be carried out in Shropshire. The dorse of the document declares that this secular inquisition found Thomas innocent.[23] Things went rather differently in the diocese of Lincoln. On 9 June 1293, Edward I wrote to the sheriff and coroners of Bedfordshire about Thomas's compurgation before the bishop of Lincoln for John's murder in much the same terms. Here, however, Thomas was less successful. The secular inquisition was delayed until just after Michaelmas of that year, and when it was made, Thomas was declared to be guilty by twelve men whose surnames suggest that they were largely from the Cranfield area.[24] Edward refused to return Thomas's goods,[25] although Thomas kept his benefice of Cranfield until his death, which happened sometime before 17 December 1295.[26]

Thomas's story is a complicated one. Just as these events challenged his contemporaries, so they challenge us as historians. They raise important questions about what it might mean to be a parish clergyman in the thirteenth century, in the eyes of both the clergy themselves and the law. If for a moment we focus on the main section of the story, John of St Edward's murder, it raises particularly interesting questions. Thomas does not behave as a rector accused of a felony might be expected to. This was a crime by a clergyman, whose trial could have been expected to start with an accusation in the secular courts, but then to move very quickly under the Church's jurisdiction. In fact, this case was almost entirely settled in the king's court. Finding clergy in the records of the King's Bench, and other secular English medieval courts is not unusual. Clergy often found themselves in the secular courts as plaintiffs and defendants in cases where their opponents could sometimes be groups which included other clerics, this might happen, in civil law pleas of trespass or debt, for example. The relationship between laws of Church and State could be complex and some clergymen certainly benefited from pursuing secular rather than ecclesiastical justice.[27] But a felony with a clerk as defendant should not

23 TNA, C 144/8, no. 23.

24 TNA, C 145/54, no. 36.

25 Thomas's temporal goods, valued at £24 14s. 11d., continued to be demanded by the king well into the fourteenth century from Ramsey Abbey, the patrons of Cranfield. Ramsey declared there were no goods. Bishop Sutton, however, thought in 1291 that the parishioners of Cranfield were holding them, and Thomas certainly had immoveable property in the diocese of Lincoln: in February 1289 he admitted that he owed William de Holecook, clerk, sixteen marks which were to be levied from Thomas's Lincoln lands. So perhaps the Crown's persistence was justified: W. H. Hart (ed.), *Cartularium monasterii de Rameseia*, 3 vols (London, 1884–93), III, 31–4; *CCR 1288–96*, pp. 34, 341, 343; *CCR 1296–1302*, p. 371; Hill (ed.), *Reg. Sutton,* III, 172.

26 This was when his successor, John de Wistow, was instituted. The benefice was vacant because of Thomas's death: Hill (ed.), *Reg. Sutton,* VIII, 116.

27 Komornicka, *'Saisie du Temporel'*, 43–6; Philippa M. Hoskin, 'Church, State and Law: solutions to lay contumacy in the Anglo-Scottish borders during the later

have been tried in the king's courts without ecclesiastical intervention. We might think that this was Thomas's misfortune. He tried in the early part of the case to claim benefit of clergy, naming the archdeacon of Westminster as his ordinary – that is, as the ecclesiastical official who had jurisdiction over him.[28] For reasons that are not clear, the archdeacon did not claim him – it is also unclear why he thought the archdeacon had the authority to do so – and so the case remained before King's Bench.[29] Thomas's first instinct had been to present himself as a clergyman, which we might expect. Perhaps this discouraged him from seeking similar protection from a more relevant bishop. Left to the mercy of the secular courts we might even accept that the case was tried – and eventually died – there. What we would not expect is that Thomas would request the writ *odio et athia*. This strategy was that of a layman not a cleric.

By requesting this writ, pursuing this as a secular case, Thomas shows us that John's murder was certainly part of a secular quarrel which appears to us in the guise of a dispute about ecclesiastical preferment.[30] Thomas's and John's rivalry was, then, part of tensions between the Pontesbury and St Edward families. The writ *de odio et athia* was used in long-standing disputes; it was intended to call an end to repeated, unfounded accusations made by an opposing party, and played a role in feuding by litigation.[31] That Thomas risked bringing renewed attention to the case through such a writ, when he

---

thirteenth century', *Historical Research* 84 (2011), 559–69; G. B. Flahiff, 'The writ of prohibition to court Christian in the 13th century', *Medieval Studies* 6 (1944), 261–313.

28 TNA, KB 27/121, rot. 38.

29 The archdeacon of Westminster did have authority over several churches in Westminster's possession and could have claimed their rectors from the secular courts to be tried in his own jurisdiction. There is no evidence that Thomas was a rector of any Westminster benefice or had any other connection to the abbey (I am grateful to Dr Matthew Payne, archivist of Westminster abbey, for his help with this). Thomas had a poor grasp of the way in which the Church worked, and he may simply have claimed help from the wrong jurisdiction.

30 Although disputes over presentations to benefices could be parts of advowson cases (N. Adams and C. Donahue (eds), *Select Cases from the Ecclesiastical Courts of the Province of Canterbury c. 1200–1301* (Selden Society, 1981), p. 76) this case was not. In 1291, when Philip Marmion, head of his family died, the advowson was firmly in their family's hands. The most recent dispute was in 1268, and was settled amicably: *CIPM*, III, nos 29, 279; *CCR 1288–96*, pp. 262, 265, 269, 270; *CFR 1272–1307*, pp. 303, 367; Robert Eyton, *Antiquities of Shropshire*, 12 vols (London, 1854–60), VI, 203.

31 Elizabeth Papp Kamali, *Felony and the Guilty Mind in Medieval England* (Cambridge 2019), p. 109; Warren C. Brown, *Violence in Medieval England* (London, 2014), pp. 212–13; Paul Hyams, *Rancour and Reconciliation* (Ithaca, New York, 2003), pp. 175–181, 246–8. I am grateful to Dr Nicholas Karn for conversations about this writ.

could have walked quietly away from the court, suggests the depth of hostility between the families. Thomas was not just accepting his accusers' defeat but trying to drive it home by counterattack in the courts. We have no idea how a quarrel between the St Edward and Pontesbury families began, or how it had proceeded before John's murder. What is clear, though, is that the spheres of influence of the two families, secular and spiritual, were geographically close. The St Edward family's landed base was in Wootton in Bedfordshire.[32] Wootton was only five miles from Cranfield, where Thomas held his legitimate benefice. At the same time, Thomas's known secular property, and his family name, place him in Pontesbury,[33] only five miles from Pulverbatch, where John of St Edward was rector at his death, and within thirty miles of Whitton, where the lords of the manor were the Wudeton family. Robert de Wudeton was the father of John's wife Laurentia.[34]

There were ample opportunities for the families to clash. In 1291, Thomas misjudged. Too confident after escaping justice, he tried to press home his advantage against the St Edward family, but in doing so made himself vulnerable again to the secular courts. By accusing members of the St Edward family of making malicious accusations, he started a procedure where Hugh of St Edward would claim his right to have the accusation against him considered by a local jury, that is, by men who knew him in the local Bedford area. This meant that men in Hugh's own area of influence would not only have to assess the accusation against Hugh but – of necessity – to offer an opinion on again on whether Thomas had murdered John. Thomas was also someone

32 In the thirteenth century they held a fee there. We can see several generations of the family making small land grants to a local religious house, Newnham Priory, and appearing in small disputes with their secular neighbours. In the late thirteenth century, Hugh of St Edward appeared before the local coroner at Bedford, with a William Freman of Wootton, to request the enforcing of the peace against William Astel, also of Wootton, who was threatening to burn down his property, while John de Enesley and Master Walter de Covelye can also be found waging peace to the same Hugh. The family also undertook some local royal service. In 1301 a Hugh of St Edward was keeper of the king's goshawks in Bedford: *CCR 1261–4,* p. 206; Joyce Godber (ed.), *The Cartulary of Newnham priory,* 2 vols, Bedfordshire Historical Society, 42–3 (1963–4), II, nos 467, 480; Charles Gross (ed.), *Select Cases from the Coroners' Rolls A.D.1265–1314* (Selden Society 9, 1896 for 1895), pp. 35–6; R. F. Hunnisett, *Bedfordshire Coroners' Rolls*, Bedfordshire Historical Record Society 41 (1961), pp. 93–4; *CCR 1302–7*, p. 386.

33 TNA, CP 25/1/193/6, no. 33, Westminster, 18 November 1290, by which Agnes Bundy admitted a messuage in Shrewsbury (eight miles from Pontesbury) to be the property of Master Thomas of Pontesbury, in return for which she received one sparrowhawk.

34 Eyton, *Antiquities of Shropshire*, VII, 65. A Robert de Wudeton was also one of the assessors for the tenth in Shropshire in 1233: *CPR 1232–47*, p. 18.

they knew as rector of Cranfield, and they were clearly conversant with events in Pulverbatch. Unsurprisingly this led to a fresh accusation against Thomas, an accusation that could have been avoided.[35]

Even then, Thomas continued to act with the instincts of a layman. A fresh accusation, before the sheriff of Bedfordshire, was a new chance to claim benefit of clergy. In fact, while he did turn to the protection of the Church, he did only what any English layman could have done, he took sanctuary. Only when sanctuary failed him, and he found himself at the Bedford gaol delivery sessions of May 1292, did Thomas claim benefit of clergy again. From then on, he made use of, and engaged with, the ecclesiastical courts. He claimed benefit of clergy again later in 1292 when tried for murder in Shropshire, and he negotiated the difficulties of his position in the diocese of Hereford with the episcopal administration there.

In cases where the parish clergy so clearly considered themselves members of secular families, including turning to the secular law to solve their problems, it is unsurprising that their relationship to pastoral care in their parishes was problematic. Men such as Thomas and John did not identify primarily as servants of the Church and officers of the spiritual realm; neither could have been ideal parish clergymen. Bishops would not have found it easy to guide men whose obligations to their parishes were not something they ignored but something that, as laymen, or principally laymen, they considered inconsequential. In 1215, the canons of the Fourth Lateran Council had reaffirmed the Church's obligation to the souls of all those in its care. Pastoral care, it said (quoting Gregory the Great) was the 'art of arts'. Bishops must ensure that their parish clergy were suitably educated, and present in their parishes, performing their spiritual duties and providing examples of a good and upright life to their parishioners.[36]

These were not new ideals, but they reaffirmed the Western Church's position. They were not, however, easy to implement universally. Throughout thirteenth-century Europe, national Churches failed to provide the pastoral care

35 Thomas's miscalculation here is hard to understand. At the very beginning of the case the hearing was transferred from Bedfordshire to Shropshire, and it was delayed more than once for lack of local engagement: TNA, KB 27/121, rot. 38; KB 27/125, rot. 21; KB 27/127 rot. 52. Perhaps Thomas had become overconfident because of this and had overlooked the fact that any inquisition concerning an accusation against Hugh would be held where the St Edward family had most influence, in Bedfordshire. This would be a serious misjudgement and would overlook a simple part of the court's process. However, since Thomas's reaction to a dispute over a benefice had been murder, rather than litigation, his conflict resolution skills and his grasp of the legal implications of his actions were clearly not advanced.

36 Norman P. Tanner, *Decrees of the Ecumenical Councils* (Washington D.C., 2016), I, 235–40, 242–50, 253.

that Lateran IV set out as an aspiration.[37] There continued to be clergy who held more than one church at a time (either because of poverty or greed) or who aspired to high level clerical careers that involved travel, and for those reasons did not reside in their parishes. A lack of more than a basic education led to parish clergy whose understanding of the Bible and the sacraments, and whose ability to preach, scarcely reached the necessary level to serve their parishes.[38]

The immediate dispute leading to John's murder was, as we have seen, over a benefice with cure of souls, where the rector's prime focus should have been working to save the souls of his parishioners, through the administration of the sacraments and the example of a good life. Yet compromises needed to be made, and canon law allowed a rector who was reluctant to serve his parish church in person to nominate a properly qualified substitute, termed a vicar, to do that duty on his behalf. Thomas was a pluralist with no desire to be a resident rector in a small parish church,[39] even though in 1288 he used the performance of mass at Pulverbatch – the work of the resident clergyman – as a statement of his authority there.[40] He may, however, still have been a better pastoral option than Pulverbatch already had in John of St Edward.

If Thomas was no parish clergyman in terms of character, conduct and ambition, and very possibly no priest, John was no clergyman at all. He was not, at his death, even in higher orders, and what we know of him demonstrates

37 Perron, 'Metropolitan Might and Papal Power on the Latin-Christian Frontier', 197; Gorecki, 'Parishes, Tithes, and Society in Earlier Medieval Poland', 53–4; Pixton, *The German Episcopacy and the Implementation of the Fourth Lateran Council*, pp. 450–4.

38 See J. R. H. Moorman, *Church Life in England in the Thirteenth Century* (Oxford, 1941), p. 30 and H. G. Richardson, 'The Parish Clergy of the Thirteenth and Fourteenth Centuries', *TRHS*, 3rd series, 6 (1912), 124–5 for the clergy as ill-educated. See Jeffrey H. Denton, 'The Competence of the Parish Clergy in Thirteenth-Century England', in Caroline M. Barron and Jenny Stratford (eds), *The Church and Learning in Later Medieval Society: Essays in Honour of R. B. Dobson* (Stamford, 1999), pp. 273–85 and William Dohar, 'Sufficienter Litteratus: clerical examination and instruction for the cure of souls', in Jacqueline Brown and William P. Stoneman (eds), *A Distinct Voice: medieval studies in honor of Leonard E. Boyle* (Notre Dame, Indiana, 1997), pp. 313–17, as a partial challenge to this.

39 As we have already seen, he not only held the church of Cranfield but was eager to obtain the rectory of Pulverbatch.

40 Another interesting hint here is that sacraments may have been carried out by people not in proper orders. We know this happened with confession as the Council of London notes the problem (*Councils & Synods* 2, I, 250). There is no reason to think that Thomas was ordained priest at the time of John's murder, although he was in higher orders.

that he had no intention of a clerical career of any sort. He was familiar to the people of Pulverbatch certainly, but then his wife was a member of one of their local prominent families and he died in the parish, so he certainly spent time in the area. His murder was brought to the attention of the court by his wife, Laurentia,[41] and, as we have already seen, she was not the sort of woman who would have entered a dubious marriage and whom the Church would have called a concubine.[42] She was from a family of minor gentry, her marriage would have been a matter of careful negotiation; this was a legitimate marriage recognised by the courts. John was the type of quasi-clergy man we glimpse from time to time in medieval England, who were amongst the pluralists and absentees often thought of as career clergy. They held rectories without being ordained, for their monetary value, without even a long-term nominal career in the Church planned.[43] Although John's place in the parish could, and should, have been filled by a vicar – a properly ordained and resident

41 TNA, KB 27/124, rot. 26.

42 What the church called a concubine the parish clergy may well have considered legitimate wives, but these were not women from families like Laurentia's: Ruth Mazo Karras, *Unmarriages: men, women and sexual unions in the Middle Ages* (Philadelphia, 2012), pp. 118–22.

43 In 1245, the monastic chronicler Matthew Paris noted that one John de Gatesdene was knighted at Christmas following his recent marriage. Now that he was a married man and a knight, he resigned all his rich benefices. As Paris says, with obvious approval, he 'gave up the danger of the cure of souls and was advanced to the level of the higher nobles'. This seems to have been perfectly acceptable. There is no suggestion that a man ordained only to lower orders (he cannot have been in higher orders if he was able to marry) had done wrong in holding benefices with cure of souls. In about 1240, a roll of *sede vacante* actions by the archdeacons in the vacancies between the episcopates of Hugh of Lincoln and Hugh of Wells and those of Hugh of Wells and Grosseteste, was drawn up. Amongst the entries in it is the institution of Richard of Healing to the church of Healing, Lincolnshire, dating from the start of the thirteenth century. The 1240 scribe described Richard as 'now a knight' (*nunc miles*). He was probably a member of the family that held the manor and the patronage of the church of Healing. Presumably, at this point he had taken up his secular role and no longer needed the benefice income. However, for several years the parish had been in the hands of a man who had no long-term commitment to the cure of souls. Careful reading of earlier bishops' rolls and registers reveals several rectors who take their positions agreeing to resign in circumstances which include their marriages. That is probably a standard form of words, but the inclusion of marriage demonstrates that it was a possible move for a man with a rectory. All these rectors had not been ordained to higher orders: *Chronica Majora,* IV, 403; LA, Dij/62/1/1a, printed in C. W. Foster, 'Institutions to Benefices in the Diocese of Lincoln', *AASRP* 39 (1928), 186; Philippa M. Hoskin (ed.), *Robert Grosseteste as bishop of Lincoln: the Episcopal Rolls 1235–1253*, LRS, Kathleen Major Series of Medieval Records 1 (Woodbridge, 2017).

priest – there is no sign of such a man in the contemporary telling of John's murder. Vicars could disappear from the official records, but when Thomas twice performed mass in the church after John's death, including on a Sunday, he was not challenged by any other resident clergyman. For John, Pulverbatch was a source of income, not a place to exercise pastoral responsibility.

If individual clergymen could regard themselves primarily as laymen rather than clerks, it is unsurprising to see the king's courts sharing this view. Whilst by the thirteenth century they had acknowledged the rights of the criminous clerk to escape capital punishment by being tried under ecclesiastical law, it is interesting to observe here that Edward I's courts had not abandoned all their authority over clerical felons.[44] We could read this as a pushing back against the Church's authority. When the secular courts handed a clerk to the bishop's men and said that he was guilty of a felony, they knew that the bishop's courts would probably find the clerk innocent. And they were aware of how many rectors were not ordained clergy, and hence they saw no problem with describing a man like Thomas as rector but trying him as a layman. In the fourteenth century it would become possible for clergy not to be able to clear themselves by compurgation if they were publicly and notoriously defamed (which we may think Thomas was) but in the thirteenth century they could not expect this.[45] This, as well as a feeling that all clergy accused of felonies were escaping justice, may have fuelled their determination to assess every man's guilt by English law. They might not be able to hang a criminous clerk, but they could seize his property on the basis of a judgement by the secular courts.[46]

44 More research in these overlooked records at TNA is necessary to see whether Henry III also used this process. However, given Edward I's administration's ability to adapt and develop legal process it would not be surprising if this was their innovation: Gwilym Dodd, *Justice and Grace: Private Petitioning and the English Parliament in the Late Middle Ages* (Oxford, 2007), pp. 20–4; Michael Prestwich, *Edward I* (New Haven, 2008), pp. 267–98.

45 This was the case both for the notoriously defamed and for those who confessed: which Thomas was clearly not willing to do: Ralph Pugh, *Imprisonment in Medieval England* (Cambridge, 1968), p. 49; Sara M. Butler, *Pain, Penance and Process: peine forte et dure in Medieval England* (Cambridge, 2022), p. 56.

46 English kings had long expressed their opposition to the consecration of a bishop they disapproved of by withholding the temporal property of that bishopric – asserting their authority over the bishop as secular lord – even while they could play no part in an episcopal election. In 1244 the diocese of Chichester had elected Richard Wich as its bishop; the pope had approved this through his grant of the pallium to Wich, leading to his consecration by the archbishop of Canterbury. Henry III had opposed this election and he expressed this by refusing to induct Wich into the bishop's secular property until 1246: D. Jones, *St Richard of Chichester, the sources for his life*, Sussex Record Society (1995), pp. 173, 175–6.

During a trial for felony, the accused's property was seized by the state, but then returned if they were found innocent.[47] When a cleric had undertaken successful compurgation, his bishop would write to the king requesting the return of his secular property, as the secular courts would request the return of the property of any of the laity found innocent of a felony.[48] But just as the Church ignored the State's judgement when it received an accused clergyman and proceeded to compurgation, so Edward I's administration now ignored the judgement of the Church. It proceeded to trial by secular process again – through a local inquisition – and the return of the clergyman's property became dependent upon the decision in that secular arena. This was no meaningless process: in this case, although Thomas regains his property in Shropshire, where the secular inquisition agrees he is innocent, the Crown refuses him the right to any Bedfordshire property he has because of the findings of the sheriff's inquisition there. Thomas is one of many surviving examples of this royal exertion of authority, whose records survive in The National Archives, and which have not received careful consideration.

Thomas's is a story which challenges what we know about the appointment of clergy, how rectors viewed their roles, and the treatment of criminous clerks by the State. How could a man think he could claim a rectory by murdering the rector? How could the murdered rector be legitimately married? How could the State ignore the Church's decisions in the case of criminous clerks and inflict secular penalties even on clerks found innocent? But if these things look to us like obstacles, then perhaps we have misunderstood the progress of ecclesiastical reform, the nature of the clerical caste and the relationship between Church and State in thirteenth-century England. Some rectors, even those with cure of souls and responsibilities for undertaking duty in their parishes, were still essentially lay, not just in character, but also in attitude and outlook: they were not merely men who saw the Church as a career involving no active involvement in any parish duties they might obtain, they had no interest in the Church at all. Married men like John could accept or retain rectories, and men ordained to higher orders like Thomas could pursue cases through the secular courts, not because they ignored their duties and their obligations to their bishops, but because these duties were ones they simply did not prioritise, and their relationship with the Church was not their main concern.

These attitudes need to be part of our assessment of episcopal struggles to enforce medieval pastoral care in England, and possibly also beyond. While the Church had been unable to create a committed clerical body, late

[47] Pollock and Maitland, *History of English Law,* II, 466.

[48] See for example Bishop Swinfield on behalf of Thomas: Capes (ed.), *Reg. Swinfield*, p. 297.

thirteenth-century royal administration was taking an active interest in, and had extended its claims over, clerical criminality further than has been noticed. Edward I could not force the Church to accept a secular court's judgement of a clerk's guilt. The king could, however, refuse to accept the Church's judgement of a clerk's innocence in so much as he could confiscate and retain a clerk's secular property, in direct opposition to the judgement of the Church courts. Thomas's is an unusual and unusually complicated case, and we might at least hope that serial murderers were rare amongst the medieval clergy. But in the way he regarded his relationship to the Church, he may not have been unusual. His story has a broader significance, because it challenges us to look from another angle at challenges to the Church's authority, not from rulers and lords but at a parish level, and through the actions, not of the laity, but of its own clergy.

6

Indomitable Countesses: Katherine Swynford, Alice de Lacy and Resistance to the Crown[1]

DAVID STOCKER

Nicholas Bennett has been a significant influence for good in the historical life of Lincoln and Lincolnshire for as long as I can remember. When I first came to the city in 1980, he was the key figure in Lincolnshire Archives to consult about those tricky archival problems that accompany all historical work. Somewhat later I found that Nicholas also wrote, in a lively, stimulating and revealing fashion, about the documents in his charge – nowhere better than in his wonderful history of the Lincoln Record Society,[2] *an organisation that he has served with great distinction for forty years. Latterly he has been a worthy successor to Canon Foster himself as the Honorary General Editor. The following paper – linking Nicholas' beloved Cathedral Close with wider national politics around 1400 – was first given in 2015, at one of the many conferences he organised (alongside his indomitable wife Carol) as part of Lincoln Cathedral Library's programme of public outreach, another cause in which Nicholas has played a fundamental role. It is offered as a sincere tribute to a great Lincolnshire scholar, and to a good friend.*

Both Alison Weir and Jeanette Lucraft have written about the 'huge influence' on modern perceptions of Katherine Swynford exerted by the publishing

1 I would like to express my gratitude, firstly, to Nicholas Bennett himself, who encouraged me to write about this topic in the first place, and to Marianne Wilson, who saw an early draft of the paper and continued the encouragement. Since then I have been given very useful specific guidance by Professor Louise Wilkinson and Professor Jocelyn Wogan-Browne, who both suggested important avenues for further research.

2 N. H. Bennett, *Wonderful to Behold. A Centenary History of The Lincoln Record Society 1910–2010*, LRS 100 (Woodbridge, 2010).

sensation that is Anya Seton's *Katherine*.[3] Nevertheless, despite exhaustive studies, both writers – as well as Anthony Goodman[4] – have struggled to find a convincing historical figure behind Seton's romantic heroine. Lucraft draws attention to Katherine's exploitation of heraldry as evidence that she was well able to assert her personal identity. This detail exemplifies Katherine's capacity to 'play the game'; it is evidence that she had the necessary skills and accomplishments of diplomacy, learning and personality, Lucraft supposes, to convince John of Gaunt that she could be a credible wife for him, and not just a discrete mistress.[5] Following their marriage in 1396, at Lincoln Cathedral, Katherine used a similar range of skills to establish herself as the leading woman amongst the respectable ladies at court – as required by her new position as duchess of Lancaster after that date. Whilst agreeing that Katherine Swynford was no mere 1950s romantic heroine – lost without her man – the intention behind this paper is to expand this revisionist view of Katherine. It explores the evidence that, following her marriage to John of Gaunt, and particularly after his death in 1399, she continued to demonstrate a strong and independent political personality.

In fact, neither Lucraft nor Weir have much to say about Katherine following her marriage. Documentary sources for her life after 1396 are not extensive, and consequently neither writer does much to dispel the obfuscation of 'deep, unexpectant peace' that Seton supposed descended between 1396 and her death in 1403.[6] Both Lucraft and Weir observe that, as the consort of John of Gaunt between 1396 and 1399, Katherine evidently overcame the initial hostility of the senior women at Richard II's court. Despite their initial opposition to her, Katherine was entrusted with the most sensitive of public roles, appropriate to her status.[7] But both writers also believe that any political influence Katherine might have had between their marriage in 1396 and John of Gaunt's death in 1399 was due entirely to Gaunt's unrivalled position. Furthermore, not unlike Seton, both Weir and Lucraft also suggest that, after Gaunt's death in 1399, Katherine 'retired' into a sort of eremitical existence, disappearing from the

3 A. Seton, *Katherine* (London, 1974); J. Lucraft, *Katherine Swynford. The History of a Medieval Mistress* (Stroud, 2006); A. Weir, *Katherine Swynford. The Story of John of Gaunt and his Scandalous Duchess* (London, 2008).

4 A. Goodman, *Katherine Swynford* (Lincoln, 1994); idem, *Katherine Swynford: Honourable Lady or She-Devil?* (Honywood Papers 5, 2004); idem, *'My Most Illustrious Mother, the Lady Katherine': Katherine Swynford and her daughter Joan* (Lincoln, 2008); idem, *The Enigmatic Philippa Chaucer: Katherine Swynford's Sister* (Honywood Papers 9, 2013).

5 Lucraft, *Katherine Swynford*, chapter 5, pp. 133, 136.

6 Seton, *Katherine*, p. 574.

7 G. Brereton, trans & ed., *Froissart Chronicles* (Harmondsworth, 1978), pp. 418–19.

historical record as a personality completely, and becoming a vowess in the Lincoln Cathedral Close waiting for death.

This paper proposes that this is an unsatisfactory picture of Katherine's final years. It suggests that contemporary perceptions of Katherine after her husband's death were very different, and that she made a dramatic and independent political statement in 1399, that was entirely commensurate with her role as a powerful dowager duchess of Lancaster, and, importantly in the more local context, as a countess of Lincoln. It also offers evidence that Katherine may not have simply faded away in 1399, following Gaunt's death, but that she continued to exercise significant political influence in her own right.

John of Gaunt died at Leicester Castle on 3 February 1399. Katherine – who attended the deathbed – followed the hearse, accompanied by their son Henry Beaufort (recently installed as bishop of Lincoln), in a great public procession from Leicester to St Paul's Cathedral, London, for burial there on 16 March.[8] This great spectacle was probably similar to that organised in the following year by Henry Bolingbroke, when Richard II's body was brought from Pontefract to London to be viewed by the masses and then taken on to King's Langley in Hertfordshire for burial.[9] But then, as far as we can tell, Katherine left London immediately after Gaunt's burial for Lincoln – perhaps on 17 March. On 18 March, Richard II's special commission announced that the Crown had seized Gaunt's entire estate. Surely Katherine's rapid departure was contrary to his expectations? Richard would have found it helpful, politically, to have a compliant dowager duchess at his side when announcing the Crown's seizure. Surely leaving the court at this critical political moment can only be seen as a dramatic and symbolic act of political resistance on Katherine's part. Furthermore, Katherine was publicly known to have been on good terms with her stepson Henry Bolingbroke, John of Gaunt's heir,[10] and that connection can only have underscored the political message of her hasty departure and must have deepened Richard's concerns about her loyalty.

Katherine's destination might also have been viewed as a significant political gesture. She could have gone anywhere on 17 March, taking her pick of the most comfortable and lavish accommodation in England – Hertford Castle, Kenilworth Castle, Leicester Castle, Pontefract Castle or Tutbury Castle, all places within the duchy of Lancaster where someone at her social zenith

8 A. Goodman, *John of Gaunt. The Exercise of Princely Power in Fourteenth-Century Europe* (London, 1992), pp. 168–9.

9 N. E. Saul, *Richard II* (New Haven and London, 1997), pp. 426–8. Richard's body was only exhumed and reburied at Westminster upon Henry V's accession in 1413: J. H. Wylie and W. T. Waugh, *The Reign of Henry V*, 3 vols (Cambridge, 1914–29), I, 207–11.

10 Goodman, *Katherine Swynford: Honourable Lady or She-Devil?*, pp. 15–16.

might be installed against a suitably fitting panoply during her widowhood.[11] Katherine could even have stayed in London through March 1399, where (since their great house at the Savoy on the Strand had been damaged in 1381) the Lancasters had used the comfortable modern palace of the bishops of Ely, off Holborn.[12]

Even if Katherine had wanted to come to Lincolnshire specifically, she could have gone to Bolingbroke Castle, a Lancastrian stronghold favoured by Gaunt's first wife, Duchess Blanche, perhaps because it was considered a suitable retreat for 'lying-in', though we only have a single record of Gaunt visiting himself – long ago in 1365.[13] Or she could have gone to Kettlethorpe Manor, a few miles west of Lincoln, held by her son by her first husband, Thomas Swynford, where she had lived during her first marriage and visited subsequently.[14] But Katherine chose none of these residences. Instead, she established her household in what was, by comparison, a very modest rented house in Lincoln Cathedral Close: 'The Priory'. By doing so, of course, she was avoiding all possibility of falling into Richard's hands, as she would have done by taking-up residence in any of the Lancastrian palaces, which – following their seizure on 18 March – would have placed her directly under his control. This further gesture of independence from the Crown at this point must surely have been noticed by all contemporaries. Not only was the famous duchess hurriedly leaving court, but she was doing so in order to live at liberty as a tenant in a small house within Lincoln's fortified close. Uncommitted bystanders at court may have sympathised with the dispossessed duchess, which may have also been partly her intention.

It is very likely that Katherine Swynford became tenant of The Priory in March 1399, although we have no evidence for her occupation until the following year, and she probably died there in 1403.[15] The contrast, for both the public and for Katherine herself, between The Priory and the Lancastrian palace accommodation to which she had been accustomed throughout most of her life was

11 Goodman, *John of Gaunt. The Exercise of Princely Power*, pp. 301–26.

12 *ibid.*, p. 255.

13 Duchess Blanche is said to have been born at Bolingbroke and was confined there in 1360 for the birth of her daughter Philippa. In 1366–67 she gave birth to her son Henry there: N.W. Webster, *Blanche of Lancaster* (Driffield, 1990), pp. 38–55. Webster also says that Blanche died of plague at Bolingbroke in September 1369, but Weir follows Palmer in saying that she died in childbirth at Tutbury Castle: J. J. N. Palmer, 'The historical context of the Book of the Duchess: a revision', *Chaucer Review* 8 (1974), 253–61. Long believed to have died in 1369, Palmer demonstrates that she died the year before: Weir, *Katherine Swynford*, pp. 79, 86–7.

14 'Kettlethorpe Hall': www.kettlethorpe.com/kettlethorpe%20hall.html (accessed 2005).

15 S. Jones, K. Major and J. Varley, *The Survey of Ancient Houses in Lincoln I: Priorygate to Pottergate* (Lincoln, 1984), p. 25; Goodman, *Katherine Swynford*, p. 27.

Plate 1. 'The Priory' (No. 2 Minster Yard), Lincoln Cathedral Close from southwest (*photograph & copyright Richard Croft*).

enormous. Kenilworth Castle – the largest of Lancaster's palaces – occupied hundreds of acres and contained hundreds of rooms, whereas the handful of rooms at The Priory took up less space than the dais end of Kenilworth's showy new great hall, completed by her husband between 1391 and 1393.[16]

Katherine's flight from London to Lincoln in mid-March 1399, then, was both a dramatic action, and one packed with political symbolism. Nevertheless, in line with their thesis that Katherine was 'retiring' from the world at this moment, both Weir and Lucraft suggest that her reasons for choosing such humble accommodation in Lincoln were basically sentimental.[17] Her first husband, Hugh Swynford (who had died as long ago as 1372), had been a minor Lincolnshire landowner, whilst her marriage to her second husband, John of Gaunt, had taken place at the cathedral in 1396. It is also true that Katherine's son by Gaunt, Henry Beaufort, who had been legitimised in 1396, had been consecrated bishop of Lincoln in 1398 (and remained in post until 1404), but we may legitimately question how much time bishops spent in their cathedral cities.[18] A recent study shows that thirteenth-century bishops of Lincoln were rarely to be found in the city, preferring to reside at one of their rural palaces, particularly at Buckden (Huntingdonshire), which was centrally placed within the diocese and within easy reach of London.[19] Lincoln Cathedral Close was probably not, then, somewhere Katherine might retreat, if her intention was to spend time with her son Henry.

Furthermore, between 1372 and 1396, Katherine did not give up her contacts with Lincoln and Lincolnshire; indeed, there is good evidence for her occasional residence at Kettlethorpe during this period.[20] Her son by her first marriage, Thomas Swynford, was baptised at St Margaret's, Pottergate, in the

16 *The Survey of Ancient Houses in Lincoln I*, pp. 23–32; M. W. Thompson, 'Three stages in the construction of the hall at Kenilworth Castle, Warwickshire', in M. R. Apted, R. Gilyard-Beer and A. J. Saunders (eds), *Ancient Monuments and their Interpretation. Essays presented to A. J. Taylor* (Chichester, 1977), pp. 211–18.

17 Lucraft suggests that Katherine was drawn to Lincoln through her devotion to St Katherine: Lucraft, *Katherine Swynford*, p. 149. This paper adopts a more political view.

18 G. L. Harriss, *Cardinal Beaufort. A Study of Lancastrian Ascendancy and Decline* (Oxford, 1988).

19 P. Everson and D. Stocker 'A divers panoply: the far-flung residences of the medieval bishops of Lincoln', forthcoming.

20 S. Armitage-Smith, *John of Gaunt's Register Part 1 (1371–1375)*, Camden Society, 3rd series, XX & XXI (London, 1911), pp. 279–80, no. 1608 (January 1375), pp. 316–17, no. 1711 (July 1375); E. C. Lodge and R. F. Somerville (eds), *John of Gaunt's Register, 1379–1383*, Camden Society, 3rd series, LVI & LVII (London, 1937), pp. 44–6, nos 108–15, 335, no. 1060 (November 1379); R. E. G. Cole, 'The Manor and Rectory of Kettlethorpe in the Parts of Lindsey in the County of Lincoln', *AASRP* 31 (1911–12), 41–86, at pp. 54–9.

Close, in which parish he was said to have been born in 1368.[21] Katherine had also previously rented another house in Lincoln Cathedral Close between 1386 and 1392 – the Chancery.[22] Between 1372 and 1396, however, Katherine had neither the status nor the household of a duchess of Lancaster, no matter how well known was her informal relationship with John of Gaunt. Furthermore, even in her official role as governess (and as mistress) throughout much of this period, she was obliged to travel with the duke's household, which meant spending most of her time in London and at the Lancastrian palaces, and she is unlikely to have seen very much of her rented house in Lincoln Cathedral Close.

No evidence has yet been produced that either Katherine or John of Gaunt had visited the city since 1391; indeed, John of Gaunt's itinerary (which is accessible only for the period between 1370 and 1383) suggests that Lincoln was not a regular port of call on his travels around duchy lands.[23] In fact, Gaunt's itinerary suggests that he only called at the city once during those thirteen years: for no more than two days, and probably less, around 25 September 1374. Subsequently, we know of only one further visit to Lincoln by the duke and his entourage: in 1386, when Henry Bolingbroke and Thomas Swynford were admitted to the cathedral confraternity.[24] It has been suggested that Gaunt, and/or senior elements of his entourage, stayed in the purpose-built guest range of the great house built by his vassal John de Sutton in Wigford on such occasions.[25] Katherine was probably present in the duke's entourage in both 1371 and 1386; indeed, the latter visit might have occasioned the contract to rent the Chancery from the Dean and Chapter for the ensuing five years.

Even so, it is surely unlikely that Katherine's principal reason for returning hurriedly to Lincoln in March 1399 was because she had previously 'hidden away' here from life's pressures. Although such impulses might have played some small part in her thinking, there had been an enormous change in her circumstances since her last documented visit in 1391. She was now the great

21 Cole, 'The Manor and Rectory of Kettlethorpe', 58, where Cole discusses the discrepancy between the date of Thomas' birth and the certification of his date of birth in 1394–95.

22 Katherine Swynford began renting the Chancery from the Dean and Chapter in 1386, and was still renting it in 1391–92; whilst the then Chancellor John Huntman had to seek alternative accommodation: *The Survey of Ancient Houses in Lincoln I*, p. 53; Goodman, *Katherine Swynford*, pp. 2, 25. Weir suggests that Katherine presented Huntman to the rectory of Kettlethorpe on 4 December in 1398 in order to compensate him for her occupation of his official residence: Weir, *Katherine Swynford*, p. 225.

23 *John of Gaunt's Register, 1379–1383*, passim.

24 J. F. Hill, *Medieval Lincoln* (Cambridge, 1965), p. 258 n.4 with references.

25 D. Stocker, '"A Very Goodly House Longging to Sutton ...". A Reconstruction of 'John of Gaunt's Palace', Lincoln', *Lincolnshire History and Archaeology* 34 (1999), 5–15.

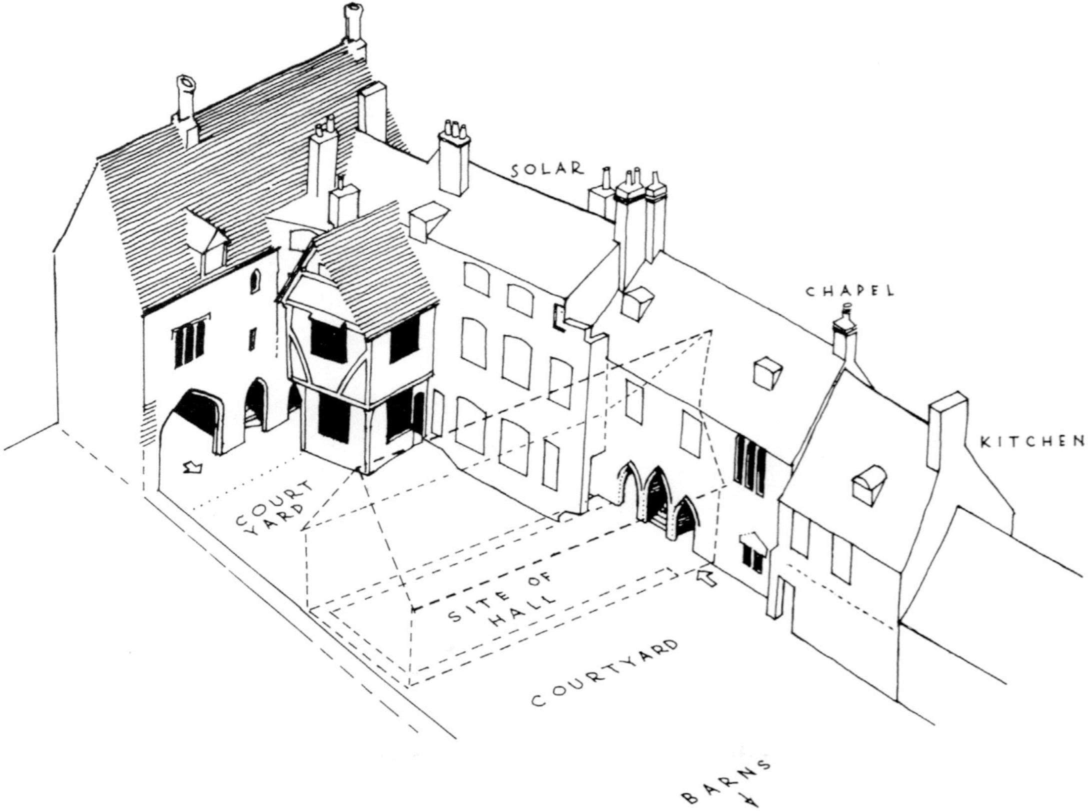

Plate 2. Reconstruction of 'The Chancery' (No. 11 Minster Yard) from the southeast, (*reconstruction drawing by Stanley Jones, copyright Lincoln Civic Trust*).

duchess of Lancaster and, as such, her actions would have been scrutinised by her contemporaries for their political meaning. Consequently, the rapid removal of the newly widowed duchess of Lancaster from court to occupy a small house in the Lincoln Cathedral Close in March 1399 must be considered as a potentially significant political gesture. Unlike Weir and Lucraft, then, we are not obliged to view Katherine's return to Lincoln as a meek 'retirement' from the world, but we should understand it, rather, as a decisive political and symbolic act.

Furthermore, it was provocative. Katherine's symbolic act of resistance may have been one factor weighed by her stepson Bolingbroke when making the momentous decision to mount his invasion in early July, which – we should recall – was initially undertaken, not to seize the crown, but to recover the duchy of Lancaster from Richard's hands. Katherine was able to mount her act of political resistance to Richard, not only because she knew enough about court politesse to gauge its effect, but also because she knew enough about property law and about recent English history to know how to behave to make a symbolic threat of rebellion against a deeply unpopular king, without actually taking up arms herself. Indeed, we can propose that Katherine's actions in March 1399, and throughout the remainder of her life in Lincoln, were intended to remind national politicians – and Richard II in particular – of the actions of her direct predecessor in the role of dowager of Lancaster and Lincoln, Alice de Lacy, seventy-seven years earlier. We can suggest that, in March 1399. Katherine's dramatic political and symbolic actions bore intentional similarity to those of Alice de Lacy, in a previous successful rebellion of a countess of Lancaster and Lincoln against an autocratic monarch – a comparison that was unlikely to have been lost on contemporary observers of politics.

First, though, it is important to understand that, in pursuing this meaningful course of action, it may be that Katherine was performing the role of countess of Lincoln, rather than that of duchess of Lancaster. Although the dukedom of Lancaster was the senior of the English titles held by John of Gaunt, the critical titles for explaining Katherine's choice of Lincoln as her retreat in March 1399, and as her home until her death in 1403, may have been those of the earldom of Lincoln and the constableship of Lincoln Castle, both of which had been held by John of Gaunt.[26] The earldom of Lincoln was just one of four earldoms Gaunt held, alongside Richmond, Derby and Leicester. Henry of Bolingbroke, of course, was invested with the earldom of Derby but not with the earldom of Lincoln.[27] It seems clear – from the jointure arrangements

26 Goodman, *Katherine Swynford: Honourable Lady or She-Devil?*, p. 2.

27 Proof that Henry of Bolingbroke never acquired the earldom of Lincoln during the lifetime of his father is provided by the fact that the honour of 'carver' – an hereditary appurtenance of the earldom of Lincoln – was devolved to his step-brother John Beaufort at his own coronation in 1400. Richard II seems to have given John

between King Richard and John of Gaunt in 1397, and from a grant made by King Richard dated 9 March 1399 (some five weeks after Gaunt's death) – that it was Katherine who held those key parts of Gaunt's former estate that had come to him through the earldom of Lincoln, by descent from his first wife, Blanche, for her lifetime.[28]

This also explains why, once Richard had been dethroned, it was the income from estates within the earldom of Lincoln, particularly, that maintained Katherine in Lincoln Cathedral Close for the final three years of her life.[29] Amongst these lands and incomes, one of the most ancient and symbolic – even if one of the least valuable in monetary terms – was the earl of Lincoln's 'third penny', an ancient fee paid to the earl in lieu of customary rents from the county.[30] The earl was able to claim this 'third penny' because he was constable of Lincoln Castle and lord of the manor of the Bail. These titles were important symbols of political power over the enormous Lincolnshire estate within the duchy of Lancaster; they were the tokens of authority over the city and county. The authority these lordships conveyed over the city of Lincoln, for example, had previously located John of Gaunt as arbiter in the long-running dispute with the city's council over jurisdiction within the Bail and the western part of the cathedral close. These lordships of the earldom of Lincoln were not at all obscure or unknown in Lincoln in 1399, then. Indeed, their contemporary importance as significant tokens of authority over the city is illustrated by Richard's moves to retain them in his own hands, the moment he realised where Katherine was headed. On 20 March 1399, Richard granted these key lordships to his uncle, Edward duke of York, but by the time the news reached Lincoln, Katherine would have been ensconced in the city.[31]

By 1399, the earldom of Lincoln was known for a succession of historical countesses and aristocratic women who had played significant military roles as constables of Lincoln Castle. In contemporary legend, at least, Countess Lucy had held the castle militarily for Henry I.[32] More certainly, Nicholaa de la Haye had held the castle for both John and Henry III against the forces of the Barons and the Dauphin, Louis; she being confirmed as constable and receiving the earl's third penny in token of her rights in the Bail.[33]

Beaufort the earldom by June 1399, contradicting, but not cancelling, the previous jointure that allocated it to Katherine for her life: *CPR 1396–9*, p. 516.

28 *CPR 1396–9*, pp. 76, 516. Goodman, *Katherine Swynford*, p. 15.

29 *CPR 1396–9*, p. 516; Goodman, *Katherine Swynford*, p. 15.

30 Hill, *Medieval Lincoln*, pp. 90–1 & note. In 1331 it was worth a mere £20 in monetary terms.

31 *CFR 1391–9*, p. 297; Hill, *Medieval Lincoln*, pp. 262–9, 312.

32 Hill, *Medieval Lincoln*, pp. 92–4.

33 L. J. Wilkinson, *Women in Thirteenth-Century Lincolnshire* (Woodbridge, 2007), pp. 13–26.

Although these great countesses of Lincoln of the twelfth and thirteenth centuries would undoubtedly have been remembered in late fourteenth-century Lincoln, the actions of a more recent countess would surely have come much more readily to the minds of the contemporary political class, both in the city and at court. This was Alice de Lacy, the sole heiress of the enormous estates and wealth of the de Lacy family, who was married to Henry III's grandson, Thomas earl of Lancaster (1278–1322), and who brought that great de Lacy inheritance into the Lancaster family. Thomas of Lancaster was the pre-eminent figure in English domestic politics during the reign of Edward II.[34] Leader of the baronial opposition to Edward's wayward rule, on more than one occasion he took up arms and, with a baronial army at his back, he sought to enforce reform on Edward's government.

The parallel between the role played by Thomas of Lancaster and Henry of Bolingbroke seventy-seven years later was not lost on contemporaries, and was reflected, for example, in the advice issued in parliament by the duke of Gloucester and Bishop Arundel in 1386.[35] Indeed, the lords who grouped themselves to protest against the personal rule of Richard II were sometimes descendants of the rebels against Edward II. Edward II's reign reached a crisis in 1322, when, in March, Thomas was defeated at the Battle of Boroughbridge, and the leaders of the rebellion were tried and executed – including Thomas himself. The earldoms of Lancaster and Lincoln were promptly seized by the crown, and Alice de Lacy – hereditary countess of Lincoln in her own right – was placed in a similarly perilous position to that of Katherine Swynford seventy-seven years later, in 1399. Alice retreated rapidly to Lincoln in 1322, just as Katherine was to do in 1399, and she and her agents went through a period of tense negotiation with Edward II aimed at salvaging her independent power-base from the wreck of the Lancastrian estate.[36] Likewise, Katherine sent her agents to London in Spring 1399 to sue for the return of a fraction of the Lancastrian estates for her own use.[37] In Alice de Lacy's case, this took some time to achieve, but by 1323 her agents had secured her rights to what were called her 'personal' properties: the Bail before the Gate of Lincoln Castle; the castle itself; and the earls' third penny (or rather £20 per annum in lieu thereof). By 1323, then, following the systematic royal destruction of her husband's earldoms, Countess Alice had salvaged for herself the ancient core property and status of the earldom of Lincoln, based in Lincoln itself.

34 J. R. Maddicott, *Thomas of Lancaster, 1307–1322: A Study in the Reign of Edward II* (Oxford, 1970).

35 A. Steel, *Richard II* (Cambridge, 1961), p. 122.

36 P. Everson and D. Stocker, *Custodians of Continuity? The Premonstratensian Abbey at Barlings and the Landscape of Ritual*, Lincolnshire Archaeology and Heritage Reports 11, HTL/EH (Heckington and London 2011), pp. 368–70.

37 *CPR 1396–9*, p. 555; Goodman, *Katherine Swynford*, p. 16.

Alice, known again as the countess of Lincoln, now bided her time on her Lincolnshire estates.

Out of the moderate fraction of the earldom of Lincoln she had recovered, Alice made a huge donation to the comital abbey – Barlings, ten miles to the east of the city. Alice's gift, also made in 1322, was of the large and valuable – and highly symbolic – manor of the earls of Lincoln at Swaton, on the Kesteven fen edge. Swaton was a major Lincolnshire holding of the earldom. Swaton church may have been the burial place of Alice's famous forebear, Nicholaa de la Haye[38] and it may be that Alice later had the entire nave of Swaton church rebuilt – to a distinctive 'military' design – and re-furnished with stained glass (of which a few armorials survive), as a belated memorial to her famous predecessor. A monument at Swaton, made at this time, may also have been intended to commemorate Nicholaa in effigy, and may also have been intended by Alice de Lacy as a tribute to her illustrious forebear.[39] No doubt the donation of this valuable, and symbolically meaningful, estate to Barlings Abbey, at precisely the same moment that Alice's lawyers were seeking royal confirmation of her rights as countess of Lincoln, was also intended as divine insurance for the status she claimed.

Edward II's regime took longer to disintegrate than did Richard II's, following military victory in 1322, and it was not until 1330 that Edward's regime, and its equally troubling successor, governed by his queen, Isabella, and her possible lover Roger Mortimer, by then first earl of March, were eventually overthrown by supporters of the young king Edward III – prominent amongst whom was Alice de Lacy. Remarried to Ebulo le Strange in 1324, and with the entirety of the earldoms of Lincoln and Lancaster restored to her in her own right, Alice embarked on funding further spectacular building works at the comital abbey (Plate 4).[40] There is very little in her resolute insistence on her rights, or in her obdurate resistance to Edward II in the 1320s, to suggest that Alice was merely a willing pawn in Ebulo's hands, as suggested by Linda Mitchell. Rather, these appear the actions of a self-confident countess quite capable of playing her allotted political role. As Mitchell herself points out, Ebulo was never called earl of Lincoln.[41]

38 Everson and Stocker, *Custodians of Continuity?*, pp. 364–7.

39 *ibid.*

40 *ibid.*, chapters 3 & 11.

41 L. Mitchell, 'Martyr to the Cause: The Tragic Career of Alice de Lacy', in L. Mitchell (ed.), *Portraits of Medieval Women, Family, Marriage and Politics in England, 1225–1350* (Basingstoke, 2003), pp. 105–24. J. G. Nichols, 'The decent of the Earldom of Lincoln', in *Memoirs Illustrative of the History and Antiquities of the County and City of Lincoln*, Archaeological Institute of Great Britain and Ireland (London, 1848), pp. 253–79, at p. 276.

Plate 3. St Michael's church, Swaton, Lincolnshire, from the northwest. Given to Barlings Abbey from the comital estate by Alice de Lacy in 1322 – and possibly rebuilt as a memorial to Nicholaa de la Haye lady of Brattleby (d. 1230) (*photograph & copyright D. Stocker*).

Plate 4a & 4b. Barlings Abbey church – Left,'cut-away' reconstruction from the northwest. Right, following the rebuilding campaign of *c.* 1330–*c.* 1360, instigated by Alice de Lacy, with comital burials in the north transept (*Everson and Stocker 2011 (note 32), fig.3/48. copyright Heritage Trust of Lincolnshire*).

The campaign of rebuilding at Barlings saw the abbey completely transformed into a major burial church, fit for a comital mausoleum, with a huge transept in which both Alice and Ebulo were eventually to be buried. Whilst making these exceptionally generous gifts to Barlings, Alice was – it is suggested – establishing a kind of memorial to the ancient earldom of Lincoln. Alice was now too old to have children and so, according to the terms of the re-establishment of her lands in 1330, the earldom of Lincoln would die out with her. The rebuilt abbey, then, was apparently conceived by Alice as the earldom's mausoleum, now that it was to become extinct, and not as a place in which a continuing family would be celebrated.[42]

But Alice's ambitions were only partly realised. When she finally died, full of honour, in 1348, her titles and landholdings did not become anonymously merged with the royal estate, as seems to have been intended in 1330. Instead, in 1349, Edward III recreated the earldom of Lincoln and granted it to Thomas of Lancaster's nephew, Henry of Grosmont (d. 1361), who would soon be elevated as first duke of Lancaster.[43] On its recreation, however, the Lincoln title became an 'entail male' (no longer 'entail general'), meaning that the title could no longer descend through the female line. Thus it was that this huge estate passed, through Henry of Grosmont's daughter and sole heir, Blanche of Lancaster, to John of Gaunt.[44] Consequently, it was the terms of Gaunt's second marriage jointure that settled elements of the comital estate on Katherine Swynford for her lifetime, and for which she was fighting in 1399.

When Richard II seized the duchy of Lancaster on the death of John of Gaunt on 18 March 1399 (including within it the earldom of Lincoln), he was placing Katherine in a very similar situation in which Edward II had placed Alice in 1322. Furthermore, we have already seen that, although Henry Bolingbroke had been exiled by Richard II, following the judgement at Coventry in September 1398 (rather than being beheaded like Thomas of Lancaster), the parallels between the two protagonists must have been very evident amongst the political classes. Like Edward though, Richard was also playing with fire here, and he must have known it. He was well aware of the parallel between his own situation and that of Edward II because, at the height of the political revolution known as the 'first tyranny' in 1386, he had sought to have Edward II canonised, presumably in order to declare publicly that anointed kings could not be overthrown by their subjects.[45]

42 Everson and Stocker, *Custodians of Continuity?*, pp. 364–70.

43 K. Fowler, *The King's Lieutenant. Henry of Grosmont, First Duke of Lancaster 1310–1361* (London, 1969), p. 173.

44 Webster, *Blanche of Lancaster*.

45 Steel, *Richard II*, p. 122. Mowbray apparently told Henry of Bolingbroke that Richard II was intending to reverse the pardon of Thomas of Lancaster in December 1397, which would disinherit both John of Gaunt and Bolingbroke himself. There

In the febrile political atmosphere of March 1399, then, following the death of John of Gaunt, Katherine Swynford had before her Alice de Lacy's reputation as an outstanding countess of Lincoln, and her example of passive opposition to the Crown. Would the parallel between the two women not have been obvious throughout the entire political class? Alice de Lacy's example would have offered Katherine a course of action in this moment of crisis, a model of how a dispossessed countess of Lincoln could behave when mistreated by the Crown. Countesses of Lincoln did not retire quietly in such circumstances; first they retreated to the seat of their power, Lincoln itself, from where they fought their rebellious corner, hoping for better times for the comital estate and for change in the Crown's stance towards them. Surely this is why Katherine came to Lincoln specifically in March 1399 to live in her rented house, because she foresaw a period of passive political opposition to the king, focused around negotiations for the immediate return of a small portion of the enormous Lancastrian estates – that portion which had been the core estates of the Lincoln earldom. Like her predecessor, Countess Alice, Duchess Katherine would wait in her Lincoln heartlands for better times.

A great difference between Katherine Swynford and Alice de Lacy as dispossessed countesses of Lincoln, however, was that in Henry of Bolingbroke Katherine had a stepson capable of taking military action to restore the family estates, and who would re-establish Katherine's position. Meanwhile, just as Alice de Lacy had done, Katherine sent envoys to London to negotiate with Richard in April 1399, and it seems that he relented more readily than had Edward II. Things moved faster in 1399 than they had in 1323, and by the time King Richard (now at Haverfordwest awaiting passage to Ireland) made a brief – and unspecific – grant of Katherine's properties held prior to her marriage to Gaunt at the end of May 1399, rumours of Henry of Bolingbroke's intentions were already reaching London.[46] Henry's small flotilla left the French coast in mid-June and, when he landed at Ravenser on 4 July, he was met by a number of Yorkshire and Lincolnshire knights – vassals of the earldom in the two counties.[47] It seems likely, then, that elements amongst the earldom's tenantry were taking their lead from Katherine, and also offering their gesture of

---

is some corroborative evidence for this plot, and the controversy rumbled on well into 1398 (Weir, *Katherine Swynford*, pp. 239–40). In February 1398 John of Gaunt sought reassurance from Richard II that he would not revoke the pardon of Thomas of Lancaster: *ibid.*, p. 241).

46 *CPR 1396–9*, p. 555. See also the entry in the Fine Rolls for 1 May 1399: *CFR 1391–9*, p. 303; *CCR 1396–9*, p. 476 (23 May 1399); and Lucraft, *Katherine Swynford*, p. 123, n. 90.

47 Hill, *Medieval Lincoln*, p. 269, citing Harding's Chronicle. For a more detailed enumeration of the Lincolnshire tenantry, see S. K. Walker, *The Lancastrian Affinity 1361–1399* (Oxford, 1990), pp. 31 & n. 98, 33 & nn. 109 & 112, 35 & n. 118.

resistance to the Crown. Some days later, Henry's growing army was joined at Pontefract Castle by William, Lord Willoughby d'Eresby, and John, Lord Darcy of Knaith, the highest-ranking Lincoln/Lancaster tenants in Lincolnshire, and by Ralph Neville, 1st earl of Westmorland, Katherine's son-in-law.[48] Furthermore, it has been widely thought that the 'N. Swynford', who was said (by Adam of Usk) to be the 'chief agent' in Richard II's death at Pontefract Castle, which had occurred by 14 February 1400, was related to Sir Thomas Swynford, Katherine's son by her first marriage, and who was then constable of Pontefract.[49]

A reputable argument can be made, then, that Katherine Swynford's dramatic reaction to Richard II's seizure of the Lancaster estates in March 1399, her retreat to Lincoln and her demand for reinstatement of key rights and properties as countess of Lincoln were all calculated to remind Richard – as well as contemporary observers of the political scene – of her illustrious predecessor Alice de Lacy. Given the eventual fate of Edward II, this must have been seen as a symbolic gesture aimed at Richard's authority.

Significant though Alice's model may have been as an inspiration for Katherine's behaviour in 1399, however, it does not explain why Katherine remained in Lincoln after Bolingbroke's assumption of power at the end of September 1399, and until her death in 1403. For the final three years of her life she did not reoccupy one of the Lancastrian palaces, and this might be thought evidence that it was indeed a 'sentimental' attachment to the city that had attracted her in March 1399, and not an act of political resistance. The palaces of the duchy of Lancaster now belonged – legitimately – to the new king, of course, but on 12 February 1400, Katherine re-acquired substantial former duchy lands, some of which had formerly belonged to the de Lacy earldom of Lincoln, yet she still did not leave the cathedral close.[50]

Perhaps, as Alison Weir suggested, she wanted to live near where she intended to be buried. Indeed, we know that she formalised that intention by becoming a vowess, and she is depicted as such on her memorial brass.[51] Her image was probably similar to that recently engraved on the brass to Eleanor de Bohun (d. 1399) in Westminster Abbey.[52] Motivations for women taking the veil were various, and they have been set out with admirable clarity by

48 M. L. Bruce, *The Usurper King, Henry of Bolingbroke 1366–1399* (London, 1986), p. 187.

49 E. M. Thompson (ed.), *Chronicon Adae de Usk. 1377–1421* (London, 1876), p. 199; Hill, *Medieval Lincoln*, p. 269.

50 Weir, *Katherine Swynford*, p. 261.

51 *ibid.*, p. 262. Katherine's depiction in brass on her monument showed her in the vowess's kirtle, mantle and veil: BL, Loan MS 38, fol. 107 – 'Dugdale's Book of Monuments'.

52 L. D. Pascual, 'Piety and Dynastic Memory: The Brass of Eleanor de Bohun, Duchess of Gloucester', *Transactions of the Monumental Brass Society* XXII (2021),

Mary Erler.[53] Erler shows that taking a formal vow of chastity in the prescribed ceremony before a bishop did not imply obedience to any 'rule'. But it was itself sometimes seen, indeed, as an act of passive rebellion, in that a widow's vow prevented further machinations aimed at securing the woman's residual estate, through attempts to make her remarry. Indeed, it may well be that Katherine's vow (presumably signed on her son, Henry Beaufort's knee during mass, as was customary) was of exactly this 'rebellious' type – a public gesture on her part aimed at securing title to that part of Gaunt's estate which she had been given as jointure on their marriage, and which she secured for herself, legally, during the Spring of 1399. By becoming a vowess she would have avoided any attempt by the Crown to have her remarried. Unfortunately, we have no confirmation of the date of Katherine's profession but, if she did view her vow as a further act of resistance, a date soon after she arrived back in Lincoln in March 1399 is most likely.

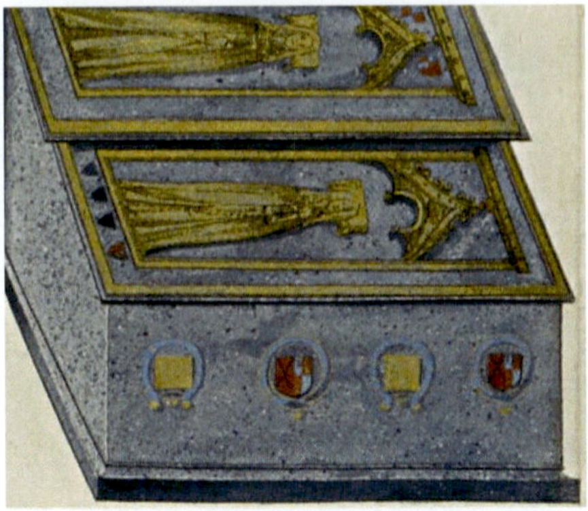

Plate 5. Drawing of the monument to Katherine Swynford and her daughter Joan, 1st countess of Westmorland, from William Dugdale's 'Book of Monuments' (*BL, Loan Ms. 38 fol. 107 – copyright Lincoln Cathedral Library*).

47–73, esp. pp. 70–2. The only evidence that the pious Eleanor 'took the vow' following the murder of her husband Thomas in 1397, is her depiction as such on this monument.

53 R. B. Dobson, *The Church, Politics and Patronage in the Fifteenth Century* (Gloucester, 1984), pp. 106–9 & n. 55; M. C. Erler 'Three Fifteenth-Century Vowesses', in C. M. Barron and A. F. Sutton (eds), *Medieval London Widows 1300–1500* (London and Rio Grande, 1994), pp. 165–81, esp. pp. 165–7. See also M. C. Erler, 'English Vowed Women at the End of the Middle Ages', *Medieval Studies* 57 (1995), 155–203. For an archaeological perspective on vowesses, including their depiction on brasses, see R. Gilchrist, *Contemplation and Action. The Other Monasticism* (London and New York, 1995), pp. 150–1.

Plate 6. Reconstruction of the image in brass of Katherine Swynford from her monument, derived from the surviving indent and other sources by Dr Roger Joy (*copyright Dr Roger Joy and the Katherine Swynford Society*).

So, we must be careful not to perpetuate the view, restated in the case of Alice de Lacy less than a generation ago, that, by taking such a vow, powerful and intelligent dowager duchesses were without effective agency.[54] Alice de Lacy had also publicly declared a vow of chastity in 1337, so Katherine can also be seen as following her example in this respect.[55] According to Linda Mitchell these women were only given direction by the political ambitions of their husbands. In fact, the evidence is that Katherine continued to play her public role as though she were dowager countess of Lincoln during the first three years of her stepson's reign, even though the political pressure on her to do so had been relieved.

Katherine Swynford continued to follow Alice de Lacy's example in her relations with the comital abbey, for example. Katherine was a generous patron of Barlings, and her patronage was impressive. John of Gaunt himself had been mindful of his responsibilities towards the comital abbey, and in 1386 he made arrangements for a substantial obit there at Pentecost – staffed by five canons during his lifetime and four after his death.[56] But this endowment (substantial though it was) was superseded by a considerably enlarged obit founded in 1402/03 by Katherine herself, which was to pray for the souls of John of Gaunt and all three of his wives, both on the anniversaries of their deaths and on subsequent days. Indeed, more than a century later, when the canons of Barlings were questioned in their annual visitations, they usually declared '*Dux Lancastrie est fundator*' to the inquisitor.[57] By this stage, then, the canons seem to have forgotten the major role of Alice de Lacy in refounding the abbey between 1330 and 1348, and their house's tradition had replaced her with the family of John of Gaunt, and specifically with the gifts of Katherine Swynford, made on their joint behalves.

Impressive though they were, the various obsequies at Barlings Abbey were never intended to be John of Gaunt's principal chantry; that was undoubtedly at St Paul's in London, where he was buried alongside his first wife. Second in his affections, however, possibly due to the influence of Katherine herself, was his support for Lincoln Cathedral. Katherine would presumably have been present when the generous bequests of furnishings, jewels and plate that had belonged to his own household chapel were made to the cathedral under the terms of her husband's will, in 1399. They were worth the fabulous sum

54 Mitchell, 'Martyr to the Cause', or even more starkly, J. G. Ruddock, *Alesia De Lacy 1281–1348* (Lincoln, 1993).

55 R. E. Archer, 'Piety in Question: Noblewomen and Religion in the Later Middle Ages', in D. Wood (ed.), *Women and Religion in Medieval England* (Oxford, 2003), pp. 118–40, at p. 128.

56 Everson and Stocker, *Custodians of Continuity?*, p. 372.

57 I. A. Gasquet (ed.), *Collectanea Anglo-Premonstratensiana. Documents drawn from the Original Register of the Order, Now in the Bodleian Library, Oxford, and the Transcript of another Register in the British Museum*, Camden Society, 3rd series, 6, 10, 12 (1904–6).

of £387.[58] The installation of Henry Beaufort as bishop of Lincoln in the previous year had incurred considerable opposition, on account of his youth (he may have been just twenty-one), but the great gift of valuables made by John of Gaunt to the cathedral might have been aimed at easing his awkward situation amongst the local clergy.[59]

John of Gaunt obtained a royal licence for a chantry foundation within the cathedral in 1398, to pray for his own soul and that of Katherine, but there is no evidence that the chantry was actually established either in 1399, following Gaunt's death, or in 1403 when Katherine died.[60] Indeed John Harvey made a strong case that the chantry licenced in 1398 was never actually established at all, due to confusion in Lancastrian estate management following John of Gaunt's demise. Consequently, Harvey argued that the chantry in the south aisle of Lincoln's Angel Choir was actually established *de novo* by Katherine's daughter, Joan, in 1437, though Harvey dates Katherine's monument itself to the period shortly after her death in 1403.

Even so, after her dispossession in 1399, it seems clear that Katherine's own investment during what remained of her lifetime went not into her husband's chantry foundation at Lincoln Cathedral, but into the elaborate obsequies she provided for both of them at Barlings Abbey, and in doing so she was – yet again – following the example of Alice de Lacy. In the end, however, Katherine did not make provision for her own burial alongside Alice at Barlings. It seems clear, from the documentation surrounding the establishment of the Swynford chantry in 1437, that it was established in the cathedral on the site of Katherine's actual grave, south of the high altar.[61] But, even so, it also seems clear that the only major obsequies performed for Katherine between her death in 1403 and 1437 were not held within the cathedral at all, but at Barlings Abbey, where they were the most well-funded such institution

58 J. F. Wickenden, '"Joyalx" of John of Gaunt, bequeathed to the Cathedral Church of Lincoln', *Archaeological Journal* 32 (1875), 317–18; Goodman, *John of Gaunt. The Exercise of Princely Power*, p. 248; idem, *Katherine Swynford*, p. 24 and references there; idem, *Katherine Swynford: Honourable Lady or She-Devil?*, p. 5.

59 Beaufort's appointment had required a papal bull (dated 27 February 1398), by which Boniface IX translated Bishop Buckingham to Coventry and Lichfield. But Buckingham continued to officiate in Lincoln until 12 July, when he finally 'retired' to Canterbury on grounds of infirmity. Beaufort received the temporalities of Lincoln at Tutbury on 19 July 1398: Weir, *Katherine Swynford*, p. 241 and references there.

60 The licence for the chantry in Lincoln Cathedral for Katherine and John of Gaunt was granted only one day after Richard II's sentence on Henry of Bolingbroke at Coventry (17 September 1398): J. Harvey, *Catherine Swynford's Chantry*, Lincoln Minster Pamphlets, 2nd series, no. 6 (1972), pp. 9–12; Weir, *Katherine Swynford*, p. 244. Katherine must have chosen Lincoln as her own burial place by then, possibly because she was a member of the confraternity there, or because she had been occasionally resident in the Close.

61 Harvey, *Catherine Swynford's Chantry*, pp. 9–12.

that the canons possessed. Her investment in major obsequies at Barlings is, therefore, best seen as another example of Katherine playing the role expected of the dowager countesses of Lincoln, in which she was once again following a model pioneered by Alice de Lacy.[62]

This contribution to our celebration of the work of Nicholas Bennett has posed two simple questions. Why did Katherine Swynford flee from the court immediately following the burial of John of Gaunt, and immediately before the seizure of her deceased husband's estates by Richard II? And why did she choose to establish herself in a small, rented house in Lincoln Cathedral Close? Previous accounts – in so far as they have considered the matter at all – have suggested that she was returning to a city and an area with which she had long-standing personal connections, and to which she had returned occasionally 'seeking a refuge' from the pressures of John of Gaunt's household.[63] Anya Seton explained these actions as a desire to 'live quietly' and in obscurity, once John of Gaunt had died.[64]

Such sentimental understandings of the motives of a powerful dowager seem entirely inconsistent with the known facts. They do not do justice to the independent and capable woman we suspect Katherine to have been. Such explanations do not account, either, for contemporary expectations once she assumed the mantle of duchess of Lancaster and countess of Lincoln in 1396. Instead, we should perhaps see Katherine's actions between 1399 and 1403 as the actions of a clever, brave and skilful politician. We can glimpse here Katherine playing a high-profile, high-risk and undoubtedly political role with great skill and understanding. This was her predestined role as countess of Lincoln and she played it to the full, initially in 1399 as a gesture of political resistance to Richard II, and thereafter she continued to inhabit the role until her death.

Furthermore, this paper has also suggested that Katherine may have been explicitly associating herself with her militant predecessor, Countess Alice de Lacy, seventy-seven years earlier, who had behaved in this very fashion, in very similar circumstances. Following the death of Katherine's husband, the political gestures she made would have thus been well understood by her contemporaries. It was a role originally performed by Countess Alice de Lacy in similarly testing times and, like Alice, Katherine also championed the rights of the earldom of Lincoln against tyrannical kings.

62 Gaunt and Katherine were also amongst the beneficiaries of the chantry established by Canon Thomas de Aston at the chapel of the re-founded Spital Hospital on the Roman road to the Humber, ten miles north of the city: N. H. Bennett and D. Marcombe, *Thomas de Aston and the Diocese of Lincoln* (Lincoln, 1998), p. 46; Weir, *Katherine Swynford*, p. 181.

63 Weir, *Katherine Swynford*, p. 255.

64 Seton, *Katherine Swynford*, p. 575.

7

The Estates of the Honour of Richmond in Lincolnshire at the End of the Fourteenth Century

MICHAEL JONES

A general survey of the settlement of Bretons in Lincolnshire after the Norman Conquest together with an account of the development of the honour of Richmond in the county, held for some two-thirds of the period to 1399 by the dukes of Brittany or their cadets, has recently been published.[1] In it attention was drawn to some manuscript material, now housed at Nantes in the departmental archives of Loire-Atlantique, relating to late fourteenth-century Boston and other Lincolnshire estates of the honour, which has not been seriously exploited by previous scholars. The opportunity to offer a short contribution to this volume of essays for Nicholas Bennett, who has spent so much of his life making available to others through his own published research and as general editor of the Lincoln Record Society the wealth of documentary evidence available for the historic diocese of Lincoln, is an appropriate one to further highlight the value of this evidence for the social and economic history of medieval Lincolnshire.

The immediate political context explains why these documents are now to be found in Nantes. Following renewal of the general Anglo-French war in 1369, to cement a new alliance with his former ward, John IV, duke of Brittany (1364–99), in 1372 Edward III returned to him the earldom and honour of Richmond that had traditionally been held by his ancestors since shortly after the Norman Conquest. They had last been held briefly by the duke's father, John de Montfort, some thirty years earlier at the beginning of the Breton War of Succession (1341–65), but then used, following Montfort's capture by the French and subsequent early death (1345), to maintain Queen Philippa's

1 Michael Jones, 'Bretons in Medieval Lincolnshire: the Honour of Richmond and other connections, 1066–1399', *Archaeologia Cambrensis* 170 (2021), 1–61.

household and provide the king's third son, John of Gaunt, with an earldom.[2] With the resumption of the Anglo-French war and English diplomatic needs, in 1372 Gaunt was persuaded to release Richmond in return for other lands, so that it could be returned to John IV. But the Anglo-Breton alliance provoked a violent reaction among most leading Breton nobles, clergy and townsmen who were strongly opposed to their duke's pro-English stance, whilst it also alarmed the duke's liege lord, Charles V, king of France (1364–80).

The despatch of a small English force of some 600 men to Brittany, led by John, lord Neville, in the autumn of 1372 prompted Charles V to send his own forces to the duchy. A short expedition to bring John IV to heel in the late autumn was headed by the king's brother, Philip the Bold, duke of Burgundy. Then, as the duke's position seriously deteriorated over the next few months, in the following spring there was a more substantial invasion led by Bertrand du Guesclin, the Breton constable of France. This compelled John IV, fearing for his life, to flee his duchy in late April 1373. Seeking refuge in England, where he had spent most of his youth, he left a handful of strongholds in the hands of his own supporters, Brest (where John, lord Neville, took over command when the castle was besieged by Du Guesclin in the summer)[3] and Auray chief amongst them, but the rest of the duchy was lost to him.

With such a reversal of fortune, the resources provided by the recently restored honour of Richmond assumed an entirely new importance for the exiled duke. Apart from whatever charity Edward III was prepared to extend to his ally, or loans the duke might negotiate, using Richmond estates as collateral,[4] they represented his principal source of income for maintaining his family and the small body of retainers and officers who had accompanied him into exile, or for financing any attempt to secure a return to the duchy should diplomatic or military events permit. Over the next few years, he strove hard to achieve that end.[5] Not surprisingly, in doing so, a major concern was the efficient exploitation of his English estates, as the documents under discussion here testify. For a few years, until his exile came to an end in 1379, when a major political error by Charles V in attempting to tighten his grip

2 Michael Jones, *Ducal Brittany, 1364–1399. Relations with England and France during the reign of Duke John IV* (Oxford, 1970), pp. 60 ff. for events from 1369, and pp. 172–98 for the Richmond connection.

3 Michael Jones, 'Confusion confounded? The contrasting military fortunes and careers of Sir William Neville (d. 1391) and Sir William Neville of Pickhill and Rolleston (d. *c.* 1420)', *Fourteenth Century England* XII (2022), 179–202 for a recent discussion of the siege of Brest, 1373.

4 John, lord Neville, was the most important private creditor in the first years of John IV's exile, exercising almost complete control over most of the honorial finances as some Lincolnshire evidence reveals though it is a theme that cannot be pursued here.

5 Jones, *Ducal Brittany*, pp. 76–92.

on the duchy provoked the duke's former rebellious nobles and townsmen to invite him to return, John IV and his officers were able to pay close attention to the administration of the honour of Richmond in a way few of his predecessors had done. The surviving records, though only a small percentage of those that must have been produced, provide a fair guide to their activities.

For the most part the surviving documents relate to the years 1372–79, as will be shown in more detail below. This suggests that they were taken to Brittany in the duke's baggage on his return in August 1379. However, their fate between then and the late nineteenth century, when they were classified in 1871 at the departmental archives in Nantes, is obscure. Usually records that had once belonged to the *Trésor des chartes des ducs*, the main ducal archival repository first organised in the late fourteenth century and preserved in the *Tour neuve* at the castle of Nantes until the Revolution, bear dorsal references first assigned to them between 1566 and 1579 when a major inventory of the *Trésor* was compiled by René de Bourgneuf, seigneur de Cucé, first president of the Parlement de Bretagne.[6] These endorsements indicated their then location in wooden boxes (*cassettes*) stored in cupboards (*armoires*) in the form 'Armoire A, cassette A, inventarié I', Cupboard 1, box 1, no. 1. They remained there until they were reclassified in the nineteenth century. They then formed the first 248 *liasses* in the *série E* containing just over 4,000 individual documents, now all digitised and readily accessible to users world-wide.[7]

Currently those concerning the administration of the honour in the 1370s are within the modern subsection 'Relations des ducs avec la couronne d'Angleterre', E 114–E 123. The surviving accounts and subsidiary documents such as ducal orders and quittances occupy E 117 (36 items) and E 118 (64 items).[8] *Liasses* E 114 and E 115 chiefly contain individual treaties, charters and other documents issued by kings of England from Henry III to Richard II, the majority relating to grants of the earldom and honour of Richmond, while E 116 contains a single item, a register, feodary and extent of the honour drawn up in 1398. This includes an important section listing seventy-four 'homagers' in Lincolnshire, that is those owing homage to the lord of the honour, headed by the previous lord, John of Gaunt, and a further 443 free tenants and fifty-two

6 Nantes, AD Loire-Atlantique, E 243; see Michael Jones, *Le premier inventaire du Trésor des chartes des ducs de Bretagne (1395). Hervé le Grant et les origines du* Chronicon Briocense (Rennes, 2007), for the history of the ducal archives. Since all the manuscript material used in this article is found in Nantes, it will simply be cited by the current class/call number.

7 To be found at https://archives-numerisees.loire-atlantique/fr under the opening menu at Trésor des chartes des ducs de Bretagne.

8 Since the summaries offered on the website are often very general, with many errors of dating and identification, a revised check-list of the contents of E 117 and E 118 is provided in Appendix II below.

bondmen, all tenants of the honour, together with charters relating to earlier ducal grants and confirmations or others particularly concerning Boston.[9] The remaining *liasses*, E 119–E 123 include a very wide range of diplomatic and financial documents, most dating from Edward III's later years to the reign of Henry VII.

Only one of the Lincolnshire documents relating to Richmond bears a dorsal reference. This is an account of Adam Wandesford, bailiff of Boston, for three months in 1377.[10] Likewise very few endorsements are found on similar accounts for honorial lands in other counties or for estates delivered by Richard II to John IV, such as Sevenhampton, Wiltshire, or Penrith, Cumberland, in exchange for the duke leasing the castle of Brest to him for the duration of the Anglo-French war in 1378. One is on a mandate for the payment of one of John IV's English estate officials in 1384, whilst the same reference that occurs on Wandesford's account (KD 1) also occurs on that of Stephen Wynne, reeve (*prepositus*) of Swaffham, Norfolk, in 1377–78.[11] Thanks to René de Bourgneuf's inventory, it is also clear that some at least of the other documents in E 117 and E 118 must have been stored together with those two accounts in the *Trésor* so that their archival history to the present seems assured.[12]

The Lincolnshire documents in E 117 and E 118 confirm that, by the 1370s, the honorial lands in the county were organised into groups for administrative purposes. These either centred on an individual manor (of which the most important was that of Boston itself), to which lands or rights in other places might be attached, or on a number of small estates forming a soke, whose origins as in the case of Gayton[-le-Wold] (Louthesk wapentake) or Skirbeck (Skirbeck) date back to late Anglo-Saxon times. These sokes had passed to Count Alan Rufus and his successors in the years after the Conquest as the

9 E 116 fols 13r–16v, for the courts held by ducal commissioners in Lincolnshire between 1 and 17 July 1398 which list tenants present acknowledging fealty; fol. 23v, charter of Piers *Walsokyn*, chaplain, granting to Ranulph de Lincoln, several houses in Wormgate, Boston, between the houses of Robert *Arneysson'* on the north, the cemetery of St Botulph's south, abutting the land of the rectory east and *sour la file de l'yaue vers le west*, Boston, 27 March 1321, property later conveyed by Ranulph, now described as Ranulph de Kyme, citizen and merchant of Lincoln, to John de *Wendlyngborgh*, merchant of Boston, mentioning the 'mansion' of the rectory, 20 July 1325, and by Wendlyngborough to John Horn of Boston, 30 November 1348.

10 E 118/40 (KD 1); see also note 12 below.

11 E 117/4 (OD 35), published in the *Recueil des actes de Jean IV, duc de Bretagne, 1357–1399*, ed. Michael Jones, 3 vols (Paris, 1980–83, and Rennes, 2001), ii, no. 486; E 118/21 (KD 1), Wynne's account.

12 E 243, fol. 126v, 'Vng viel compte en Rolles de parchemin non signé ny daté d'ung Recevour de duc Jehan de la despens par luy faicte en Angleterre durant le temps il y a esté avecques pluseurs autres aquitz et lettres servant a la verificacion de la despaise dudit compte'.

honour of Richmond took shape. An extent of the honour compiled in 1280–82 shows that the administrative structure functioning in the late fourteenth-century records was already firmly in place.[13] The 1398 register confirms that it remained so at the point when the duke-earls last held the honour. What the records from the 1370s also show is that in addition to the reeves and bailiffs administering individual manors or sokes, there was a general receiver of ducal income for Lincolnshire. He collected money from the reeves and bailiffs, which he then delivered directly into the hands of the duke, to his two main financial officers, a receiver-general of the honour and the treasurer of his household, or to the steward (*senescallus*) of Richmond, who exercised his authority as senior ducal officer throughout the whole honour.

A similar administrative structure also seems to have been operative in some other counties where there were extensive honorial lands, such as Norfolk.[14] In Lincolnshire, William Harcourt, who had some experience of honorial administration from the days of John of Gaunt,[15] acted as receiver for the county between at least Michaelmas 1373 and Michaelmas 1376, as three surviving accounts testify.[16] These show that in 1373–74 his receipts came to £956 1s. 4½d., to £509 18s. 7¾d. in 1374–75 and £628 12s. 3½d. in 1375–76, an indication of the important contribution that Lincolnshire estates made to honorial finances, since they seem to have represented around 40% of the duke's income from his honour, although these accounts cannot be used as the equivalent of a modern balance-sheet. Their figures should be considered indicators of scale rather than as exact figures of annual receipts and expenditure. For instance, they often included accounting arrears from previous years that disguise actual annual income and expenditure.[17]

Boston (Skirbeck) was by far the most important honorial holding in Lincolnshire and the accounts, together with a rental of 1372–73, distinguish

[13] Roger Gale, *Registrum honoris de Richmund* (London, 1722), Appendix, no. VIII, pp. 29–42 for the inquiry in Lincolnshire.

[14] E 118/62 and 63, accounts of Thomas Tynteshale, receiver of moneys in Norfolk, 1374–75.

[15] In 1366 he was granted the farm of the *tronage et pesage* of wool at Gysor's Hall for life: Pishey Thompson, *The History and Antiquities of Boston and the villages of Skirbeck, Fishtoft, Freiston, Butterwick, Benington, Leverton, Leake and Wrangle, comprising the hundred of Skirbeck in the County of Lincoln* (Boston, 1856, reprinted London, 2018), p. 339. This classic work of local history is a daunting *omnium gatherum* of information on Boston not always easy to extract or synthesize. Harcourt accounted for £36 10s. 8½d. for *tronage* and the farm of houses for half a year in 1373–74 (E 118/38), for £53 6s. 1d. in 1374–75 (E 118/36) and £40 14s. 4¾d. in 1375–76 (E 118/37). In 1377 the *tronage* was farmed for three years but the name of the farmer is not given (E 118/40).

[16] E 118/36–38.

[17] Jones, 'Bretons in Medieval Lincolnshire', 22–4 for a fuller discussion.

between the actual manor of Boston and the honorial properties or rights in the rest of the town. There has been some debate over the location of the earl's manor since Pishey Thompson, in the mid nineteenth century, placed it close to where the current Grammar School is sited to the southeast of the town,[18] The 1372–73 rental helps to confirm this by showing that most of the places mentioned in Henry VIII's grant in 1546 of Hallgarth and other Richmond properties in the town to the new borough of Boston are identical with those listed as parcels of the manor in the late fourteenth century.[19] Wandesford's account as bailiff of the town in 1377 provides the earliest known description of the manor house and its immediate surrounds. It consisted of *une salle et IIII chambres*, a hall and four chambers, a large timber-frame open ground floor hall with attached chambers, some at first-floor level.[20] They were set within a gated enclosure, a porter receiving 2d. a day for guarding the door. Extensive repairs, described in some detail, were being carried out in preparation for an expected rare visit to Boston from the duke and duchess which eventually happened in early October 1377. Fortuitously surviving ducal household accounts provide elaborate details on the ceremonial of the occasion, including a banquet hosted by the couple for leading townsmen.[21]

The foundation of Boston was originally owed to the patronage and encouragement of Count Alan and his successors. Building a sluice and bridging the Witham in the twelfth century helped to create a port, whilst the earls and their leading vassals, the Craon and Tatteshale families, who held land on the west side of the river, encouraged the development of a fair, which soon gained an international reputation.[22] Already by 1200 income from the fair represented the most important single source of revenue for the honorial lord from any of his estates. By 1300 Boston had become the main port for exporting English wool to the continent and rivalling London as the country's leading port. The fourteenth century saw a decline in the town's economic fortunes, but it was still nationally ranked tenth by tax population in 1377, so that its exploitation by John IV in straitened circumstances is hardly surprising. The drawing up of a rental in 1372–73 shortly after the duke had taken possession of the honour, together with later annotations and revisions for 1374–76, is indicative of this.[23]

The three accounts submitted by William Harcourt, for the years 1373–75, one rendered in 1376–77 by Philip Gernoun, as lieutenant for the bailiff,

18 Pishey Thompson, pp. 63–4. For careful modern discussion see Stephen Rigby, *Boston 1096–1223. A medieval boom town* (Lincoln, 2017), pp. 19–20.

19 Appendix I below.

20 E 118/40; see also Jones, 'Bretons in Medieval Lincolnshire', 26 for further discussion.

21 *ibid.*, 27–9, citing E 206/1, m. 1.

22 Rigby, *Boston 1096–1223*, pp. 9–12, 23–6.

23 E 118/1, printed in Appendix I below.

Edmund Stokes, another submitted by William Blacden, receiver of moneys at Boston, for the period 29 March–16 June 1377, and one by his successor, Adam Wandesford for 16 June–28 September 1377, provide further important evidence on the physical layout of the town, on vacant tenements, arrears and waste and on the activities of its inhabitants.[24] Damage from flooding, which had affected houses *mersum in mare*, submerged in the sea, in Wormgate in 33 Edward III (1359–60) was still affecting tithe revenues in 1376–77.[25] Perhaps the most interesting feature revealed is that the bridge over the Witham was very comparable in form, if not in scale, to Old London Bridge, with a roadway flanked by houses and shops built out over the river on either side from which substantial rents were exacted.[26] There is also mention of a crane and a rope-house,[27] while the rental also provides much earlier evidence for street and other minor names in the town than those found in Pishey Thompson. It draws attention to a wide range of crafts and trades practised in the town and the diverse geographical origins of townsmen, including some from the Low Countries. It notes, for instance, that the merchants of Brabant failed to come to the town in 1372–73.

Boston apart, all the other honorial lands in Lincolnshire were in rural manors and sokes. Close to Boston were the manors of Frampton[28] and Wykes in Donington and the sokes of Skirbeck and Kirton. On the southwestern side of the county was the manor of Leadenham (Loveden), just to the east of Lincoln the manor of Washingborough (Langoe), with the soke of Mumby (Calcewath) with its coastal and inland estates further to the east, while in the northeast, close to Grimsby and the Lindsey marsh, lay the soke of Gayton-le-Wold (Louthesk). All these estates, apart from Washingborough, which was acquired in the early twelfth century,[29] had belonged to Count Alan in 1086. In the 1280–82 extent the soke of Skirbeck (valued at around £89)[30] and Washingborough (£82) appear to have been the most remunerative, followed by Wykes (£67), Frampton (£40–£50) and the soke of Gayton (£29), with

24 E 118/13 (Gernoun), 36–8 (Harcourt), 39 (Blacden) and 40 (Wandesford).

25 E 118/13.

26 Jones, 'Bretons in Medieval Lincolnshire', 26–7.

27 Roger Lyon, chaplain, was farming the Malthouse in 1376–77 for 1 lb. of pepper per annum (E 118/13).

28 One of three manors in the parish, one of which was held of the honour by the Moulton family, leading tenants since the twelfth century: Jones, 'Bretons in Medieval Lincolnshire', 24–5. Their later history is best recounted in Peter R. Coss, *The Foundations of Gentry Life. The Multons of Frampton and their World, 1270–1370* (Oxford, 2010).

29 Jones, 'Bretons in Medieval Lincolnshire', 18.

30 Figures have been rounded up and, because of discrepancies in accounting practice or imperfections in the extent itself, are simply intended as indicative.

Leadenham (£17) the least profitable (the value of the soke of Mumby at that point has not been fully elucidated). By 1398 these relative positions had changed with Wykes (£100) and Frampton (£82) heading the list followed by Washingborough (£66), the sokes of Gayton (£42), Kirton (£36) and Skirbeck (£22 – a very considerable fall since 1280) with Leadenham (£11) and Mumby (£8) at the bottom. The surviving accounts from the 1370s show how fluctuating receipts and expenses could be from year to year.

At Frampton, for instance, in 1374–75, the reeve German Nelisson paid £80 13s. 11d. to William Harcourt on one occasion and £53 14s. 3d. arrears; in 1375–76 he paid Harcourt £83 6s. 8d. for the year and in 1376–77, the reeve Adam Bosevyl accounted for £160 5s. 5d. of income, double what it seems to have been in 1398. From the soke of Kirton the bailiff John Busy paid Harcourt in 1373–74 £85 13s. 4d., and there was also a further payment of £34 7s. from a previous bailiff; in 1374–75 Busy delivered £35 17s. 4½d. to Harcourt; his successor Roger Rolleson paid £69 8s. 2d. in 1375–76 and in 1376–77 acknowledged revenues of £81 4s. 2½d. From the soke of Mumby, John Antoynesson, bailiff, paid in 1373–74 £36 and arrears of £20 18s. 7d. to Harcourt; in 1374–75 £20, together with £24 4s. 11d. in arrears and in 1375–76 only £19 15s. At Washingborough, John Rasisson, reeve, paid £77s 5s. 2d. to Harcourt in 1374–75; in 1375–76 Robert Wodelef, reeve, paid him £74 18s. 1½d., and in 1376–77 William Elyot, reeve, accounted for revenues of £124 18s. 1¾d. All the other manors showed similar widely fluctuating variations.

The accounts also provide evidence on farming practices and other activities associated with managing estates, as well as on social conditions, For instance, at Swineshead (Kirton) between 1372 and 1374, John Attleden farmed the marsh for £10 13s. 4d. p.a., and in 1376–77 fines paid by Adam Bosevyl, reeve of Frampton, levied for transgressions of customary practices in that marsh totalled £6 13s. 4d., while expenses incurred transporting turves from the marsh to Swineshead amounted to the surprising sum of £13 19s.[31] Land at farm brought in £9 15s. 1d. that year. Bosevyl also accounted for £6 tallage and 13s. 4d. chevage on bondmen, while assize income arising from customary rents and dues brought in £50 12s. 2d. and perquisites of the manorial court £3 15s. 5d. Sales of hay and herbage (£5 8d.), turves (26s. 8d.) and sheep (24s.) were recorded, and 15s. 4d. was spent on maintaining the mill. At Leadenham in 1376–77, Nicholas Blank, a bondman appointed reeve, accounted for pannage fees paid by twenty-one peasants.[32] William Elyot, reeve of Washingborough, in the same year was unable to pay any money collected from farming lakes and ponds because of damage caused by John of Gaunt's officers when they

31 E 118/2 and 4.

32 E 118/12, and cf. 11 for his main account. In 1398 Nicholas, together with Hugh and John Blank, gave sureties as bondmen (E 116, fol. 16v).

held the manor.[33] Among his expenses were the usual costs of mill maintenance, in this case £2 paid to carpenters for repairs, and 12d. spent on the pinfold. All other accounts submitted by reeves and bailiffs contain similar snippets. They particularly underline the importance of assize income and court perquisites as sources of revenue. This is also fully confirmed in the 1398 extent.[34]

This brief discussion of the accounts and other documents surviving from the 1370s for the history of the honorial lands of Richmond in Lincolnshire has been couched in very general terms. A more detailed analysis would bring out further regional differences in economic fortunes or social structure. Such an analysis should also make use of some comparable material from the 1380s when the honorial lands were in royal hands so that a more comprehensive view of the honour at the end of the fourteenth century could be established.[35] Nevertheless, it will have served its purpose if some of the evidence presented, especially that for the topography and life in late fourteenth-century Boston, reaches a wider audience and encourages further investigation of this little-exploited cache of documents.

Appendix I

Rental for the Honour of Richmond in Boston, 29 September 1372–29 September 1373 (Nantes, AD Loire-Atlantique, E 118/1, a single sheet of parchment)

*Rentale de Sancto Botholpho a festo Sancti Michaelis anno regni regis Edwardi tercii XLVI*to *usque idem festum subsequentem anno XLVII*o *per j annum integrum*

Terminis Purificacionis beate Marie, Sancti Botholphi et Sancti Michaelis[36]

33 E 118/20.

34 E 116, fols 13r–16v. Among expenses in 1398 at Kirton 2s. 6d. was spent on repairing the sea dyke (fol. 15v).

35 Jones, *Ducal Brittany*, pp. 178–9, 182 for a brief discussion based on this later material.

36 2 February, 17 June and 29 September respectively.

Barregate[37]

De Johanne Glasenwrighte		13s. 4d.[38]
De Thoma de Claceby		18s.
Summa	Summa	31s. 4d.

Memorandum quod omnes nove ex alterius vel diminuciones sequenti incip' primo anno XLIX° ad sanctum Michaelem[39]

Bucheria[40]

De Johanne Lyghthed		15s.
De Johanne Wawayn		15s.
De Johanne de Lusseby		15s.
De Johanne de Sibsey		15s.
De Alano Perkyn		15s.
De[41] Waltero Heved		15s.
	Summa	4 li. 10s.

Orientalis pars le Fisherowe[42]

De Johanna Hopcrowe	28s.
De Simone Candeler	24s.
De Petro de Neuland[43]	22s.
De eodem Petro pro alia shop' ibidem	22s.

37 The earliest mention of this and most of the following street/minor names in Pishey Thompson, *Antiquities of Boston* date from Henry VIII's grant to the Corporation in 1546 of Hallgarth manor and the other honour of Richmond rights and possessions in the town (pp. 63–4).

38 Sums given in Roman numerals in the original.

39 Comment added by auditors in left margin.

40 Pishey Thompson, pp. 218–19, for a discussion of the Butchery, sited near the northwest corner of the Market Place, from the mid sixteenth century onwards.

41 In the left margin, usually opposite the last entry of a block as here, auditors have noted the *summa* which is formally given in concluding each section. These marginal sub-totals have not been included except where they add information.

42 Now Church Street. The accounts of Philip Gernoun, lieutenant of Edmund Stokes, bailiff of Boston, in 1376–77 mention a tenancy in *Le Fysshrowe* held by Gregory Milly, formerly by Simon Gyldyng, abutting the foot of the bridge, for which he owed 1 lb. rent in pepper (E 118/13).

43 A Pierre de Neuland performed fealty at Boston in 1398 (E 116, fol. 14r). Following references for fealties in 1398 are taken from this same source (fols 13v–14r).

De Galfrido de Langrake	20s.
De Willelmo Fisher	13s. 4d.
De eodem Willelmo pro alia shopp' ibidem	15s.
De Benedicto de Menes	15s.
De Roberto de Selby	15s.
De Ricardo Abraham	30s.
Summa	10 li. 14s. 4d.

Nova bucheria

De Ricardo Abraham	26s. 8d.
De Willelmo Abraham[44]	13s. 4d.
De Adam Bucher	13s. 4d.
De Alano Perkyn	13s. 4d.
De Roberto Rous	13s. 4d.
De Thoma Pay	13s. 4d.
De Thoma Drop'[45]	13s. 4d.
De Johanne Wynche	13s. 4d.
De Willelmo de Pomfreyt	13s. 4d.
De Luca Dust	26s. 8d.
De Simone de Fenne	53s. 4d.
De Isabella la Rede[46]	46s. 8d.
De eadem Isabella pro alia domo in Lopholme	55s. 4d.
De eadem Isabella	8s.
De Radulfo Oskheved	12s.
De Dulcia Tapester	18s.
De Ricardo de Jernemuth	16s.
De Alano Taillour	16s. et in annis sequentibus 12d. plusque
De Johanne de Driffeld	20s.
De Alicia de Wenham	24s.

[44] William Abraham, butcher, performed fealty at Boston in 1398 while Henry Abraham was a tenant in Skirbeck and Nicholas and Robert Abraham at Kirton.

[45] He, or a homonym, performed fealty at Boston in 1398.

[46] In 1398 Reynald Rede performed fealty at Boston, while Thomas was a tenant at Wykes and William at Kirton.

De Roberto Catour		16s.
De Willelmo del House[47]		60s.
	Summa	25 li. 5s. 4d.

In medio ponte ex parte boreali

De Thoma Furbour		15s.
De Roberto Shether'		15s.
De Willelmo de Massyngham		36s. 8d.
De Willelmo de Scouby et Thoma Stalworth 100s. et in annis subsequentibus 4s. plusque		
De Roberto Catour		20s.
~~De eodem Roberto pro j placeam vasti 6s. 8d.~~ quod stetit vacuum hoc anno		
De Petro Fisher		20s.
De Rogero del Loft ~~20s.~~ 10s. quia stetit vac' per dimidium annum		
De Nicholao Bedeman		40s.
De Stephano Croun		20s.
De Ricardo Stalworth pro j placeam vasti ibidem		6s. 8d.
	Summa	14 li. 3s. 4d.

Ex australi parte pontis

De Roberto Wautoun		15s. 6d.
De Hugone Wright pro ij shopp' ibidem		30s.
De Johanne Bailly Errant[48]		40s.
De[49] Thoma Furbour ~~20s.~~10s. et non plus quia stetit vac' per dimidium annum		
De Willelmo Lyghtfote[50]		34s.
De Johanna de Burton		26s. 8d.
De Willelmo de Hesill' aurifabro		20s.
De Roberto dicto Broun Robyn		26s. 8d.
De Johanne Lambert tavernario		4 li.
	Summa	14 li. 4s. 4d.

47 He, or a homonym, performed fealty at Boston in 1398.

48 Not otherwise identified.

49 In left margin: *a[nno] XLVIII 20s.*

50 In 1376–77, William *Lythfot* was being pursued for arrears allegedly stretching over twenty years (E 118/13).

Le Escheker ad pedem pontis

De Ricardo Stalworth		6 li. 13s. 4d.
De Johanne de Halton		13s. 4d.
De Ricardo Garlekmongre		20s.
De Willelmo de Goushill		16s. 8d.
De Rogero del Loft		20s.
De Ricardo Kerver		40s.
De Johanne Birch		20s.
De Henrico de Leverton		40s.
De Petro Palmere		18s.
De Benedicto Watkynsoun		20s.
De Johanne Clementsoun		36s.
De Ricardo Cartersoun		30s.
De Willelmo Barbour[51]		20s.
De Willelmo Yole		20s.
De Willelmo Symsoun		20s.
De Willelmo de Benyngtoun		30s.
	Summa	24 li. 17s. 4d.

Neusent

De Johanne Coke potterer	40s.
De Waltero Pescod[52]	40s.
De Johanne Hadelay	40s.
De Johanne Molde[53]	40s.
De Thoma de Chosell'[54]	40s.
De Ricardo de Thymelby	40s.
De Willelmo de Thorntoun[55]	40s.

51 Jacques Barbour performed fealty at Boston in 1398.

52 Pishey Thompson had difficulty finding any early members living in Boston of this family, which gave its name to the still standing Pescod Hall (p. 222). This Walter, or a homonym, performed fealty in 1398.

53 In 1398 Agnes Mould performed fealty.

54 In 1398 Cecile Chosell performed fealty.

55 He, or a homonym, performed fealty in 1398.

De Edmundo Claver		40s.
De Thoma de Gosberkirk		46s. 8d.
De Henrico Cok		15s. 5d.
	Summa	19 li. 20d.[56]

Cranerowe

De Stephano Baxter et Waltero de Hareby		40s.
	Summa	40s.

Vertatur pro consimilibus firmiis in dorso

Dorse

Quinque selarii in Gasconrowe

De Rogero Broud		20s.
De Johanne Chapman		20s.
De Henrico Botell'		26s. 8d.
De Roberto de Toft		30s.
De Johanne de Castell	~~20s.~~15s. et quia stetit vac' per j quarterium anni	
De ij selariis ibidem[57]		
De le Crane[58]		8s. 4d.
	Summa 8 li. 5s., 25s. plus a[nno] XLVIII°	

Parcelle nostra maneria

De Johanne de Edelyngton	5[...] 8d.
De heredibus Johannis Thomasson pro Roperhous'	26s.
De Magota de Welbourn	~~13s. 4d.~~[59]
De Johanne de Westoun	26s. 4d.
De Johanne de Braunstoun	15s.
De Ricardo Coupe junior'	52s.[60]
De eodem Ricardo	40s.

56 *Recte* 19 li. 2s. 1d.

57 There follow various, largely illegible, additions, indicating rents of around 70s.

58 The earliest reference in Pishey Thompson to a crane for unloading ships dates from 1600 (p. 343).

59 This item has been illegibly glossed.

60 E 118/40 for his messuage in 1377.

De Johanne Besage		3s. 4d.
De Henrico Cok		20s.
De Thoma Bosse		3s. 4d.
De Henrico Wright		3s. 4d.
	Summa	13 li. 9s. 8d.
	plus a[nno] XLVIII°	12 li. 16s. 4d.[61]

Item de Willelmo Hares pro XVI partic' vast' exopell' venell' firmiis predictis 5s.

Summa totalis firmiis domorum 137 li. 12s. 4d. anno XLVII
Summa totalis firmariis domorum 139 li. 9s. anno XLVIII°

Stallag'[62]

De Pannatoribus[63]		2s. 4d.
De Parvis merceriis[64]		15s.
De Pictreariis London'		6s. 8d.
De Siccoris pro Stallagio		6s.
De Losemarket nulla quia aliter superius in parvis merceriis[65]		
De parva piscariis[66]		10s.
De mensa olei		26s. 8d.
De Stallagio taintatoriis[67]		3s. 8d.
	Summa[68]	70s. 4d.

Frontag'

De heredibus Willelmi de Flete pro ij plac' equaliter solutis	6s. 8d.

[61] Added above the original sum and in the same hand as the following entry.

[62] It is probable that most if not all of the stalls mentioned were in the Market Place.

[63] Cloth was already being manufactured in Boston in 1201 (Pishey Thompson, p. 37).

[64] *ibid.*, p. 226, mentions 'a row of mean houses' called Mercer's Row in the Market Place in 1564.

[65] There are some illegible notes in the right margin.

[66] To be distinguished from the main fish market, called Fish-stones in 1564 (Pishey Thompson, p. 226)?

[67] Around 1200 local merchants were already being accused of sharp practices over the dying of cloth (*ibid.*, p. 37).

[68] Two small subtotals in left margin *55s.* and *66s. 8d.* struck out.

De eisdem pro j plac' vasti ante ostium sim'		6d.
De Ricardo de Wrangle		7s.
De heredibus Willelmi de Ketilby		13s. 4d.
De Johanne de Toft		6s. 8d.
De Saiero de Rocheford milite[69]		13s. 4d.
De Johanne de Slotheby		10s.
De Priore de Frestoun[70]		6s. 8d.
De Willelmo de Flete		10s.
De fenestris Hales de Deest,[71] nulla quia merceriorum de Brabaunt non venit[72] nulla hoc anno		
De Willelmo Harcourt pro *les holmes* cum molend'		4 li. 3s. 4d.
	Summa	7 li. 17s. 6d.
Summa totalis stallag' et frontag'.		11 li. 7s. 10d
Summa totalis huius rotulus.		149 li. 2d
		392 li. 8s. 5¼d.[73]

Appendix II

Check-list of accounts and other documents relating to the household and estates in England of John IV, duke of Brittany, earl of Richmond, 1372–79 (Nantes, AD Loire-Atlantique, E 117 and E 118).[74]

E 117

1 List of lands in the open fields and of tenants at Sevenhampton, Wilts., mid-late 14th c., small parchment roll of four membranes with the modern endorsement 'vers 1351' (m. 1), following 2 below.

69 Pishey Thompson, pp. 319–30 for the Rochford family.

70 *ibid.*, pp. 508–20 for Freiston Priory, a dependency of Crowland Abbey.

71 *Hales de Deest* was almost certainly originally from Diest, Flemish Brabant, Belgium.

72 Explanation added in different, smaller hand.

73 Added in a small hand at the bottom right, with no explanation.

74 The titles and brief summaries found of these two *liasses* on the departmental website are, almost without exception, adapted from those of Léon Maître, the archivist who heroically between 1869 and 1871 catalogued the *Trésor.* Many dates are very general while identifications of persons and places are often imprecise. Unless otherwise mentioned all documents consist of a single parchment membrane, written in Latin.

2 Similar, presented by R. Russell, keeper (*custos*) of the manor, *anno xxiiij*, 1 membrane, 1350–51?[75]

3 Order of John IV to John Cropwode, bailiff of the Rape of Hastings, to take horses, carriages and other goods of which the duke had need for his ship, Burwash, Sussex, 1 December 1377, French (= *Recueil* (cited in full, note 11 above), i, no. 263).

4 Order of John IV to John FitzNichol, steward of the duke's lands in England, to pay various debts to Jannequin Derneford, Nantes, 1 March 1384, French, old archival reference OD 35 (= *Recueil*, ii, no. 486).

5 Inquiry and extent by Richard Whitemarsh and Simon de Flutheman into the value of Castle Rising, Norfolk (damaged), 29 August 1378.

6 Letters of Edward, prince of Wales, leasing the Tollbooth at (King's) Lynn, Norfolk, 24 (month unknown), 47 Edward III (1373–74).

7[76] Order of John IV to the reeve of Cheshunt, Herts., to provide Guillaume Briz, chaplain, with various victuals for the duke's household, 1 (*recte* 5) February 1378, French (= *Recueil*, i, no. 266).

8 Quittance of Guillaume Le Briz, ducal chaplain, for victuals worth £10 7s. 11d., 4 April 1378, French.

9 Quittance from John FitzNichol to Piers Flynthard, reeve of Cheshunt, Herts., for £9 9s., Friday next to Pentecost, 1 Ric. II, i.e. 4 June 1378?, French.

10 Order of John IV to John Wodeward, receiver-general of the county of Richmond, to pay various men-at-arms, Cheshunt, 23 May 1378, French (= *Recueil*, i, no. 278).

11 Indenture issued by William de Wyndesore, treasurer of John IV, recognizing receipt from Piers Flynthard, reeve of Cheshunt, of various victuals for the lord's household, Cheshunt, 18 September 1378, French.

12 Expenses of Piers Flynthard/t, reeve of Cheshunt, when the duke and his household were staying at the manor. Undated, French.

13 Order from John FitzNichol, steward of Richmond, to Piers Flynthard, to repair houses at Cheshunt, London, 2 November 1377, French.

14 Order of John Wodeward, receiver-general of the duke, to Piers Flynthard, to pay Thomas Haket according to the duke's letters and taking a quittance from him, Cheshunt, 23 May 1378, French.[77]

15 Quittance from Thomas Haket for £8 2s. owing to him from the duke's gift for the period 20 April 1378–29 September 1378, French.

16 Order from John IV to Piers Flynthard to pay John Breton for the guard of the manor and parks of Cheshunt and for surveying carpenters and

[75] Suggested by Maître to be 24 Edward III (1350–51). Sevenhampton was delivered to John IV in 1378 along with Castle Rising in exchange for the castle of Brest, leased to the English (Jones, *Ducal Brittany*, p. 175).

[76] Nos 7–16 are currently all tied together.

[77] cf. *Recueil*, i, no. 266, for the duke's grant to Haket of 12d. a day on revenues of Cheshunt, Cheshunt, 20 April 1378.

other labourers, and for other debts, Cheshunt, 3 March 1378, French (= *Recueil*, i, no. 269).

17[78] Indenture by which William de Wyndesore, treasurer, recognizes the receipt from John Wodeward, receiver-general of Richmond, of £80 for the duke's household, *Botulpheston* (Boston), Lincs., 16 June 1378, French.[79]

18 Similar, for £94 13s. 4d., Castle Rising, 17 October 1378, French (seal of William de Wyndesore).

19 Similar, for £12 5s. 4d., Cheshunt, 2 May 1378, French (fragment of seal).

20 Similar, for £40, received by Wyndesore from Wodeward, by the hands of Adam Wandesford, receiver of the town of Boston, Cheshunt, 21 July 1377, French.

21 Similar, for various sums received for household at Swineshead, Lincs., 21 October–8 February 1378 and at Castle Rising, Norfolk, 10 February–29 September 1378, at Cheshunt, 21 July 1378 and at Cambridge, 14 September 1378, French.

22 Indenture whereby William de Wyndesore recognizes receiving from John Wodeward by the hands of Thomas Ty[n]tteshal, receiver of Swaffham Market, Norfolk, £20 for the household, 27 June 1377, French.

23 Similar for £147 17s. 11½d., Cheshunt, 17 August 1377, French.

24 Similar for £15 7s. 8d., Cheshunt, 4 September 1378, French.

25 Similar, for £13 6s. 7d. from Wodeward by the hands of Janekyn Curteys, Castle Rising, Norfolk, 1 March 1378, and a further £4 on 7 April 1378, French.

26 Order of John IV to John Wodeward to allow Piers Flynthard £6 14s. 1½d. when he renders his account for what he had spent on the household as attested by Janekyn Curtis and Guillaume Le Briz, 10 April [1378], French (= *Recueil*, i, no. 274).

27 Indenture by which William de Wyndesore recognizes receipt from John Wodeward of £44 6s., Castle Rising, 26 September 1378, French

28 Quittance from the prioress of *Stiksewould* (Stixwould, Lincs.), for receipt of 13s. 4d. from John IV for the term of St James the Apostle (25 July), received on 8 May [1377], Stixwould, 29 September 1377.[80]

29 List of tenants and lands in the open fields at Sevenhampton, Wilts., small parchment roll of four membranes, later 14th c. as 1.

30 Similar, one membrane.

[78] Nos 17–28 are currently tied together with a piece of modern (?fishing) line.

[79] E 118/50 for the accounts of John Wodeward, receiver-general of the duke's lands in England, 6 September 1377–6 March 1378.

[80] Eustachia de Ravenser, prioress of Stixwould, 1376/7–1403 (David M. Smith & Vera C. M. London (eds), *Heads of Religious Houses, II: 1216–1377* (Cambridge 2001), p. 611).

31 Accounts of William de Wyndesore, treasurer of the household, 22 September 1377–29 September 1378, paper, roll of three sheets (damaged), written on both sides.

32 Expenses of the ducal household at Castle Rising, Norfolk. late September–26 October 1378, quire of thirteen folios, paper, French.[81]

33 Accounts for the ducal household, 3 August–22 September 1377, large paper roll, twenty-three sheets, French.

34 Fragment of accounts of William Windsor, clerk, treasurer of the duke, 29 September–26 October 1378, paper, two sheets, probably originally part of a roll.[82]

35 Expenses of John IV's household in England, 14 September–2 November 1377, long paper roll, thirteen sheets, damaged at head, French.

[36] *La Retenue des gentz d'armes et archers assignez pour le Nief Mons.*, listing the names of sixty-two men-at-arms, fifty-eight archers and four minstrels [1377], loose sheet of paper at the end of 35, French.[83]

E 118

1 Rental for the Honour of Richmond estate in Boston, Lincs., 29 September 1372–29 September 1373, with additions for 1373–75 (edited in Appendix I above).

2 Accounts of John Attelden, farmer of the marsh at Swineshead, Lincs., 26 June 1372–29 September 1374.

3 Accounts of John Godwyph, bailiff of Skirbeck, Lincs., 29 September 1376–29 September 1377.

4 Accounts of Alan Bosevyl, reeve of Frampton, Lincs., 29 September 1376–29 September 1377.

5 Accounts of Ralph Phelyp', reeve of Wykes [in Donington], Lincs., 29 September 1376–29 September 1377.

6 Accounts of Roger Rolleson, bailiff of Kirton, Lincs., 29 September 1376–29 September 1377.

7 Particulars of accounts of Roger Rolleson, 1376.

8 Particulars for an account [of Roger Rolleson?] in same hand as 7, *c.* 1376.

[81] Of which twelve used, containing lists of purchases etc. for *Butterie* (f. 1v), *Garderie* (2r–v), *Cuisine* (3r), *Mareschaucie* (3v), and various expenses in considerable detail for period 29 September–26 October 1378 (5r–12v).

[82] For the counter-roll kept by Janekyn Curteys for the period 24 September–26 October 1378 when the duke was chiefly at Castle Rising, see E 206/3.

[83] An original retinue list for the duke's forces *pour le voiage sur le mier* with Thomas, earl of Buckingham in the winter of 1377 is found in TNA, E 101/42/13 (cf. *Recueil*, iii, no. 1259).

9 Particulars of an account as 7 and 8 for Kirton, 1 Richard II, 1377–78.

10 Accounts of John Antoynesson, bailiff of Mumby, Lincs., 29 June 1376–29 September 1377.

11 Accounts of Nicholas Blaunk, reeve of Leadenham, Lincs., 29 September 1376–29 September 1377.

12 Particulars for 11.

13 Accounts of Philip Gernoun, lieutenant of Edmund Stokes, bailiff of Boston, Lincs., 29 September 1376–29 September 1377, two membranes.[84]

14 Accounts of John Pope, reeve of Swaffham [Market], Norfolk, 30 September 1376–29 September 1377.

15 Contemporary transcript of accounts of Roger Hobbes, reeve of Sevenhampton, Wilts., 29 September 1374–29 September 1375.

16 Accounts of William Maupas, feudal bailiff of John IV in Norfolk, 29 September 1374–29 September 1375.

17 Similar, 29 September 1375–29 September 1376.

18 Accounts of bailiff of Swaffham Market, Norfolk, *c.* 1371–72, together with (m. 2) transcript of accounts of Thomas de *Titeshale*, bailiff of fees of the liberty of Richmond in Norfolk and Suffolk, 1372.

19 Accounts of Thomas de *Tynteshal,* bailiff of fees in Norfolk, 27 June 1372–29 September 1372, 29 September 1372–29 September 1373 and 29 September 1373–29 September 1374.

20 Accounts of William Elyot, reeve of Washingborough, Lincs., 29 September 1376–29 September 1377.

21 View of accounts of Stephen Wynne, reeve of Swaffham, Norfolk, 29 September 1377–10 January 1378, with 16th c. archival reference KD 1.

22 View of account of William Taillour, reeve of Sevenhampton, Wilts., 29 September 1378–7 March 1379.

23 Accounts of William Maupas, lieutenant of Adam Blakemore, keeper of the duke's fees in Norfolk, 29 September 1376–29 September 1377.

24 Particulars of accounts of Roger Hobbes, reeve of Sevenhampton, Wilts., 29 September 1377–30 April 1378.

25 Similar, 5 April 1378–29 September 1378.

26 Accounts of Robert Loundys, receiver of the duke in the Rape of Hastings, Susssex, 29 September 1377–29 September 1378.

27 Accounts of William Comdenne, reeve of *Byvelhame (*Bivelham manor, Crowhurst), Sussex, 29 September 1377–29 September 1378.

28 Accounts of Thomas Turnour, reeve of Burghersh, Sussex, 29 September 1377–29 September 1378.

84 Gernoun had served as bailiff himself, 1374–76, as Harcourt's accounts show (E 118/36–38).

29 Expenses of ?Piers Rine of Crowhurst, Sussex by command of the duke from Monday, 23 Nov. [1377] when the duke arrived for supper, paper, French.

30 Accounts of John Kyng, reeve of Crowhurst, Sussex, 29 September 1377–29 September 1378.

31 Accounts of John Crowyshersh, receiver of the duke in the Rape of Hastings, Sussex, 29 September 1376–29 September 1377.

32 Accounts of William Dosy, reeve of the duke at his manor of Bivelham, Sussex, 29 September 1376–29 September 1377.

33 Accounts of Philippe Fysshe, reeve of Burghersh, Sussex, 30 September 1376–29 September 1377.

34 Accounts of Henry Natalee, reeve of Crowhurst, Sussex, 29 September 1377–30 September 1378.

35 Accounts of Peter Flynthard, reeve of Cheshunt, Herts., 29 September 1377–30 September 1378.

36 Accounts of William Harcourt, receiver of moneys of the duke in the county of Lincoln, 29 September 1374–29 September 1375.

37 Accounts of William Harcourt, receiver of moneys of the duke in the county of Lincoln, 29 September 1375–29 September 1376.

38 Accounts of William Harcourt, receiver of moneys of the duke in the county of Lincoln, 29 September 1373–29 September 1374.

39 Accounts of William de Blacden, receiver of moneys of the duke at Boston, Lincs., Easter (29 March) 1377–Vigil of St Botulph (16 June) 1377, when Adam Wandesford was instituted.

40 Accounts of Adam Wandesford, bailiff of the duke at Boston from the Vigil of St Botulph (16 June) 1377–28 September 1377.

41 Transcript of the accounts of Thomas Watresson, reeve of Bassingbourn, Cambs., 29 September 1370–29 September 1371.

42 Transcript of the accounts of Richard de Brotherton, reeve of Cheshunt, Herts., 29 September 1370–29 September 1371.

43 Accounts of John Swan, reeve of Cheshunt, Herts., 29 September 1376–29 September 1377.

44 Accounts of Adam Studham, reeve of Bassingbourn, Cambs., 29 September 1375–29 September 1376.

45 Quittance of John FitzNichol, steward of Richmond, attorney of Thomas Melbourne, to Adam Studham of Bassingbourn for £40 3s. 10d. in part payment of 100 marks owing to the duke on last Easter and Michaelmas terms, Bassingbourn, Cambs., 20 November 1374, with seal (red).

46 Quittance of William de Overbury to Adam Stodham for 100s. for last St John the Baptist term, part of £20 p.a. assigned by the duke to him and his wife, Isabella, on Bassingbourn manor, Bassingbourn, *le jour de Goule d'Augst* (1 August) 1376, sealed on tongue (red wax) – Cf. *Recueil Jean IV*, I, no. 227, 29 September 1374, for ducal grant (French)

47 Duplicate of 46.

48 Quittance by William Overbury to Adam Stodham for £5 for Easter term, Bassingbourn, Cambs., 23 April 1376 (French).

49 Quittance by William Overbury to Adam Stodham for 46s. 8d., part of £5 for Christmas term, Bassingbourn, Cambs., 1 March 1376 (Latin).

50 Account of John Wodeward, general receiver of moneys for the duke, 6 September 1377–6 March 1378.

51 Particulars of an account, location *Pykenham* uncertain, possibly Suffolk, late 14th c.

52 Account of William de Cros, keeper of lands belonging to the Chapel of the lord at Swaffham, Norfolk, 1372–74.

53 Account of John Wombe, collector of money for the Chapel (?at Swaffham), 29 September 1376–29 September 1377.

54 Account of John Wombe, collector of rents and farms of lands of the Chapel (?at Swaffham), 1376–77.

55 Particulars of expenses of Thomas Leygton, reeve of Cheshunt, Herts., 29 September 1378 et seq.

56 View of accounts of Thomas Leygton, reeve of Cheshunt, Herts., 29 September 1378–21 May 1379.

57 Accounts of John Wodeward, receiver of moneys for the duke for manors acquired from the king, 5 April 1378–29 September 1378.

58 View of accounts of John Kyng, reeve of Crowhurst, Sussex, 29 September 1378–12 May 1379 (paper).

59 View of accounts of John Houchoun, reeve of Burghersh, Sussex, 29 September 1378–12 May 1379 (paper).

60 View of accounts of Richard Trippe, reeve of Bivelham, Sussex, 29 September 1378–12 May 1379 (paper).

61 View of accounts of Robert Loundes, receiver of moneys of the duke in the Rape of Hastings, Sussex, 29 September 1378–12 May 1379.

62 Accounts of Thomas Tyteshale, receiver of moneys in the county of Norfolk, Swaffham, 1374.

63 Accounts of Thomas *Tyteshale*, receiver of moneys in the county of Norfolk, 29 September 1374–29 September 1375.

64 Letters of John de Neville, lord of Raby, governor of the county of Richmond, assigning to William de Blacden, as one of the auditors appointed to hear accounts of lands of *mons. de Bretaigne* in Norfolk, to make payments of various sums due to him via accounts in the county of York, London, 12 November 1375.[85]

[85] Since this paper was first drafted, seven documents in Appendix II have been edited in Michael Jones, Comptes de Jean IV, duc de Bretagne (1364–99) (Paris, Académie des Inscriptions et Belles-Lettres, Recueils des Historiens de la France, Documents financiers et administratifs, XII, 2025, et Rennes, Société d'Histoire et d'Archéologie de Bretagne, Sources médiévales de l'histoire de Bretagne, 11, 2025), pp. 75–82 (E 117/31), 82-4 (E117/34), 85–92 (E 118/50), 93–4 (E 118/57), 94–121 (E 117/33), 122–41 (E 117/35) and 168–92 (E 117/32).

8

'Directed according to the judgement of the Dean and Chapter?' Fifteenth-century Chantry Chaplains in Lincoln Cathedral

MARIANNE WILSON

I think back very fondly on the time I spent during my PhD working in the Exchequergate Library (often wearing fingerless gloves in winter!). Alongside Nicholas Bennett, the oracle as regards the records of Lincoln Cathedral in the Middle Ages, I spent many hours perusing the core manuscripts produced by the dean and chapter. In so doing, I became very interested in the people who had lived and worked in the cathedral close, which was the focus of my thesis, but I also developed a secondary project exploring the expectations and behaviour of a particular section of the lower clergy connected with the Cathedral: the chantry priests. I gave several conference papers on this topic, which were shaped by Nicholas's own preliminary work, tracing chantries through the medieval records, that he generously shared with me. It is apt, therefore, that this chapter should appear in a volume to honour the mentorship and munificence of Nicholas, to whom I owe an enormous debt of gratitude for his steadfast support of my work on medieval ecclesiastical records.

Introduction

On 6 August 1457 John Copuldyk, priest and vicar choral of Lincoln Cathedral, made an oath before the dean and chapter which was copied into the Chapter Acts in the first person. promising that 'if it should happen in future that I am convicted of any crime or excess then I wish and consent that then I should be completely removed both from my vicarage and chantry which I hold in the said church and from any other office of ministering by the said dean and

chapter, forever and ever, suspended by these words'.[1] The repetition of this oath upon John's institution as a chantry chaplain[2] provides an example of what a chantry founder and the dean and chapter believed that a good chantry chaplain ought to be, and that failing in their moral and spiritual obligations or committing a crime rendered a vicar unworthy of carrying out their duties.

The reality, however, did not always match the aspirations of the chantry founders or the initial good intentions of the chantry priests. In another example taken from the Lincoln Cathedral Chapter Acts, Thomas Marshall, chantry chaplain of the Gynewell chantry, and William Sargeaunt, junior vicar, were convicted on 11 July 1489 of fighting with each other, with swords drawn, in a street in the Bail of Lincoln. They were cautioned by the dean and chapter to keep the peace, on pain of a payment of 6s. 8d.[3] This example shows how the dean and chapter aimed to uphold their role of responsibility to the chantries, by cautioning any chaplains who behaved badly and brought shame and disrepute on their chantries. But, more widely, what exactly did chantry founders and the dean and chapter believe that a good chantry chaplain ought to be and why was this so important? And, on balance, how faithfully did the chaplains of Lincoln Cathedral fulfil their responsibilities towards their chantries? This chapter attempts to understand more fully the standards of behaviour expected by chantry founders, under the supervision of the dean and chapter, of chantry chaplains living and working around Lincoln Cathedral during the fifteenth century.

Chantry chaplains became a permanent fixture in cathedrals such as Lincoln following the growth of chantries in the later Middle Ages. Lincoln Cathedral was the mother church of the largest diocese in medieval England, stretching from the Humber Estuary in the north to the Thames Valley in the south, and as such possessed great wealth and importance among secular cathedrals. The cult of masses for the dead and the focus on encouraging prayer and intercession to speed one's soul through Purgatory in the later medieval period motivated the arrangement of chantries in Lincoln Cathedral.[4] The celebration of mass was central to catholic devotion – the acceptance of the doctrine of transubstantiation made mass the focal point at which to appreciate the corporeal humanity of an incarnate God.[5] A chantry provided for the daily celebration of masses, usually at an existing altar in a church or cathedral, and

1 LA, D & C A/2/34, fol. 57v.

2 It is not known to which chantry John was collated. It is not specified either here or later in the Chapter Acts, where John is referred to as chantry chaplain and vicar in the choir.

3 LA, D & C A/3/1, fol. 64v.

4 G. H Cook, *Mediaeval Chantries and Chantry Chapels*, 4th edn (London, 1968), p. 7.

5 R. N. Swanson, *Religion and Devotion in Europe c. 1215–c. 1515* (Cambridge, 1995), p. 137.

was founded following successful application to the Crown for a licence to endow a perpetual chantry. It was supported either by the endowment of lands or churches, rents, pensions from churches or religious houses or a sum of money and could be established during the founder's lifetime or as fulfilment of their wishes after their death.[6] Chantries could be established for a finite time or in perpetuity. However, only the very wealthy could afford to endow a perpetual chantry and many were established for as long as the founder's goods would endure. In spite of Lincoln Cathedral's position as one of the most powerful ecclesiastical establishments in medieval England, its chantries have largely been neglected in recent historiography and have not been paid the attention that has been given to those in similar institutions, such as York Minster or St Paul's Cathedral.[7]

Evidence for Chantries in Lincoln Cathedral in the fifteenth century

Primary evidence for chantries in Lincoln Cathedral can be found in a variety of sources: the chantries' cartulary and selected episcopal registers both contain copies of the foundation deeds of a number of perpetual chantries. The *Liber de Ordinationibus Cantariarum* is a cartulary containing copies of the foundation deeds of the chantries established in Lincoln Cathedral between the twelfth and fourteenth centuries and supervised and managed by the dean and chapter.[8] The cartulary also contains copies of the deeds to properties given to endow chantries in the cathedral. It is unique to Lincoln as the only English secular cathedral to have a cartulary specifically dedicated to chantries; this suggests the importance placed on recording this information by the cathedral authorities.[9] The cartulary is very detailed and carefully written by a number of fourteenth- and fifteenth-century scribes and, although in some of the later sections of the cartulary the hand appears rushed and untidy, the information throughout seems to be reliable.

6 C. Burgess, '"Longing to be prayed for": death and commemoration in an English parish in the later Middle Ages', in B. Gordon and P. Marshall (eds), *The Place of the Dead: Death and Remembrance in Late Medieval and Early Modern England* (Cambridge, 2000), p. 57.

7 R. B. Dobson, 'The Foundation of Perpetual Chantries by the Citizens of Medieval York', in G. Cuming (ed.), *The Province of York* (Leiden, 1967); idem, 'Citizens and chantries in late medieval York', in D. Abulafia, M. Franklin and M. Rubin (eds), *Church and City 1000–1500* (Cambridge, 1992); M. Rousseau, 'Chantry Chaplains at St Paul's Cathedral London CA. 1200–1548', *Medieval Prosopography* 26 (2005), 197–314; eadem, *Saving the Souls of Medieval London* (Farnham, 2011).

8 LA, D & C A/1/8.

9 G. R. C. Davis (ed.), *Medieval Cartularies of Great Britain, A Short Catalogue* (London, 1958).

Medieval episcopal registers were, in the main, a contemporary record of the acts of bishops. The registers for Lincoln in the period 1450–1500 are currently unpublished; there are five covering this period and its five bishops, Marmaduke Lumley (1450), John Chedworth (1452–71), Thomas Rotherham (1472–80), John Russell (1480–94) and William Smith (1495–1514), as well as several periods of vacancy.[10] Each register contains a remarkable variety of information and is organised in a range of forms. They are largely divided into three sections: institutions to each archdeaconry; ordinations; and memoranda. The memoranda registers were not complete records of a bishop's acts from day to day but contained miscellaneous material including foundation deeds for chantries, which provide invaluable information about how the founders wished their chantries to be established.[11] These deeds provide the most detail about the original arrangement of each chantry as desired by the chantry founder, such as how many priests were to serve and what type of priest they wished to employ, along with various stipulations to keep the chantry priest focused on his work. Most valuably, the foundation deeds usually include the founder's specific instructions regarding the employment and behaviour of chantry chaplains.

Another important source of information for the chantries of Lincoln Cathedral is the contemporary Chapter Acts, the minute books of the weekly meetings of the dean and chapter. At Lincoln, for the fifteenth century there are ten volumes of Chapter Acts and altogether these volumes cover ninety-seven years of the century.[12] They remain unpublished, with the only printed Acts for Lincoln covering the mid-sixteenth century.[13] Kathleen Edwards has commented that the Lincoln Chapter Act Books were neither so well written nor as carefully kept as those of Salisbury. Her critique was that the Lincoln folios were not always numbered consecutively, memoranda of different years had been combined and not arranged according to subject matter, there were many crossings out and interlinear additions, and the writing was usually small and heavily abbreviated. It seems that the Lincoln Acts, more so than those

10 LA, Episcopal Register 19, fols ir–82v (28r–82v *sede vacante*); Register 20, fols 1r–323r; Register 21, fols iv–197v; Register 22, fols 1r–281v; Register 23, fols 1r–408v.

11 C. W. Foster, 'The Lincoln Episcopal Registers being the substance of an address delivered to the Canterbury and York Society', *AASRP* 31 (1932), p. 160.

12 LA, D & C A/2/29 (1403–17); A/2/30 (1403–20); A/2/31 (1420–7); A/2/32 (1421–40); A/2/33 (1438–48); A/2/34 (1448–62); A/2/35 (1452–74); A/2/36 (1465–78); A/2/37 (1479–92); A/3/1 (1479–1502).

13 R. G. Cole (ed.), *Chapter Acts of the Cathedral Church of St Mary of Lincoln A.D. 1520–1536*, LRS 12 (Horncastle, 1915); idem (ed.), *Chapter Acts of the Cathedral Church of St Mary of Lincoln A.D. 1536–1547*, LRS 13 (Horncastle, 1917); idem (ed.), *Chapter Acts of the Cathedral Church of St Mary of Lincoln A.D. 1547–1559*, LRS 15 (Horncastle, 1920).

of Salisbury, appear to be notes 'hastily jotted down at chapter meetings'.[14] All the same, these notes contain valuable information about the institution and management of chantries. Entries in the Chapter Acts record important details about chantries including resignations, nominations, institutions and collations of chantry priests to particular chantries, discipline meted out to misbehaving chaplains, disputes between chantry priests, licences granted to chantry chaplains for improving their chantries, the texts of wills made on behalf of chantry priests and so on. Of particular value for this article is the information regarding the behaviour of chantry priests and how this was managed by the dean and chapter.

The chapter accounts are a further rich source for chantries. The accounts were kept in great detail at Lincoln and were copied into volumes known as the Audit Accounts of the dean and chapter.[15] These volumes, which cover much of the fifteenth century with few gaps, are often two or three times as thick as the Lincoln Chapter Act Books for the same period. The accounts are particularly useful as they record payments from various institutions to chantries and from chantries to chantry chaplains. This provides additional evidence regarding endowments of chantries and also outlines within a timeframe the periods when chantries became impoverished. The chapter accounts were kept regularly throughout the year and indicate when chantries changed hands between chantry priests.

The records of the English royal chancery can also provide useful material for the historian of chantries. The Patent Rolls exist in almost unbroken series from 1201 and record copies of letters patent through which the sovereign conferred a privilege or communicated their will. These rolls encompass a wide variety of documents which were issued under the great seal and which include licences to alienate lands or properties as endowments for perpetual chantries. Many people wished to grant land or property to the Church to endow their perpetual chantries in the expectation and belief that land and property were permanent fixtures whose value would be able to sustain their chantries in perpetuity. The Statutes of Mortmain, enacted in 1279 and 1290, prevented people from granting land to a corporation such as the Church for provision of religious services, and therefore removing it from the control and taxation system operated by the state, without first gaining royal consent in the form of a licence.[16] This was part of a response by the secular government to what Edward I and his advisers deemed as uncontrolled acquisition by

[14] K. Edwards, *The English Secular Cathedrals in the Middle Ages*, 2nd edn (Manchester, 1967), p. 29.

[15] LA, D & C Bj/2/10 (1399–1409); Bj/2/11 (1420–5); Bj/2/12 (1440–1); Bj/2/13 (1443–5); Bj/2/14 (1446–8); Bj/2/15 (1448–51); Bj/2/16 (1452–6); Bj/3/2 (1479–96).

[16] S. Raban, *Mortmain Legislation and the English Church, 1279–1500* (Cambridge, 1982), pp. 18–28.

religious institutions.[17] Conversely, the Patent Rolls cannot be used reliably to verify the existence of a chantry, as many licences were issued for perpetual chantries which were never founded. Nevertheless, in order to receive a licence for a perpetual chantry, it was necessary to make a payment to the Crown, which certainly highlights a serious intention to found on the part of the applicant. It also outlines a range of dates when the foundation of a perpetual chantry was being considered; this is valuable information which would not exist without the record making and record keeping practices of Chancery. At Lincoln, there is not the same depth of source material surviving for the foundation of perpetual chantries in the fifteenth century compared to previous centuries, which makes this Patent Roll evidence particularly useful.

Moving into the period of the dissolution of religious institutions in the sixteenth century, the *Valor Ecclesiasticus* stands out as a survey of the value of church finances. Commissioned by Henry VIII and compiled under the supervision of Thomas Cromwell in 1535, this monumental survey records the value of the endowments of chantries still in existence. There are, however, problems with using the *Valor*: it has rightly been criticised for being incomplete, for its tendency to undervalue (generally by more than 15%) the worth of many ecclesiastical institutions, and it was subsequently more precise and informative about the larger foundations than the smaller ones.[18] Nevertheless, the *Valor* can provide a useful comparable figure for the wealth of the remaining chantries as well as confirmation of which chantries still existed by 1535.

Another centrally commissioned source of information is the so-called Chantry Certificates. These were returned under acts of parliament in the late 1540s and assessed the value of remaining perpetual chantries before they were dissolved and their revenues directed into royal coffers. These are considered to be the most reliable and informative indicators of the number and nature of the chantries pre-Dissolution.[19] The extant certificates for Lincoln and Lincolnshire were returned in 1548 under the act of parliament by King Edward VI. They have the disadvantage of belonging to the returns made under the second chantries act, which are generally briefer and contain less information than the certificates drawn up following the earlier act of parliament.[20] It is possible to use these two sources, the *Valor* and the Chantry Certificates, in conjunction with one another to find discrepancies. The most noticeable discrepancy between the records concerns the Lincoln Cathedral chantries: in 1535 there were fifty-three chantry priests serving thirty-six

17 *ibid.*, p. 23.

18 A. Kreider, *English Chantries: The Road to Dissolution* (London, 1979), p. 9.

19 *ibid.*, p. 11.

20 C. W. Foster and A. Hamilton Thompson (eds), 'The Chantry Certificates for Lincoln and Lincolnshire, returned in 1548 under the Act of Parliament of Edward VI', *AASRP* 36, II (1922), p. 1.

chantry foundations but by 1548 only seventeen chantry priests are recorded, serving eleven foundations.[21] The Chantry Certificates are particularly significant because some contain information copied from the original foundation deeds of chantries for which other records no longer exist. We will now turn to examine those fifteenth-century chantries in Lincoln Cathedral in more detail.

Chantries in Lincoln Cathedral in the Fifteenth Century

Masses would have been celebrated almost continually throughout the day in the cathedral in the later Middle Ages due to the vast number of chantries. Between 1200 and 1547 approximately seventy-one chantries were founded, which places Lincoln just behind St Paul's, the largest English cathedral, in terms of total numbers of chantries.[22] By the beginning of the fifteenth century the majority of chantries in Lincoln Cathedral had already been founded, a total of forty-eight. However, the evidence shows that the remaining twenty-three were founded in the fifteenth century. In the Chapter Acts from that 100-year period 174 individual chantry chaplains are named, although each would have served particular chantries for different episodes. Chaplains would probably also have moved between chantries if the opportunity arose, especially if a larger stipend or better benefits were on offer. As a consequence, it is difficult to discern how many chantry chaplains would have been part of the cathedral community at any one time in the fifteenth century. At Lincoln in 1535 the *Valor Ecclesiasticus* indicates that fifteen vicars held chantries, but that there were also thirty-three other chantry chaplains in the cathedral attached to twenty more chantries.[23] The figures for the fifteenth century may well have been slightly higher than those from the sixteenth, as a result of localised economic decline throughout the period, but these chantry chaplains would certainly have formed a considerable presence in the late medieval cathedral. But how did chantries operate?

Chantry Foundation Deeds and Management

The founders of chantries in Lincoln Cathedral, similar to chantry founders elsewhere, issued prescriptive instructions in the foundation deeds regarding how their chantries were to be managed. They often left the responsibility of supervising the chantry chaplain's performance up to the dean and chapter, who had the power to deprive or otherwise punish any chantry chaplains who

21 *ibid.*, p. 3.

22 Rousseau's study suggests that there were eighty-four chantries in total founded at St Paul's Cathedral throughout the medieval period. Rousseau, 'Chantry Chaplains at St Paul's Cathedral London CA. 1200–1548', 197.

23 Edwards, *The English Secular Cathedrals in the Middle Ages*, p. 296.

defrauded the souls of their benefactors by neglecting to celebrate divine service.[24] Additional priests were employed by the dean and chapter to attend some of the chantries; out of the 174 chantry chaplains noted as serving chantries in the cathedral in the fifteenth-century Chapter Acts, thirty can be identified as being vicars choral and the rest would have been chantry priests. The position of chantry priests who were not vicars choral in secular cathedrals would have been unique, as they would not have been directly involved in supporting the daily liturgy of the cathedral in the same way that vicars choral would have. Chantry priests were primarily concerned with special services that were subsidiary to the main cathedral offices. They were supported by separate endowments not connected to the chapter's common fund but were still considered by the dean and chapter as belonging to the cathedral foundation. As such, they were subject to a large measure of control.[25]

Some chantry founders, notably Bishop Oliver Sutton (1280–99), did not mind whether the chaplain serving their chantry was a vicar choral or a chantry priest.[26] Seven founders of chantries in Lincoln Cathedral, however, specified that their chaplains were not to be vicars choral.[27] In addition to serving their chantry, the vicars choral would have had other responsibilities in the cathedral, such as attending a certain number of daily services and the canonical hours as well as other endowed anniversary masses, representing the canon of a particular prebendal stall. The foundation deed for the chantry of Nicholas de Cantilupe, for instance, stipulated that none of the chaplains was to hold any office in the cathedral that would involve him in duties outside the church. The foundation deeds of Bishop John Buckingham (1363–98), moreover, insisted that the chaplains of his chantry should hold no other benefice.[28] This highlights the strength of feeling among many chantry founders that their chaplains should not be distracted by other duties from their obligation to follow the founders' intentions and continually pray for their souls.

The chantry founders were also concerned about the longer-term management of their chantries. The issue of who was to have the right of presentation of priests to a chantry after the founder's death was clearly an important issue evidenced by the prescriptive instructions left by seventeen founders in their foundation deeds. For example, Nicholas de la Hiche (subdean of Lincoln Cathedral, 1265–73), intended that his executors should have the right to

24 *ibid.* p. 289.

25 *ibid.*, p. 297.

26 C. W. Foster (ed.), *The Registrum Antiquissimum of the Cathedral Church of Lincoln, Vol II*, LRS 28 (Hereford, 1933), pp. 303–4.

27 Henry and Batholomew Burghersh, Nicholas de Cantilupe, Richard of Faldingworth, John Gynewell, John Buckingham, Hugh de Walmesford, Richard Whitwell.

28 LA, Register 10, fol. 21v.

present a suitable chaplain to the chantry while they lived; then after their deaths the dean and chapter were to have the right to appoint within eight days of vacancy but after this period had elapsed the right to appoint would pass to the bishop.[29] Other chantry founders such as William son of Fulk (archdeacon of Stow, 1222–23), were content to leave the right of presentation solely to the dean and chapter.[30] It is important to see that all of the chantry founders who left instructions regarding the right of presentation to their chantries made allowance for the right of the dean and chapter to appoint chaplains at some point in the proceedings. The main preoccupation of the founders was to ensure that a new chaplain was appointed promptly so that services could continue with as little interruption as possible and the role of the dean and chapter was clearly important in facilitating this.

Behaviour of Chantry Chaplains

Another overriding concern among chantry founders was the quality of the chaplains serving their chantries. William Skelton, treasurer of the cathedral from 1477 to 1501, was clear in his instructions that he did not want the chaplains who celebrated his masses to be of ill repute, as he sets out in this extract from his last will and testament:

> Also I will that … if thei be nott of honeste and good conversacion butt wanton prowid and nott araide lyke honest prestes then to be put owt of ther service and other takyn in to ther service that be of good name and fame.[31]

Some chantry founders such as Richard Ravenser, canon of Lincoln Cathedral in the late fourteenth century, specified the priests whom they wanted to serve the chantry initially; he left instructions for William Baron and Robert Scotour to be his first chantry priests as he must have known that these men were of good reputation.[32] Ten of the chantry founders insisted that the chaplains should swear an oath on admission to observe the terms of the ordination of the chantry.[33] Most of these stipulations are along the

29 LA, D & C A/1/8: 67, fols. 17–17v.
30 LA, D & C A/1/8: 71, fol. 19v.
31 LA, D & C A/3/2, fols 12v, 13.
32 LA, D & C A/1/8 564, fol. 164.
33 LA, D & C A/1/8: 1238 (Hervey Beek); D & C A/1/8: 77 (Henry de Beningworth); Register 10, fol. 21v (John Buckingham); D & C A/1/8: 1251 (John Gynewell); D & C A/1/8: 78 (Robert and John Lacey); D & C A/1/8: 79 (Robert Lacey, Richard Rothwell and Hervey de Luda); D & C A/1/8: 114 (Henry Mansfield); D & C A/1/8: 564 (John Ravenser); D & C A/1/8: 1225 (Walter Stauren); D & C A/1/8: 82 (William Wynchecombe).

lines of those set out in the John Gynewell chantry foundation deeds, namely that the chaplains were under the jurisdiction of the dean and chapter in all things. If they were found criminous or otherwise defective, then they should be punished by the chapter. But if the nature of the offence required it then they should be removed from their chantries by the dean and chapter.[34] Others went into more specific details about the types of behaviour that were considered unacceptable. For example, John Buckingham's chantry foundation deed stated that:

> If any chaplain is quarrelsome, a sower of discord, haunter of taverns, unchaste, a night prowler, guilty of serious crime or intolerance in the company and if after three warnings from the supervisor he has not, in the judgement of the chapter, amended his ways, he is to be removed from the chantry.[35]

The impression given by the chantry foundation deeds is that observation of the foundation statutes was of paramount importance for the chaplains but that it was also important for them to behave in a manner that would not bring the chantry into disrepute.

The founders of chantries in Lincoln Cathedral were aware of the temptations that would be facing their chaplains as they carried out their duties and some made efforts to prevent them from falling out of line. Richard Whitwell, canon of the prebend of Empingham from 1331 to 1361, indicated in the foundation deeds for his chantry that the chaplains were not to be absent from the Close without special licence of the dean and chapter. They were also not to have too frequent access to the city of Lincoln, nor were any of them allowed to go there without the company of a fellow chaplain and without necessary cause.[36] The city may have provided temptation as many chantry chaplains and vicars choral were recruited from the cathedral cities where they lived and were not therefore secluded from the disruptive influences of their families, male contemporaries and women.[37] Another strategy employed by the chantry founders with the intention of relieving their chantry priests from the monotony of the repeated services was to allow them a certain amount of time off per year. Richard Ravenser allowed his chantry priests, with the licence of the dean and chapter, to be absent up to three times each year to visit friends or to go on pilgrimage, provided that the total number

34 LA, D & C A/1/8: 1251, fol. 363.

35 LA, Register 10, fol. 21v.

36 LA, D & C A/1/8: 1236, fol. 347v.

37 R. B. Dobson, 'The English Vicars Choral: An Introduction', in R. Hall and D. Stocker (eds), *Vicars Choral at English Cathedrals: Cantate Domino* (Oxford, 2005), p. 9.

of absences did not exceed thirty days in the year or, in the case of foreign pilgrimage, permitted once in his lifetime, for a whole year, but in this case the priest was bound to provide a suitable substitute.[38] This emphasises the licence of approved opportunities for recreation by chantry founders as an alternative to illicit ones.

In 1293 Bishop Oliver Sutton had recognised the moral dangers arising from the vicars choral living separately and decreed that they should be provided with a residence: 'seeing that for the most part solitude is the occasion of all evils amongst them'.[39] By the fifteenth century the chantry chaplains who were vicars choral lived within the cathedral close in a common house of senior vicars known as Vicars' Court. Various measures were undertaken to enforce communal living: for example, the vicars, choristers, poor clerks and chantry priests were obliged to eat together regularly.[40] The same reasoning most probably lay behind ten chantry founders' instructions that their chantry chaplains were to live in common houses.[41]

In the fourteenth and fifteenth centuries it was becoming fashionable for wealthy benefactors to found chantries for more than one or two priests; these were sometimes called colleges. Lincoln Cathedral had three or four chantry colleges of a similar kind: the Cantilupe chantry was the largest of these, founded by Nicholas de Cantilupe in 1345 and amended by his wife Joan in 1358 to include a warden and seven chaplains.[42] The Burghersh family chantry college, consolidated by Bartholomew Burghersh on 3 September 1345, consisted of six chaplains, a clerk and seven boys. The chaplains also lived communally, and the arrangements made by Burghersh for his chantry priests were clearly desirable, as another chantry founder, John Buckingham, bishop of Lincoln, attempted to emulate this provision for the chantry he established in 1371. He stated that the chaplains and clerks of his chantry were to dwell together in the rooms which he had caused to be built at the front entrance of the Burghersh chantry house and they were to follow the good example of the Burghersh chantry – to dwell with them, and to eat and drink

[38] LA, D & C A/1/8: 564, fol. 164.

[39] D. Owen, 'Historical Survey, 1091–1450', in eadem (ed.), *A History of Lincoln Minster* (Cambridge, 1994), p. 148; P. Wragge, 'Lincoln Cathedral', in W. Page (ed.), *A History of Lincolnshire, Vol II*, 2nd edn (London, 1988), p. 81.

[40] M. Bowker, 'Historical Survey 1450–1750', in Owen (ed.), *A History of Lincoln Minster*, p. 170.

[41] John Buckingham, Henry and Bartholomew Burghersh, Nicholas de Cantilupe, John Gynewell, Henry Lexington, Works chantry, Richard Ravenser, Richard Faldingworth, Hugh de Walmesford, Richard Whitwell.

[42] Foster and Hamilton Thompson (eds), 'The Chantry Certificates for Lincoln and Lincolnshire, returned in 1548 under the Act of Parliament of Edward VI', pp. 221–2, *CPR 1364–7,* p. 335.

with them.[43] The arrangement of the vicars in communal quarters was an attempt by the cathedral authorities to keep unlawful activities to a minimum and bring order and discipline to their lives.

Despite the best efforts of the chantry founders to regulate their chantry chaplains' behaviour, not all chaplains serving Lincoln Cathedral in the fifteenth century were able to maintain the high standards of behaviour that were expected; the Chapter Acts provide evidence of this. On 29 October 1452, Richard Brygg, senior vicar choral, was warned by the dean and chapter, on pain of privation of his vicarage, that he should attend divine service in the choir more vigilantly, day and night, singing and psalmody.[44] Also that he should abstain from suspect places and taking part in illicit games or other games of any kind, especially when divine service was being celebrated. Finally, that he should behave properly towards the succentor and vice-chancellor and clergy brethren and not abuse the succentor. It seems that some chantry chaplains found it difficult to maintain the level of commitment and good behaviour that the chantry founders desired for the office. There were also lapses in moral standards among the chantry chaplains. Sir John Bett, former chantry chaplain of Katherine Swynford's chantry, was accused of holding 'Katherine Aleyn within his bedchamber, alone, with the door closed, suspectly and wretchedly in adulterine embraces', in October 1454.[45] He expressly denied this but he was lambasted by the dean and chapter for bringing the cathedral into 'a scandal not modest of the church and a shame on the priestly order' as he was unable to find eight clergymen who were all willing to swear his virtue. Nevertheless, there are no further references to these particular chaplains' behaviour in the Chapter Acts so perhaps the dean and chapter's warnings were sufficient embarrassment and punishment to prevent further lapses.

There are, however, examples of certain chaplains offending repeatedly over a span of years, such as Robert Swaby, chaplain and warden of the Cantilupe chantry. He was accused on 16 March 1426 of playing dice in the house of William Hert in Lincoln with a man from the West Country and again with John Routh and John Walpole, chaplains in the Close, on which occasion Swaby lost 6s. 8d. and a fight ensued between him and Walpole.[46] Swaby was warned to desist his gambling on pain of payment of £20 to the fabric.[47] It is evident that in spite of the penalty this chantry chaplain's misbehaviour persisted to the further detriment of his chantry, as on 5 May 1431 Swaby was accused of playing dice on the Sunday before the feast of SS Philip and James

43 LA, Register 10, fol. 21v.
44 LA, D & C A/2/34, fol. 26.
45 LA, D & C A/2/34, fol. 47v.
46 LA, D & C A/2/32, fol. 39r.
47 LA, D & C A/2/32, fol. 43r.

in the house of William Belle, a Lincoln mercer, through the whole night until the fourth hour on the following Monday. He returned to his chamber at the fifth hour to get more money and did not say matins, vespers or mass that day but went back to the house of William Belle and played at dice as before until the fourth hour on Tuesday when he returned to the chantry in a weak and feeble state. Swaby denied the articles and was given until 12 May to find clergy brethren to testify for him but was unable to and was found guilty.[48] He also appeared before the dean and chapter later in the same year for, in spite of his oath on admission to the Cantilupe chantry, he was serving as parochial chaplain in the parish church of St Augustine, Lincoln, contrary to the will of the precentor to whose dignity the church was annexed, with the result that he was only celebrating at his altar at most once or twice a week.[49]

The dean and chapter appear to have been adept at determining the offences of this particular chaplain but his punishments were not forceful enough to prevent him from pursuing other more lucrative interests than performing his chantry services. It was very rare for the dean and chapter to take exceptionally strong measures against chantry chaplains. In the fifteenth century there is only one example of a chaplain being removed from his position: Alan Strangman, chaplain of the chantry of William Cawse, was excommunicated by the dean and chapter for obstinate disobedience on 16 July 1446.[50]

Conclusion

In concluding this survey of fifteenth-century chantries within Lincoln Cathedral, and the behaviour of the priests who served them, we can highlight several key points. The level of detailed provision in the surviving documentation concerning chantries emphasises that chantry founders clearly desired to employ chaplains who would be obedient to the foundation statutes of the chantry and would not be distracted from following the designated programme of masses and prayers. They required chaplains who were well behaved and with proven reputations to serve their chantries and were clear that any behaviour that was considered immoral or sinful was to be punished. As far as the chantry founders were concerned, a chaplain failing in his moral and spiritual obligations or committing a crime rendered him unworthy of carrying out his duties. It seems that there was a concern that the reputation of the chantry priest reflected on the legacy of the chantry founder. The overriding concern of a chantry founder was to create a good quality, well-maintained chantry which would project an impression that the founder was an upstanding,

48 LA, D & C A/2/32, fol. 57r.
49 LA, D & C A/2/32, fol. 57v.
50 LA, D & C A/2/33, fol. 16v.

pious citizen and therefore was more worthy of the respect and prayers of the living for their soul long after their death.

The fifteenth-century Chapter Acts indicate that there were many accusations of disorderly living directed at the chantry chaplains and vicars choral, including disobedience, absenteeism, fornication and violence. The chantry founders appear to have been content to trust the ever-changing group of individuals who constituted the dean and chapter of the cathedral to ensure that their chantries would be well maintained and their chaplains would be well disciplined. The dean and chapter seem to have been consistently strict with chantry chaplains about maintaining an accepted standard of behaviour and also punishing chaplains when they failed to maintain the chantry masses. They were not, however, always successful at protecting the chantry founders' interests as they meted out justice. In some cases, such as that of Robert Swaby, perhaps the dean and chapter could have been harsher with their punishments as his behaviour continually harmed the work of the Cantilupe chantry. However, perhaps external factors impacted upon how severely they could afford to punish their chantry priests in the fifteenth century as there may have been a shortage of priests willing to accept a relatively small stipend for maintaining a chantry instead of pursuing a more rewarding position with a parish in the post-plague period.

It is interesting to note that Robert Swaby was a chaplain of the Cantilupe chantry and he was involved in illicit activities such as gambling with the promise of financial gain. Over the course of the fifteenth century, the Cantilupe chantry suffered decline as a result of the economic circumstances of the period. The general loss of property value meant that the original endowments of this chantry had lost their value to the extent that they could no longer cover the full cost of maintaining it; the number of chantry chaplains decreased and the stipends for the chaplains diminished. So in this case there may have been a link between the misbehaviour of chaplains from chantries that were having economic problems. On the other hand, whilst attempting to judge the fifteenth-century chantry chaplains for their faults, we should also consider that it is mainly the clerical misdemeanours that were recorded in the Chapter Acts and that there are no similar surviving records documenting the virtues of the chantry chaplains and vicars choral to balance out the potentially disproportionate picture painted by these documents. Nevertheless, on balance, the dean and chapter at Lincoln certainly supervised the chantries to a reasonably high standard. This was because they understood the crucial importance of the chantry priests' good behaviour and diligent attitude towards their work not only for the souls of the chantry founders but also for the good reputation of the Cathedral.

9

The Wainfleet Haven Railway: Anatomy of a Failed Project

R. C. WHEELER

Introduction

The 'Railway Mania' is a term used primarily for the period 1844–46 when investment in railway projects became an all-consuming passion for a significant portion of the population. A bubble developed and eventually burst (or at least deflated). Many investors lost money. Nevertheless, a high proportion of the country's railway routes were promoted and commenced in those hectic years. There were no railways at all in Lincolnshire prior to 1844. By 1847, almost half the county's route-mileage had been authorised by Parliament.

Contemporary accounts alleged that many of the projects floated in those years were fraudulent. Railways were promoted, it is said, with no possible prospect of success, merely so that their promoters could allocate shares to themselves and sell them at a profit after their price had risen.[1] Lawyers and even surveyors, it is said, arranged for lines to be promoted for the sake of the fat fees they could charge. Parliament had introduced certain Standing Orders on railway bills to act as a check on the powers of compulsory purchase that railways were granted in their Acts. By 1845, the House of Commons was enforcing these rigidly, as a way of throwing out a small proportion of the bills which threatened to swamp its sessions. Crooked promoters, it is alleged, would deliberately introduce certain errors in the plans they were obliged to deposit as a convenient way of killing their projects: they had made their money and had no wish to proceed further.

These allegations have been repeated in more modern accounts of the Railway Mania. None of these authors have given examples of fraudulent

1 'There were projects for hundreds of lines which had not the slightest chance of success, which their very authors never had any intention of really carrying out, and whose sole purpose indeed was to enable the directors to squander the deposits, and to make fraudulent profits from the sale of the shares' (1850) – K. Marx and F. Engels, *Collected Works*, 10 vols (London, 1978), vol. 10, 491–2.

projects, and some more recent work has cast doubt on such assertions.[2] Of the eighty-eight projects for railways through Lincoln listed by Ruddock & Pearson,[3] one in particular – that of the Wainfleet Haven Railway – seemed to trigger at least two of the suggested indicators for fraud: the purpose of the line as set out in its prospectus seemed implausible; and it failed Standing Orders because of a height datum error – allegedly a favourite device of fraudulent promoters. It therefore seemed worth investigating the project further.

It rapidly became clear that there was no reason to suppose that the project's failure indicated fraud; but this well-documented scheme provides a useful case study of the challenges facing railway promoters. In particular, it shows the extent to which they identified gaps in their knowledge and found ways to fill those gaps.

The Promoters

The four men who convened the first formal project meeting at Spilsby were James Smith, George Bourne, J. H. Bourne and W. C. Calthrop. Smith was Lord of the Manor of Wainfleet, and his status explains why he was invited to chair the first meeting; but he was only leasing the manorial rights and he only attended nine out of the thirteen meetings he was entitled to attend. He appears to have been a useful member of that initial group but not the driving force. George Bourne became the project's interim chairman and attended every meeting bar one. His age and experience gave him additional influence, especially as many of those involved with the project were quite young. John Henry Bourne was his younger brother, a major farmer in nearby Partney. He attended regularly but seems not to have been a forceful personality. Calthrop was a surgeon who had settled in Crowland and had been appointed by the Poor Law Union as medical officer and registrar for the Crowland District. He had married in 1843, but the following year he resigned his posts and a sale was announced of his furniture, and even his hunters. This suggests a financial crisis at the very least. He moved to Spilsby, where he failed to be appointed medical officer.[4] George Bourne had a connection with the family going back many years,[5] and may perhaps have offered a helping hand. From 14 October, Calthrop was made the project's Secretary at a salary of £300 per

2 Andrew Odlyzko, 'The Railway Mania: Fraud, disappointed expectations, and the modern economy', *Journal of the Railway & Canal Historical Society* 215 (November 2012), 2–12.

3 J. G. Ruddock and R. E. Pearson, *The Railway History of Lincoln*, 2nd edn (Lincoln, 1985).

4 *Lincs Chronicle*, 5 May 1843 and 7 March 1845; *Stamford Mercury*, 3 January 1845 and 21 February 1845.

5 LA, MF 2/70, 10 February 1811.

year. His out-letters survive and provide a more vivid picture of what was going on than do the more formal minutes.[6]

George Bourne is so important to the project that it is worth enlarging on his background and character. Fortunately in his younger days he kept a diary, a record of his travels and the places he saw rather than of his emotions, although these creep in sometimes.[7] His father, another George, was a younger son of John Bourne of Dalby Hall and had farmed extensively, with at least one appointment as an inclosure commissioner.[8] George junior was born in 1780 and was commissioned Lieutenant, serving first in the Royal North Lincs Militia, then in a garrison regiment in Ireland, then in a regular Light Infantry regiment, taking part in the Walcheren expedition of 1809. Unlike most of his fellow officers on that expedition, he returned whole in body and health but was evidently determined to avoid any more campaigning.[9] He married in 1810, spent two years on recruiting duties and, being recalled to regimental duties, he exchanged into the Life Guards (at a cost of 500 guineas). Living in London as a married man proved too expensive, so he sold his commission, becoming Paymaster to the Oxfordshire Militia and buying a house outside Banbury. His timing was poor: following the defeat of France, the Militia was disembodied and there was nothing for a Paymaster to do. Returning to Lincolnshire in 1818 he took a farm at Skendleby, augmenting his income by working as a valuer and land agent.[10] He later moved to Halton Holegate and by 1845 was (briefly) occupying East Keal Hall.

The diary suggests that as a young man George was highly sociable, less than conscientious so far as regimental duties were concerned, practical in the sense of being able to march a body of recruits halfway across the country, but impulsive when it came to big decisions, being too much of an optimist to see problems lurking. He certainly had a knack for cutting his losses when his situation became difficult. As a sixty-five-year-old, he remained impulsive: in November 1845, having received an anonymous letter claiming that one of his daughters had been stabbed in the breast by her husband, he drove directly to the couple's house, accompanied by one of his sons (in case force was needed) and his unmarried daughter Catherine (whose role seems to have been to conduct any intimate examination). Arriving at the house, he barged in as guests were arriving for afternoon tea and dragged his brother-in-law

6 Both are at LA, Misc Don 588/7. The out-letters, as was fairly common business practice at this date, were copied into a book. Letters are filed in date order.

7 LA, MF 2/70.

8 Tattershall, 1796–98.

9 For the expedition see Martin R. Howard, *Walcheren 1809: the Scandalous Destruction of a British Army* (Barnsley, 2012).

10 A little under 200 acres, to judge by the Land Tax duplicates: LA, LQS/LAND TAX/Candleshoe (followed by the year and parish).

before a magistrate. The brother-in-law subsequently brought an action for damages: presumably the allegation was completely unfounded.[11]

In discussing personalities, we should not neglect the solicitors to the project. Titus Bourne and his son were in partnership at Alford; Titus was George's brother, so an obvious choice. Marcus Huish of Castle Donington may seem a curious choice as solicitor, but he was Titus's son-in-law; perhaps more important, his cousin Captain Mark Huish was Secretary of the Grand Junction Railway.[12] The London solicitors were Scott & Tahourdin of Lincoln's Inn Fields; they seem to have had little involvement with railways and were perhaps keen to gain experience in such remunerative work.

Prehistory

Titus Bourne had been solicitor to the Alford Canal, a project of 1820 which obtained its Act but failed to raise enough capital in shares. Its aim had been to bring coal into Alford and to export agricultural products from the Alford markets, thereby enhancing the prosperity of the town. If the Wainfleet Haven Railway had started with the aim of bringing coal in to Spilsby and exporting agricultural produce, that would be unsurprising; other early railways were promoted with similar objects.[13] It is likely that a very local line, little more than a tramway, would be seen as insufficiently attractive to investors, who were largely focused on long-distance traffic. It may even have been Captain Mark Huish who suggested extension westwards to link up with other projected lines and offer an outlet to the North Sea for the manufactures of the Midlands and the North-West. The Derby men who eventually became directors of the Wainfleet Haven line were the Deputy Chairman and a director of the Derby & Crewe Railway, which was a *protégé* of Mark Huish's Grand Junction Railway.

By August, the promoters envisaged a line extending east of Wainfleet to a new quay at the mouth of Wainfleet Haven; westwards from Spilsby it would serve Horncastle and would cross the river at Bardney to connect with either the projected London & York Railway or the alternative scheme via Cambridge.

At the prorogation of parliament on 9 August 1845, none of the competing schemes for a line south-east from Lincoln had been approved. The only line through Lincoln that had obtained its Act was the Nottingham & Lincoln Railway. Accordingly, the plans were changed so that the line continued from Horncastle north of the River Witham, crossing the river just east of Lincoln and making an end-on junction with the Nottingham & Lincoln Railway. The

11 *Northern Star*, 25 July 1846.
12 John Burke, *Commoners*, 1838, 417.
13 For example, the Canterbury & Whitstable Railway.

project at this stage was called the Lincoln, Horncastle, Spilsby and Wainfleet Haven Railway.

The interim prospectus was issued in August and starts off by explaining that the railway:

> will form a direct … communication between the important grazing Country of the Lincolnshire marshes and the large manufacturing and consuming districts of the Midland and Northern Counties. It will also establish an immediate connection between the East Coast and South Wolds of Lincolnshire with the various Coal Fields … expediting the transfer of Corn, Wool, and other Agricultural produce … and introducing Timber, Stone, Slate, Seeds, Oil-cake, and Artificial manures.

That is a very elegant way of saying it will be a rural branch line. It goes on to claim that:

> By this Chain of communication, with other contemplated Lines of Railway (some of which have obtained legislative authority) the important towns of Birmingham (as the centre of the Manufacturing districts) Liverpool, Manchester, Leeds, Sheffield, Wakefield, Nottingham, Worksop, Derby, Stafford, the Potteries, and other important places of Trade and Manufacture, will be placed in direct connection with the central parts of the Continent of Europe, for Import and Export at Wainfleet Haven.

Why should the manufacturers of Leeds send their goods to Wainfleet Haven, when they already had a railway to Hull? The only answer the prospectus offered was that 'This Haven is the most Central one on the East Coast and possesses Roadsteads of a superior description …'. But railway investors in August and September 1845 were not disposed to raise such niggling questions. The Railway Mania was still prevalent: all railway shares could be expected to rise.

The Provisional Committee

The main item of business at the first meeting on 1 September 1845 was co-opting a Provisional Committee. It was common practice for railway projects to have a smattering – often a more sizeable number – of the nobility and gentry on their Provisional Committees, who usually played no part in their proceedings but were willing to lend their names. In this case the list was headed by Lt Gen. Thomas Birch-Reynardson of Holywell Hall. He had been Deputy Quartermaster-General for the Walcheren expedition and was presumably an old acquaintance of George Bourne. At the age of seventy-two, it was probably assumed he would never travel to Spilsby to attend meetings.

James Whiting Yorke, of Walmsgate Hall near Alford, was the other prominent name; again, he never attended.

More important, not just for the credibility their presence gave the project but also for their advice, were men who already had experience as railway directors. Marcus Huish had a brother and erstwhile partner, John, who was Secretary to the projected Derby & Crewe Railway. He had presumably recruited one of its directors, Thomas Parker Bainbrigge of Derby, who at the start of September was the only member of the Provisional Committee with actual railway experience. Bainbrigge was heir to his uncle Thomas Bainbrigge (1751–1818) of Woodseat Hall, Rocester, Staffs, an extraordinarily dissolute man, and was currently engaged in a lawsuit over his late uncle's will, a suit which consumed most of the contested estate and which brought the entire family into disrepute. That lawsuit certainly casts doubt on the soundness of Bainbrigge's judgement but in September 1845 the sordid details had yet to come to the attention of the newspaper-reading public.

Of the other ten co-opted, one was a banker, the others were selected from communities along the line, from Lincoln to Wainfleet and the marshes. Another five were added a fortnight later, three of whom had railway experience; there was clearly a recognition that they needed more than one man in that line. Three more names were added on 29 September, four more on 7 October, three more on 18 October. It was quite usual for Provisional Committees to grow in this way.

The intention seems to have been originally that the Provisional Committee should be the primary decision-making body: a fee of two guineas per attendance was agreed at that first meeting. On 19 September just thirteen members were elected directors, without any indication of their role. A revised list of sixteen was agreed on 14 October; and that was the last occasion the Provisional Committee met. Thereafter all decisions were taken by the directors, sometimes augmented by a couple of invited committeemen. The intention, expressed on 7 November, was that the Provisional Committee would meet monthly, the directors (at least at this very busy period) weekly. It was not clear how such a two-tier structure would actually work, and it was never implemented.

There were hopes of persuading Lord Scarbrough to accept the chairmanship but they settled for Lt Col. Sir Edward Brackenbury, of Skendleby Hall near Spilsby. He was a soldier with a distinguished war record and was well connected. Five years younger than George Bourne, he failed to attend any meetings but may have done valuable work behind the scenes. By early November, the line's advertisements included a baronet on the Provisional Committee[14] along with the chairman's elder brother, Sir John MacPherson

14 Sir Richard Charles Henry Rycroft, 3rd bt, of Marydown Park, Basingstoke. The connection was that his daughter was Lord Yarborough's niece.

Brackenbury. Better still, the advertisements appeared 'under the express sanction of the Rt Hon. Lord Willoughby d'Eresby, Lord Bayning and the Governors of the Bethlem and Bridewell Hospitals'. In other words, the major landowners of the district may not have been willing to have any formal association but were at least prepared to lend their names.

Initial Tasks: Engineer and Shares

Any new railway project had three concrete tasks to address: find an engineer; attract sufficient subscriptions for shares; and survey a proposed line. With regard to the engineer, there had been hopes of appointing Joseph Locke. This may well have been Bainbrigge's suggestion: the Derby & Crewe railway was closely associated with the Grand Junction to which Locke was engineer. The problem was that with so many railways being promoted it was not easy to find any engineer willing to take on yet another project, let alone one of the leading men. In the end they settled on Thomas Page, whose experience had been gained as resident engineer for the Thames Tunnel. Currently he was working on a plan to embank the Thames and to construct a central railway terminus on reclaimed land, connected to the various trunk lines by lines running along the new embankments. He seems to have been considered something of an expert in estuarine muds, which will have made him seem qualified for the work at Wainfleet Haven.

The second task was to attract subscribers for the 30,000 shares, along with the 10% deposits which Parliamentary Standing Orders now required. Several commission agents were appointed for this. Locations suggest that Marcus Huish's contacts were involved. It was resolved that no single individual should subscribe for more than 200 £25 shares, implying total calls of £5000 and an immediate deposit of £525.[15] One is struck by the enthusiasm of the entire Bourne family:

George Bourne – 200 shares
Titus Bourne – 200 shares
John Henry Bourne – 200 shares
George Bourne – 200 shares
John George Bourne (Titus's eldest son) – 50 shares
Timothy Bourne Bourne of New Brighton (another of Titus's sons) – 150 shares
Eliza Bourne (Titus's eldest daughter) – 20 shares
Thomas Bourne of Radstock (brother of George) – 50 shares.

15 A deposit of a little over 10% – in this case £2 12s. 6d. per share – was required to pay immediate expenses and still have the 10% of capital in hand when the bill went before Parliament.

Other significant investors were:

T. P. Bainbrigge of Derby – 200 shares
William Charles Calthrop – 200 shares
James Smith of Wainfleet – 200 shares

along with two other residents of the neighbourhood.[16]

In view of Calthrop's presumed financial difficulties, one suspects that he either bought his shares in order to sell them on immediately, or else he was acting as a nominee; but the pattern of subscription by so many members of the Bourne family suggests they bought with the intention of holding. There was no particular difficulty in subscribing – there were vast numbers of subscribers who had no particular connection with the railway – and the Bourne family were subscribing on the same terms as everyone else, yet they made up almost 50% of all those subscribing for more than eighty shares. The only plausible explanation is that George Bourne's (and perhaps Titus Bourne's) enthusiasm for the scheme persuaded them that this was an unparalleled way of making money, as well as being good for the neighbourhood. Curiously, a resolution of 29 September allowed all the officers and members of the Provisional Committee a second allotment of 200 shares if they wished: none seem to have taken this up.

By the end of October the project was, in effect, fully subscribed. A small number of shares had been held back so that the board could oblige influential landowners. Thus it was agreed on 10 November that Lord Willoughby's friends, whom he should nominate, might be accommodated with shares.

The Survey

The third task was to make a detailed survey of the proposed line, to the standards laid down in Parliamentary Standing Orders. The newly-appointed Provisional Committee addressed this at its first meeting on 1 September 1845, directing that Mr William Bourne, of Partney, should 'take the levels and prepare a plan of the proposed line'. This looks like jobbery: William Bourne had little experience as a surveyor – one tithe map is all he is known to have produced at this date – and he appears to have been engaged because he was the son of a promoter. However, there is an alternative explanation. From the Preliminary Prospectus, it appears that the initial survey of the line – usually a task for the Engineer – had already been undertaken. Indeed, in easy country like East Lincolnshire it hardly needed an engineer to lay out a railway. That initial

16 *Accounts and papers of the House of Commons*, vol. 38 (1846) 'List of Subscribers of £2000 and upwards to the Railway Subscription' provides a readily searchable list of the larger subscribers. The full subscription contracts are at LA, Padley 4/2.

survey must have been undertaken by the promoters. Quite possibly William Bourne had joined that party and may even have been responsible for the resulting sketch map. It would not be normal at that stage to determine exact levels: experienced engineers often seem to have relied on visual inspection to declare that gradients would be acceptable, but it would be foolish to rely on the judgement of a group of amateurs. Thus, young Bourne is being paid to establish exact levels along or adjacent to the intended line, a task which would require him to engage two labourers to carry the fore- and back-staves and also for a fair copy of the initial survey; perhaps even he is being paid retrospectively for his attendance on that initial reconnaissance.

At any rate, the meeting on 19 September divided the line into three portions, so far as the main survey was concerned. Mr Percy Brackenbury of Ollerton, who had been recommended by Page, was to take one portion, the Lincoln surveyor J. S. Padley took another – naturally enough, he did the Lincoln end – and William Bourne was to do the third.

The deadline for the deposit of plans was 30 November. The directors were sufficiently concerned about this to appoint a subcommittee to monitor progress with full powers to hire and fire. Given the massive difficulty of engaging surveyors in the critical month of November, these powers were something of an empty threat. More seriously, the final stage in the preparation of plans was the drawing of sections showing the level of the land and the proposed level of the rails. This was regarded as a job for an engineer so was Page's responsibility. The work was increased by the decision to add a branch to Boston. Indeed, on 24 November, just six days before the deadline, a further branch at the Boston end was added, in order to comply with an ill-considered demand of that corporation. Clearly, informal discussion had already taken place; Page had been given considerable delegated authority, including the authority to hire surveyors, and he appears to have started work on this second branch in advance of the formal decision.

There were some hectic days leading up to the deadline. Calthrop wrote, on 30 November, in his best literary style:

> The Tumult in London [on the 29th] was tremendous, Lithographers being kept from the commanding influence of Sleep by Golden Bribes and the largesse, high as it was, could scarcely prevail over the demands of nature.

The evening of the 29th was when the precious parcels of plans would be sent out by the night coaches to the local solicitors, for formal deposit the following day. The Clerk of the Peace for Lindsey received his copy at 1pm.[17] This was fairly relaxed timing: one encounters copies of such plans deposited as late as 11:40pm.

17 LA, Lind Dep Plans 1/14.

The Datum Error

What went wrong? There are two sources which enable us to advance a tentative explanation. The first is the system being used by the lithographers, Standidge of London. One problem Standidge faced was that surveyors were remarkably sloppy about writing titles and numbers on their plans. Standidge had therefore developed a practice of starting all their lithographed plans by transferring the appropriate scale bar which had their name underneath it.[18] To this name was added a number with a suffix letter. The letter indicated the project: the Wainfleet Haven line was 'g'. The numbers were allocated sequentially as plans came in. We do not know the *dates* of receipt but we do know the *order*. The other source is a letter from Calthrop in which he explains that the surveyor Corbett had refused to hand over his sections and levels until W. H. Bourne guaranteed payment of his bill. Until it received its Act, a railway project had no legal personality: it could not sue or be sued. Corbett wanted to ensure there was a reputable individual he could sue in the event of non-payment.

Corbett was not one of the surveyors appointed by the Board; he must therefore have been appointed by Page in the final few weeks. Demand for surveyors being so high, Corbett may well have demanded an extremely high rate, and Page may have agreed for lack of any alternative; that would explain why Corbett was so concerned that he might not be paid. The levels along the main line had been taken by young Bourne back in early September; but the Boston branch had only been agreed after that date. The terrain was more or less flat, so there would have been no need to worry about levelling until the time came to draw the sections.

Longitudinal sections were lithographed by Standidge with up to five on each sheet. The sheets with sections 11 to 16 of the main line (the middle) formed their sheets numbered 39 to 41. These were done in good time. The Lincoln end, sections 1 to 10, came in as sheets 43 to 45. Then came the southern half of the Boston branch, sections B1 to B5, as sheet 46; then the final part of the main line, sections 17 to 20, on sheet 47. Then came most of the remainder of the Boston branch, with just two sections B6 and B7 on sheet 48. Sheets 49 and 50 had plans and sections of the additional branch at Boston; the combination of plans and sections on the same sheets implies that the work was all done by Page's subordinates. Sheet 51 had the cross-sections, where levels of roads needed to be altered so that they could cross the railway. Finally, sheet 52 had the northernmost section of the Boston branch, B8, in splendid isolation.

Clearly, the levelling of the Boston branch was done from south to north. All levelling has to be done with respect to some datum. Projects were required to

18 Lithographic transfer is an easy way of copying standard detail without redrawing it.

draw their sections with respect to a single datum; this one used the springing of the door arch at Wainfleet Grammar School. (Unlike Ordnance surveyors, railway surveyors did not have authority to cut benchmarks, so needed to describe in some way a vertical level on a feature.) Working from south to north would require the surveyor of the Boston branch to use a temporary datum; when he reached the main line he could then relate his temporary datum to the Wainfleet one and adjust all the levels accordingly. That final stage required section B8 and it looks as though Corbett had been holding this back until he received his guarantee. The lithographers had drawn sections B1 to B7 using the temporary datum; perhaps someone had decided that it would be acceptable to place a note on the sections relating their zero mark to the zero used on the main line. In the event, nothing was done to relate these levels. If one reads off the height of the land (and the rails) at the northernmost point of the Boston branch, it does not agree with the height read from the corresponding point of the main line.

From an engineering point of view, it did not really matter: one could work out from the deposited plans what was intended. The trouble was that Parliamentary hearings for Private Bills worked like a court of law and that included the Standing Orders Committee. A precedent had already been set, that inconsistent datums were unacceptable. However, the problem would remain undiscovered until February.

Strategy

Throughout its life, the Wainfleet project managed to steer a middle course between the two Great Powers of the railway world in Lincolnshire: George Hudson's lines and the London & York.[19] This was forced on it by circumstances: it planned to make an end-on junction with Hudson's Midland Railway, but it needed the support of the local landowners, who were predominantly behind the London & York. There was scope for an alternative connection at Lincoln with the London & York, so the promoters may even have been hoping that, once they had obtained their Act, they could sell out to one camp or the other. Several such deals were made about this time whereby the acquiring company guaranteed dividends of 6% to the shareholders of the company being bought out. That may have been seen as an ideal outcome: the promoters could rest from their labours, Spilsby would have its railway and the shareholders would have received an ample reward. This middle course

[19] Playing off powerful interests against one another may have been advice from Mark Huish who in 1845 had advised the Grand Junction's shareholders that the railway was contemplating adding broad-gauge track to its main line, as a way of signalling its independence to the London & Birmingham: C. Hamilton Ellis, *British Railway History*, vol. I (London, 1954), pp. 104–5.

is apparent as late as 20 January 1846, when the directors were considering which MP should be asked to introduce their Bill: George Hudson was their third choice, only to be asked if the first two were to refuse.

In other matters of railway politics, the directors seem to have relied on three of their number connected with other railways: they appear at less than half the meetings but are usually present when railway politics are to be discussed. The addition of the first Boston branch took place at one of those meetings, on 19 September. It seems to have been Bainbrigge's idea: although the minutes are silent about the reason for the branch, Bainbrigge was to set out his views in a letter to the engineer; he was also included in the delegation that visited Boston to 'confer with the Mayor and Corporation' about it. The rather secretive manner in which this was done suggests possibly that there was no real intention to build the branch and it was seen largely as a bargaining chip with the East Lincolnshire Railway, part of whose line it would duplicate. If that is the case, it was a singularly ill-judged move: if Parliament had to choose between a line from Boston to Wainfleet and a line from Boston to Grimsby with onward connections to Hull, it was clear they would choose the latter. So it was a hostile act of little tactical value.

Where the directors needed to give their attention was at the Lincoln end. They were one of several projects seeking to continue the Nottingham to Lincoln line along the north bank of the Witham. One of the others was the Great Grimsby, Louth, Horncastle & Midland Junction Railway (hereafter the 'Great Grimsby line'). It was unlikely that Parliament would authorise more than one of these projects. If one of them built the final part of the line into Lincoln, allowing the others to use it, that company would have the choice of whether to connect with the Midland Railway or the London & York; the other would have to go along with that choice. The Wainfleet directors initiated no action on this issue, waiting for others to approach them. The Great Grimsby line, which had the advantage of having one of its directors on the Wainfleet board, proposed that the Wainfleet line abandon its line west of Horncastle. The Wainfleet board were naturally unwilling but proposed an alliance whereby they would share a common station at Lincoln. Bainbrigge was thanked in the minutes for his 'energetic services' on the matter. But he seems to have fudged the issue: Parliament would not approve two parallel lines from Horncastle to Lincoln; if neither project was willing to act as a feeder to the other, then their interests were fundamentally opposed and there could be no question of an 'alliance'.

Not much is known about the Great Grimsby line but all the signs are that it enjoyed George Hudson's moral and technical support, if not his financial support. It appears to have been intended to secure territory in East Lincolnshire for the Midland Railway. It planned to build a main line from Lincoln to Wragby, from which branches would diverge to Market Rasen (having a junction there with the Sheffield & Lincolnshire Junction Railway), to Louth and to Horncastle. If Parliament was going to choose one scheme among the several that planned a route along the north side of the Witham, this was the one that would appear to offer the most general utility.

Normally, railway projects could afford not to worry unduly about competitors until the year had ended: a fair proportion might be expected to have folded by then, having failed to raise the necessary capital. But the Great Grimsby line showed every sign of succeeding; the directors of the Wainfleet project needed to develop a plan for how they would address this threat, and there is no sign that they realised this.

Winter of Despair

Once the critical deadline of 30 November was past, the directors' meetings became fortnightly, and we become more dependent on Calthrop's letters to follow what was going on. One of those developments was a stock market decline: by 11 December, the Wainfleet shares were trading at 45s., a fall of 7s. 6d. from the deposit that had been paid; by 29 January they were selling at 25s. At one level, this was irrelevant: the necessary number of subscription contracts had been signed and there were no plans to issue any further shares. But the mood was different. When the shares were trading at a premium, the promoters had the option of selling out at a profit; now they were committed – unless they pulled out at a loss – and that commitment extended to a total of £5,000 for most of the promoters. It is unlikely that any of them had £5,000 in ready cash. Like so many investors in railway shares, they had been planning to sell other assets when calls were made. With the decline in stocks those assets were now worth less. In fact, it has been suggested that the main cause of the drop in share values in the autumn of 1845 was that those railways approved by Parliament in 1845 were making calls on their shareholders to finance construction, and those shareholders were already starting to sell other assets to meet those calls.

Concern extended beyond the shareholders to those of the gentry who had previously been willing to be associated with the project and who now sought to distance themselves. Sir Edward Brackenbury and General Reynardson had both declined to be named in the Bill as chairman. In the end, the list of directors for the Bill had Reynardson at the top but followed by Joseph Hunt of Addlethorpe, (a major shareholder and another surgeon) as chairman, with Bainbrigge as vice-chairman. George Bourne was listed as an ordinary director; perhaps his enthusiasm was waning.[20]

If this fall in share prices had the effect of causing the directors to look more critically at the line's prospects, that was a development to be welcomed; and

20 Letter from Calthrop, 21 November 1845; minutes of directors' meeting, 20 January 1846: LA, Misc Don 588/7.

nowhere was more in need of critical examination than their engineer's plans east of Wainfleet. Page was planning to recut the existing Haven to lead the water to an area enclosed by embankments, which extended like pincers into the North Sea to enclose the port. The water of the Steeping River would flow out between these pincers at right-angles to the coast, rather than flowing along the coast as it had done hitherto (and still does). The plan invited three questions:

1) Would a bar form at the exit from the harbour? (John Grundy's view when a previous proposal had been made for Steeping River to flow out at right-angles was that it would certainly silt up.)
2) Would the earthen embankments be eroded by the along-shore currents?
3) With turbid water entering the port area on every tide and depositing its silt, how rapidly would the port area silt up?

There is no sign that the directors articulated these questions; but their underlying concerns are apparent in their repeated requests to Page to produce his report quickly with particular emphasis on the port. Part of the problem was that none of the directors had any knowledge of shipping or of ports. They were reliant on Page, who was almost as ignorant.

Page was also ignorant of land drainage – certainly of the politics of land drainage. Perhaps to facilitate the re-cutting of the Haven, he (or rather Scott & Tahourdin) had given formal notice, back in November, that their Bill would seek to modify sundry drainage Acts, going back to the great Witham Act of 1762. No prior consultation appears to have taken place, so, naturally enough, the reaction of the various Drainage Trusts was to petition against the Wainfleet project's Bill. Perhaps the issues might be resolved and the counter-petitions withdrawn, but there was a secondary effect that all the members of drainage trusts – generally quite influential men – were thoroughly annoyed. This was bad for the railway. It was also bad for the promoters insofar as *their* ongoing businesses depended on maintaining good relations with such people.

The board had initially lacked expertise on land drainage, but this was something it had been able to rectify. David Martin, a land agent from Wainfleet, had been co-opted to the Provisional Committee on 7 October and had been made a director just a week later. He was one of the deputation sent to London to tell Page to make his works at Wainfleet Haven less extensive – and less expensive. The deputation was given authority to consult another engineer if they thought it necessary. Calthrop wrote to Page: 'Mr Martin's knowledge of all kinds of practical business and workmanship is great and he could I dare say furnish you with some idea of the cost of the items you mention'. This is astonishing: Calthrop is implicitly questioning Page's professional competence. Originally the deputation was to report back on 14 January, but this was delayed because Page was unable to rework his plans in time. They reported on 20 January that 'Mr Page has altered his plans so that the Drainage is not interfered with, thus negativing the opposition of the Commissioners of the respective Drainage systems in the neighbourhood of the Haven'. Clearly, their engineer was willing to accept instructions if they were given firmly; it is regrettable that he had been left unsupervised for so long in November.

Meanwhile, shareholders were becoming 'impertinent'. One reported that 'at Spalding and Boston the project is stigmatized as chimerical'.[21]. It seems likely that the allegations about fraudulent projects mentioned at the start of this article were already gaining currency. The delay to Page's formal report did not help. Nor did the announcement in *The Times* that the Lincoln, Horncastle, Spilsby and Wainfleet Haven Railway had not filed the necessary papers to proceed in this session. That was because the name had changed and papers had been filed under the new name. Nothing was amiss, but it increased shareholders' concern.

Near-Amalgamation and Oblivion

By January, the directors should have been aware that the competing projects at the Lincoln end were two in number: the Great Grimsby line and a branch of the Sheffield & Lincolnshire Junction Railway. As before, it was the Great Grimsby line which took the initiative, proposing once again that the Wainfleet project should use their line from Horncastle to Lincoln. The Wainfleet board proposed a joint line from Horncastle to Lincoln; that was unacceptable to the Great Grimsby directors. The idea of complete amalgamation was viewed with caution, not least from a fear that Spilsby and Wainfleet Haven would be seen as a lesser part that might never be built at all. However, it was agreed that 'the united attention of both companies should be fixed on Wainfleet Haven' and on that basis amalgamation was agreed. There seems to have been no attempt at what would now be called 'due diligence'. Perhaps the fact that W. H. Brook of Lincoln was a director of both projects allowed him to assure the other Wainfleet directors that the affairs of the Great Grimsby line were entirely healthy. Or perhaps the Wainfleet directors were so depressed by their own problems that they were only too glad to hand them over (along with their shareholders) to a larger concern.

All this was agreed on 20 January. Nine days later, Calthrop was writing as though an announcement was about to be made. However, Scott & Tahourdin, who had been given the job of sorting out the details, learned in early February that the Great Grimsby line were unwilling to proceed. 'United attention' had always been an ambiguous expression; perhaps the Great Grimsby directors decided that a verbal fudge was no basis on which to run a combined project. In any case, by then the datum error had come to light and a meeting was called at Westminster for 12 February to decide what to do.

21 Letter, Calthrop to Page 31 December 1845: LA, Misc Don 588/7.

That meeting could almost be made into a play. It seems to have opened with Page wringing his hands in contrition: he took full responsibility for the error; he left the matter of his remuneration entirely in the directors' hands; he would not go so far as to advise the directors that they should not go before the Standing Orders Committee but he was clearly anxious that his professional failings should not be made public in that way. The directors were clearly undecided about what they should do. Interspersed with this were delegations from the Great Grimsby line (whose directors appear to have been meeting nearby) pressing for some form of agreement about the line west of Horncastle. In the end, the Wainfleet board agreed (by seven to three) to offer to withdraw now and resubmit the line east of Horncastle next year in exchange for a payment of £2,000 towards their expenses. (Some might term this a bribe.) This offer the Great Grimsby directors promptly accepted. There was then an astonishing 'joint protestation' from the line's assembled solicitors (orchestrated no doubt by Scott & Tahourdin) that abandonment in this way would be contrary to the interests of the line's shareholders. The directors (who, of course, included most of the line's biggest shareholders) ignored them.

The lawyers then worked with exemplary speed: a formal agreement was drawn up and was signed by both sets of directors the following day. It was important to have everything signed before anything leaked out about the datum error. In fact, it is not clear whether anything did leak out: the project simply failed to present itself to the Standing Orders Committee and so the Bill was not proceeded with. Deposits were returned to shareholders, less 11s. per share for the expenses incurred. Thus the promoters with 200 shares lost £110 from embarking on this venture, a substantial enough sum for a middle-class professional but not a disaster.

The idea of resubmitting a Bill in 1847 was quietly dropped, but the project was not immediately wound up. The idea seems to have remained of promoting a line from Wainfleet through Spilsby and Horncastle to a junction with the Market Rasen line (which was the only route from Lincoln in that general direction actually built) – when conditions were such as to justify it. Not that there is anything about this in the formal minutes, but it may be significant that the project only wound itself up in 1858, three years after Horncastle had been connected to the railway network by its own branch.

A Grain of Truth?

This paper was motivated by allegations of fraudulent schemes promoted – in some cases, it was said – for the sake of the fees that could be earned, and terminated by a convenient error. It has become clear that there was nothing fraudulent about the conception of this project: the promoters genuinely believed their project would be useful and profitable.

Notwithstanding this, it does appear that the discovery of the datum error proved a convenient opportunity to abandon a project that the promoters and shareholders no longer believed in. It was of course possible for the promoters to withdraw their Bill anyway; but it was difficult in the hurly-burly of promoting a Bill to stand back and ask whether they really wanted to continue. It is striking that no one seems to have asked whether it was possible to withdraw the Boston branch – which was where the datum error occurred – and continue with the rest of the scheme. Nor was there any discussion of whether they should return deposits or hold on to them pending a new application in 1847.

Several of those involved with the project made some curious decisions which seem to be related at least in part to their personal financial interests. Calthrop, the Secretary, wrote in January 1846 that many shareholders 'are wanting money from over speculation and would vote for anything even at a loss for present convenience', so it was important that no meeting of shareholders be called which might allow them to take such a vote. One cannot help noting that Calthrop's present convenience was greatly aided by his salary of £300 per annum as Secretary, rather more than he would be earning as a struggling surgeon.

The astonishing joint remonstrance of the solicitors has already been noted. The surveyors were, if anything, worse, having seemingly agreed jointly to demand payment at the rates current in November, even though they had been engaged in September.[22] The directors raised the matter with Page, who had had a hand in their appointment. By 23 February, Padley had settled for £300 less than his original claim, Bourne for £200 less. Brackenbury was threatening legal action.[23] As for Lewis Kennedy, Lord Willoughby's agent, he saw the railway as a splendid opportunity to use his position to advance his family: the directors were placed under considerable pressure to appoint his architect son George Penrose Kennedy as their valuer, a post for which he was quite unsuited. They compromised by agreeing that he should be retained 'in the Architectural Department'.[24]

Barriers to Fraud

It has also become apparent just how difficult promotion of a wholly fraudulent scheme would be. Potential shareholders liked to see some prominent local landowners on a Provisional Committee. It is clear that the promoters of

22 Padley and Bourne charged £25/mile, Brackenbury £28. The extra charge by the latter probably reflects the fact that he was working away from home.

23 Letter from Calthrop, 23 February 1846: LA, Misc Don 588/7.

24 Minutes, 17 November 1845. Just a week later, Owen Jones was appointed 'one of the architects', perhaps to stop young Kennedy from presuming too much. How large an architectural department did a rural branch line need?

this project were fully aware of this. They wanted the great landowners of the district but had to content themselves with a reference to their 'express sanction'. They managed to recruit a handful of lesser men to their Provisional Committee, but even that was not easy.

Some promoters, it is said, would simply add names to their Provisional Committee without so much as asking the individuals concerned; but here the position of the project's local solicitors becomes pertinent. If the Wainfleet promoters had added Lord Willoughby to their list without his consent, it is clear that Bourne & Bourne of Alford would have been held responsible. In the event of Lord Willoughby's displeasure, how many of their clients would continue to employ them? In the great cities, there were doubtless crooked lawyers whose reputation was already so soiled that they had nothing to lose, and in such places the number of solicitors was so great that potential shareholders would scarcely expect to recognise the solicitors the line was employing. However, even lines promoted between great cities – like the London and York – normally had a phalanx of local solicitors all along their route. Such men would know of reputations within their profession and would scarcely become involved with schemes whose principal legal advisers were regarded as disreputable.

That would not prevent fraudulent promoters from floating railway projects linking great cities with no 'names' or solicitors from the intervening country. No doubt they might attract subscriptions from foolish urban investors. But investors who restricted their attention to schemes with Provisional Committees who were respected in their localities and which employed local solicitors of repute ought to have enjoyed a substantial measure of protection against the outright fraudsters. Those lengthy advertisements in the newspapers with long lists of Committeemen and solicitors really did serve a purpose.

A postscript

After his dispute over fees, one might suppose that J. S. Padley would have nothing more to do with the Bourne family. One would be mistaken. In December 1846, Padley, a widower, married the Catherine Bourne we encountered earlier being whisked off to Wragby to conduct an intimate examination of her sister. In his will, George Bourne left his 'written books', plans, maps, and surveying instruments to his son-in-law. J. S. Padley's antiquarian interests scarcely embraced railways; nevertheless, he and his descendants retained the minutes, out-letter book and subscription contracts, in due course donating them to Lincolnshire Archives, which is why we know so much about this scheme.

Padley also drew on his experience, seeking in 1848 to benefit his profession, by publishing Padley's Tables, which amongst other things explained how to set out the 'kerbs of a railroad' at a given radius, starting from a line tangential to that curve.[25] By 1848, the railway mania was long past, setting out railways was a specialist job, and the work was never published. It serves as a memorial for the brief period when surveyors up and down the country dreamt of making their fortunes from the sudden mania for promoting railways.

25 LA, LCL4968: *Padley's Tables for Measuring Timber, Stone &c and kerbs of Railroads etc,* unpublished draft, 1848.

10

Debating the Vote for Women at the Lincoln Diocesan Training School: National and Regional Testimonies to Women's Suffrage, 1909

ANDREW J. H. JACKSON, CLAUDIA CAPANCIONI, SIAN HOPE-JOHNSON, ELAINE JOHNSON AND JASMINE MILLS

Introduction

In 2018 and 2019, the touring exhibition *Vote 100: A Lincolnshire View of Women's Suffrage* celebrated one hundred years of British women's right to vote. It narrated national events from a regional perspective, and brought stories back to life with the support of archival material, including letters, and national and local newspapers. The exhibition was created by staff and students at Bishop Grosseteste University (BGU), in collaboration with Lincoln Central Library, the City of Lincoln Council and the Lincolnshire Branch of the Fawcett Society.[1] The exhibition invited visitors to engage with the arguments for and against women's suffrage by asking them to leave their comments, using a card that reproduced the form and style of a 'Ballot Paper' (Fig. 1).

1 Claudia Capancioni, Andrew Jackson, Sian Hope-Johnson, Elaine Johnson and Jasmine Mills, *Vote 100: A Lincolnshire View of Women's Suffrage,* exhibition booklet (Lincoln, 2019). For a coinciding and interrelated project, see: Jackson, Capancioni, Johnson and Hope-Johnson, 'Provincial Newspapers, Sports Reporting and the Origins, Rise and Fall of Women's Football, Lincolnshire, 1880s–1940s', *Midland History* 45:2 (2020), 244–57.

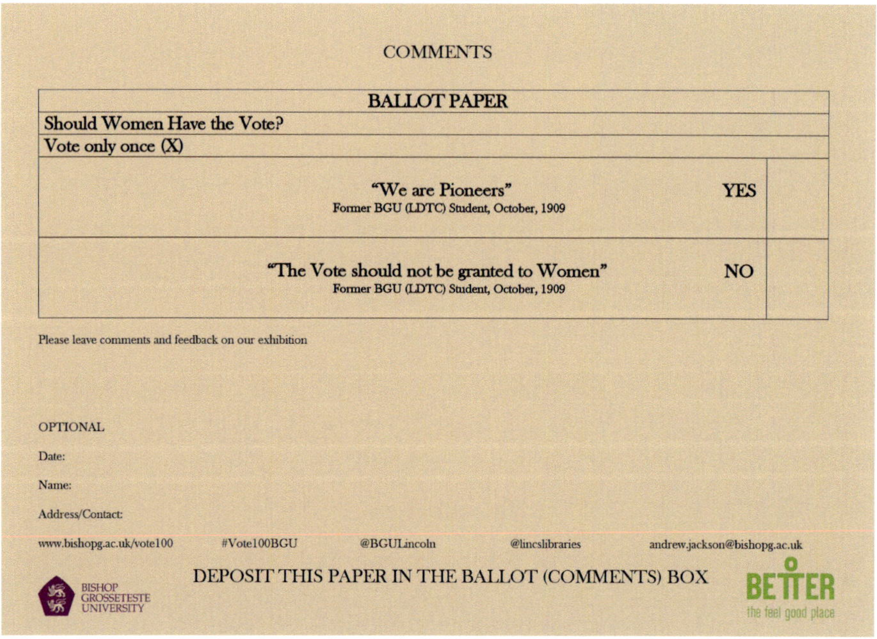
COMMENTS

BALLOT PAPER		
Should Women Have the Vote?		
Vote only once (X)		
"We are Pioneers" Former BGU (LDTC) Student, October, 1909	YES	
"The Vote should not be granted to Women" Former BGU (LDTC) Student, October, 1909	NO	

Please leave comments and feedback on our exhibition

OPTIONAL

Date:

Name:

Address/Contact:

www.bishopg.ac.uk/vote100 #Vote100BGU @BGULincoln @lincslibraries andrew.jackson@bishopg.ac.uk

BISHOP GROSSETESTE UNIVERSITY

DEPOSIT THIS PAPER IN THE BALLOT (COMMENTS) BOX

BETTER the feel good place

1. 'Ballot paper' visitor comments card for visitors' comments on *Vote 100: A Lincolnshire View of Women's Suffrage.*

The comments card incorporated as 'slogans' abridged quotes extracted from two features written by two teachers who studied at the Lincoln Diocesan Training College (LDTC, now BGU), at the time a women-only institution. Their conflicting opinions were published in 1909 in the *Lincoln Training College Magazine*, a publication launched in 1895 to which current students and alumni contributed. Their opinions outlined the long-standing contrast between supporters for, and opponents to, the women's campaign for the vote. Their contrasting views encapsulated the complexity of the historical debate so effectively that they became a central inspiration for *A Lincolnshire View of Women's Suffrage*, and several public events associated with it.

The comments card, as the exhibitors intended, captured the responses of visitors to the historical content of the displays. These charted the contribution of Lincolnshire from the origins of the women's movement to the 1918 Act, which gave propertied women after the age of thirty the right to vote in the UK. Furthermore, the exhibition also reflected on the wider achievements of the vote for women, and opinion on how favourably democracy and equality in the present day might be judged in the light of the campaign run around one hundred years ago. It created a conversation between different and multiple perspectives on women's rights now and then, highlighting how life stories can offset accounts of political activism recorded in the press and providing new interpretations on the past and the ways in which they reverberate in the present.

This contribution aims to recover the voices of these two alumnae of the Lincoln Diocesan Training College, Winifred Waller (1883–1947) and Annie Royce (1885–1954), in order to reflect on the difficulties that the debate on women's right to vote brought to the surface for female teachers at the beginning of the twentieth century. The exhibition proposed new interpretations of the British history of women's suffrage through the lens of the lives of men and women connected specifically to Lincolnshire, such as Emilia Jessie Boucherett, Emily Massingberd, Sara Jessie Stephenson, the bishop of Lincoln, Edward Hicks, Margaret Wintringham, Maria Elizabeth Nevile, the first woman to be elected Mayor of Lincoln in 1925, and Emily Gilbert, the first to be appointed Sheriff in 1936. After contextualising the history of women's suffrage with that of BGU, the discussion unfolds the voices of LDTC alumnae Annie Royce and Winifred Waller, whose writing opens a window onto an intergenerational perspective connecting women who trained to become teachers with those who were already teachers at the time. Their professional and personal experiences bring to the fore questions that remain relevant today about agency and political activism, and how being policitcally engaged affects differently those whose profession is linked to concepts of character, respectability, and impartiality.

These two teachers who trained in Lincoln offer opposing standpoints on women's suffrage, and their thoughts are analysed here for the first time as they originally appeared in the *Lincoln Training College Magazine*: Royce's argument for the women's right to vote precedes Waller's argument against it. They were published in 1909, the year when force-feeding of hunger-striking suffragettes began; and a year after ten militant suffragettes, including Florence E. M. Macauley and Mary Leigh, interrupted the Home Secretary, H. J. Gladstone, in Lincoln Corn Exchange, while he was addressing the public in the Cornhill in October 1908. Their writing marks a significant moment in the city's history of women's suffrage. It also reflects the influence of the Training College's debating society, to which staff and students contributed, and which facilitated independent thinking and agency. The LDTC students' debating society had started discussing women's right to vote in 1898 and, from 1922, the students held mock elections, including speeches from the local candidates when parliamentary elections occurred.

The year 2018 hosted a number of major anniversaries in the history of the widening of the franchise and the extension of the political representation of and by women: the centenary of the passage of the Representation of the People Act of 6 February 1918; the ninetieth anniversary on 2 June 2018 of the Equal Franchise Act, which established the minimum voting age at twenty-one for men and women; the ninetieth anniversary on 14 June 2018 of Emmeline Pankhurst's death; and the centenary of the General Election of 12 December 1918, when many newly enfranchised women could vote for the first time. These anniversaries stimulated new activities among scholars attracted to identifying local and regional connections and associations with these significant events. The topic of the movement to secure votes for women also offered considerable public-history appeal and contemporary relevance, attracting much media attention.[2] In 2018 and 2019, queries about the past were addressed, evaluating, perhaps most evidently, the contribution and experience of the suffragettes, and, with it, revisiting the controversies surrounding militant action, and the punishment imposed upon the imprisoned. Against the background of the centenary years of the First World War, the following long-standing questions also remained: had the case for votes for women been secured by women themselves, and by 1914? Alternatively, would progress depend ultimately upon the moral argument won for the vote through the war service and sacrifice of women during wartime? Did the breakthrough come finally as a pragmatic response to a more general urgency to extend the franchise to men as well as women? Equally, there was reflection upon how the past has shone light on the present, and how far issues such as equality of political representation, integrity in the conduct of parliamentary business, adequate enfranchisement of the young people, equal pay, reasonable equal protection under the law, and openness of opportunity for women in the workplace, have been overcome one hundred years on.

A Lincolnshire View of Women's Suffrage was a research-based, community engagement project that celebrated the 2018 centenary in collaboration with Lincoln Central Library, the University of Lincoln and the Lincoln Book Festival. It was curated from material accessed through Lincoln Central Library and BGU's archive, the county's branch of the Fawcett Society, Lincolnshire Archives, the Lincolnshire Cooperative Society, Gunby Hall, British Newspapers Online and the Women's Library at the London School of Economics. Displays were organised in five sections: the 'Origins of the movement', emerging through the middle decades of the nineteenth century; the 'Broadening of the movement' during the last quarter of the 1800s; 'Mounting pressure' in the opening decade of the twentieth century; 'Militant action and force-feeding' between 1909 and 1914; and 'Aftermath, legislation and representation' from 1918. Following its installation in Lincoln Central Library through the summer of 2018, it travelled in sequence to: Robert Pattison School, North Hykeham, and Sleaford Town Hall at the request of North Kesteven District Council, including for its Local Democracy Week; the Lincoln Labour Club

2 Gay Gullickson, 'Militant Women: Representations of Charlotte Corday, Louise Michel and Emmeline Pankhurst', *Women's History Review* 23:6 (2014), 837–52; Joyce Kay, 'It Wasn't Just Emily Davison! Sport, Suffrage and Society in Edwardian Britain', *The International Journal of the History of Sport* 25:1 (2008), 1338–54; June Purvis, '"A Glass Half Full"? Women's History in the UK', *Women's History Review* 27:1 (2018), 88–108; Purvis, 'Gendering the Historiography of the Suffragette Movement in Edwardian Britain: Some Reflections', *Women's History Review* 22:4 (2013), 576–90.

for its suffrage centenary event; Bishop Grosseteste University, as part of the Being Human Festival; the ancient Stonebow Guildhall, at the invitation of the City of Lincoln Council; The Sessions House, Spilsby; and Caistor Heritage Centre. The exhibition also formed a backdrop to collaborative activities with the University of Lincoln at Lincoln Central Library: such as an 'EqualiTeas' event for National Democracy Week in July 2018; talks in September as part of the Lincoln Book Festival; and a commemoration in December of the 1918 General Election.

BGU's Victorian origins as a teacher training college for women only, from 1862, and its legacy in women's education, were important reference points and sources for inspiration for the exhibition, given the institution's historical commitment to supporting and promoting the education and learning of women and the widening of participation. The University today holds an extensive and well-preserved archive. Interest in its content has increased in recent years: among students and staff exploring the life of the LDTC during the centenary years of the First World War and investigating Victorian and Edwardian women's lives through their education, teaching professions and life writing. BGU's uninterrupted archival material enables the recovery of the lives of students and staff who remained attached to their alma mater after they left. The run of the college magazine, for current students and alumni, is a particularly rich source for shedding light on contemporary opinion and activity. This includes a number of illuminating references to the course and cause of female suffragism from the end of the nineteenth century to the eve of the First World War.

This chapter's focus – the articles published in the magazine by Winifred Waller and Annie Royce – form compelling primary material, for one is written by a securely positioned anti-suffragist, and the other by an engaging author who was in transition from suffragist to suffragette, respectively. The two women, who shared their learning and training, were faced with the question of a woman's right to vote, and whether to share their views on the debate with the training college's students through the college magazine. Published together, their opposing perspectives provide stimulating testimonies on the women's activism, and teachers' activism in particular, at the start of the twentieth century. Furthermore, they remain a thought-provoking basis for discussing equality and the right to vote today.

Suffragism: selected perspectives

The history of the suffrage movement has its place within the wider history of women. Indeed, for June Purvis, the study of suffragism has been one of the 'constant themes' in women's history in the UK over the last fifty years, and through the last two decades it has endured as a leading interest. Its handling has been informed by the early and central concerns of women's history, driven by the influences of, and interconnections between, feminist politics, socialist and radical approaches and 'history from below'. In this context, interest in the intersection of the themes of class and gender have been prominent. The history of women has diversified and evolved, losing some of its feminist edge, while the term 'gender studies' emerged, including the recognition of the growth of work on masculinities and the LGBTQ+ communities. The main characteristics of women's history of more recent times provide a clear space for the ongoing exploration of suffragism, most evidently its emphasis on the modern period in Britain, its broad-ranging empirical-level investigation of women and gender relations, and, particularly enriching, the development of interest in life story, personal narrative and biography.[3] Indeed, the production and collecting together of biographical material was actively promoted by the pre-war activists themselves through the work of the Suffragette Fellowship. Their analysis supports reassessment of the dynamics of suffragette activity and the role and character of leading figures.[4]

The history of suffragism is also positioned in relation to histories other than women's history. Set within the context of political and constitutional history, with its traditional male-dominated 'masculinist' approaches, it can certainly be described as 'a field that is riven by debate and controversy'.[5] Within the masculinist paradigm the role of the women's movement is diminished, and, more especially, the suffragettes are marginalised and dismissed, perceived as forming a self-serving, single-issue campaign, and acting counter-productively and divisively. The greater 'constitutional' influence of Millicent Garrett Fawcett and her National Union of Women's Suffragist Societies and the more centre-grounded Sylvia Pankhurst are accorded more recognition than the more militant, 'Deeds, not words', women-only organisation, the Women's Social and Political Union (WSPU), and its leading figures of Emmeline and Christabel Pankhurst. More attention is paid to the relationship of women with politicians and the political process than an understanding of what motivated the women themselves and the suffragettes more particularly. Some feminist historians have also been dismissive of the WSPU in placing gender and women-centred politics above issues of class. Others, meanwhile, have challenged masculinist assumptions and attitudes, drawing attention to the relations across classes, and both the militant and constitutional approaches; and the connections between the

3 Kay, 'It Wasn't Just Emily Davison!', 1350–1; Purvis, '"A Glass Half Full"', 89–95; Purvis, 'Gendering the Historiography', 581–2.

4 Krista Cowman, 'A Footnote in History? Mary Gawthorpe, Sylvia Pankhurst, *The Suffragette Movement* and the Writing of Suffragette History', *Women's History Review* 14:3–4 (2005), 447–66.

5 Purvis, 'Gendering the Historiography', 576.

rational political activism among suffragettes and the progress of the wider social-reform campaign.[6]

Suffragist history also connects with the history of education. The expansion of education has a well-recognised and instrumental role in the development of suffragist sentiment and activism, and female emancipation more broadly.[7] Some leading suffrage activists were from teaching backgrounds. Mary Gawthorpe, for example, of working-class background, had been a pupil teacher and had been involved in the work of the National Union of Teachers, becoming a salaried organiser in the WSPU.[8] Joyce Kay observes that women's gymnastics as a sport had the clearest association with suffragism, while the suffragist ranks included those with backgrounds in gymnastics and physical training, including leading figures in the field of physical education. The challenges were also recognised of holding a professional position in education and training while also engaging in too prominent a role in suffragist activity.[9]

At the LDTC, the curriculum for 'Mistresses of Elementary Schools in connection with the Church of England' placed an emphasis on religion. Its church foundation was also reflected in other aspects of student life, such as attendance in the college chapel, and at local cathedral and parish church services. The 1862 Trust Deed also states that the training should aim to meet the requirements of the National Society for 'promoting the education of the poor'. Moreover, a Practising School was set up in an adjoining building in the institution's campus to serve 'the labouring manufacturing or other poorer classes in the said United Parishes of Saint Nicholas and Saint John Newport'. From 1862 to 1892, under the first Principal, the Rev. Canon Hector Nelson, the size of the institution was deliberately limited. This created a successful atmosphere that was best described as 'a family' and earned a good reputation for the care and training of its students. Moreover, Nelson demonstrated an active interest in the students' professional lives that extended beyond their term of training. By the early 1900s, the title of College was adopted, and the size of its student body had doubled. The students took up employment not only in church foundation schools but also in new local authority Board schools and beyond Lincoln. The College also admitted the first of its nonconformist students, although they would come to be housed separately in hostels.[10]

6 Kay, 'It Wasn't Just Emily Davison!', 1338–41; Purvis, 'Gendering the Historiography', 580–2; June Purvis, 'Emmeline Pankhurst (1858–1928), Suffragette Leader and Single Parent in Edwardian Britain', *Women's History Review* 20:1 (2011), 87–108.

7 Gullickson, 'Militant Women', 844.

8 Cowman, 'A Footnote in History?', 449, 457.

9 Kay, 'It Wasn't Just Emily Davison!', 1347–50.

10 Andrew Jackson, 'Bishop Grosseteste University College Lincoln', in Andrew

The pursuit of women's suffrage had commenced by the time of LDTC's establishment in 1862: petitions were presented through the middle and later nineteenth century, with the build-up towards parliamentary and electoral reform taken as opportunities to press for a step forward. In April 1898, a note in the college magazine gives some sense of the position that the college community had reached. Its Debating Society came together to consider the motion 'That women should be allowed a vote in parliament'. The entry is very short, but notes that the 'very womanly and conservatively-minded household', which included most of the staff, soundly defeated the proposition, expressing a 'very feminine dread of women's home duties being neglected'. There is no further reference to the deliberations of the Debating Society in relation to the progress of suffragism, except for a fleeting student's note in April 1904 stating, 'it is a pity that the Woman Suffrage Bill had not been passed'. In 1914, the magazine echoes a change in attitudes and expectations as the Society considered two motions. The first confronted the issue of militancy: 'that militant methods in the cause of women's suffrage are justifiable', an occasion that 'attracted a large and argumentative audience'. It was not carried, with sixty-three in opposition, although the record notes that fourteen were of the opinion that militancy was justified. A second motion, 'that women should be allowed to sit in Parliament', turned to ends rather than means. Fewer Debating Society members cast a vote, although the community was content to show favour, thirty-nine to eleven.

Between the two accounts of the deliberations of the Debating Society, are two letters by Annie Royce and Winifred Waller of 1909. It is not clear how they came about, whether it was coincidental that they should be presented to the magazine at a similar time, or that they were requested of the authors to appear side-by-side representing opposing viewpoints. On the pages of the magazine they are under the following titles, 'Some Glimpses of the Women's Suffrage Movement' and 'The Case Against Women's Suffrage'. If not the intention of the authors, this editorial decision on titling underlines their different angle and style. The close reading below addresses them in the same order in which they are shown in the magazine's pages and follows their content's original structure.

'Some Glimpses of the Women's Suffrage Movement': The Arguments For

Annie Royce was a student at the LDTC in the years 1905–07 and, in 1909, she was an elementary teacher in Ringland School, Norwich. Her piece reflects on the militant action of the suffragettes by offering four scenes that

Walker (ed.), *Survey of Lincoln vol. 5. Uphill Lincoln 1: Burton Road, Newport, and the Ermine Estate* (Lincoln, 2009), pp. 33–8; Donald Henry John Zebedee, *Lincoln Diocesan Training College* (Lincoln, 1962).

summarise her personal journey from a sceptic – who 'believed in the enfranchisement of women, [but] thought that Mrs. Pankhurst and her friends were shrieking horrors who were harming the excellent cause by their unruly and riotous methods' – to a suffragette, a pioneer who 'feels the necessity of militant methods' to achieve social change.[11] Royce's standpoint is clear: she is an enthusiastic proponent of the extension of the franchise. Her writing expresses the power and influence of the campaign, and how its very mood and manner drew the admiration, allegiance and support of women like her, and the two other teachers who are included in her narrative. She describes some glimpses or scenes, as they are referred to within the text, which depict most significantly her transformation during the previous year from a woman with suffragist sympathies to a local suffragette activist.

'More than a year ago', she opens, describing how she proceeded 'half amusedly and half ashamedly' to her first 'Suffragette "At Home"'. 'We looked furtively round', she continues, 'wondering if perchance any gimlet-eyed friend, passing at that identical moment would taunt us on the morrow with having been seen near the haunts of those obnoxious persons, the Suffragettes', who are distanced and rendered as 'other'. Royce draws on some of the typical and diverse modes of media-enforced stereotyping that can be found in earlier depictions of the militant woman. This ranged considerably, Gullickson observes, encompassing the 'hysterical, fanatical, sexually deprived, menopausal, intellectually pretentious, delusionally ambitious, man-hating, and devoid of talent … pathological unhappy, sexually unfulfilled … unbalanced and unfulfilled'.[12] The experience constituted an overturning of preconceived ideas. In appearance, Royce expects to find:

> some mannish-looking women with strident voices and rough manners would be shrieking their views to an audience of other women – all of them freaks, with their hair screwed into tight little knobs, and wearing thick, square-toed boots, stiff collars and sailor hats; these individuals, we presumed, scorning creature comforts, would be seated on hard wooden forms in a room quite destitute of anything that was not grim and hard and business-like.

Instead, she discovers that in 'a prettily-decorated apartment with dainty little tables scattered about … there were seated a number of ladies in the most becoming of spring costumes'. Yet, these same women were also the supposed 'most rampant and rabid of those who had faced angry election crowds and interrupted grave political meetings'. Royce pays attention to the mode of their address, 'mostly quiet and restrained, though in deadly earnest', while

11 *Lincoln Training College Magazine*, October 1909, 13–17.
12 Gullickson, 'Militant Women', 837, 848.

one, 'with her hand stretched out when declaiming', reminds her of the statue of Boadicea at Westminster Bridge. Suffrage activists were conscious of the significance of deploying the imagery of historical figures of heroic and warrior women, and how they helped normalise the place of female militancy.[13]

Then, the real central figure of this first scene, Christabel Pankhurst, enters, heralded by others displaying 'anxious sidelong looks towards the door':

> through the room tripped a sweet-looking girl with a beaming smile on her face, which made her look like a veritable ray of sunshine. 'Christabel'! the contented murmur went round as she stepped on the platform, and in a few minutes we were all under the spell of Miss Pankhurst's silvery eloquence. She was grave, she was playful, she was satirical by turns; now she touched ever so lightly, some foible of one of her sworn foes, the cabinet ministers, and her audience bubbled with laughter; for a few moments she gave a lawyer-like exposition of some point of law, and left her audience gasping.

The former LDTC student is enchanted by Pankhurst's ability to entice the audience by making legal matters into the light subjects of her talk. Royce is aware of writing at a moment when negative stereotypes of the militant woman were ranged against those of the ideal woman, the former typically stressing various unappealing qualities, which were perpetuated in masculinist narratives, as well as neglectful and derogatory representations of Emmeline and Christabel Pankhurst.[14]

Royce also identifies some of the features of an anti-suffragist opposition that rose more to prominence as militancy was stepped up from 1912, and more pathological and medical in character, one which gave emphasis to 'mental instability and fanaticism … and childishness'.[15] She is clearly struck by the qualities of what the WSPU modelled in defence: the ingénue suffragette, who was 'calm, practical, brave, self-sacrificing, well educated, and physically attractive … elegant … stylishly dressed … young, energetic … articulate, and anything but dour'. The focus on leading suffragette figures has generated a conventional view of the serious activist, devoted to the cause, while the reality was a more broadly engaged woman, taking up opportunities in terms of employment, sport, social and cultural club membership, and shopping, all of which were part of the emancipation process.[16] There was a connection

13 Katharine Cockin, 'Cicely Hamilton's Warriors: Dramatic Reinventions of Militancy in the British Women's Suffrage Movement', *Women's History Review* 14:3–4 (2005), 527–42.

14 Cowman, 'A Footnote in History?', 449; Purvis, 'Emmeline Pankhurst', 90; 'Gendering the Historiography', 585.

15 Gullickson, 'Militant Women', 847.

16 Joyce Kay, '"No Time for Recreations till the Vote is Won"? Suffrage Activists

between gymnastics and physical education and training, and those engaged in suffrage activism. Studies of the leisure activities of suffragists and suffragettes show considerable numbers engaging in the growing popularity of sports and other leisure activities at the time. Indeed, the failure to counter this contemporary representation of the militant women was highly significant in the failure of the anti-suffragist cause.[17]

Addressing them directly, Royce continues her 'history of the Women's Suffrage Movement' through scenes she wants her readers to 'watch with [her]'. Set in Trafalgar Square in early June, the second scene depicts the spectacle of a suffrage procession:

> Women in carriages, women on foot, marching with a firm and steady tread … Here are the graduates of the Universities, wearing their hoods and gowns … Next come the hospital nurses in their neat uniform, the house-wives, the teachers, the clerks, the poor factory workers, – these have travelled the whole night long, from a great town in the north, in order to be present to-day, and these have crossed the seas to cheer on their English sisters. In their hands they carry gorgeous banners, and for a while one is carried back to some medieval festival, and here are the insignia of the various trade-guilds, one thinks.

She pays attention to the social inclusivity of the parade, and to the prowess and commitment of suffragettes coming from all over the country for an event that demands future equality, whilst also paying homage to the country's past. The development of suffrage history in more recent years has been drawn to the significance of the spectacle and performance of its parades, and of its national and transnational networks.[18] The suffrage movement engaged with the well-established cultural practices in the processions and festivities associated with the labour movement, utilising the contemporary popularity of the pageant. They also developed plays to promote the cause.[19] 'What does it all mean?', Royce asks emphatically to underline how the procession is an example of political agency in response to a government's challenge to demonstrate that women 'of all classes desire the vote'. It is also a scene that shows the movement's inclusivity, reach and resilience. This inclusiveness and cohesiveness have attracted scrutiny, including a revisionist view in recent

---

and Leisure in Edwardian Britain', *Women's History Review* 16:4 (2007): 535–53, pp. 539–49; Kay, 'It Wasn't Just Emily Davison!', 1347–50.

17 Gullickson, 'Militant Women', 848–9.

18 Cowman, 'A Footnote in History?', 449, 456; Purvis, '"A Glass Half Full"', 93–4; Purvis, 'Gendering the Historiography', 585.

19 Cockin, 'Cicely Hamilton's Warriors', 528; Purvis, '"A Glass Half Full"', 93–4; 'Gendering the Historiography', 585.

research acknowledging a fuller place for working-class socialist women within the ranks of the WSPU.[20]

The third, shorter scene adds more sensory dimensions: 'a great organ peals out the stirring tones of the "Women's Marseillaise"' in a London concert hall, she recalls. Described as 'a great day in the history of the militant movement', the event is a welcoming of Suffragette leaders from prison: 'Mrs. Pankhurst, Miss Pankhurst, Mrs Pethwick Lawrence, and many another, we can see on their faces the marks of the struggle they have been through'. Royce recalls the cheers in 'admiration of the courageous women who have suffered as truly for conscience' sake as any Reformation martyr', and William Wordsworth's lines from 'The French Revolution as It Appeared to Enthusiasts at Its Commencement' (1804), a poem that contemplates the poet's disenchantment with the French Revolution. Conversely, she adapts his line about past youthful hope to emphasise her confidence that it is 'bliss to be alive' at a time of 'a glorious struggle for liberty'.

For her conclusion, Royce chooses a 'far different scene illustrat[ing] the methods by which the work of the Union is spread', the forming of a new branch. A member of the Union, she makes use of the first-person plural in emphasising her participation in a communal cause whose influence is empowering. She lists a variety of activities others opt to do and acknowledges how she needs to consider 'the risks that teachers run professionally, in being present at any place where there is likelihood of arrest'. Direct action could result in losing everything she worked for at LDTC; hence, in her view, imprisonment is a 'sacrifice which leisured and richer women are so willing to make', and which she would consider, '[s]hould the necessity arise'. Switching to the first person and associating her militancy to biblical language, she ends on her belief in her role in the story of women's rights, in her contribution to changing the world. The vote for women is a future certainty and suffragettes are perceived through biblical images as 'sowing the harvest of the great To-be'. Newspapers, she writes, are ready enough to give distorted accounts of scenes from a suffragette's life, and argues that, '[w]hile every Suffragette feels the necessity of militant methods, there is not one who glories in or likes them'.

In the manner of other personal testimonies, Royce provides insightful glimpses into what it 'meant' to be a suffragette, what motivated WSPU members, and what supported their depth of commitment, whatever the extent of their political influence and impact.[21] She wants her readers to partake in her experiences by seeing, hearing, and feeling what it means to be involved in the Women's Suffrage Movement. She also signals the difficulties of holding

20 Purvis, '"A Glass Half Full"', 93; 'Gendering the Historiography, 579.

21 Kay, 'It Wasn't Just Emily Davison!', 1350; Purvis, 'Gendering the Historiography', 581–2.

a professional position in education and engaging in suffragism and more especially militant action. Her writing is also about the life of the ordinary suffrage woman. This is a story that has been rather neglected, if for a general lack of evidence, in favour of leading figures, and one that has sometimes been distorted in its representation of the typical activist. Royce reflects the 'countless rank-and-file suffrage workers throughout Britain [...] the very women about whom so little is known'.[22] She does not specify what actions might demand of her a more direct contribution; however, the timing of her feature is significant. It follows the founding of the WSPU and its call for civil disobedience and disruption. It falls in the year when, from September, the force-feeding of imprisoned suffragettes who chose to be on hunger strike begun to be reported. It is also four years away from the scale of criminal damage that erupted in early 1913, following failures to secure legislative progress. This is a phase that attracted much notoriety and controversy at the time and has continued to do so since.[23] Royce expresses the sense of comradeship that would give rise to an outpouring of memoirs from the 1920s and find encouragement from a form of 'alumni association', the Suffragette Fellowship.[24]

'The Case Against Women's Suffrage': Reason and Analysis

Winifred Waller attended LDTC before Royce, over the years 1902–4. Her feature is signed 'Oxford, Sept 1909', and exposes the case against the vote for women as if to a jury. She dismisses the arguments for it, and what she calls the 'grievance[s] of the Suffragists', and presents her 'justification of the Anti-Suffragist position'.[25] The article opens from her perspective of, and perhaps appealing to, what constitutes the 'average woman'. This is an appeal that regularly features in contemporary campaigns.[26] Waller observes:

> One of the most astonishing things about the Woman Suffrage Movement is the number of women in England who are unaffected by it, for all practical purposes, and who remain almost entirely ignorant of what the 'Extension of the Franchise' to their sex involves, or why one body of women claim it so insistently, while another body of women repudiate their claim. Incidentally this is a very strong argument against granting it, but quite apart from that, it is a fact that has to be reckoned with by all those who regard it as a vital issue, from whatever point of view.

22 Kay, '"No Time"', 536.
23 Kay, 'It Wasn't Just Emily Davison!', 1339–41.
24 Cowman, 'A Footnote in History?', 447–8.
25 *Lincoln Training College Magazine*, October 1909, 17–22.
26 Kay, 'It Wasn't Just Emily Davison!', 1351.

The Movement, she states, has no impact on most women, and their franchising claim might be considered 'at once selfish and unconvincing', and indeed a reason to repudiate it. Furthermore, this rather negative line of argument maintains that, for such women, to have the vote would constitute 'a serious responsibility'. It would bring both 'an obligation to read the papers', and to endure parliamentary debates that 'were so stupid and dull'. 'More feebly still', she adds, the vote is not desired simply 'because women never had had one', and the average woman 'did not see why they wanted one now'. Waller feels such perspectives are also vulnerable to an 'obvious and crushing' retort in the face of a Suffragist, and the average woman would be left to feel 'selfish and indifferent to the interests of the community', or 'obstinately conservative as to make her partly ludicrous'. She lists three possible outcomes for her average woman: to try and put the 'whole question out of her head'; to feel 'somehow to her discredit' that she should be 'better informed and larger minded'; or to convert into a 'staunch upholder of Women's Rights', despite the fact that 'most women in their heart of hearts retain a strong personal dislike to the idea' – 'guided by their instinct, and following the light of nature, in spite of their feeble illogical arguments'.

For Waller, 'to inflict the vote on women would be mischievous and unjust', and the strong arguments of the Anti-Suffragist could counter 'the specious arguments' of Suffragism. The Anti-Suffragist position appeals to the impartial, but also does not dismiss the place of 'finer feelings'. It will enable a woman to feel that 'she has on her side the deepest thinkers and the most practical philanthropists', and be able 'to face the most militant Suffragette. She argues that:

> it is unwise to attempt to under-rate the strength of the Suffragist position. Their arguments are often very clever and plausible, and they set out to instruct the ignorant with an air of breadth and candour which is eminently prepossessing. And though nothing is easier and, up to a certain point, safer than to dismiss the whole thing with a laugh, and to make shelter behind the doing of the 'martyrs,' yet it is certainly wiser and more honest to examine their contentions and study their literature, and thus be able to repudiate their claims, with all the force of an intelligent conviction that they are mistaken.

Waller makes no explicit reference to her education. This was one of the themes that had lessened in the critique of the militant women, when earlier stereotyping would draw on attitudes that women were variously uneducated, 'over-educated, under-educated', or 'mis-educated'. Moreover, the WSPU could draw on education as one of the attributes of their contemporary militant ingénue suffragette, and certainly there is a noticeable connection between physical education and training and suffrage activism.[27] If implicitly, she seeks to build a more 'educated' Anti-Suffragist case. She opens with 'one or two of their main propositions'. The first relates to an area of primary interest among historians of Suffragism, and within women's history more broadly, the comprehension of gender relations and the place of masculinities in contemporary attitudes and debates. Moreover, the targeting of sporting facilities may be seen as deliberate given their association with male dominance and exclusivity.[28] 'They assert, with loud-voiced insistence, that woman is the equal of man, intellectually and morally, if not physically, and that therefore she has an equal right to the vote'. Conversely, she contends, 'since physical force is still the controlling element in national affairs, only those who are able to exercise it have the right to vote'. The power of the vote rests with those who can enforce it physically, and power in the world relies on physical force, whatever the status of moral and spiritual influence. Furthermore, spiritual force is not something expressed through ballot.

Waller then proceeds to another of the leading arguments:

> The Suffragists contend that since some women pay taxes, they have the right to the franchise. 'No taxation without representation,' that hard-worked and distinctly debatable party-cry is raised again on their behalf.

The study of gender and class against the context of the development of capitalist relations has been an early concern of women's history, and, more specifically, their relative significance and how they intertwine in the course of Suffragism. The degree to which the WSPU placed the broad concerns of women over issues of class has come under scrutiny, as has the Union's inclusiveness and breadth of interests in the wider reform movement for women.[29] Waller argues that the extension of the franchise proceeds through class categories, with more classes progressively represented, not by gender. Moreover, men of each class are able to represent the women of their class, and it is the rule of law, rather than the payment of taxation and right to the franchise, that is the protector of person and property.

Turning to a third argument, she declares that:

> But most mischievous and misleading of all the Suffragist arguments is that with which she goes among working women, and persuades them that their work will command better prices and that they will be paid better wages if they get the vote.

27 Kay, 'It Wasn't Just Emily Davison!', 1347–50; Gullickson, 'Militant Women', 844, 848.

28 Kay, 'It Wasn't Just Emily Davison!', 1346; Purvis, '"A Glass Half Full"', 90–1.

29 Purvis, '"A Glass Half Full"', 89; 'Gendering the Historiography', 579.

She is most condemning of the Suffrage Movement here. While the nature of the 'labour', 'struggles' and 'sorrows' of women ought to be acknowledged, it is a 'monstrous thing indeed' to exploit passions and ignorance to suggest that the franchise is an enabler of reform of wage levels. 'Surely the most casual student of economics' is aware that these are controlled not by legislation but the market. 'That women's work is underpaid is miserably true', she writes. But unchangeable facts are for her that men are relatively more organised and unionised; that in areas of female employment there is more oversupply; and that women are perceived by employers to be less regular in their level of performance, less able to be offered full career prospects.

Waller turns then 'to the last great grievance of the Suffragists; they complain bitterly of women's position under the law', making a reference to John Stuart Mill. She also observes that 'Suffragists are very careful to suppress' the considerable progress made since 1870 in removing the disabilities of women under the law. Inequality remained conspicuously in relation to divorce; however, this form of inequality had already been attended to in Scotland, and, more generally, parliaments 'of men, elected by women', had been securing the progress of legislative reform, and, therefore, 'it is quite unnecessary to give her the vote'.

Having demonstrated that the case of Suffragism does 'not bear investigation', Waller outlines some 'positive' arguments against votes for women. She links her feature to the intersection of gender and class relations, a topic which is of interest to historians of women who investigate how inclusive in class terms Suffragism was, how concerns relating to class or gender vie for influence and interrelate, and how far perceptions of men determine attitudes and approaches. For the Pankhursts, this was a cause of tension: whilst Emmeline and Christabel and the WSPU favoured a woman-centred approach, Sylvia was drawn to socialist and Independent Labour Party affiliation.[30] The process of extending the franchise to women was in effect a course towards the universal vote. Waller argues that most Suffragettes would 'shrink from the disastrous consequences which even they are bound to admit would ensue'. Even modest extension to unmarried women with the property qualification would raise the question of leaving out 'the very women who might be considered to know most about the needs of ordinary women and children – the mothers. It would create a majority of female voters, leading in turn to agitation for 'women M.P.s and women in the cabinet'. In parallel, widening the male franchise further would also be inappropriate:

> No one denies that there are many women in England who are eminently fitted to use the vote usefully and well or that there are hundreds of women who would use it at least as well as the average

[30] Purvis, '"A Glass Half Full"', 89–93; Purvis, 'Emmeline Pankhurst', 88–9.

> man; but the fact that a great many men are ignorant and prejudiced voters, is a very poor reason for wishing to add to their numbers.

She returns to counter a Suffragist argument that granted the franchise women will be intellectually regenerated and rise to leadership. She refers to the international context where progress has been made in colonial systems, certain other European countries, and US states; but she points out, such countries lack the responsibilities of 'foreign or imperial policy', 'great army or navy', and without the 'concerns of a world empire like our own … the great Powers are steadily refusing to have anything to do with Woman Suffrage'.

Waller's case against the extension of the vote ends with a final flurry of 'positive' arguments, which receives less elaboration. She reiterates what constitutes the average woman and her nature and role. She ponders the 'miserable divisions that it would cause in the home, for after religion there is no subject upon which men feel more deeply than on politics' and estimates that 'most women would be guided by some man on the exercise of her vote' anyway, because women are far more easily 'got at than men'. She moves from her depiction of the average woman, with which she opens the letter, to that of the ideal woman, before she draws to a close. The representation of the latter can be found elsewhere in media depictions of the opposite to the militant woman. In Gullickson's study, the ideal woman 'was still a charming, loving, morally pure, and devoted wife and mother who dedicated her life to caring for her home and family'.[31] Waller concludes by returning to her main argument, that it is a majority of 'women in England who do not want a vote', and begs her readers to understand that the right to vote 'is unworthy of them' and that 'it need not come, and it will not come, if women will only unite in refusing to be led into a false position by a noisy minority'. Significantly, she recognises that her 'justification of the Anti-Suffragist position is, unhappily, long and dull', and suggests reading other 'pamphlets on the subject'.

Waller's writing is different in style and tone to that of Royce, but as forceful as a call to arms with little by way of a clear indication of what is personally of greatest interest or concern. She endeavours to position herself objectively, representing many and varied opposing arguments and reminding her readers that the case against also has many supporters, and that there is much good cause in encouraging fuller and further consideration of the arguments. After more than one hundred years, her words may appear incongruous and out of touch. This is also a view expressed by Helen Pankhurst in *Deeds Not Words: The Story of Women's Rights, Then and Now* (2018), a volume that, like this chapter, also uses life-writing to recover the history of suffragism. There, she ponders 'the absurdity of the government's long-drawn-out opposition to women voting', recalling the words of her great-grandmother in 1911 in the

31 Gullickson, 'Militant Women', 846.

preface to Sylvia Pankhurst's *The Suffragette*. In imagining future readers of the history of women's vote, Emmeline Pankhurst foresaw our dismay 'at the blindness that led the Government of the day to obstinately resist so simple and obvious a measure of justice'.[32]

Conclusion

In a field that is 'exciting and dynamic', 'evolving and vibrant' and 'expanding and diversifying',[33] it may seem rather counterintuitive to reduce this analysis to two articles written by two women in a particular year in the progress of the women's suffrage movement. Nonetheless, by applying the now broader and multi-faceted lenses through which we might gaze upon suffragism, these accounts are stimulating and revealing. They incorporate a number of the perspectives and experiences that informed contemporary debates on women's suffrage. Equally, they represent views and considerations that are not included, but may have enlightened discussions among the students and alumni of LDTC from the early twentieth century. It can only be speculated how representative the two letters are of the thoughts and feeling of LDTC students, the college community, and its alumni. They are both in their own way impressive and worthy of respect. Their common and primary theme is that of gender and the representation of women. It is with this that Waller opens and closes her discussion, and it forms the basis for how Royce positions herself culturally and politically.

The conclusion that women led the way in winning the vote is a powerful and compelling one. It is all the more convincing when one considers their contribution over the long years up to 1914. This was a period of remarkable patience, persistence and sacrifice that is to be rightly commemorated as much as it is celebrated. With regards to the years from 1914, however, ease of historical interpretation is challenged and clouded by the intervention of the First World War. Confounding the analysis is consideration of other perspectives: in particular, was the extension of the franchise to women an adjunct perhaps to a more pressing need to broaden the franchise for men, most evidently serving soldiers, and to ease concerns surrounding general and mounting civil unrest? Was it Home Front service by women during the war that proved essential in securing the moral argument over their entitlement to the franchise? Moreover, the pace and operation of the political reform process was ultimately the preserve of a male governing elite, who had regularly thwarted democratic progress over many decades up to 1914.

The magazine of the Lincoln Diocesan Training College and the two contributions by Annie Royce and Winifred Waller do not bring resolution to the

32 Helen Pankhurst, *Deeds Not Words: The Story of Women's Rights, Then and Now* (London, 2018), p. 12.

33 Purvis, '"A Glass Half Full"', 93; 'Gendering the Historiography', 585.

historical debate in the present. They relate to a point in the long campaign up to 1914, rather than to circumstances and events during the war years up to 1918. Their interpretation requires sensitivity to timing. 1909 was a particular moment in a protracted process that shifted in its character. A few years earlier, Emmeline Pankhurst had issued her call for militant action; however, it was also a few years away from all that would surround the Cat and Mouse Act or the action of Emily Wilding Davison. The two testimonies give a glimpse into how individual women who trained as primary school teachers, within a wider but distinctive community, came to terms with prevailing thoughts and feelings, and expressed them to their peers. This chapter has considered what the personal testimonies of Royce and Waller meant, rather than their impact. They are to be appreciated as sources to understand how much the struggle felt like for those fighting the cause, and how much it meant for those resisting it. It is a study of thought, feeling and action, opening up fresh insights into how hearts, minds and behaviours were influenced through the exchange of ideas and collective association.

11

Addressing the Diocese in Wartime: Edward Lee Hicks, Bishop of Lincoln, and the *Lincoln Diocesan Magazine*, 1914–19

ANDREW WALKER

Introduction

As bishop of Lincoln, Edward Lee Hicks has attracted some considerable historical attention.[1] This is partly due to the availability of his diaries, of which substantial parts have been published in a Lincoln Record Society volume.[2] His extensive correspondence in the pages of the *Lincoln Diocesan Magazine*, however, has not generated a significant amount of consideration.[3] One of the bishop's biographers explains that these regular contributions read 'rather drily today'.[4] The following chapter, not discouraged by this verdict, seeks to examine the bishop's letters to his diocese during the First World War and suggests that these were of some considerable significance at the time of their publication in ensuring his views on matters relating to the war and other issues were widely distributed amongst the diocese's clergy and laity. Some consideration will also be given to the bishop's hopes for

1 See, for example: M. C. Curthoys, 'Hicks, Edward Lee (1843–1919), ODNB; G. R. Evans, *Edward Hicks: Pacifist Bishop at War. The Diaries of a World War One Bishop* (Oxford, 2014); J. H. Fowler (ed.), *The Life and Letters of Edward Lee Hicks (Bishop of Lincoln 1910–1919)* (London, 1922); Graham Neville (ed.), *The Diaries of Edward Lee Hicks, Bishop of Lincoln 1910–19*, LRS 82 (Lincoln, 1993); and Graham Neville, *Radical Churchman: Edward Lee Hicks and the New Liberalism* (Oxford, 1998).

2 The original diaries comprise approximately 270,000 words. The selections included in the Lincoln Record Society volume amount to 120,000 words. The original diaries are held by Lincolnshire Archives. Neville (ed.), *The Diaries of Edward Lee Hicks*, p. viii.

3 There are, for example, just five entries referring to the *Lincoln Diocesan Magazine* in the index to Neville, *Radical Churchman*, p. 356.

4 Neville (ed.), *The Diaries of Edward Lee Hicks*, p. xi.

the diocese and the country at large following the cessation of hostilities, as expressed in his contributions to the *Lincoln Diocesan Magazine*. During the period from the outbreak of war in August 1914 until its end in November 1918, the bishop published fifty monthly letters in the *Lincoln Diocesan Magazine*, with most being of between 750 and 1,000 words in length, comprising just under 50,000 words in total.

Through focussing upon such evidence, particular experiences of life on the Home Front in Lincolnshire during the First World War can be gleaned from the writings of a man, described by one of his obituarists, J. R. Elliott as someone who 'some may call a "political bishop"' and whose views on certain subjects some may consider 'to have been extreme and even dangerous'.[5]

Before considering the content of the bishop's letters in the *Lincoln Diocesan Magazine*, it is perhaps worth giving some consideration to Edward Lee Hicks' career prior to his becoming bishop of Lincoln from 1910. A brief examination of the diocesan magazine as a publishing genre and a short history of the *Lincoln Diocesan Magazine* in particular since its first publication in 1886 will also be presented.

Edward Lee Hicks: Before Becoming Bishop of Lincoln[6]

Hicks had a reputation as a formidable scholar. He won a scholarship at Brasenose College Oxford and obtained a first-class degree, winning the University's Latin prize; he then obtained a fellowship at Corpus Christi College. He served as a classical tutor at Corpus from 1866 to 1873. Amongst his senior colleagues during his time there was John Ruskin, who exercised a strong influence over him. Hicks developed an interest in Greek inscriptions and spent much time examining these in the British Museum's collections, when, generally, English classical scholars paid little attention to these artefacts, placing instead most emphasis upon literary sources.

Hicks decided to join the Anglican clergy and, in 1873, he became rector of Fenny Compton in Warwickshire, which was a Corpus living. During his time at Fenny Compton, he continued to engage in scholarly work, editing several Classical Greek volumes. These included a *Manual of Greek Historical Inscriptions*, published in 1882, which became the standard textbook on the subject. Whilst at Fenny Compton, he married the daughter of a clergyman, Agnes May Trevelyan Smith, with whom he had two daughters and four sons.

A number of experiences during his time as a rector of a rural Warwickshire parish informed his later actions as Bishop of Lincoln. Through the agricultural

5 J. R. Elliott, 'His Episcopate in Lincoln', *Lincoln Diocesan Magazine* XXXV, no. 399 (September 1919), 134.

6 This section draws heavily upon Curthoys, 'Hicks, Edward Lee (1843–1919)', ODNB.

Figure 1. Edward Lee Hicks, bishop of Lincoln (1910–19)
(© National Portrait Gallery, London, Ref Ax39059)

depression he was much taken with the example of rural labourers setting up a temperance society in his parish and he was converted to the cause of restricting alcoholic consumption. He became a teetotaller and a member of the United Kingdom Alliance for the Total Suppression of the Liquor Traffic.

In 1886 he left Fenny Compton and he was appointed the Principal of Hulme Hall, Manchester, a Church of England hall of residence for students at Owens College. Hicks continued his research and gave lectures on classical archaeology at Owens College. In 1892, he was also appointed as a Canon at Manchester Cathedral and he undertook work in St Philip's Salford, a large slum parish. Here, he sought to improve living conditions, and in doing so became a strong critic of slum landlords. He also set up a club to support the welfare of female millworkers.

Hicks was very critical of the Boer War and, in 1900, one of his sermons on the subject was published by the Manchester Transvaal Peace Committee as 'The Mistakes of Militarism'. Between 1904 and 1910, as 'Quartus', he wrote a regular column for the *Manchester Guardian*. The newspaper was edited at the time by one of his former Corpus students, C. P. Scott.

The radical views of Hicks no doubt harmed his career progression within the Church of England. However, in 1910, at the age of sixty-six years, he was offered the position of bishop at Lincoln by the Liberal Prime Minister, Herbert Asquith, who overruled the opposition of the Archbishop of Canterbury, Randall Davidson. At his enthronement in June 1910, Hicks declared that his 'sympathies lay with the friends of democratic reform'. Unsurprisingly perhaps, given the nature of the diocese, he was initially regarded with some suspicion, though as J. R. Elliott observed, his strong convictions never 'caused him to be uncharitable to his opponents'.[7]

It is against this background that Edward Lee Hicks' time as Bishop of Lincoln during the First World War needs to be seen. From his appointment, Hicks was keen to engage fully with the diocesan clergy: his diaries reveal his busy schedule of visiting the parishes within the extensive rural diocese, which included some 700 parish churches and parochial chapels in 1914.[8] He saw the need to supplement these visits by other means of communication, and the monthly diocesan magazine gave him an ideal vehicle in which to deliver significant messages to his audience of clergy and key diocesan workers.

7 Elliott, 'His Episcopate in Lincoln', 134. An example of Hicks' diplomacy in dealing with contentious issues can be found in Nicholas Bennett, 'A case of simony', *News Review*, LRS, 1 (2012), 4.

8 Nicholas Bennett, *Lincolnshire Parish Clergy, c. 1214–1968. A Biographical Register. Part I: The Deaneries of Aslacoe and Aveland*, LRS 103 (Woodbridge, 2013), xxix.

Diocesan Magazines – and the *Lincoln Diocesan Magazine*

The diocesan magazine began to appear in many Anglican dioceses in the second half of the nineteenth century. The earliest seems to have been one produced in the diocese of Lichfield in 1867.[9] Lincoln's *Diocesan Magazine* was first published in 1886, a year after Edward King became bishop.[10] The *Lincoln Diocesan Magazine* had much in common with those published elsewhere. In addition to regular letters from the bishop, the publication regularly included some theological reflections, details of the bishop's forthcoming engagements; comments on recent national and local news; details of future meetings and events; and the particulars of recent clerical appointments. In a letter published in January 1886 introducing the forthcoming magazine, initially called the *Diocesan Gazette*, its first editor, and rector of Snitterby, Canon R. E. Warner, expressed his hopes that the new publication would provide 'great benefit to the work and system of the Church' and 'will it is hoped be received as a welcome help to unite the scattered parishes of this great county'.[11] As if to underline the remoteness of some of the diocese's parishes, his letter ended by encouraging enquiries or communications to him, but he requested that 'no telegrams be sent because of the distance from railway stations'. Some uncertainty was evidently initially felt in several quarters regarding the role of the magazine: Canon R. E. Warner noted that 'it will not attempt to take the place of, or interfere with, parish magazines'. In reviewing the first issue of the *Diocesan Gazette*, the *Grantham Journal* indicated that the new publication is 'intended to give an easy means of communication between the Bishop, the clergy and members of the Church generally'. It was also hoped to form 'a kind of permanent record of the Diocesan history'.[12] The *Grantham Journal* commented positively as well upon the production quality of the magazine, which was printed by the Lincoln firm of G. Gale, situated in the High Street.[13]

9 An advertisement for *the Lichfield Diocesan Magazine*, issue V (January 1868), appeared in the *Derby Mercury* on 22 January 1868, p. 6, though, since no copies appear to have survived, it is unclear how regularly this was published; advertisements for the *Lichfield Diocesan Churchman* appeared in 1876, indicating that it was a monthly publication (see for instance *Derby Mercury*, 3 May 1876, p. 4). The *Lichfield Diocesan Magazine* was published monthly from January 1880. As the *Lichfield Mercury* reported: '*Lichfield Diocesan Magazine* – the first number of this monthly record of Church work in the Diocese of Lichfield will appear on 1 January. The magazine will evidently supersede the *Diocesan Churchman*'. (10 October 1879, p. 4).

10 The first issue of the *Lincoln Diocesan Magazine*, (hereafter *LDM*), was published in May 1886.

11 This and the two following quotations are taken from *Lincolnshire Chronicle*, 22 January 1886, p. 6.

12 *Grantham Journal*, 8 May 1886, p. 4.

13 A succession of Lincoln-based printers was contracted to produce the *Lincoln*

Upon taking on increased duties as vicar of Gainsborough, Canon Warner relinquished the editorship of the *Diocesan Magazine* in 1889, which then passed on to Canon William Weekes Fowler, headmaster of Lincoln Grammar School and a naturalist of national standing. During the early years of Foster's editorship, it is clear that the magazine was thriving with a rising circulation and covering its costs.[14] At this time, following the first bloom of diocesan magazines, many of them were beginning to struggle. Having indicated that the *Lincoln Diocesan Magazine* was paying its way with a considerable circulation outside as well as within the diocese, *The Globe,* a trade journal for booksellers, reported in January 1894 that this magazine 'occupies what we are afraid is a unique position among similar publications ... Few if any of them either pay their way or command a considerable circulation'.[15]

Canon Fowler edited the magazine until he left Lincoln in 1902.[16] Soon after his departure, a committee was set up at the 1903 Diocesan Conference, led by Rev. T. Hill, which sought to explore 'improving the Diocesan magazine'.[17] Some ten years after *The Globe* had observed that 'diocesan magazines are apt to be the dullest of dull reading', such observations were still being made.[18] An editorial in the *Wellington Journal*, with the *Lichfield Diocesan Magazine* in mind, declared that 'diocesan magazines are generally pitifully dull and meagre reading ... Church literature and church magazines will only be read if they are made readable'.[19] Some clergy in other areas besides the diocese of Lincoln attempted to bring about change. At a meeting in the diocese of Worcester in 1907, Rev. A. C. Deane 'moved a resolution asking for the appointment of a committee to confer with the editors of the *Diocesan Magazine* with a view of improving its character and usefulness to the Diocese ...'[20] The discussion that was then reported as following did not suggest a radical change was imminent

Diocesan Magazine. These businesses included G. Gale, High Street (1886–91), Clifford Thomas, High Street, (1892–1902), and, for over fifty years, Keyworth and Sons, Swanpool Court from 1903 until 1954, In 1955, the company became Keyworth & Fry and continued to produce the magazine until 1975.

14 See, for instance, *Nottingham Evening Post*, 14 October 1891, p. 4; and *Stamford Mercury*, 14 October 1892, p. 6.

15 *The Globe*, 6 January 1894, p. 6.

16 Following his departure from Lincoln, Canon Fowler became vicar of the Berkshire village of Earley, where he took on the inaugural editorship of the *Oxford Diocesan Magazine*, a post he held for twenty-one years until his sudden death in his parish church's vestry, where he was 'robed for morning service' in June 1923: *Berks & Oxon Advertiser*, 8 June 1923, p. 6; *Banbury Guardian*, 5 July 1923, p. 5.

17 *Lincolnshire Chronicle*, 9 October 1903, p. 8.

18 *The Globe*, 9 December 1893, p. 6.

19 *Wellington Journal* 10 October 1903, p. 8.

20 *Evesham Standard,* 18 May 1907, p. 6.

when it was noted that 'all speakers praised the devotion of the editors, Mr Lawson and Mr Bourne, who were awarded hearty thanks'.[21]

A more incisive analysis of the problems with diocesan magazines was presented by in a paper given at the Bath and Wells Diocesan Conference in October 1904 by Rev. Colin A. F. Campbell, the rector of Street. He asked what diocesan magazines were for: were they to represent the bishop to the clergy, or the clergy to the bishop, or were they to express the views of the laity in the diocese? He argued that what the church needed was 'an official diocesan magazine run on constitutional lines which shall bind church men together in the diocese'.[22] Campbell went on to observe that 'Nobody knows which is the best model diocesan magazine in England and few care to know. Its possibilities are disregarded and that it is so is an object lesson on the Church's appreciation of the power of the Press'.[23]

Despite the concerns expressed there seemed to be little conspicuous change in the content or presentation of diocesan magazines at the time. However, as will be seen, arguably these critics did rather underestimate the reach of these publications' articles. In the case of Lincoln, at the time of the appointment of Edward Lee Hicks in 1910, the *Diocesan Magazine* was edited by Canon George Frederick Wilgress, the newly-appointed rector of Kettlethorpe. Prior to this, Wilgress had been domestic chaplain to Bishop King, his uncle, from 1894 to 1910. Wilgress left Lincolnshire to take up a post as secretary for preventive and rescue work in the diocese of Winchester, and the editorship of the magazine was then passed on in 1913 to Canon James Bell, whom Wilgress had succeeded at Kettlethorpe.[24] Bell was rector of Riseholme from 1913 to 1915, and then, until his death in 1918, vice-chancellor of Lincoln Cathedral.[25] In January 1918, it was announced in the *Diocesan Magazine* that a committee, chaired by the bishop, was going to oversee the reorganisation of the magazine, under the new editorship of Canon J. R. Elliott., who at the time was secretary of the Cathedral Library, and, a strong supporter of the bishop.[26] It stated boldly that 'a vigorous effort will be made by the Committee to render the Magazine of practical utility both to the clergy and to the laity'.[27] According to the bishop's diary, however, much time was spent not necessarily discussing the magazine's content but dealing with the printers on production challenges, including escalating prices, scarcity of labour and especially the shortage of paper.[28]

21 *Evesham Standard,* 18 May 1907, p. 6.
22 *Bath Chronicle*, 20 October 1904, p. 2.
23 *Bath Chronicle* 20 October 1904, p. 2.
24 *Boston Guardian*, 7 December 1912, p. 7.
25 *Sleaford Gazette*, 6 April 1918, p. 3.
26 See Canon Elliott's obituary, *Lincolnshire Echo*, 20 January 1936, p. 5.
27 *LDM*, vol. XXXIV, no. 379 (Jan. 1918), 5.
28 Neville (ed.), *The Diaries of Edward Lee Hicks*, 1158, 19 December 1917, p. 196.

It seems that, similarly to many diocesan magazines, there was a suspicion through Bishop Hicks' period in office that the *Lincoln Diocesan Magazine* was not widely read. During his visitation at Grantham in June 1918, for instance, the bishop 'made an appeal to the churchwardens to take in the *Diocesan Magazine*'.[29] Notwithstanding the concerns about the extent of the circulation of the magazine, however, one aspect of its content received much coverage in other considerably more widely-read publications. During much of his time as bishop, Edward Lee Hicks' monthly letters in the *Diocesan Magazine* were reported, often *verbatim*, within the pages of the Lincolnshire press. In the *Boston Guardian* and *Lincolnshire Echo*, for instance, the bishop's monthly letter within the *Diocesan Magazine* was fully reported during the First World War on sixteen and fifteen occasions respectively.[30] Regular and detailed reports of the bishop's letters were also included in other newspapers published across the county including the *Grantham Journal*, *Skegness News* and the *Sleaford Gazette*.[31] Indeed, on occasion, newspapers beyond the diocese extracted the bishop's letter from the *Diocesan Magazine*: the *Yorkshire Post* for instance published one letter in its entirety under the headline 'The Bishop of Lincoln and women's work in the church'.[32]

Particular attention will be paid in the remainder of the chapter to examining a number of recurring themes which emerge from Edward Hicks' monthly letters in the *Diocesan Magazine* during the First World War, which draw attention to a range of issues with which the bishop was grappling during the conflict.

Edward Lee Hicks' Letters in the *Lincoln Diocesan Magazine*

Attitude to War

Hicks' earlier stance on the Boer War had shown that his position on any military action was, broadly speaking, to oppose it. As a leading member of the Church of England Peace Society he had hesitated in 1913 about the hallowing of regimental colours. On Sunday 2 August 1914, immediately prior to the declaration of war, he addressed a Church Army service at the beach at Cleethorpes where he protested loudly against the 'embroiling of Great

29 *Grantham Journal*, 1 June 1918, p. 4.

30 The *Boston Guardian* and *Lincolnshire Echo* were viewed using the online British Newspaper Archives (https://www.britishnewspaperarchive.co.uk/), which has complete runs of both titles for the First World War period.

31 See, for instance, articles referring to various of the bishop's letters in the *Diocesan Magazine* in the following newspapers: *Grantham Journal*, 7 November 1914, p. 6, and 8 April 1916, p. 3; *Skegness News*, 9 June 1915, p. 3, and 7 December 1917, p. 3; and *Sleaford Gazette*, 7 November 1914, p. 3, and 13 December 1915, p. 3.

32 *Yorkshire Post*, 1 September 1916, p. 3.

Britain in European complications'.[33] This had caused some criticism within the diocese. However, once war was declared on 4 August 1914, the bishop accepted its necessity, whilst clearly articulating his hatred of its effects. He spelt out his position in his letter in the *Diocesan Magazine* of September 1914. Entitled 'the Terrible War', his letter first outlined the reasons for his loathing of war:

> its stoppage of industry, its heaping up of debt and taxation, its unemployment, its famine, its misery at home, its paralysis of all effective work and expenditure on Social Reform, not to mention on horrible carnage of the battlefield, the agonies of the wounded, the visitations of disease and pestilence that always follow campaigns of battles.[34]

He then disclosed the content of a letter he had sent out to all of the clergy in the diocese in which he urged them to 'pray for our country, for our Sailors and Soldiers at the front; and for our Rulers that they may be wisely guided …' He urged the diocese's inhabitants to:

> behave ourselves as brave English men and women without panic, without excitement – steadily and quietly we will try to do our duty; we will be content to live plainly and waste nothing; and bear discomforts without grumbling … We will be very kind one to another, and very strict with ourselves, living as people should live who look for the blessing of God.[35]

In the early months of the war, the bishop sought to maintain a positive tone in his commentary on the war. In December 1914 his diocesan letter noted that:

> it is wonderful that we have gone so far into a great European war with so little of national suffering and with so large a measure of success. God be thanked for it all … In our prayers let us remember not only our own soldiers and sailors and statesmen but those of all of our allies – France, Belgium and Russia. Let us pray for the Belgian refugees and for the families who are now both destitute and dispersed through the war. We shall be more humbly thankful to God that England has been spared these miseries if we remember before God the sufferings of our neighbours and friends.[36]

33 Fowler (ed.), *Life and Letters*, p. 250.

34 *LDM*, vol. XXX, no. 339 (September 1914), 130.

35 *LDM*, vol. XXX, no. 339 (September 1914), 131.

36 *LDM*, vol. XXX, no. 342 (December 1914), 179.

During the early part of the war, for seven months the bishop and his family accommodated six Belgian refugees within the Old Palace.

The tone of his letters towards the war varies significantly through its duration: the positive account in December 1914 compares with a more despairing attitude in June 1915. He noted that 'As the awful tragedy rolls on, as the area of slaughter and devastation widens, as horror succeeds horror, we are driven to feel that it is wrong and not right to go on as usual'.[37] He advised his readers that 'We must change our habits, we must shape our lives to the new circumstances. Things that were well enough in quiet times of peace are out of place in the days of national peril and agony'.[38] Perhaps the lowest ebb articulated by the bishop was in his letter written in December 1916 and published in January 1917, at a time when he was laid low with a severe bout of influenza. He wrote that: 'The Old Year closed in darkness, blood and sorrow. The agonies and horrors of the war have been such that if the *homes* of all the belligerents were polled, an overwhelming majority would be found voting for peace all round'.[39] He declared that: 'Everybody hates the war more and more. But no one at present dares to breathe a proposal of peace … And so war goes on in its murderous, relentless, devastating course. How long, O Lord, how long?'[40] He exhorted all in the diocese to continue to pray 'for the safety and welfare of our land and Empire'.[41]

Throughout his letters, interestingly he was at pains to point out who the enemy was – not the regular German soldiers – but the 'German Government',' the 'German High Command', 'the Kaiser'.[42] Indeed, Hicks pointed out in his letters that the British troops themselves, in their discussions with him, 'speak kindly and nobly of their enemies'.[43]

Whilst Hicks' critical view of warfare is expressed consistently throughout his letters, his description of the military personnel he comes across in his own work is uniformly positive. He makes reference on a number of occasions to the 'citizen soldiers'. In September 1915, he wrote at length of the military he had encountered in the last six months:

> I have visited repeatedly the camp at Belton as well as Louth and Luton and St Alban's. I have watched the troops billeted not only in Lincolnshire, but also in Somersetshire and in North Wales. Everywhere I find the same qualities, the same behaviour. I do not want to sentimentalise or

37 *LDM*, vol. XXXI, no. 348 (June 1915), 82.
38 *LDM*, vol. XXXI, no. 348 (June 1915), 82.
39 *LDM*, vol. XXXIII, no. 367 (January 1917), 4.
40 *LDM*, vol. XXXIII, no. 367 (January 1917), 4.
41 *LDM*, vol. XXXIII, no. 367 (January 1917), 4.
42 All *LDM*, vol. XXXIII, no. 367 (January 1917), 4.
43 *LDM*, vol. XXXI, no. 351 (September 1915), 131.

> ignore facts. But I do thank God and take courage … Their favourite song expresses their feelings exactly – 'It's a long, long way to Tipperary, but we're not down-hearted yet'. And they carry this spirit into the trenches and into the horrors of the battlefield … Who are these men? … They are drawn from all classes and grades. I know a Squire's son who is a private in the Yeomanry. There are hundreds, thousands of gentlemen rankers. But for the most part the recruits come from the plough and the stable, from the factory and the forge, from the quarry and the mine. They come from our schools and colleges, from our warehouses and our shop, from all kinds of occupations and professions. I go to a Church and I hear that half of the choir men are serving; I go to another and all the servers at the altar, the best Church-workers, are gone. … it is highly encouraging to find how many of the men that have enlisted are among our most upright, valued and zealous Churchmen.[44]

However, although the bishop was impressed by the range of occupations represented within the citizen army, he was keen to deter the diocese's clergy from signing up as he argued they had an important part to play at home. Consideration will now be given to how the bishop urged his diocesan clergy to respond to the war – on the Home Front.

The Bishop and His Clergy on the Home Front

In one of his first letters in the *Diocesan Magazine* following the outbreak of war, Hicks explained why the clergy should not enlist as soldiers. In October 1914, he stated to his readers – many of them clergy – that:

> You will find everywhere in Church Law the assumption that no clerk may bear arms or serve in the wars. This is why Statute Law makes an exemption in favour of the clergy: they cannot be called upon to serve. Two reasons seem to underlie this prohibition. One is that the work of the priest is so necessary for the community that he must not leave it for anything else. The moral soundness of a nation is as vital to the safety and prosperity as the size and courage of its fleets and armies. The present war is a war of Christian *versus* anti-Christian ideals; and if the war is protracted England will need her clergy at home more than ever. Even now, every parish priest is more than busy. The other reason surely is that war is felt to be an abnormal condition of human society … the life of the clergy is intended to represent and exemplify the Christian ideal. To engage in war would sacrifice this great advantage, and thereby do harm and not good to the national cause.[45]

44 *LDM*, vol. XXXI, no. 351 (September 1915), 131.

45 *LDM*, vol. XXX, no. 340 (October 1914), 147.

Interestingly, Hicks went on to state that this was a view he knew that was shared with the archbishop of Canterbury. Given the manner of his appointment as Bishop of Lincoln, it is perhaps unsurprising that the Archbishop of Canterbury's views on a subject were rarely invoked to support Hicks' own position. Throughout the war, from time to time, Hicks continued to assert this position – that the diocese's clergy could not be spared to take on military service. Perhaps in order to defend his clergy from alternative viewpoints, Hicks was at pains in several letters to highlight the fact that a good many clergymen's offspring were contributing to the war effort. As he declared in November 1917, six months after losing one of his own sons, Edwin, in France (to meningitis):

> We are a married clergy; and we sent our sons from the Parsonage. Nay; they needed no sending. At the outset of the war they went off to the Recruiting Stations with their mothers (as I know), and enlisted at once; by hundreds and thousands they went; and this county has had a large share in this glory. And let me add, most of them will never come back again; or if they do, it will be with wounds and scars and a narrow escape from death. That is my answer to the parrot cry. You and I have no reason to be ashamed of the war record of our quiet English villages and certainly not of their parsonages.[46]

Of Hicks' other sons, one saw service in Burma and Mesopotamia; and another was wounded both at Gallipoli and in France.[47]

Whilst Hicks was at pains to deter his clergy from enlisting, he was prepared for them to become involved in war work on the Home Front. In April 1916, for instance, he encouraged clergy to take on land work in order to bring in the forthcoming harvest. In May 1917, the bishop referred to a village in the diocese where the vicar worked several hours a day as a 'striker' for the village blacksmith, in the absence of the regular man, having gone to war. Hicks declared that 'we may be proud of the versatile ability of our parish priests'.[48]

In Spring 1917, a directive from Government was sent to diocesan bishops calling upon them to make their clergy available, where appropriate for National Service. As Hicks explained in his letter of May 1917, four methods of National Service were made available: the manufacture of munitions; the helping forward of food supplies; the assistance of Elementary Education; and the undertaking of clerical duties to relieve neighbouring clergy involved in the first three methods of National Service. Hicks commented positively within his letter on the number of clergy within the diocese who were involved in

46 *LDM*, vol. XXXII, no. 377 (November 1917), 164.
47 Fowler (ed.), *Life and Letters*, p. 251.
48 *LDM*, vol. XXXIII, no. 371 (May 1917), 68.

this National Service. He reported that the Government Registers contained the names of a hundred or more clergy from the Lincoln diocese who were being drafted into agricultural work, munition making or supplementary work. He gave the example of the archdeaconry of Stow where already nineteen members of the clergy were working in agriculture; sixteen in the Lincoln foundries (munitions); eight as chaplains to the forces; eighteen in supplementary work; four on government work; nine as officiating Ministers to the Forces; two in Elementary Schools; and one in Post Office work. Hicks commented that:

> as their Bishop I look with a jealous eye upon their withdrawal from their proper parochial labours. But their country needs their service and they will return to their normal duties with an enlarged experience of life and (I hope) with a new sense of brotherhood with the lay folk and the manual toilers. Certainly the work of the clergy in the Foundries is having a very satisfactory result. It is thoroughly appreciated by masters and by men. Perhaps, please God, the "parsons" will come to be better understood when they are found to be really human beings with a readiness to do hard work and submit to the rigorous discipline of the great 'Works'.[49]

The bishop was clearly quite taken by the opportunities the Munitions Works offered the clergy to interact with hard-to-reach members of the flock. A year later in May 1918, he wrote in his monthly letter that 'The Munitions Works stands most in need of the sort of help the Clergy can tender. Much of it is not really heavy work and an intelligent man soon masters its difficulties'.[50] He went on to observe that: 'The withdrawal of large numbers of men for active service is creating an urgent need for more hands. In many cases, also, munitions work allows a man to return to his home and his Church for the Sunday'. He concluded helpfully, 'we must all work harder and pray better'. It is not recorded how many clergy responded positively to the bishop's plea at this stage in the war.

In a number of ways, the onset of war merely brought into sharper focus several issues that the bishop had already been seeking to confront. He was keen to tackle the perceived 'remoteness' of the clergy: his enthusiasm for the clergy to work alongside laypeople during the war can be seen as a way of addressing this issue. However, there were other means by which he sought to encourage his clergy to overcome perceptions of remoteness. In both November and December 1914, for instance, the bishop exhorted his clergy to speak up – quite literally. In a letter entitled 'On reading in Church' Hicks

49 *LDM*, vol. XXXIII, no. 371 (May 1917), 68.
50 *LDM*, vol. XXXIV, no. 383 (May 1918), 87.

wrote about bad reading, which he considered to be a grave and common fault: 'I hear lessons read so swiftly and so inarticulately that I am confident that few people can hear the words and fewer still can follow the sense of what is read'.[51] The bishop encouraged his clergy to recollect that many of our congregations are 'only half-educated, many of them unacquainted with the Bible in general, some of them liable to the interruptions caused by coughing or movements [in a] … large congregation, then the reasons become very strong for a careful, devout, distinct and leisurely reading of Holy Scripture'.[52] He concluded: 'This matter is so serious that I desire to call universal attention to it. We stultify ourselves if we are not understood'.[53]

During the early months of the war, the bishop issued strong advice regarding the need to ensure that the diocese's churches were regularly open during the week to enable prayer. In November 1914, he wrote:

> I hope that not one parish in our Diocese is so lacking in religion and in patriotism as to keep its Church unused and its people unsummoned for prayer from Sunday to Sunday. If your Church has been thus unused and unfrequented hitherto, now is the opportunity and the call for better things. Let the Church be used and the plain direction of the Prayer Book be no longer quite a dead letter. Happily, in most cases our people are eager to use such opportunities and a constant stream of earnest and united prayer is rising up to the throne of God.[54]

Hicks also had some words of advice for his clergy regarding the content of their sermons. In January 1915, he wrote about 'Services for the Men in Khaki'. When conducting services to congregations including a significant number of soldiers and other recruits, he reminded his clergy 'that there are now in our camps and barracks, or billeted up and down our towns and villages hundreds and thousands of our best young churchmen – our choir-men, our servers, our Sunday teachers – in a word, the very pick of our people'.[55] The bishop went on to instruct those conducting such ceremonies that 'When, therefore, our men in khaki come to a service let us especially think of these devout and well-trained churchmen and so shape our services and our sermon to minister to their needs'.[56]

Hicks was quite clear that his clergy should show some imagination, both in terms of their sermon subjects and hymn selection. As he commented, a young officer had mentioned to him that he wished the clergy 'would forget

51 *LDM*, vol. XXX, no. 342 (December 1914), 178.
52 *LDM*, vol. XXX, no. 342 (December 1914), 179.
53 *LDM*, vol. XXX, no. 342 (December 1914), 179.
54 *LDM*, vol. XXX, no. 341 (November 1914), 163.
55 *LDM*, vol. XXXI, no. 343 (January 1915), 3–4.
56 *LDM*, vol. XXXI, no. 343 (January 1915), 4.

their uniforms' and he 'longed for some other hymns besides "Onward Christian Soldiers"'.[57]

The bishop's distaste for bellicose imagery in church was also made clear in his letter of March 1915 in which he observed critically that: 'Many Sermons on the War have tended to degenerate either into recruiting sermons or even mere denunciations of Germany. Neither of these objects is suitable for a Christian pulpit. Let us not preach always about the War …'[58] Hicks went on to comment:

> If we speak of the faults of Germany, let us own that in ourselves there are tendencies to some of the same vices. Have we never boasted of our national greatness, wealth and strength? Have we never been tempted to trust in our soldiers and Navies? Have we never desired the British Empire to dominate the world? Have we never forgotten the Lord? It is by self-humiliation for our national sins and by placing ourselves frankly under the Divine protection that we shall win.[59]

The Bishop and Drink

The bishop's continuing radical position on a number of issues can clearly be seen in evidence during the war. In addition to urging his clergy to guard against excessive jingoism in sermons, he also maintained a strong line on two other issues that caused some discomfort in the diocese: drink and the rights of women.

In the case of drink, his opposition to this before the war was well known. During the war, his criticisms of drink were tailored to the new circumstances. In his letter of February 1915, for instance, he expressed concern about how the younger new recruits to the military were too easily exposed to the temptations offered by drink. As he noted, 'Drink is the soldier's most obvious temptation; and when drink has entered, immorality can easily slip in'.[60] He compared the British authority's disinclination to deal with what he perceived as the drink problem unfavourably with the actions taken by the governments of Russia and France. He complained of the 'regular treating of soldiers to drinks; the open drink shops; the feeble policy of our local licensing authorities; and the silence of our Press on this matter of vital importance to our national efficiency'.[61] He returned to the theme in September 1915 when he complained of slowness of the authorities to shield 'our citizen soldiers

[57] *LDM*, vol. XXXI, no. 343 (January 1915), 4.
[58] *LDM*, vol. XXXI, no. 345 (March 1915), 35.
[59] *LDM*, vol. XXXI, no. 345 (March 1915), 35.
[60] *LDM*, vol. XXXI, no. 344 (February 1915), 19.
[61] *LDM*, vol. XXXI, no. 344 (February 1915), 19.

from obvious temptations'.[62] He declared that 'Nothing but the power of evil custom and the tenacity of vested interests could have kept the public-houses open so long … near the camps and the billets of the men. This anti-social cupidity amounts to a national crisis'.[63] In April 1917, his readers learnt once more of the bishop's grave concerns regarding drink and the need to safeguard 'our noble lads'. He stated that:

> we want the temptations to drink and immorality much more courageously put down. Nor can we think it right that the little children of the poor should be stinted in sugar or in bread because the drinkers of alcoholic liquors demand enormous quantities of sugar and of foodstuffs for the brewery and distillery.[64]

The bishop's references to drink prompted a certain amount of minor irritation amongst some of his clergy. However, a subject that prompted rather more strongly-held objection to the bishop's progressive views related to his attitudes towards women's position within society.

The Bishop and Women's Rights

Hicks was President of the Church League for Women's Suffrage. Consequently, perhaps, it is unsurprising that from the outset of the war, at a time when others were doubtful, Hicks expressed his full approval of women's involvement in war work. In April 1916 he wrote at length of the valuable work 'committees of ladies' were undertaking – enlisting women and training them for field and harvest work. He wrote that: 'I observe that our women have been displaying their skill and courage in ploughing. This war has brought out the bravery and the enterprise with which English women are endowed'.[65] He went on to identify the types of work women were undertaking: 'They have done wonders in the Red Cross Hospitals and in every kind of war work. They have taken the place of men in our ticket offices, in our banks, on the railway platform and in the tram cars. We are proud of them and thankful too'.[66]

In September 1916, Hicks dedicated much of his letter in the *Diocesan Magazine* to supporting the increased use of women as laity within the work of the church. He was prompted to engage with this subject following what he referred to as a 'hue and cry' in the *Church Times* and secular press which had claimed that the National Mission 'were plotting to make use of

62 *LDM*, vol. XXXI, no. 351 (September 1915), 130.
63 *LDM*, vol. XXXI, no. 351 (September 1915), 130.
64 *LDM*, vol. XXXIII, no. 370 (April 1917), 51–2.
65 *LDM*, vol. XXXII, no. 358 (April 1916), 52.
66 *LDM*, vol. XXXII, no. 358 (April 1916), 52.

the Mission to promote the Women's Movement'.[67] Hicks within his letter outlined the ways in which women were replacing men very capably in a wide range of jobs during the war; he highlighted the increasing proportion of women who were benefitting from higher education and were, he explained, 'now competent to offer to the State a kind of service which they could not have offered a generation or two ago'.[68] He continued:

> a silent but tremendous revolution has taken place and what seemed odd, or unseemly, or impossible before is now taken for granted by the younger generation. But if this is true may it not be – must it not happen – that the status of women within the laity of the Church is undergoing a like modification?[69]

Hicks concluded that 'we shall be wise in treating women as important members of our laity'. This was a point he returned to in the final year of the war. In March 1918, he noted how, during the war, owing to the other duties of parish priests, significant work in church was being undertaken by devout laymen, and especially by the members of the ever-growing Lay-Readers' Association. He also noted how recently some six million women had been enfranchised by the Reform Act. Hicks observed that:

> Women who are now called to share with us in the vital task of self-government have already been asking what share they will be expected by the Church to take in promoting the spiritual welfare of their country. Does the Church want their help? What place, what work are we assigning to them? The question is urgent and demands an answer.[70]

Hicks went on to make his views on the subject clear. He drew attention to the fact that 'women are the more numerous, the more devout and usually the more intelligent portion' of the laity. He concluded that 'we dare no longer permit mere prejudice, or antiquated custom or sheer ignorance to deprive women of their rightful place in the ranks of the churchmen or rob us of the help that (under God) they may render'.[71] The roles that women should be able to undertake within the diocese were the subject of a later letter by the bishop in the first issue of the *Diocesan Magazine* following the war's end. In December 1918 he observed that the arrival of peace would 'liberate large numbers of church-women from tasks nobly pursued as war

67 *LDM*, vol. XXXII, no. 363 (September 1916), 130.
68 *LDM*, vol. XXXII, no. 363 (September 1916), 131.
69 *LDM*, vol. XXXII, no. 363 (September 1916), 131.
70 *LDM*, vol. XXXIV, no. 381 (March 1918), 47–8.
71 *LDM*, vol. XXXIV, no. 381 (March 1918), 48.

service … and many of these women, rendered all the more capable by their recent and varied experiences, will be willing to take up work for Christ and His Church'.[72] Hicks identified two types of women workers – the college-trained and highly-educated 'University woman … who will be glad, while living at home, to undertake some amount of congenial Church work without salary'. The bishop expected to see a place found in many parishes for such women workers 'and a large freedom allowed them to make experiments and win their way in dealing with women, girls and others'. He then identified a second group of whole-time paid women workers who would be trained and appointed to particular parishes. He concluded that 'It is hardly too much to say that an organised system of women's work in our parishes, both the rural and urban, would … bring about within a brief space, a wonderful change in the religious condition of the county'.

It is perhaps testament to the progressive thinking of an ailing bishop, now in his mid-seventies, that so much attention was being paid to future diocesan planning. Throughout the war – at least from late 1915 – the bishop's letters in the *Diocesan Magazine* regularly made some reference to preparing for a post-war world. It is perhaps appropriate to end by focussing upon his aspirations for a postwar world in which he lived just nine months, until his death at the age of seventy-five in August 1919.

Preparing for a Postwar World

At the heart of much of the bishop's thinking about postwar life in the diocese was inevitably the image of the returning soldier, and the need for the existence of a stable family unit. Right at the outset of the war the bishop had urged his clergy to do what they could to secure the futures of these family units by encouraging the soldiers to marry their partners before leaving home. As he explained to his clergy: 'It will be found in dealing with the families of our soldiers that some of their "wives" have not been married to their "husbands". Wherever it is possible, the clergy should endeavour to have those couples (who have often lived faithfully together) legally married'.[73]

Explicit references to preparing for the end of the war begin to appear in Hicks' letters from November 1915, when he expressed concern about 'the return of our troops at the close of the war'.[74] He paid particular attention to housing conditions, both what he described as the 'slums of the town' and in the country 'where the cottages are bad, or so few as to be overcrowded

72 This and the following quotes are taken from *LDM*, vol. XXXIV, no. 390 (December 1918), 216.

73 *LDM*, vol. XXX, no. 340 (October 1914), 147.

74 *LDM*, vol. XXXI, no. 353 (November 1915), 163.

…'[75] He noted that the returning troops 'will have seen something of foreign lands, and of their beauty and charm; they will want to make dear old England become all that they have dreamed of'.[76] In June 1917, he wrote once more of the return after the war of men with 'ideas enlarged by the experience of foreign lands'.[77] Again, he spoke of the importance of providing improved housing, but his principal focus was placed upon the need for an enhanced education system. He asserted that 'the village school needs to be radically changed … we need much better qualified teachers … and smaller classes. All children must be retained at school until they reach fourteen. When they begin to work, they must be allowed time for compulsory continuation schooling until the age of eighteen'. He also added that the returning labourer should have a permanent increase of wages and a larger measure of personal freedom. He concluded: 'I shall have said enough to make some people afraid and some (perhaps) even angry; while those who wish well to our dear land and its people will thank me for speaking so plainly in time before the dawn of the Day of Peace'.

Four months later, Hicks again returned to the theme of the postwar preparations in which he drew attention to the housing problems within the diocese which needed urgent attention: He wrote: 'Already in Lincoln and elsewhere the scarcity of house room is such that it is impossible to await the close of the War: houses must be built here and now … and the need of houses in our villages is often just as acute'.[78] He observed how the social order was in flux, with large properties being eagerly sold and 'the land losing its old masters'. He noted as well that 'some of our country towns are fast being overshadowed by the … growing populations of our new Camps and Flying Stations'. As part of this reordering of society, the bishop took the opportunity to urge for an end to the yearly hiring system of agricultural servants. He wished to see the destruction of what he described as 'the evil custom of uprooting a family every twelve months and compelling all its members, old and young, to find a new home, a new school, a new Church and parson, a new social environment. That this should exist is a sufficient condemnation of the present Lincolnshire village-system'.[79]

75 *LDM*, vol. XXXI, no. 353 (November 1915), 163.

76 *LDM*, vol. XXXI, no. 353 (November 1915), 164.

77 This and the following two quotations are taken from *LDM*, vol. XXXIII, no. 372 (June 1917), 83.

78 This and the next two quotations are taken from *LDM*, vol. XXXIII, no. 376 (October 1917), 147.

79 *LDM*, vol. XXXIII, no. 376 (October 1917), 148.

Concluding Remarks

The bishop's postwar agenda was, then, a consistent one, urging both clergy and laity, to involve themselves in debates regarding the return of the 'citizen army' and associated matters such as temperance, the place of women within society, educational reform, social improvement, particularly with regard to housing, and the campaign to transform employment methods in agriculture. The content of his letters in the *Diocesan Magazine* echoed issues raised in his diaries, and invariably linked directly to causes with which he was active both within the diocese and beyond. These often connected to causes with which he was close before his time as bishop.

The discursive and engaging writing style adopted by the bishop in his letters certainly encouraged several Lincolnshire newspapers to publish these, often in their entirety, and sometimes notwithstanding their support for the issues being advocated.[80] This provided him with a much wider readership, and thus potential influence, than could have been achieved through the *Lincoln Diocesan Magazine* alone, which, like so many other church-based publications of its type, rather struggled to find an audience and a clear purpose in the early decades of the twentieth century. That the bishop's thoughtful and thought-provoking letters had a life beyond what many at the time agreed were the rather dull pages of diocesan magazines has perhaps been somewhat overlooked.[81]

80 In the case of the *Lincolnshire Echo*, for instance, the newspaper provided coverage of the bishop's views regarding extending the rights of women although the newspaper itself had long opposed women's suffrage. On 6 May 1911 (p. 2), the newspaper expressed the hope regarding the Women's Suffrage Movement that 'it may be many years before such a change comes over the country'. Seven years later, it argued that giving votes to women without first obtaining the approval of the existing electorate would be 'to accomplish a revolution' and would be 'a betrayal of constitutional government': *Lincolnshire Echo*, 24 May 1917, p. 2. Nevertheless, the newspaper provided a detailed account, without immediate comment, of the bishop's Lenten address, previously printed in the *Lincoln Diocesan Magazine* (vol. XXXIV, no. 381 [March 1918], 48), which included the bishop's arguments for women's rights to be extended beyond 'self-government' to include a more active part in the work of the church: *Lincolnshire Echo*, 6 March 1918, p. 4.

81 The comment by *The Globe* that diocesan magazines 'are apt to be the dullest of dull reading' (9 December 1893, p. 6) was echoed by Canon W. W. Fowler, editor of the *Lincoln Diocesan Magazine* for thirteen years and then of the *Oxford Diocesan Magazine* for twenty-one years. In response to a suggestion advanced at the Oxford Diocesan Board of Finance that the magazine could be made more interesting, Canon Fowler replied that, given the vast amount of official notices to be accommodated 'there was not space enough to make it interesting'. He then remarked that 'if they looked at some of the other diocesan magazines they would agree that they were not only dull but deadly dull. (Laughter)': *Banbury Guardian*, 15 February 1923, p. 2.

12

The Enthronement of Bishop Buckingham[1]

ALISON MCHARDY

In 1363, after a long and successful career in crown administration, John Buckingham left royal service, and the people of the diocese of Lincoln finally got a new bishop.[2] They had had over a year to wait. John Gynewell died on 4 August 1362, but the appointment of his successor was not straightforward. Buckingham was the king's candidate, but it seems likely that there was a rival whose local supporters were prepared to thwart the royal will.[3] In the end, though, the king got his way, and in June 1363, before he was consecrated, let alone enthroned, Bishop Buckingham commenced his diocesan duties.

The start of his episcopate is mysterious, for it is likely that the first folios of his memoranda register (Lincolnshire Archives, Register 12) have been lost. These would doubtless have contained his bulls of provision which were read both at his consecration and his enthronement, but his memoranda register indicates that he was working on diocesan administration from early in that month. The first surviving memoranda entry is a commission to act as sequestrator in the archdeaconries of Oxford and Buckingham.[4] It is followed by commissions to sequestrators in the other archdeaconries. Most other entries were of three routine types of business: licences for non-residence, letters dimissory, and permissions to have oratories in private places. One such

1 My warmest thanks go to the late Professor David Smith, who, back in 1969, drew my attention to this document, and who, very recently, applied his learning and kindness to improving my text.

2 For details see A. K. McHardy, 'Buckingham, John (*c.* 1320–1399), administrator and bishop of Lincoln', *ODNB* online, and *The Age of War and Wycliffe* (Lincoln Minster Pamphlet, 2001), p. 9.

3 A. K. McHardy, 'The Promotion of John Buckingham to the See of Lincoln', *Journal of Ecclesiastical History* 26 (1975), 127–35.

4 The commission was printed by Colin Morris, 'The Ravenser Composition', in *Lincolnshire AASRP*, vol. 10 pt. 1 (1963), 24–39; this entry is on pp. 29–30 but is now illegible in the ms.

permission was to William Courtenay, who was already described as being skilled in law, to have a portable altar in his lodging at Oxford, on 15 June.[5]

Courtenay was the fourth son of the earl of Devon and a future bishop of Hereford, London, and archbishop of Canterbury from 1381 to 1396. At that point Buckingham was in 'London', though not yet, apparently, using the episcopal town house, the Old Temple. This routine work was interrupted by his consecration, on Sunday 25 June. It took place in the parish church of Wargrave, Berkshire, which lay in Salisbury diocese, but where the bishop of Winchester had a manor house. It was that bishop, William Edington, who performed the ceremony, assisted by Robert Wyville, bishop of Salisbury, and by John de Tatenhale, bishop of Ossory, a Dominican friar.[6] Edington and Wyville were both veteran bishops, and Edington had made something of a cottage industry as a consecrator of colleagues, having already consecrated an archbishop of Dublin, and bishops of Rochester, London, Whithorn, Norwich, St. Davids, Ely, and Worcester, between 1350 and 1362.[7]

From Wargrave the new bishop journeyed (almost certainly crossing the Thames at Henley) to the episcopal manor at Wooburn, in Buckinghamshire, which was his base until 23 August.[8] The picture is then confused, but suggests great energy on the part of the new bishop travelling through Oxfordshire and Northamptonshire before arriving at the manor of Lyddington, in Rutland, which would be his preferred residence during the first years of his episcopate, on 25 August.[9] The day of his enthronement was not the first time Buckingham was in Lincoln, since he had transacted business there on the day before, but he then evidently went out to Nettleham, two miles to the northeast, where the bishops' manor lay just south of the village.

The account of Buckingham's enthronement printed here is not unique, but it is one of the few surviving eye-witness accounts of an episcopal enthronement. The enthronement of a bishop came within the authority of his cathedral chapter. It was among cathedral statutes that rules for this service were set out, and it was usually, as here, that the event was recorded among the chapter acts. Most of these remain unprinted.[10] Exceptional is the account of

5 LA, Reg. 12, fol. 1v.

6 *The Register of William Edington Bishop of Winchester 1346–1366*, ed. S. F. Hockey, 2 vols Hampshire Record Series, 7, 8 (London, 1986, 1987), II, no. 550, p. 72; E .B. Fryde, D. E. Greenway, S. Porter, and I. Roy (eds), *Handbook of British Chronology*, 3rd edn (London, 1986), p. 369.

7 Hockey (ed.), *Register of William Edington*, II, nos 523, 525, 532, 535, 544, 545, pp. 69, 70, 71–2.

8 LA, Reg. 12, fols 2v–6.

9 *ibid.*, fol. 12v.

10 Kathleen Edwards, *The English Secular Cathedrals in the Middle Ages*, 2nd edn (Manchester, 1967), p. 102 and n. 1 for references.

the enthronement of William Courtenay as bishop of Hereford on 15 September 1370, which was recorded in his register.[11] This is longer than the account here, and is laced with proper names, in contrast to the brief notice of Buckingham's enthronement. Although the others involved in Buckingham's ceremony are anonymous, the account is detailed in its liturgical information. The choice of psalm, 132 in the Vulgate, is interesting, for this very short psalm begins, 'Behold, how good and joyful a thing it is: brethren, to dwell together in unity!' It was not the psalm of the day, but was surely chosen to heal the disagreement which there had been over the choice of a new bishop. It is possible that the image of St John Baptist which Buckingham presented to the chapter on this occasion did not long remain in its possession. For much of the fourteenth century the chapter was in dispute with the city of Lincoln, a dispute which was resolved by the (very biased) arbitration of John of Gaunt in 1392. The chapter was so delighted with his ruling that they presented him with an image of John the Baptist; 'and, since there is no record of expenditure on it except two shillings … for cleaning it, it seems probably that it was one they already had in the Treasury'.[12]

In the following transcription editorial extensions are indicated by underlining. The punctuation has been modernised. The use of capitals in the manuscript has been maintained. Interlineation is indicated \ /

Lincolnshire Archives, Lincoln Dean and Chapter Muniments (The Book of John de Schalby), A/2/3, fol. 43v.

Memorandum Installationis Johannis Bokyngham' Lincoln' episcopi [looks like episcopum] a Nettelham ad Lincoln venien'.[a]

Memorandum quod anno domini millesimo ccc lxiij x^{o} Kalendae Novembris fuit Johannes de Bokyngham Episcopus Lincoln' installatus modo et ordine sequentibus: pello pulsato ante solis ortum, missam beate marie, primam in choro, preciosa[b], et horam terciam consueto more cantabant; et post horam iii^{am} tam canonici quam vicarii et ceteri de choro qui tunc presentes fuerunt, induti capis sericis processionaliter venerunt ei obviam usque ad ostium occidentale, ut habetur in registro; et ibi steterunt maiores proximi ostium predictum, ordine quo stant in

[11] W. W. Capes (ed.), *Diocesis Herefordensis: Registrum Willelmi de Courtenay*, Canterbury and York Society 15 (London, 1914), pp. 4–5.

[12] Kathleen Major, 'The finances of the Dean and Chapter of Lincoln from the Twelfth to the Fourteenth Century: a Preliminary Survey', *Journal of Ecclesiastical History* 5 (1954), 149–67. The quotation is from p. 163. For much background material see Gwilym Dodd and Alison K. McHardy (eds), *Petitions from Lincolnshire c. 1200–c. 1500*, LRS 108 (Woodbridge, 2020), pp. 192–6.

processione sabbatorum ad vesperas. Cum autem Johannes episcopus prenominatus intrasset ecclesiam, precentor[13] in dextera parte, quod decanus[14] non erat presens, Thesaurarius[15] in sinistra, duxerunt eum, absque incensario vel alio officio, ad magnum altare. Succentore[16] incipiente Responsorium 'Honor virtus' et ibant per medium chori. Cum autem venissent ad altare, Inclinavit se Episcopus, genuflectens coram altare, supra cathedram ferream ad hoc ibidem preparatam et tunc dixerunt Psalmum 'Ecce quam bonum'[c] cum 'gloria patri' et 'kirie' et 'pater noster'; deinde dixit precentor \preces/ et oracionem, ut habetur in collectarium. Tunc allata erat sibi oblacio sua, videlicet quadam ymago Sancti Johannis Baptiste, quam, genuflectens, optulit super altare, et unum anulum cum saphiro, et conversus ad fratres suos, osculato precentore et Thesaurario dixit, 'hanc ymaginem offero in honore Sancti Johannis Baptiste, quod natus fui in vigilia illius, ut medius sit inter me et illam gloriosam virginam ad supplicandum pro me quod me reputo indignum'. Et tunc directe ivit in vestiarium ad lavandum pedes, quod nudus pedibus venit de Nettilham ubi pernoctabat nocte preterita, et tunc indutus fuerat pontificalibus, processit et fuit installatus et ibi fuerant lecte bulle sue et eodem die celebravit ad magnum altare.

a The margin flag is in a different hand.

b Psalm 115 v. 15, in the Vulgate, 'Preciosa est in conspectu Domini', the versicle said after Prime.

c Psalm 132 in the Vulgate.

[Memorandum that on 23 October 1363 John Buckingham, bishop of Lincoln, was installed in the following manner. The bell was rung before sunrise, and they sang the Mass of the blessed Mary, prime in the choir, *Preciosa*, and the hour of terce, in the usual way; and after the third hour both the canons and vicars and others of the choir who were then present, wearing their silken copes, came in procession and met him at the west door, as is found in the register. And there stood the senior men close to that door, in the order in which they stand in procession on Saturday at vespers. When, however, the said bishop

13 Mr. Anthony Goldsborough, John le Neve, *Fasti Ecclesiae Anglicanae 1300–1541, I, Lincoln Diocese*, comp. H. P. F. King (London, 1962), p. 20.

14 John Stretley, *Fasti*, p. 4. He was then chancellor of Guyenne. For his distinguished career in crown service see A. B. Emden, *A Biographical Register of the University of Oxford to 1500* 3 vols (Oxford, 1959), vol. 3, p. 1804.

15 John Welbourne, *Fasti*, p. 22.

16 The succentor's name is unknown; he was not a canon. For the office see Edwards, *English Secular Cathedrals,* pp. 169–72.

John had entered the church, the precentor on his right, because the dean was not present, the treasurer on his left, they led him, without incense or other ceremony, to the high altar. The succentor began the response *Honor virtus* and they went through the middle of the choir. When however, they had come to the altar, the bishop bowed, genuflecting before the altar, he [sat] on an iron chair prepared, and then they sang the Psalm *Ecce quam bonum* with the *Gloria patri* and *Kyrie* and *Pater Noster*. Then the precentor said the supplications and prayer, as in the book of collects. Then there was brought to him his offering, namely an image of St John the Baptist which, genuflecting, he placed on the altar, and a sapphire ring, and turning to his brethren, he kissed the precentor and treasurer and said, 'I offer this image in honour of St John the Baptist because I was born on his vigil, to be an intermediary between me and that glorious Virgin, to supplicate for me because I consider myself unworthy'. Then he went straight to the vestry to wash his feet, because had had walked barefoot from Nettleham where he had spent the previous night, and then he was clothed in his pontifical robes, he processed and was installed, and there were read his bulls [of provision], and the same day he celebrated at the high altar.]

13

The Lost Rolls of Bishop Oliver Sutton of Lincoln (1280–99)

DAVID M. SMITH

Professor Rosalind Hill, the editor of the magisterial eight-volume edition of the rolls and register of Bishop Oliver Sutton of Lincoln (1280–99),[1] considered with some justification that John de Schalby, Sutton's registrar, had developed registrational practices at Lincoln to their finest point when, in 1290, the rolls were replaced by the register format. From the bishop's accession until that year Schalby had followed the practice of keeping separate archdeaconry rolls, first devised at Lincoln under Bishop Hugh of Wells (1209–35), but in 1290 he abandoned the rolls in favour of the register, which enabled a more flexible subdivision of recorded business into many different category sections (by keeping a system of loose quires designated for each particular type of business and/or geographical area). What now survives for Sutton's episcopate, in addition to this large register covering the years 1290–99, are five earlier institution rolls (for the Lincoln, Northampton, Stow, Bedford and Leicester archdeaconries, the last mentioned incomplete) and a custody roll for the whole diocese. Institution rolls for the remaining archdeaconries of the diocese (Buckingham, Huntingdon and Oxford) are missing.

Dodsworth MS 107 in the Bodleian Library, Oxford, contains Roger Dodsworth's abstracts from early medieval Lincoln episcopal registers, including Sutton's, made in 1641. The principal value of these notes is that at the time Dodsworth was consulting this material, the now lost institution rolls covering 1280–90 for the archdeaconries of Buckingham, Oxford and Huntingdon and the earliest portion of the Leicester archdeaconry roll 1280–86 were still extant. Dodsworth's notes on these lost rolls cover ten folios of the manuscript, and, as might be assumed, were clearly very selective in content, and were confined to brief notes of what was of particular interest to the

1 *Reg. Sutton*.

antiquary. There was no attempt to systematically note the entire contents of the rolls (in the later Leicester material covering 1287–90, which still survives, we can see that Dodsworth chose sixteen entries out of a possible total of fifty). Nevertheless, we must be grateful that he noted at least 210 entries that would otherwise be lost to us.

In the following calendar, I have numbered the entries for convenience and abstracted them in English (the original notes are written in Latin). The entries are not individually dated, only by the sectional heading giving the bishop's pontifical year. As can be seen from a typical institution entry, Dodsworth was much more interested in the patrons than the presentees to the benefices: invariably all patrons are noted but rarely incumbents. I have attempted to identify all place names by their modern version but have placed the version given by Dodsworth in italics after the current spelling. Abbreviations Ds for *Dominus*, Dna for *Domina*, and Mag. for *Magister* have been retained where written before certain personal names.

Bodleian Library, Oxford, Dodsworth MS 107
[fol. 138r]

ARCHDEACONRY OF LEICESTER

Annus Primus [19 May 1280–18 May 1281]

1. Ds William de Kileby [?Kirkeby presents to the church of Saxby [*Saxeby*]. [The Kirkby family presented to this church.]

2. Dna Ellen la Zuche presents to the church of Laughton [*Laucton*], and in the 5th year [1284 × 1285].

3. John the chamberlain [*camerarius*], elected as abbot of Owston [*Osolueston*], licence to elect having previously been sought from the king as patron.

[John the chamberlain was abbot of Owston 1280–84 (*Heads*, II, 442).]

4. Ds Richard de Grey presents to the church of Knipton [*Gnipton*].

5. Ds William le Botiller presents to the church of Narborough [*Northburg*].

6. Ds Robert de Nuers, knight, presents to the church of Knossington [*Knossinton*].

7. Ds Robert de Wyvile presents to the church of Stoughton [*Stouton*].

8. Simon Basset, layman, presents to the church of Stanton under Bardon [*Stanton*].

9. William de Beauchamp [*Bellocampo*], earl of Warwick, presents to the church of Kibworth Beauchamp [*Kibworthe*], and in the 5th year [1284 × 1285].

10. Ds William de Morteyn presents to a mediety of the church of Misterton [*Minsterton*].

11. Reginald son of Ds Roger de Sadington, layman, presents to the church of Bruntingthorpe [*Brantingthorp*] [see no. 37 below].

Annus Secundus **[19 May 1281–18 May 1282]**

12. William Moton presents to the church of Congerstone [*Congiston*]. [At the next recorded institution to this benefice in 1298 the reason for the vacancy was given as the institution of the previous incumbent, Robert de Belchford, to Peckleton church (*Reg. Sutton*, VIII, 69).]

13. Ds Richard de Harecurt, knight, presents to the church of Sheepy [*Sepeya*].

[Sheepy church was divided into medieties at this time and at the next recorded institution to the mediety in the Harecurt patronage in 1290, the reason given for the vacancy was the resignation of Thomas de Tefford (*Reg. Sutton*, VIII, 47).]

14. William de Warewyke, chaplain, presented by br. Roger de Akeney, preceptor of the Knights Templars in Scotland, lieutenant [*locum tenens*] of the Master of the Knights Templars in England, then absent, to the vicarage of Rothley [*Rolley*].

[William de Warewyke died as vicar of Rothley in 1297 (*Reg. Sutton*, VIII, 67) and his will is mentioned in TNA, CP 40/119, rot. 141d.]

15. Ds Nigel de Charnels, knight, presents to the church of Swepstone [*Sueppeston*].

16. Ds William le Waleys presents to the church of Wanlip (*Anley recte Anlep)*.

[At the next recorded institution to this benefice in 1288 William le Waleys was instituted on the resignation of Walter [*sic*] le Waleys (*Reg. Sutton*, VIII, 40).]

17. The prioress of Farewell [*Fairewell*] is elected as prioress of Langley [*Langele*].

[Most probably this is Christina de Wynchestre who occurs as prioress of Langley in the 1280s and resigned in 1296 (*Heads*, II, 578).]

[fol. 138v]

18. Simon Basset, knight, presents to the church of Sapcote, and to the church of Stanton under Bardon [*Stanton*] in the 3rd year [1282 × 1283].

[Possibly the presentee to Sapcote on this occasion is to be identified with John, parson of Sapcote, who occurs in Hilary term 1284 (TNA, CP 40/52, rot. 37d).]

Annus Tertius [19 May 1282–18 May 1283]

19. Ds Robert de Ros, knight, presents to the church of Harby [*Herdeby*].

20. Ds Nicholas de Segrave, knight, presents to the church of Kegworth.

21. Ds Andrew de Estle, knight, presents to the church of Broughton Astley [*Bructon*].

[At the next recorded institution to this benefice in 1296 the reason for the vacancy was given as the resignation of Mag. Walter de Hida (*Reg. Sutton*, VIII, 66).]

22. Ds John de Bolemer, knight, presents to the church of Pickwell [*Pikewell*].

23. Ds John de Kirkeby presents to the church of Medbourne [*Medburne*].

[In the Leicestershire eyre roll for 1284 there is a note that King Henry III had granted the advowson of Medbourne to John de Kyrkeby who gave the church to Robert Samson who now holds it (TNA, JUST 1/457, rot. 38; JUST 1/458, rots 24d, 33). See G. F. Farnham and A. Hamilton Thompson, 'The manor and advowson of Medbourne

1086–1550' in *Transactions of the Leicestershire Archaeological and Historical Society*, 13 (1923–4), 91–135.]

24. Ordination of the vicarage of the church of Dalby on the Wolds [*Dalby super le Woldes*], which church is appropriated to the use of the prior and brethren of the Hospital of St John of Jerusalem in England.

25. Ds William Murdak, knight, presents to the chapel of Mirabel [*Mirable*].

[At the next recorded institution to this benefice in 1293 the reason for the vacancy was given as the death of the previous incumbent, Adam (*Reg. Sutton*, VIII, 52).]

Annus Quartus [19 May 1283–18 May 1284]

26. Proctor of Mag. Roger de Martiwall presents to a mediety of the church of Hallaton [*Halgton', Halugton*], which advowson Master Roger de Martival recovered in the king's court against William Bardolfe.

[For the advowson dispute between Mag. Roger de Martivaus and William Bardolf see TNA, CP 40/49, rot. 58.]

27. The dean and chapter of Lincoln Cathedral present to the church of Gumley [*Guthmundele*].

28. Edmund, earl of Cornwall, by reason of the custody of the land and heir of Henry de Hastings, presents to the church of Wistow [*Wystandstowe*].

[At the next recorded institution to this benefice in 1293 the reason for the vacancy was given as the death of the previous incumbent, Mag. Salvagius (*Reg. Sutton*, VIII, 54).]

29. The prior of Lewes presents to the vicarage of Melton Mowbray, which church is appropriated to the prior (and see the 7th year) [nos 46–7 below.]

30. Ds Richard Gobien, knight, presents to the church of Knaptoft [*Knapetoft*].

[There was a dispute over this advowson in 1284 between William son of Thomas de Graystock (Craystok, Creystok), John his son, Robert de Somervill (Somervile) and Isabel (*occasionally* Sybil) his wife v.

Richard Gubyon (Gobyon, Gobyoun) (TNA, JUST 1/457, rots 1, 31; JUST 1/458, rot. 1; JUST 1/459, rots 2, 21; JUST 1/460, rots 1, 14, 25; JUST 1/461, rot. 1; JUST 1/462, rots 1, 29; CP 40/54, rot. 9d).]

Annus Quintus [19 May 1284–18 May 1285]

31. Robert de Folevile and John de Lek, guardian of the said Robert, present Roger Chaumberlayn to the church of Rearsby [*Reresby*]. The same Roger, on 3 June 1284 (in the 5th year) at the celebration of orders held in the conventual church of St Leonard outside Stamford, is ordained subdeacon.

32. Ds Simon de Ellesworth, by reason of the custody of John de Bakepuiz and his land, presents to the church of Allexton [*Adelaxton*], dna Margery de Bakepuiz opposing.

33. John de Hauthirne, brother, was elected as Master of the hospital of St John, Lutterworth, licence to elect having been sought from Ds Theobald de Verdon, knight, the patron.

[John de Hathern had died as master of the hospital by February 1299 (*Reg. Sutton*, VIII, 70).]

[fol. 139r]

34. Ds Richard de Grey, by reason of the custody of the land and heir of William Avenel deceased, presents to the church of Knipton [*Gnipeton*].

[At the next recorded institution to this benefice in 1298 the reason for the vacancy was given as the death of Hugh, the previous incumbent (*Reg. Sutton*, VIII, 69).]

35. Peter Chaynel [*recte* Charnel(s)], lord of Elmesthorpe, presents to the church of Elmesthorpe [*Thorp iuxta Lilleburn*].

36. Ds Ralph Basset, knight, presents to the church of Ragdale [*Rakedale*].

37. Reginald de Sadington presents Roger Brabazun, acolyte, to the church of Bruntingthorpe [*Brantingthorp*], vacant because Thomas Brabazun was admitted rector of the church of Hungarton [*Hungerton*].

[In 1283 × 1284 there was probably another vacancy in this benefice, for the advowson was then disputed between Reginald de Sadington

(Sadinton) and Agnes de Bosceby (Bosseby) (TNA, JUST 1/458, rots 9, 9d; JUST 1/459, rot. 7d; JUST 1/460, rots 16, 16d; JUST 1/461, rot. 15; JUST 1/462, rot. 18d).]

Annus Sextus [19 May 1285–18 May 1286]

38. Ds Edmund, son of the late King Henry III, by reason of the custody of the land and heir of Walter de Redeware, presents to the church of Seal [*Scheile*].

[At the next recorded institution to this benefice in 1292 the reason for the vacancy was given as the death of Ralph de Burgh (*Reg. Sutton*, VIII, 50).]

39. Ds William Murdake, knight, presents to the church of Stockerston [*Stockfaston*], vacant by the death of Hugh Murdak, last rector.

[At the next recorded institution to this benefice in 1288 the reason for the vacancy was given as the death of Hugh de Neville (*Reg. Sutton*, VIII, 39–40).]

40. Ds Hugh le Despenser, knight, presents to the church of Loughborough [*Lutheburg*].

41. Ds Edmund, the king's brother, presents to the church of Edmondthorpe [*Thorp Eymer*].

[The presentee was almost certainly William de Alkemundebir', who was re-presented by Edmund, earl of Lancaster, the benefice being vacant because William had not been ordained priest within a year of his institution. He was eventually instituted again on 13 November 1287 (*Reg. Sutton*, VIII, 38).]

42. Ds Geoffrey de Gresle, knight, presents to the church of Norton [iuxta Twycross], which presentation he recovered in the king's court against the prior of Belvoir.

[For the advowson dispute between Geoffrey de Gresle (Gresele, Greselee, Gryselegh) and Belvoir priory see TNA, JUST 1/457, rot. 7; JUST 1/458, rot. 2d; JUST 1/460, rot. 7; JUST 1/461, rot. 3d; JUST 1/462, rot. 6d; CP 40/46, rot. 26d; CP 40/47, rot. 112; CP 40/51, rot. 88d; CP 40/52, rot. 35; CP 40/53, rot. 37d; CP 40/58, rots 19, 57; CP 40/60, rot. 29; CP 40/61, rot. 40. At the next recorded institution to this benefice in 1288 the reason for the vacancy was given as the death of Thomas de Dreuton (*Reg. Sutton*, VIII, 40).]

43. Walter le Baud, presents to the church of Lubbenham [*Lobenham*], Peter de Wolwardynton opposing. Peter came into court and granted to Walter the presentation for this turn.

[For the advowson dispute between Peter de Wolwardynton and Walter Baud, see TNA, CP 40/60, rot. 43.]

44. Ds Edmund, earl of Cornwall, by reason of the custody of John son and heir of Henry de Hastings, presents to the church of Shackerstone [*Schakerston*], Walter de Anvers opposing. Walter granted to the earl the presentation for this turn.

[For the advowson dispute between Walter Danvers and Edmund, earl of Cornwall see TNA, CP 40/49, rot. 54d.]

Annus Septimus [19 May 1286–18 May 1287]

45. Ds Gilbert de Houby, knight, presents to the chapel [church *crossed out*] of *Alfleteby*.

[This is presumably the same chapel, but at that time described as *Alfletesford*, to which two institutions were made by Bishop Dalderby in August 1309 and February 1310, on the presentation of John de Houby (Lincoln, Episcopal Register II, fols 203v–204r). I have not managed to identify this Leicestershire chapelry. The Houby family, taking its name from the Leicestershire village of Hoby, held land in Medbourne and Sutton (*CIPM*, III, p. 20; V, p. 183; IX, p. 364).]

46. The prior of St Pancras, Lewes, has the church of Melton Mowbray appropriated to his use by grant of Robert, late bishop of Lincoln, and by ordinance of Henry, bishop of Lincoln. Afterwards Roger de Moubray, knight, [fol. 139v] claimed the right of patronage by diverse machinations against the prior and presented Ds Bogo de Clare to the same church. Subsequently, Roger de Moubray granted the right of patronage by fine in the 13th year of Edward I [20 November 1284–19 November 1285]. The beginning of the final concord is cited with Moubray as petent and the prior of Lewes as tenant, mentioning eight virgates of land in Melton Mowbray etc.

[For the advowson dispute between Roger de Mowbray and the prior of Lewes see TNA, JUST 1/457, rots 8d, 33d; JUST 1/458, rot. 3d; JUST 1/459, rot. 7; JUST 1/460, rot. 6d; JUST 1/461, rots 7d, 22, 23; JUST 1/462, rots 8d, 31; CP 40/50, rot. 71; CP 40/51, rots 70, 104d; CP 40/59, rots 88, 91d. The final concord, dated 3 November 1285, is TNA, CP 25/1/123/36/146. In 1299 there was a further case between

Lewes Priory and Rose (de Clare, sister of Bogo), the widow of Roger de Mowbray, who claimed a third part of the advowson (TNA, CP 40/126, rot. 126d; attorneys rot. 3 [199]).]

47. Ordination of the vicarage of Melton Mowbray
[The surviving portion of Sutton's Leicester roll starts some way through this vicarage ordination, printed in *Reg. Sutton*, VIII, 31–35.]

Abstracts from the remainder of the Leicester roll, which still exists from this point onwards, continue on fols 139v–140r.

[fol. 140v]

ARCHDEACONRY OF BUCKINGHAM

Annus Primus [19 May 1280–18 May 1281]

48. The abbot of St Katherine, Rouen [*Rotomagensis*], presents to the church of Tingewick [*Tyngewyke*].

[The presentee on this occasion is most likely to have been Robert de Sorteford who occurs as parson of Tingewick in a case in Common Pleas in Michaelmas term 1281 (TNA, CP 40/42, rots 107d, 152).]

49. The abbot of St Albans presents to the church of Little Kimble [*Parva Kenebell*].

[At the next recorded institution to this benefice in 1291 the reason for the vacancy was given as the resignation of Thomas de la Le (*Reg. Sutton*, VIII, 128).]

50. The prior of Chacombe presents to the church of Penn [*Lapenne*].

51. Ds John de Beauchamp [*Bellocampo*] presents to the church of Middle Claydon [*Myddyl Claydon*].

52. Br. Robert de Rameseia elected as prior of Bradwell [*Braddewell*], licence to elect having been sought from Ds Antony Bek, guardian of John son of Alan, then a minor, the true patron.

[Robert de Rameseia occurs as prior of Bradwell until 1303 (D. M. Smith, *Heads of Religious Houses: England and Wales, Supplement* (Cluj-Napoca and York, Borthwick Institute for Archives publications, 2019), p. 2.]

53. Ds William de Bechampton, knight, presents to a mediety of the church of Beachampton [*Bechampton*].

54. The Master of the hospital of Hogshaw [*Hoggesawe*] presents to the church of Creslow [*Kerslawe*].

55. The prior of Luffield presents to the church of Water Stratford [*Parva Stratford*].

56. The abbot of Gloucester presents to the church of Wraysbury [*Wirarddesbir*].

[At the next recorded institution to this benefice in 1299 the reason for the vacancy was given as the resignation of Mag. Richard de Gloucester (*Reg. Sutton*, VIII, 171).]

57. Nicholas de Hameslape elected as prior of Snelshall [*Snelleshall*], licence to elect having been sought from Ds Richard son of John, knight, the patron (as is customary).

[Nicholas de Hameslape was prior of Snelshall until his resignation in 1300 (*Heads*, II, 71).]

58. Peter de Coudre, knight, by reason of the custody of the son and heir of Hugh de Bray, presents to a mediety of the church of Walton.

59. The proctor of the prior and convent of Longueville [*Longavilla*], O. Clun., presents to the church of Newton Longville [*Neuton Longvill*], and to the church of Akeley [*Ackele*] in the 4th year [1283 ×1284], and to the church of Great Horwood [*Magna Horwode*], in the 5th year [1284 × 1285].

60. The prior of Tickford presents to the church of Sherington [*Schirington*].

61. Ds Geoffrey de Lucy, knight, presents to the church of Cublington [*Cubelington*], vacant by the death of Robert de Lucy, the last rector.

[The presentee was possibly William Frenceys who occurs as parson of Cublington in the plea roll for Michaelmas term 1289 (TNA, CP 40/80, rot. 220d).]

[fol. 141r]

62. Ds John Druel, knight, presents to the church of Newton Blossomville [*Neuton Blosmevill*]

[At the next recorded institution to this benefice in 1291 the reason for the vacancy was given as the death of William, the previous rector (*Reg. Sutton*, VIII, 127).]

Annus Secundus [19 May 1281–18 May 1282]

63. Ds Amaury de Sancto Amando, knight, presents to the church of Grendon Underwood [*Grendon*], and in the 4th year [1283 × 1284].

64. William de Chilteham, guardian of the land and heir of Geoffrey son of Hugh de Bray, presents to a mediety [*altered*] of the church of Walton, which presentation William has recovered in the king's court against Henry de Ewyas and Juliana his wife by their default. [see also no. 80 below]

[For this advowson case between William de Chilteham (Chyltham), guardian of the land and heir of Geoffrey son of Hugh de Bray v. Henry de Ewyas (Euyas) and Juliana his wife see TNA, CP 40/45, rots 17, 59, 77; CP 40/46, rot. 3.]

65. Robert de Grey and Joan his wife present to the church of Ickford [*Ikeford*], Denise [Alice *crossed out*] de Appilton opposing. Denise, in the king's court, remitted all her right to Robert and Joan and the heirs of Joan.

[For the advowson dispute between Denise de Apelton v. Robert de Grey and Joan his wife see TNA, CP 40/46, rot. 74d.]

66. The prior of Ravenstone presents to the vicarage of the church of Ravenstone [*Raveneston*], which church is appropriated to the prior.

67. Ordination of the vicarage of Ravenstone [*Raveneston*].

68. Ds Stephen DelaHaye presents to the church of Foscott [*Foxcote*].

[*no Annus Tertius noted*]

Annus Quartus [19 May 1283–18 May 1284]

69. Matilda Neyrnut elected as prioress of Little Marlow, licence to elect having been sought from the countess of Gloucester and Ds William de Cressy, knight, patrons of the house.

[Matilda occurs as prioress until 1286 (*Heads*, II, 581).]

70. Ds Hugh de Gerund [*recte* Gernun], knight, presents to the church of Dunton [*Dodington*].

71. Ds John Neyrnut, knight, presents to the church of Pitstone [*Pythelestorn*], vacant by the death of William Neyrnut, Reginald de Beauchamp [*Bellocampo*] and Isabel his wife opposing. Reginald and Isabel quitclaimed in the king's court all their right to John and his heirs.

[At the next recorded institution to this benefice in 1299 the reason for the vacancy was given as the death of Fulk Neirnut (*Reg. Sutton*, VIII, 168).]

72. Ds Ralph Pipard, knight, presents to the church of Great Linford [*Magna Linford*], and in the 8th year [1287 × 1288.]

73. Ds William Danvers, knight, presents to the church of Dorney.

[fol. 141v]

74. The burgesses of Wycombe present to the cure of the hospital of St John, Wycombe.

Annus Quintus [19 May 1284–18 May 1285]

75. Ds Jordan de Saukevile, knight, presents to the church of Fawley [*Fallegh*].

76. The prioress of Goring presents to the church of Moulsoe [*Mulsho*].

[Possibly the occasion of the institution of Richard de Sancto Egidio, who occurs as parson of Moulsoe in a case against the prioress of Goring in Easter term 1289 (TNA, CP 40/78, rot. 66).]

77. Alice de Hadeng' presents to the church of Eton.

78. Robert Malet, knight, presents to the church of Quainton [*Quenton*]. [see also no. 102 below]

79. The king, patron of Ravenstone [*Ravenston*] [*erasure in mid-entry*].

[Probably to do with the appointment of the new prior, John de Beneton, who was prior 1285–1309 (*Heads*, II, 451).]

Annus Sextus [19 May 1285–18 May 1286]

80. Henry de Ewyas and Juliana his wife present to the church of Walton. William de Chiltham opposing, [presenting] another clerk by reason of the custody of Geoffrey son and heir of Hugh de Bray. Henry and Juliana came to court and granted to William his presentation to the mediety of the church of Walton. [see also no. 64 above]

81. Ds Robert de Chetwode, knight, presents to the chapel or hermitage in the parish of Chetwode.

82. The prior of Bradwell presents to the vicarage of the church of Wolverton.

[At the next recorded institution to this benefice in 1297 the reason for the vacancy was given as the death of Ralph de Wolverton (*Reg. Sutton*, VIII, 167).]

83. Robert Chaunceys presents to the church of Bow Brickhill [*Bollebrikhill*], Richard Justyn of Oving [*Ovyng*] and Alice his wife opposing, presenting another clerk. Richard and Alice came to the king's court and granted the advowson to Robert and his heirs.

[For this advowson dispute see TNA, JUST 1/1247, rot. 13d.]

84. Ds Robert son of Roger presents to the church of Iver [*Evere*].

[There was an advowson dispute over a fourth part of this church between the abbot of Osney and Robert son of Roger, see TNA, CP 40/69, rot. 28. At the next recorded institution to this benefice in 1295 the reason for the vacancy was given as the death of Ingram de Balliol (*Reg. Sutton*, VIII, 161).]

Annus Septimus [19 May 1286–18 May 1287]

85. John de Tyngewyke presents to the church of Thornton.

86. Richard son of Ds Richard de la Vache presents to the church of Shenley [*Schenle*], and in the 8th year [1287 × 1288].

[fol. 142r]

87. Ds Miles de Hastinges, holding [*cancellation here*] the lands of Denise daughter and heiress of Peter de Goldinton, his late wife, by the law of England and guardian [*custos*] of Miles son of Philip de Hastinges and heir of the said Denise, presents to the church of Stoke Goldington [*Stoke Goldinton*].

88. Ds Robert de Chetwod, knight, presents to the church of Chetwode [*Chetwod*] and to the chapel or hermitage of St Laurence, Chetwode.

89. Ds Robert de Cave and Sybil his wife present to the church of Woughton on the Green [*Woketon*], Ds Thomas de Northwod, knight, and Hawise his wife, Robert Bragwayn and Alice his wife, Robert de Manneye and Agnes his wife, and John son of Roger de Burghill opposing. Thomas and Hawyse came to the king's court and granted to Robert and Sybil for this turn their right to the church.

[For the disputes over this advowson, Robert de Cave and Sybil his wife v. Robert de Brangweyn and Alice his wife; and Robert de Moneye and Agnes his wife, Thomas de Northwode and Hawise his wife, and John son of Roger de Burghull v. Robert de Brangwayn and Alice his wife, see TNA, CP 40/65, rots 1d, 2; CP 40/66, rots 15, 15d, 57d.]

Annus Octavus [19 May 1287–18 May 1288]

90. John son of [*blank*] de Luchton presents to the church of Loughton [*Luchton*].

91. The prior of Merton presents to the church of Hardmead [*Hardnede*].

92. Dna Joan Chaumberlayn presents to the church of Petsoe [*Petesho*].

93. Ds William de Sauntersdon, knight, presents to the chapel of Hedgerley [*Hugele*].

Annus Nonus [19 May 1288–18 May 1289]

94. Br. Robert de Turvile, Master of the Knights Templars presents to the church of Radnage [*Radenache*].

95. Ds John Peyvre, knight, presents to the church of Wavendon [*Wavyndon*].

[There was an advowson dispute over this church in Michaelmas term 1286 between John Peyvere and Nicholas Fermbaud (TNA, CP 40/564, rot. 82).]

96. The abbot of Faversham presents to the church of Tring [*Treng*].

[This entry has clearly been placed in the wrong archdeaconry roll. It should have been included in the Huntingdon archdeaconry roll. In the 1280s there was a case over this advowson between Faversham abbey and the French priory of Rumilly (TNA, CP 40/45, rot. 43d; CP 40/47, rot. 9; CP 40/48, rot. 46; CP 40/50, rots 19d, 27; CP 40/55, rot. 32d; CP 40/57, rots 16d, 18d; CP 40/59, rot. 16d; JUST 1/326, rot. 9; JUST 1/328, rot. 22d). Gilbert de Whytewey (Whiteweye, Whyteweye) occurs as parson of Tring in Hilary term 1284 and Easter and Michaelmas terms 1285 (TNA, CP 40/52, rot. 34d; CP 40/58, rot. 32; CP 40/60, rot. 44), and Gilbert de Ivyngho (? a different person or alternative surname) as parson in 1287 (JUST 1/328, rot. 25.]

97. The abbot of Woburn presents to the vicarage of the mediety of the church of Chesham [*Chesham alias Cestreham*].

[fol. 142v]

98. Ds John de Filiol, knight, presents to the church of North Crawley [*Craule*].

99. Robert [*blank*], lord of Ekeney presents to the church of Ekeney.

100. The prior of Merton presents to the church of Hitcham [*Hucham*].

Annus Decimus [19 May 1289–18 May 1290]

101. Ds Robert de Ver, earl of Oxford, presents to the church of Aston Sandford [*Aston Staunford*] and to the church of Whitchurch [*Wytechurch*], in the 10th year [1289 × 1290].

[At the next recorded institution to Aston Stanford in 1293 the reason for the vacancy was given as the resignation of Mag. Stephen de Haslingfield (*Reg. Sutton*, VIII, 156).]

102. Ds Robert Malet, knight, presents to the church of Quainton [*Quenton*].

[At the next recorded institution to this benefice in 1298 the reason for the vacancy was given as the resignation of Walter Hachard (*Reg. Sutton*, VIII, 167).]

103. The king presents to the church of Oakley [*Okle*], with the chapel of Brill [*Brehull*].

[At the next recorded institution to this benefice in 1297 the reason for the vacancy was given as the deprivation of Richard de Luda by Archbishop Winchelsey (*Reg. Sutton*, VIII, 168).]

104. Ds John Peyvre, knight, presents to the church of Maids Moreton [*Morton*].

105. William le Graunt, knight, presents to the church of Hulcott [*Huccote*].

[The name of the presentee was most probably William le Graunt. At the next recorded institution to this benefice in 1291 the reason for the vacancy was given as the fact that William le Graunt, the previous rector, had not been ordained priest within a year of being instituted (*Reg. Sutton*, VIII, 127).]

106. Ds Reginald de Grey, knight, presents to the church of Simpson [*Sweneneston*].

[At the next recorded institution to this benefice in 1292 the reason for the vacancy was given as the death of Mag. John de Morden (*Reg. Sutton*, VIII, 128).]

107. Gerard de Braibroke presents to the church of Horsenden [*Horsindon*].

108. Ds Hugh de Curtenay presents [*blotted word*? portion/corrody] which Ds Geoffrey de Ver had in the [*blotted word*? abbey] of Biddlesden [*Bitlesden*].

109. Br. William elected abbot of Notley [*Nuttele*], licence to elect having been sought from dna Matilda de Mortimer [*Mortuomari*] who was said to be patron, but the earl of Gloucester said he was patron [see no. 112 below].

[This was William de Sheringham who was abbot of Notley 1290–1308 (*Heads*, II, 440).]

110. Ds John Giffard, knight, presents to the church of Radclive [*Radeclyve*].

111. Ds John Neyrnut, knight, presents to the church of Fleet Marston [*Fletemereston*].

[In 1283 there had been an advowson dispute over Fleet Marston between John de Neyrnuyt and Robert de Vernay, TNA, CP 40/51, rot. 63d. See also the earlier 1246 final concord over this advowson between Geoffrey de Neyrnuyt and Ralph de Vernay (M. W. Hughes ed., *A Calendar of the Feet of Fines for the County of Buckingham, 7 Richard I to 44 Henry III*, Buckinghamshire Record Society, 4 (1942 for 1940), p. 87).]

[*In dorso*]

Annus Decimus [19 May 1289–18 May 1290]

112. *Contentio* between the earl of Gloucester and Matilda de Mortimer over the patronage of the abbey of Notley [see no. 109 above].

[fol. 144v]

ARCHDEACONRY OF OXFORD

Annus Primus [19 May 1280–18 May 1281]

113. The king presents to the church of Lillingstone Lovell [*Lillingston*], and in the 6th year [1285 × 1286].

[William de Holcote was presented by the king in October 1279 (*CPR 1272–81*, p. 329).]

114. Ds Richard de Leonibus presents to the church of Begbroke [*Beckkebroc*].

[At the next recorded institution to this benefice in 1298 the reason for the vacancy was given as the death of Richard de Lyuns, presumably a member of the Leonibus family, the patrons (*Reg. Sutton*, VIII, 199).]

115. Ds Elyas de Wytefeld presents to the church of Wheatfield [*Witefeld*].

116. William de Luveday presents to the church of Mongewell [*Mungewell*].

117. Edmund, earl of Cornwall, presents to the church of Rousham [*Rollesham*] and the church of Henley [*Henle*] in the 3rd year [1282 × 1283] and to the church of Mixbury [*Mixeburi*] in the 4th year [1283 × 1284] and to the church of Beckley [*Bekkele*] in the 4th year [*marg.*]

and to the church of Ambrosden [*Ambresden*] in the 5th year [1284 × 1285] and to the church of Chalgrove [*Chalgreve*] in the 6th year [1285 × 1286].

[At the next recorded institution to Rousham in 1292 the reason for the vacancy was given as the institution of the previous incumbent, William de Brueria, to the church of Hemswell (*Reg. Sutton*, VIII, 178); the next vacancy at Beckley in 1291 was given as the institution of the previous incumbent, Mag. Richard de Sotwell, to South Frodingham church (*ibid.*, 173), and the next vacancy at Ambrosden in 1298 was given as being by the death of Mag. Ralph de Martival (*ibid.*, 200).]

118. The prior of Dunstable presents to the church of North Marston [*Northmerston*].

Annus Secundus [19 May 1281–18 May 1282]

119. The prior of Deerhurst presents to the church of Northmoor [*Lamore*].

[At the next recorded institution to this benefice in 1294 the reason for the vacancy was given as the death of Hugh de Clifford (*Reg. Sutton*, VIII, 185).]

120. Mag. Geoffrey de Sancto Medardo, former archdeacon of Richmond lately deceased, was rector of the church of Enstone [*Enneston*], vacant by his death.

121. Ds Roger de Oylly, true patron of the church of Kencott [*Keincote*], presents Thomas de Sutton to the church.

122. Hugh de Sancto Philberto presents to the church of Brightwell Baldwin [*Brittewell*].

123. John Mauduit presents William de Wydehill to the church of Standlake [*Stanlake*], Ds Osbert Giffard, knight, opposing him (together with Ds John de Boys, knight, and Philip de Wylegby, Robert de Grey, Andrew de Nevile and Isabel de Grey) in the king's court. John de Bosco granted to John Mauduit his presentation for this turn and Osbert Giffard and the others granted to John Mauduit their presentation for this turn.

[For this advowson case in Common Pleas over Standlake see TNA, CP 40/44, rots 3d *bis*, 70, 70d, 92; CP 40/45, rot. 7; CP 40/55, rot. 79d.]

[fol. 145r]

Annus Tertius [19 May 1282–18 May 1283]

124. Ds Robert de Wytham, knight, presents to the church of Swalcliffe [*Sualclive*] for this turn and in the 4th year [1283 × 1284.]

[At the next recorded institution to this benefice in 1292 the reason for the vacancy was given as the institution of the previous incumbent, Peter de Shenington, to the vicarage of Wetwang in York diocese (*Reg. Sutton*, VIII, 179).]

125. Ds John Maudut, knight, presents to the church of Broughton Poggs [*Broucton*].

126. Ds William (Matthew *crossed out*] le Pouer, knight, presents to the church of Oddington [*Otingdon*].

127. Ds John de Elsefeld (Ellesfeld *crossed out*], knight, presents to the church of Bolney [*Bollehithe*].

128. The prior of Kenilworth presents to the church of Glympton [*Clinton*].

[At the next recorded institution to this benefice in 1291 the reason for the vacancy was given as the death of Robert *dictus* Schirlok (*Reg. Sutton*, VIII, 176).]

129. John son of Guy, knight, presents to the church of Wigginton [*Wyginton*] and in the 4th year, and to the church of Ardley [*Arduluele*] in the 4th year [1283 × 1284] and to the church of South Weston [*Weston*] in the 5th year [1284 × 1285].

[At the next recorded institution to South Weston in 1298 the reason for the vacancy was given as the previous incumbent, Roger, having been instituted to Shipton on Cherwell (*Reg. Sutton*, VIII, 201).]

130. Sarra de Excester was elected as prioress of Goring [*Gorings*], licence to elect having been sought from the earl of Cornwall, the patron.

[Also known as Sarah de Oxford, she had died as prioress of Goring by January 1298 (*Heads*, II, 564).]

Annus Quartus [19 May 1283–18 May 1284]

131. Ds Thomas de Parco, knight, presents to the church of Brightwell Baldwin [*Brigtewell*], and in the 9th year [1288 × 1289] [see no. 154].

132. Adam de Wodford elected as prior of Cold Norton [*Coldenorton*], vacant by the death of Simon de Rolesham. [see also nos 138 and 158]

133. The king, patron of the abbey of Godstow [*Godestowe*] and the priory of St Frideswide [*Sancte Fretheswide*].

[These entries no doubt related to the appointment of Mabel la Wafre as abbess of Godstow 1283–95 and either to the ineffective election of John de Sandon as prior of St Frideswide's, Oxford, in 1283 or to the election of his successor, Robert de Ewelme 1284–94 (*Heads*, II, 562, 444).]

134. Ds Thomas de Breaute, knight, presents to the church of Upper Heyford [*Heyford Waryn*] and in the 5th year [1284 × 1285].

135. Ds Andrew de Sakevile presents to the church of A[*blotted letters*]ton. [From earlier evidence (W. P. W. Phillimore and F. N. Davis (eds), *Rotuli Hugonis de Welles, episcopi Lincolnsiensis, A.D. MCCIX–MCCXXXV*, 3 vols, Canterbury and York Society, 1, 3, 4 (1907–9) and Lincoln Record Society 3, 6, 9 (Lincoln, 1912–14)), II, 41) the church of Emmington had Sackvilles as patrons and is probably the correct identification in this instance].

Annus Quintus [19 May 1284–18 May 1285]

136. Ds John de Pratellis, knight, presents to the church of Great Tew [*Magna Tywa*].

[At the next recorded institution to this benefice in 1290 the reason for the vacancy was given as the death of Richard, the previous incumbent (*Reg. Sutton*, VIII, 172).]

137. The dean and chapter of Lincoln Cathedral present to the church of Great Milton [*Milton*].

[fol. 145v]

138. Br. Peter de Wadington elected as prior of Cold Norton [*Caldenorton*], licence to elect having been sought from dna Isabel de Mortimer [*Mortuomari*], the patron. [see nos 132 and 158]

139. Ds Nicholas Syfrewast, knight, (by reason of the lands which were of Ds Osbert Giffard, knight, and Ds John de Bosco, knight, in the vill of Standlake), and Ds Robert de Grey, knight and Ds John Maudute, knight, present to the church of Standlake [*Stanlake*], vacant by the death of W. de Wydehill, Richard son of Thomas de Wydehill, subdeacon.

140. Ordination of the vicarage of Brize Norton [*Norton Bruer*], which church the abbot of Eynsham [*Eynesham*] has *in proprios usus*.

141. Ds Isabel de Fortibus, countess of Aumale [*Albemarle*], presents to the church of Whitchurch [*Wytechurche*].

[For the advowson dispute over Whitchurch between Roger la Ware and Isabel de Fortibus, countess of Aumale, see TNA, CP 40/58, rot. 53; CP 40/60, rot. 23d].

142. John Marmyon, knight, presents to the church of Checkendon [*Chakinden*].

143. Ds Miles de Hastings, knight, presents to the church of Yelford [*Eleford*] and in the 7th year [1286 x 1287].

144. Ds John de Patteshull, knight, presents to the church of Tusmore [*Thoresmere*].

Annus Sextus [19 May 1285–18 May 1286]

145. William, lord of Harpsden [*Harpeden*], knight, presents to the church of Harspsden [*Harpeden*].

146. Ds William de Luton, knight, presents to the church of Heythrop [*Hethrop*].

Annus Septimus [19 May 1286–18 May 1287]

147. Simon de Baliden and Thomas de Brokton, after the execution of the testament of Ds William de Perton, last rector of the church of Broughton [*Brocton*, *Bructon*], present Philip de Everdon, subdeacon, to the church of Broughton. This presentation is by reason of the custody of the land and John son and heir of John de Brocton, which is held together with the marriage of John and the advowson of the church, and which Ds William [purchased] for him and his heirs and assigns of Ds Reginald de Watervile, chief lord of the manor of Broughton, until the full age of John.

[fol. 146r]

148. William Wale of Norton presents to the chantry of the Blessed Virgin Mary in the parish church of Chipping Norton [*Chepingnorton*], which consists of a rent of 60s. and a messuage in Chipping Norton, founded by Richard Wale at the altar of St James in the old chapel of Norton.

Annus Octavus [19 May 1287–18 May 1288]

149. Ds Robert de Grey, knight, presents to the church of Rotherfield Greys [*Rotherfield Murdake*].

150. Ds Edmund, earl of Cornwall, [?patron, *blotted section*] of the priory of Studley.

[Probably this relates to the appointment of Mabel, prioress of Studley, who occurs in 1289 and died in 1292 (*Heads*, II, 612).]

151. Ds Richard de Kirkeby, knight, presents to the church of Ducklington [*Dukelington*].

[At the next recorded institution to this benefice in 1295 the reason for the vacancy was given as the death of Philip Dyve (*Reg. Sutton*, VIII, 189).]

Annus Nonus [19 May 1288–18 May 1289]

152. Ds Thomas de Ardern, knight, presents to the church of Drayton.

153. Ds Henry de Bruyly, knight, by reason of Katherine his wife, daughter and heiress of Ds William Foliot, presents to the church of Waterstock [*Waterstoke*].

154. Ds Thomas de Parco, knight, presents to the church of Brightwell Baldwin [*Brichtewell*], Thomas de Huscard opposing. Thomas [Huscard] granted to Thomas [de Parco] his presentation for this turn.

[For the advowson dispute between Thomas de Parco of Brightwell Baldwin and Thomas Huscard see TNA, CP 40/76, rot. 152d; CP 40/77, rot. 45. At the next recorded institution to this benefice in 1294 the reason for the vacancy was given as the death of John de Blewbury (*Reg. Sutton*, VIII, 184).]

155. Ds Ralph de Vernun, knight, presents to the church of Hanwell [*Hanewell*].

156. Ds Richard de Wylamescot, knight, presents to the church of Asterley [*Asterle*].

157. Ds Edmund, earl of Cornwall, presents to the church of North Stoke [*Stoke Basset*].

[The presentee was most probably Roger de Bikkerwyk, who was re-instituted in 1290 because he had not been ordained priest within a year and was again re-instituted for the same reason in 1291 (*Reg. Sutton*, VIII, 172, 176).]

[fol. 146v]

Annus Decimus [19 May 1289–18 May 1290]

158. The priory of Cold Norton [*Norton*] being vacant, br. Walter de Stratton was elected as prior, licence to elect having been sought from Robert Hastang, the patron. [see nos 132 and 138]

[Prior Walter resigned the priory in 1292 (*Heads*, II, 370).]

159. The king presents to the church of Stonesfield [*Stuntesfeld*].

160. Ds Alan de Craule, knight, presents to the church of Salford [*Salteford*].

161. Br. William de Thornberg was elected as prior of Bicester [*Burnecestr'*], licence to elect having been sought from Ds Henry de Lascy, earl of Lincoln, the patron.

[William remained as prior of Bicester until his resignation in 1300 (*Heads*, II, 334).]

162. The prioress and convent of Clairruissel [*Claro Rivo*] [diocese of Rouen] present to the vicarage of Mapledurham.

[*In dorso nichil*]

[fol. 147r]

ARCHDEACONRY OF HUNTINGDON

Annus Primus [19 May 1280–18 May 1281]

163. The queen presents to the church of Willian [*Wylire*].

164. Robert de Wotton [and Constance *word blotted*] his wife by reason of the manor of Conington which she has in dower, present to the church of Conington [see also no. 179 below].

165. Christiana de Maulea presents to the church of Hertingfordbury [*Hertfordingbiry*].

166. Ds Henry de Wymundele, knight, presents to the church of Watton-at-Stone [*Watton*].

Annus Secundus [19 May 1281–18 May 1282]

167. John son of Simon presents to the church of Graveley [*Craule*], William de la Holte of Graveley opposing. John recovered the presentation, and in the 5th year [1284 × 1285].

[For the advowson dispute between William son of Ralph de Holte [Holt] of Graveley and John son of Simon see TNA, JUST 1/1256, rots 4, 7; JUST 1/1229, rots 11d, 14 (in the latter entry John's opponent is called William son of Adam de Gravele.]

168. Ds William de Myriden, William Deloley, John son of Mathew de Wethamsted, and Roger Salina present to the chapel of St Mary, Titehurst [*Tighurst*].

[For this chapel in the parish of Shenley see *Reg. Gravesend*, p. 176.]

169. Dna Margery Corbet, widow, heiress of Richard de Monte Fiscano, presents to the church of Ayot St Peter [*Ayote sancti Petri*].

170. Ds Robert Ageliun, knight, presents to the church of Stapleford [*Stapelford*], and in the 5th year [1284 × 1285].

171. William Engayne presents to the church of Coppingford [*Coppemanford*].

172. The abbot of St Albans presents to the church of Wallington [*Waulington*].

173. The prior of Wilsford [*Wyvelford*] presents to the church of St Nicholas, Hertford.

Annus Tertius [19 May 1282–18 May 1283]

174. Ordination of the vicarage of Edworth [*Eddeworth*], which the prior of St Neots has *in proprios usus*. [Edworth is in the archdeaconry of Bedford.]

[fol. 147v]

Annus Quartus [19 May 1283–18 May 1284]

175. Ds Peter Pigot presents to the church of North Mimms [*Northmines*].

[Later in 1289 there was an advowson dispute over North Mimms between Ralph (Ranulph) de Monte Caniso (Monchesny) and John Pycot (Pykot), see TNA, CP 40/80, rots 41, 122d, which resulted (after a further dispute in 1294) in a final concord over the advowson between Peter Pycot and Ranulph de Monte Caniso dated 12 November 1294 (TNA, CP 25/1/86/46/310). See *Reg. Sutton*, VIII, 86, for details of the 1294 dispute.]

176. The prior of Bermondsey presents to the vicarage of the church of *Aynho* [*sic*, but *recte* Bengeo]. [Bermondsey priory were patrons of Bengeo vicarage.]

177. Ordination of the vicarage of the prebendal church of Brampton.

178. Ds William de Lyndeseye, knight, presents to the church of Molesworth.

Annus Quintus [19 May 1284–8 May 1285]

179. Robert de Watton and Constance his wife present to the church of Conington [*Coningeton*], which he has recovered against Ds Robert de Brus, senior, in the king's court.

[There was much litigation over this advowson, with cases between Robert de Brus senior v. Robert de Wotton [Wtton] and Constance his wife and Bernard de Brus, and also the abbot of Lindores against the preceding parties (TNA, CP 40/41, rot. 55; CP 40/42, rots 103d, 107, 107d; CP 40/43, rots 21, 95; CP 40/44, rots 11 *bis*, 90d; CP 40/45, rot. 35. At the next recorded institution to this benefice in 1294 the reason for the vacancy was given as the death of Richard, the previous incumbent (*Reg. Sutton*, VIII, 83).]

180. Dna Eleanor, the queen consort of King Edward presents to the church of King's Langley [*Langele*].

181. Alan de Charters, lord of Woolley [*Wfle*], presents to the church of Woolley [*Wolfle*].

182. William Engaine of Waresley [*Wersle*] presents to the church of Waresley [*Wersle*].

183. Ds Adam de Strattona, clerk, on the death of William de Strattona, is presented to the church of Shenley [*Schenle*].

Annus Sextus [19 May 1285–18 May 1286]

184. 12 Edward I. The king presents to the church of Essendon [*Esingdon*], vacant by the death of Ds John de Sancta Maria, last rector.

[The king presented Robert de Sancto Albano on 7 September 1285 (*CPR 1281–92*, p. 191). The reference to 12 Edward I is curious as 7 September 1285 falls in Edward's thirteenth regnal year. This is perhaps a mistake by Dodsworth.]

185. Vitalis de Grafham presents to the church of Grafham, Simon son of Burghard de Grafham opposing. Vitalis recovered his presentation.

[For the advowson dispute between Vitalis de Grafham v. Simon son of Burghard de Grafham, see TNA, CP 40/59, rot. 1d. The presentee on this occasion was possibly John de Maldon who occurs as parson of Grafham in Trinity and Michaelmas terms 1285 (TNA, KB 27/92, rot. 32; KB 27/94, rot. 35d; CP 40/60, rot. 43).]

186. Ds Ralph de Thony, knight, presents to the church of Flamstead [*Flaumstede*], and in 10th year [1289 × 1290].

Annus Septimus [19 May 1286–18 May 1287]

187. 14 Edward I. Ordination of the vicarage of Spaldwick [*Spaldwik*] belonging to the prebendal church of Stow Longa [*Longe Stowa*].

188. Br. John de Sautre was elected as abbot of Ramsey, vacant by the cession of William de Gumecestr'.

[John de Sautre was abbot of Ramsey 1286–1316 (*Heads*, II, 60).]

[fol. 148r]

189. Edmund, earl of Cornwall, patron and founder of the house of Ashridge [*Asserugg*].

[Possibly this entry relates to the appointment of Ralph who occurs as *custos* or rector of this newly-founded house in 1287 and 1288 (TNA, JUST 1/326, rot. 16; JUST 1/328, rots 37d, 38d, 39; CP 40/60, rot. 153; CP 40/70, rot. 26d; CP 40/75, rots 150, 178d, 179).]

190. [*blank*], subprioress of Rowney was elected as prioress, licence to elect having been sought from Ds John de Kirkeby, the patron.

[Probably this was Agnes de London who resigned the priory in 1291 (*Heads*, II, 602).]

191. Ds William de Ayete, knight, presents to the church of Ayot St Laurence [*Ayete*].

192. Ds John de Wengham, precentor of St Paul's London, by reason of the custody of John de Sumery, presents to the church of Bygrave [*Bigrave*].

193. Ds John de Offord, knight, and Isabel his wife, present to the church of Offord Darcy [*Offord*].

[At the next recorded institution to this benefice in 1298 the reason for the vacancy was given as the death of William de Tadcaster (*Reg. Sutton*, VIII, 90).]

194. William de Hirste presents to the church of Caldecote, and in the 10th year [see no. 207 below].

195. Giles son and heir of Ds Roger de Trumpeton, having power to present to the said [*sic, place not given*] chapel in the name of Ds Roger.

[This chapel is most probably to be identified with Eynesbury Hardwick [Puttocks Hardwick], see N. Bennett (ed.), *The Registers of Bishop Henry Burghersh, 1320–1342*, 3 vols in progress, Lincoln

Record Society 87, 90, 101 (Woodbridge, 1999–2011), II, nos 1775, 2486, 2528, 2576, 2661, 2697).]

Annus Octavus [19 May 1287–18 May 1288]

196. Ds Simon son of Ds Richard de Buckewrth, knight, presents to the church of Buckworth.

197. Ds Nicholas de Segrave, knight, presents to the church of Fenstanton [*Staunton*].

[The presentee was possibly Mag. Gilbert de Segrave. At the next recorded institution to this benefice in 1290 the reason for the vacancy was given as re-institution of the same Gilbert de Segrave who had resigned on being instituted to Aylestone and was then re-presented to Fenstanton (*Reg. Sutton*,VIII, 87).]

198. The church of Stilton is of the patronage of the bishop of Lincoln.

[At the next recorded collation of this benefice in 1299 the reason for the vacancy was given as the collation of Greetham church to the previous incumbent, Richard de Tynton (*Reg. Sutton*, VIII, 91).]

Annus Nonus [19 May 1288–18 May 1289]

199. 16 Edward I. Ds (H)umphrey de Bohun, earl of Hereford and Essex, presents to the church of Kimbolton [*Kynebauton*].

200. The abbot of Crowland presents to the church of Morborne [*Morburn*].

[At the next recorded institution to this benefice in 1296 the reason for the vacancy was given as the resignation of Robert de Greneburn (*Reg. Sutton*, VIII, 87).]

201. Dna Eleanor, queen of England, presents to the church of Great Gaddesden [*Magna Gadesden*].

[The presentee was possibly Peter Martin who was re-instituted to the church in 1291 which was vacant because he had not been ordained priest within a year of institution. Queen Eleanor had died in 1290 and the patron on this latter occasion was Alan de la Zouche (*Reg. Sutton*, VIII, 74).]

202. The king, by reason of the custody of the land and heir of Ds Thomas de Bekering, presents to the church of Catworth.

[The previous incumbent, James de Bekering, was instituted to the benefice in 1276 and re-admitted in 1279 (*Reg. Gravesend*, pp. 182, 189) and he still occurs as parson in Hilary term 1288 (TNA, CP 40/70, rots 64d, 102d; CP 40/71, rot. 81). In February 1290 it is noted that William de Holcot had been instituted to Catworth (*Reg. Sutton*, VIII, 106–7).]

203. John Cumin de Kilbride [*Kiwrd vel Kilbrid*] presents to the church of Sacombe [*Sevenecaumpe*].

[fol. 148v]

204. The abbot of Ramsey [*Rameseia*] presents to the church of Holywell [*Halywell*] with the chapel of Needingworth [*Nadingworth*], Ds Ralph de Beauchamp [*Bellocampo*], knight, opposing. The abbot recovered his presentation in the king's court.

[For this advowson dispute between Ralph de Bello Campo and the abbot of Ramsey, see TNA, CP 40/75, rot. 8d. In May 1290 a new rector was instituted to Tempsford, since the previous incumbent, Hugh de Roubir' had been instituted to Holywell (*Reg. Sutton*, VIII, 107).]

205. Ds John de Peyvre, knight, presents to the church of Willian [*Wylie*].

Annus Decimus [19 May 1289–18 May 1290]

206. Ds John de Lovetot, knight, by reason of the custody of William, son of the late Ds William le Moyne and Eleanor de Lovetot, presents to the church of All Saints, Sawtry [*Sautre*].

[At the next recorded institution to this benefice in 1300 the reason for the vacancy was given as the death of Mag. Walter de Teford (*Reg. Sutton*, VIII, 224).]

207. William de Hirste presents to the church of Caldecote [*Caldecote iuxta Ashewell*], which he recovered in the king's court against Ds Gerard de Furnivall for this turn.

[For the advowson dispute between William de Hurst and Gerard de Furnivall see TNA, CP 40/76, rot. 31d; CP 40/77, rot. 24d; CP 40/78, rot. 4d. At the next recorded institution to this benefice in December

1290 the reason for the vacancy was given as the death of Simon de Bassingham (*Reg. Sutton*, VIII, 74).]

208. Ralph Musket de Wakeley presents to the church of Wakeley.

[At the next recorded institution to this benefice in 1299 the reason for the vacancy was given as the institution of the previous incumbent, Ralph de Hackthorn, to the church of Raithby by Louth (*Reg. Sutton*, VIII, 91).]

209. Ds Robert de Beaumes, knight, presents to the church of St Andrew, Sawtry [*Sautre*].

210. Ds Adam de Cretinge, knight, presents to the church of Great Staughton [*Stockton*].

[For this advowson dispute between Adam de Creting (Cretingg) and Nichola his wife v. Anselm de Gyse and Beatrice his wife, and similarly between Creting and his wife v. Nicholas de Bathon' and Margery his wife, see TNA, CP 40/79, rots 87, 97d. At the next recorded institution to this benefice in 1292 the reason for the vacancy was given as the resignation of John de Ponte (*Reg. Sutton*, VIII, 79).]

[*in dorso nichil*]

INDEX

Numbers in round brackets () after page numbers signify entries in the checklist in chapter 7
Numbers in square brackets [] after page numbers signify entries in the calendar to chapter 13

TABULA GRATULATORIA

Ken & Lesley Hollamby
Paul Everson
Owain G. R. Gardner
David Start
Joan Coverley
Gary & Heather Phillips
Michael Burger
Jane Bailey
Hannah Boston
David Roffe
Mark Acton
Derek Wellman
Philippa Hoskin
Brian Davey
Andrew Walker
Lesley Clarke
David Stocker
Heather Hughes
Magnus Williamson
Ken Redmore
Julie L. Mell
Kathryn Dutton
Malcolm Locking BA (Hons)
Anna Marie Roos
Marian Brebner
David Crook
Rod. Ambler
Chris Johnson
Richard D'Arcy
Ian Beckwith
Wendy J. Atkin
Edmund King
Michael and Diana Honeybone
Mark Gardiner
Claire Arrand

Dr Michael J. Jones
Pearl Wheatley
Kenneth Carlisle
Angelo M. Silvestri
Ann Marcombe
Brian Hodgkinson
Sally Badham
Cliff Webb
Alan Humphries
John Ollard
Nicholas J. Day
Michael Jones
Jessica Holt
Ian George
Mike Rogers
Penelope A. Forsdyke B.A (Hons) M.A. Cert.Ed
John Manterfield
Michael R. Begley
Martin Roberts
Neil R. Wright
Alison K. McHardy
Michael Casterton
President and Council, Northamptonshire Record Society
Martin Williams and the late Gillian Darby
Mark Lockwood
Rob Wheeler
Michael C.M. Anyan
Paul Dryburgh
Professor Claudia Capancioni
Paul M. Stebbing
Professor Louise J. Wilkinson
David Boulton

Julian Haseldine
Gillian Tresidder Arca
Malcolm S. Plaskitt
Professor Andrew Jackson
Sethina Watson
Roz Mellows
Christopher Woolgar
The Trustees of the Spalding Gentlemen's Society
Richard Hillier, Peterborough.